American Literature's Aesthetic Dimensions

American Literature's
Aesthetic Dimensions

EDITED BY

CINDY WEINSTEIN

AND

CHRISTOPHER LOOBY

Columbia University Press   New York

Columbia University Press
Publishers Since 1893
New York   Chichester, West Sussex

Copyright © 2012 Columbia University Press
All rights reserved

Library of Congress Cataloging-in-Publication Data
American literature's aesthetic dimensions / edited by Cindy Weinstein
and Christopher Looby
p. cm.
Includes bibliographical references and index.
ISBN 978-0-231-15616-5 (cloth: acid-free paper)
—ISBN 978-0-231-15617-2 (pbk.: acid-free paper)
—ISBN 978-0-231-52077-5 (e-book)
1. American literature—History and criticism.
2. Literature—Aesthetics. I. Weinstein, Cindy. II. Looby, Christopher.
PS88.A49   2012
810.9—dc23   2011039141

Casebound editions of Columbia University Press books
are printed on permanent and durable acid-free paper.

Printed in the United States of America

c 10 9 8 7 6 5 4 3 2 1
p 10 9 8 7 6 5 4 3 2

References to Internet Web sites (URLs) were accurate at the time
of writing. Neither the author nor Columbia University Press
is responsible for Web sites that may have expired or changed
since the book was prepared.

To our teachers

Contents

Acknowledgments

Some of the essays included here originated as talks given at a conference at the Huntington Library on October 26–27, 2007, also with the title
"American Literature's Aesthetic Dimensions." We wish to thank Robert C.
Ritchie, formerly W. M. Keck Foundation Director of Research at the Huntington, for his support of the conference (which was generously funded
by the William French Smith Endowment), as well as Caroline Powell and
Susi Krasnoo for their kind organizational assistance. Several friends and
colleagues served as chairs and moderators (Alison Hills, Catherine Jurca,
Maria Karafilis, Samuel Otter, Nancy Ruttenburg, and Elisa Tamarkin), and
they, along with the many members of the lively audience, deserve our
thanks as well. Those who spoke at the conference (Edward Cahill, Christopher Castiglia, Max Cavitch, Julie Ellison, Jonathan Freedman, Dorothy J.
Hale, Eric Lott, Trish Loughran, Sianne Ngai, Wendy Steiner, Cindy Weinstein, and Ivy Wilson) benefited greatly from the exchanges and challenges
that the conference enabled. The published collection now includes a host
of essays not originating at the conference (those by Dorri Beam, Nancy
Bentley, Mary Esteve, Christopher Looby, Elisa New, and Sianne Ngai—
whose essay here is different from the talk she gave at the conference—as

well as the afterword by Charles Altieri), and we thank them for adding their contributions to the conversation already in progress.

Our editor at Columbia University Press, Philip Leventhal, has been interested, understanding, patient, and strongly supportive (when necessary), and we have greatly enjoyed working with such a talented editor. Our deep gratitude goes also to Alison Alexanian and Susan Pensak for seeing this volume through the editorial and production process so deftly and wisely. The reviewers for the press gave us astute and pointed advice, which we have tried to use to the collection's advantage; they deserve our sincere thanks, and it is a pleasure to express our gratitude to one of them (James Davis of Brooklyn College) by name. We would also like to thank colleagues in the field, many of whom appear in this volume's notes, for helping to bring this book to fruition. They include Hester Blum, Gregg Crane, Mark Eaton, Michael Gilmore, Karen Jacobs, Wyn Kelley, Mark Maslan, John Matthews, Geoff Sanborn, Peter Stoneley, Ezra Tawil, and Robert von Hallberg. Many thanks to Jonathan Katz, chair of Caltech's Division of Humanities and Social Sciences, for his financial support of the project.

Several of these essays have been previously published elsewhere, and we are grateful for permission to reprint them here. Max Cavitch, "Stephen Crane's Refrain," is reprinted by permission from *ESQ: A Journal of the American Renaissance* 54 (2008): 33–54, copyright © 2008 by the Board of Regents of Washington State University. Wendy Steiner's essay provided much of the material for the conclusion to her recent book, *The Real Real Thing: The Model in the Mirror of Art* (Chicago: University of Chicago Press, 2010), and is reprinted by permission of the University of Chicago Press, copyright © 2010 by the University of Chicago. Cindy Weinstein, "When Is Now? Poe's Aesthetics of Temporality," is reprinted by permission from *Poe Studies/Dark Romanticism: History, Theory, Interpretation* 41 (2008): 81–107, copyright © 2008 by the Board of Regents of Washington State University. An earlier version of Jonathan Freedman's essay, "What Maggie Knew: Game Theory, *The Golden Bowl*, and the Possibilities of Aesthetic Knowledge," was published in the *Cambridge Quarterly* 37, no. 1 (2008): 98–113 and is reprinted by permission of Oxford University Press, copyright © the author. Dorothy J. Hale, "Aesthetics and the New Ethics: Theorizing the Novel in the Twenty-First Century," is reprinted by permission of the Modern Language Association of America from *PMLA* 124 (2009): 896–905, copyright © 2009 by the Modern Language Association of America. Eric Lott, "Perfect Is Dead: Karen Carpenter, Theodor Adorno, and the Radio;

or, If Hooks Could Kill," is reprinted by permission of *Criticism: A Quarterly for Literature and the Arts* 50 (2008): 219–34, copyright © 2009 by Wayne State University Press.

The collection is dedicated to our teachers, and that is by now a very large category for both of us, given how much we know we have learned over the years from numerous instructors, colleagues, and friends—too many to be named here. But Christopher Looby wishes to single out one particular teacher to whom to dedicate his contributions to this volume—one out of many inspirational undergraduate and graduate professors he could name, along with all those fellow students, departmental colleagues, and wise friends whose intelligence and learning he has been pleased to enjoy and exploit. Sacvan Bercovitch's rare combination of acute intelligence, prodigious learning, and scholarly imagination continue to represent for him a beautiful and unmatched ideal of critical accomplishment. Cindy Weinstein has been fortunate to study with the very best of teachers (and friends) at Brandeis and Berkeley, but she wishes to dedicate her contributions to this volume to Michael Gilmore and Eric Sundquist. Their exemplary scholarship and steadfast friendship have been her foundation and ideal.

American Literature's Aesthetic Dimensions

Introduction

CINDY WEINSTEIN AND CHRISTOPHER LOOBY

The political potential of art lies only in its own aesthetic dimension.

—HERBERT MARCUSE, *The Aesthetic Dimension*

For a long time, what made American literature distinctive, even exceptional, was held to be its aesthetic particularity: its characteristic "organic
form," its embrace of romance rather than realism, its colloquial style,
or some other discovered or invented aesthetic quality.[1] Then it came
about that this critical use of aesthetic categories to identify and analyze
American literature was considered spurious and politically suspect—
held to constitute a dangerous and morally blameworthy evasion of history and political reality. So for many years the predominant approach
in American literary studies, as in many other sectors of the academic
humanities, was a politically engaged historicism, and the aesthetic
dimension was consciously dismissed (although never, to be sure, successfully avoided) as a matter of minor importance, trivial distraction,
or accidental detail. In recent years, this dismissal has come to seem,
to many of us, limiting or deforming to critical inquiry and scholarly
investigation—and so it comes about that aesthetic questions return to
the critical conversation, perhaps in fruitful conjunction with the historicist and political questions that have earned their central position in
our inquiries.

Aesthetics Redux

American Literature's Aesthetic Dimensions is inspired by the literary criticism of scholars written in the last several decades. We envision this volume as both a critical and companionate piece to Sacvan Bercovitch and Myra Jehlen's seminal *Ideology and Classic American Literature*.[2] Call it what you will—"ideology critique," "new historicism," "cultural studies"—the transformation from understanding American literature as, in the words of Richard Poirier, "a world elsewhere," as an aesthetic object removed from and resistant to the vicissitudes of historical context, to reading literature as profoundly social, has greatly illuminated and complicated our sense of literature's relation to culture.[3] None of the essays in this volume, despite their engagement with questions of aesthetics, departs from the fundamental premise that literature is engaged in what Jane Tompkins famously dubbed "cultural work," which requires a critical methodology that "looks for continuities rather than ruptures, for the strands that connected a novel to other similar texts, rather than for the way in which the text might have been unique."[4] This methodology, of course, has a politics, which Tompkins quite powerfully explains in relation to her own graduate school career, where Harriet Beecher Stowe was a footnote to Mark Twain, where an appreciation of narrative complexity meant that popular novels went unread, where Nathaniel Hawthorne's success was understood solely as a function of his genius and had nothing to do with a complicated network of publishers and reviewers who helped to establish Hawthorne's place in the canon. We do not think any of the contributors to the present volume would dispute this general account of the state of literary criticism in the late 1960s; however, what these essays do is recalibrate the relation between the literary and the social to see if and how the terms purposefully excluded, but not entirely banished, from Tompkins's account—particularly those that fall under the sign of the aesthetic—might be of value and worth acknowledging explicitly once again. She wrote, "I have not tried to emphasize the individuality or genius of the authors in question, to isolate the sensibility, modes of perception, or formal techniques that differentiate them from other authors or from one another" (xv). And yet in her influential reading of *Uncle Tom's Cabin* she wrote that Stowe's novel was "a brilliant redaction of the culture's favorite story about itself—the story of salvation through motherly love" (125). Tompkins's analysis did not isolate Stowe from cultural "modes of perception, or formal techniques," but it certainly "differentiated" Stowe from the likes of certain other authors, such as

Mary Jane Holmes and E. D. E. N. Southworth, to name just two hugely popular novelists of the period who, like Stowe, often wrote that "culture's favorite story about itself." The point to be made with this example (and we shall develop this claim further) is that even the staunchest practitioners of ideological critique deploy, whether explicitly or only implicitly, aesthetic criteria. While Tompkins may not *want* to "differentiate," she nevertheless does so. It is difficult to think of a more aesthetically loaded pronouncement (one that distinguishes *Uncle Tom's Cabin* as "brilliant" on the basis of its narrative form); that it is located in a critical text so committed to questioning the aesthetic is fascinating. The essays in the present volume think through this paradox—can one use the language of aesthetics in a way that does not reproduce the conceptual blindnesses that ideology critique worked to address? Indeed, might questions of sensibility, perception, and form now be put to use, not from a retro-position of political naïveté or New Critical "art for art's sake," but rather from a critical position informed by theoretical developments of the last several decades? Is it possible to talk about "aesthetics" and also to heed Fredric Jameson's call to "always historicize"?[5] And what would this literary criticism look like? The essays in *American Literature's Aesthetic Dimensions* answer these questions.

Let us make clear from the start that this volume does not pretend to represent all of American literature and culture. No set of essays could do so, but our goal has been to put together a collection with a breadth and depth of content that, when brought together, represents a critical intervention into how we might rethink the question of aesthetics and American literature. That said, we have tried to achieve some degree of temporal coverage, ranging from the eighteenth to the twenty-first century. The effects of the critiques of the canon, about which we will have more to say, are exemplified by the heterogeneity of the essays, which centrally address such noncanonical writers (some of them representing minority literary formations) as Phillis Wheatley, Constance Fenimore Woolson, Earl Lind, Sekou Sundiata, and Juliana Spahr (not to mention the Carpenters!), along with canonical authors such as Herman Melville, Stephen Crane, and Henry James. Despite the absence of work on Native American or Latino/a or Asian American writers, we believe that the essays assembled here (on noncanonical texts, by African American writers, gay authors, aural and visual forms, and popular culture) will provide critics working on genres, forms, and texts not featured in this volume with a valuable set of interpretive templates.

The purpose of this introduction is to delineate the place of aesthetics in literary criticism, more generally, and then to analyze the role aesthetics has played in American literary criticism in particular. Arguably, the study of American literature and culture has been as thoroughly hostile, in recent years, to aesthetic questions as any other academic field in the humanities. But what are we talking about when we talk, once again, about "aesthetics"? It will be seen quickly enough by readers of this collection that the contributors are by no means agreed upon the answer to this question— upon what counts as an aesthetic phenomenon or experience, or, indeed, what constitutes the "aesthetic dimension" of the collection's title.[6] It has always been the case that *aesthetics* was a contested term and, likewise, it has always been true that philosophers and critics have used the term in different and sometimes contradictory ways. The American writer, editor, and educator Elizabeth Palmer Peabody, who in 1849 published the first and only issue of a journal she called *Aesthetic Papers*, wrote in her introduction, explaining her choice of the word *aesthetic* in the title, that of all such terms in common use "perhaps no one conveys to the mind a more vague and indeterminable sense than this," characterizing *aesthetic* as "this vague, this comprehensive, but undefined word" and contending that it would be useless to refer to a dictionary or encyclopedia to help determine its meaning.[7] Formal philosophy has nevertheless attempted to define its meaning in various ways, to determine its intrinsic signification or legislate its normative essence, but, again, it will be seen by readers of this collection that formal philosophical definitions play a distinctly subordinate role in the essays that follow. The contributors are literary and cultural scholars and critics who tend to mean a variety of things by *aesthetic* and generally use it for heuristic rather than strictly philosophical purposes—to open up new avenues of inquiry rather than to inhibit or delimit research and criticism. A quick and dirty list of what counts as aesthetic herein would have to include the play of imagination, the exploration of fantasy, the recognition and description of literary form, the materiality of literary inscription and publication, the pleasure of the text, sensuous experience in general, the appreciation of beauty, the adjudication and expression of taste, the broad domain of feeling or affect, or some particular combination of several of these elements.[8] Given the current state of cultural studies, which has for some time been suspicious of aesthetics and even sometimes hostile to aesthetic approaches—and has largely preferred to focus its attention first and foremost on matters of society, history, ideology, politics, and power—it seems wise not to close down prematurely the possible value of a renewed aesthetic dimension to our critical researches and analyses, better not to attempt to prescribe a single definition of *aesthetic*, but to grant the term its "vague and indeterminable sense" (as Peabody said) and encourage a variety of investigations under its aegis.

Many of the essays here might be understood as efforts "to *risk* alternate forms of aesthetic engagement," in Rita Felski's terms.[9] They suspend (in some measure) or subordinate (to a degree) certain reflexive habits of critical demystification—the general attitude Paul Ricoeur famously dubbed the "hermeneutics of suspicion"[10]—to recover and redeem something that may have been nearly lost, and certainly has been usually bracketed and generally suppressed, in most Americanist scholarship of the past several decades. Felski again: "Once we face up to the limits of demystification as a critical method and a theoretical ideal, once we relinquish the modern dogmas that our lives should become thoroughly disenchanted, we can truly begin to engage the affective and absorptive, the sensuous and somatic qualities of aesthetic experience" (76). Felski is essentially appealing to a notion of the aesthetic that is quite archaic, perhaps deriving remotely from the early eighteenth-century German philosopher Alexander Baumgarten's original coinage of the term *aesthetics* and his definition of it as "a science of sensitive knowing (*scientia cognitionis sensitivae*)" or "a science of how things are to be known by means of the senses (*scientiam sensitive quid cognoscendi*)."[11] Although we might well heed Peabody's warning to stay away from dictionaries or encyclopedias in an effort to nail down the meaning of *aesthetic*, it has been almost a reflex of recent critical attempts to reopen aesthetic approaches and questions to do so, to advert to the derivation of the English term from its Greek origin. To quote one especially concise and apt philological and historical summary, from Susan Buck-Morss (who quotes another such summary, from Terry Eagleton), "*Aisthitikos* is the ancient Greek word for that which is 'perceptive by feeling.' *Aisthisis* is the sensory experience of perception. The original field of aesthetics is not art but reality—corporeal, material nature. As Terry Eagleton writes: 'Aesthetics is born as a discourse of the body.' It is a form of cognition, achieved through taste, touch, hearing, seeing, smell—the whole corporeal sensorium."[12] Buck-Morss goes on to argue that "one might rather place [aesthetics] within the field of animal instincts" (6–7) or what Eagleton calls "our creaturely life" (13). Indeed, a number of philosophers have recently undertaken to rehabilitate a form of aesthetic theorizing that is frankly prosensualist, ranging from Ekbert Faas's rereading (under Nietzsche's tutelage) of the entire history of Western philosophical reflection on aesthetic experience as a regrettably puritanical attempt to exorcise "sex, sensuality, sensuousness" from aesthetics to Richard Shusterman's proposal for a "somaesthetics," which envisions a return to "Baumgarten's broad practical vision of aesthetics,"[13] uniting reflection upon the sensorium with practical bodily disciplines, and tellingly draws much of its inspiration from the American pragmatist philosophers William James and John Dewey.[14]

Whatever direction(s) the return to aesthetics takes in the near future, whether "prosensualist" or "new formalist" or "affective" or other, these possibilities all are united by a certain negative impulse or by a negation of a prior negative impulse—what Nancy Bentley, in her essay in this volume, tellingly references as our "disenchant[ment] with disenchantment." This new resistance to the resistance to aesthetics may find some powerful inspiration in the later writings of Sacvan Bercovitch, whose influential work was so powerfully productive of the very turn to ideological analysis that has now, perhaps, started to run out of steam.[15] It is worth remembering how magnetically energizing it seemed when, for example, in *The Puritan Origins of the American Self*, Bercovitch insisted, on the book's final page, at the culmination of an intricate argument about the long historical persistence of an American myth of representative selfhood, on "the importance of ideology (in the Marxist sense) in the shaping of the United States." Less often noticed (but hiding in plain sight) is the sentence immediately following this invocation of "ideology," a sentence in which the key terms nimbly bring us back to the aesthetic dimension: the "persistence of the myth is a testament to the visionary and symbolic power of the American Puritan imagination."[16] The collection of essays Bercovitch edited with Myra Jehlen, mentioned earlier, *Ideology and Classic American Literature*, is often cited as a watershed moment, a consolidation in great form of the turn to ideology critique.[17] But an earlier collection of essays edited by Bercovitch went under the title *The American Puritan Imagination: Essays in Revaluation*, which amounted to a defense of the aesthetic in a scholarly field dominated by attention to the intellectual framework of American Puritanism (à la Perry Miller) at the expense of its creative power and imaginative value.[18] Even less often noticed, however, are several of Bercovitch's own subsequent writings in which he cautions against the divorce of ideological analysis from aesthetic analysis, two approaches he considers to be, together, the "constitutive parts of literary history." "Reverence for art, like all forms of idolatry, is the road to mystification," he bluntly asserts. But "the separation of aesthetic from cognitive analysis," he goes on to say, this "false dichotomy," comes at a high cost to searching inquiry and fruitful dialogue.[19] Elsewhere, using slightly different terms, Bercovitch grants approvingly that "cultural studies is here to stay," but expresses a "hope that as it grows and flourishes it will preserve the literary in what still remains literary and cultural studies. What is at stake here is not just an issue of aesthetics but, more important . . . the prospects of open dialogue in the humanities."[20]

These admonitions of Bercovitch's—which might be said to draw a bright line under the ineluctable interest in aesthetic questions he and others have exhibited all along—date from the 1990s, but have been remarkably slow to gain real traction. Bercovitch's celebrated book on Hawthorne, *The Office of "The Scarlet Letter,"* was itself a practical demonstration of the inextricable entanglement of aesthetic and ideological matters and the necessary critical virtue of keeping their dynamic interrelationship in constant play.[21] The professional academic resistance to aesthetics has been nearly intractable, however, and the wariness exhibited even by some of those who once again feel the pull of the aesthetic dimension is palpable. Several signal moments, large and small, might be cited as evincing the halting return to aesthetic questions in American literary studies, among them the special issue of *American Literature* coedited (with Russ Castronovo) by one of our contributors, Christopher Castiglia, in 2004, under the title "Aesthetics and the End(s) of Cultural Studies"; another collection, edited by Emory Elliott, Louis Freitas Caton, and Jeffrey Rhyne, *Aesthetics in a Multicultural Age*; yet another collection, *The Aesthetics of Cultural Studies*, edited by Michael Berubé; and a recent issue of the journal *Representations*, entitled "The Way We Read Now," coedited by Sharon Marcus and Stephen Best, that proposes a notion of "surface reading" as an antidote to the habits of symptomatic reading that have held sway for a good long time.[22] This last collection is especially interesting, and—we might say—symptomatic of what Castiglia and Castronovo in their introduction to the special issue of *American Literature* frankly called the "aversion to aesthetics" that has generally prevailed among "the public and professional cultures of academia" (1). Best and Marcus, in their introduction, eschew the language of the aesthetic nearly entirely, although it would seem to be a category perfectly well suited to their purposes; they associate aesthetics with "the broad field styled as 'New Formalist,'" but do not embrace the term as their own; among the contributors to their special issue, several are studiously averse to the term while others use it freely; and the authors of the afterword also carefully avoid it.[23] At the same time, Best and Marcus voice reservations about the political efficacy of academic work in the humanities and acknowledge that their style of surface reading "might easily be characterized as politically quietist, too willing to accept things as they are" (16).

Might abjuring the category of the aesthetic—paradoxically—have something materially to do with the risk of political quietism? Although the aims of the present volume are in many ways compatible with those of the proponents of "surface reading," we choose to adopt *aesthetic* as a usable term precisely because its history involves the discipline of a careful attention to surfaces and appearances, to the sensible textures of things, and its history also preserves the conviction that social and political life always has a sensory and perceptual dimension.

With this history of aesthetics and this summary framing of recent developments in mind, we can now discuss the deployment of this term (and category) in accounts of American literature. The critique of aesthetics assumes a variety of different forms, with differing emphases, and this is the case because aesthetics is so capaciously defined. That said, virtually all works of literary criticism that position themselves against aesthetics contain some kind of accusatory statement about aesthetics as universalizing, as dehistoricizing, as problematically privileging literary discourse over other discourses, as depoliticizing (which is, in itself, of course, politicizing). Again, we can turn to Jane Tompkins as representative of this particular position: "It is the notion of literary texts as doing work, expressing and shaping the social context that produced them, that I wish to substitute finally for the critical perspective that sees them as attempts to achieve a timeless, universal ideal of truth and formal coherence" (200). What is "substituted" for aesthetics ("timeless," "universal," "formal coherence") is historicizing, politicizing, specifying, as in taking account of gender, race, region, and class, and popularizing, as in engaging with popular texts. This substitution, however, is not a simple one. Using the language of mathematics, while discussing the relative simplicity of characters in popular novels, Tompkins argues that their "familiarity and typicality, rather than making them bankrupt or stale, are the basis of their effectiveness as integers in a social equation" (xvi). It is hard to imagine an account of character (and text) more committed to a notion of "formal coherence" than this, or a statement of universality more complete than this one: "a novel's impact on the culture at large depends . . . not on its departure from the ordinary and conventional, but through its embrace of what is most widely shared" (xvi).

Despite this and other inconsistencies in certain critical accounts skeptical of aesthetics, particularly around the issue of formalism, which we shall discuss in greater detail, this work of historicization and politicization has wrought tremendous and much-needed change in the canon of American literature as well as the methodologies, including feminism, deconstruction, and postcolonialism, that have been brought to bear on the field. Thus, Tompkins is absolutely correct when she says that "an entirely new story begins to unfold" when one approaches texts from a perspective that "reverse[s] the negative judgments" of past critics (xvii). But as necessary and hermeneutically fruitful and historically nuanced as that critical position has been, it also depends, ironically, upon reifying the aesthetic as it renders *ahistorical* questions of taste, beauty, affect, and feeling.[24] We agree that the aesthetic cannot be understood apart from ideology, but we also think that yet another "new story" might unfold if we revisit aesthetics with the methodological and theoretical knowledge gained from critics of the last several decades. In an elegant statement that anticipates this volume, Richard Brodhead presciently writes in *Cultures of Letters*, one of the most important new historicist monographs to come out of the 1990s: "The most compelling reason for studying the social relations of literary forms is that this dimension has been so long and so systematically ignored. Once this territory has been scouted as thoroughly as some others, visiting it will become comparatively less rewarding."[25] Might "the social relations of literary forms" be reintroduced to their aesthetic relations?

Along with other scholars in the profession, we have begun to wonder if the category of the aesthetic (and the artifacts that have been designated as "aesthetic") was worth revisiting with a less suspicious attitude. We wanted to examine whether aesthetics was useful only insofar as it was one more exemplification of the operations of what Louis Althusser has described as "ideological state apparatuses."[26] Or/and does that category (and do those objects) also provide us with a framework and a vocabulary that give us deeper insight into how we read, what we read, and why we read? It is time to revisit our position vis-à-vis aesthetics and specifically the way that aesthetics has been cast as a subservient handmaiden to the hegemony of ideology.[27]

As should be evident, the goal of this volume is not to resuscitate aesthetic categories in order simply to go back to a New Critical moment when the text stood alone as an object of study, cordoned off from the putatively disfiguring effects of politics, biography, production, and reception—in other words, context; rather, the aim is to reintroduce aesthetic categories—such as style, form, beauty, pleasure, imagination, in order to demonstrate the ways in which aesthetics and politics are dialectically engaged. That dialectical engagement, however, is the *donnée* of all these essays, which then seek to go beyond that and explicate how a broadly conceived notion of aesthetics—its properties, its effects, its representational status—better

equips us to analyze that engagement and, in doing so, gives a set of interpretive tools that allows us to get past the habitual reduction of aesthetics to
ideology. The essays comprising *American Literature's Aesthetic Dimensions*
open up this homology in order to provide examples of how literary critics might move forward as they reposition American literature's aesthetic
dimensions in relation to its ideological ones.

Indeed, one of the primary reasons for this volume (that sense of something missing) has to do with how that homology has defined (and limited)
analyses of American literature.[28] In offering the following partial survey of
American literary criticism over the last several decades, we have chosen
certain representative texts that we believe most directly take up the case
against aesthetics, though by no means does this survey do justice to the
wide-ranging and numerous contributions made by scholars in the field.
With that caveat in mind, let us turn again to one of the defining texts of
the 1980s, *Ideology and Classic American Literature* (1986), in which the
contested relation between aesthetics and politics is, as in this volume, the
impetus for a set of ambitious and powerful essays. When Sacvan Bercovitch, in his afterword, wished to critique the American ideology that is
"adopted from the start precisely for its capacity to transmute radicalism of
all forms, from religious protest to revolutionary war, into forms of cultural
consensus," he described that ideology as an "aesthetic flowering" (436).
Aesthetic flowering, which is the direct result for Bercovitch of the production of the "'representative' American" (436), however, comes with thorns.
We might take John Carlos Rowe's work on literature and imperialism as
representative of a critical unease with what that flowering implies; his
aim in *Literary Culture and U.S. Imperialism* is to "follow the logic of a text
without lapsing into trivial formalism or celebration of literary ambiguity or linguistic undecidability."[29] Presumably, trivial formalism (and Rowe
describes his method as "anti-formal") is one that fails to "use the text to
gain access to a wider historical and cultural field of debate and inquiry"; in
other words, a formalism that is designated by the term *aesthetics*.

"Aesthetic criteria" (23), elsewhere referred to as "conventional aesthetic
standards," are, in Rowe's analysis, the problem that animates everything
from New Criticism to structuralism to deconstruction. They cordon
off the canonical from the noncanonical, thereby limiting our exposure
to and understanding of historical contexts. They tend to focus on "the
moral conclusions and aesthetic pleasures of the middle-class novel" (15).
And they privilege literature as a domain outside ideology (in a footnote,
Rowe alludes to "traditional literary study which often tacitly supports an

aesthetic ideology" [302n36]). The solution is a cultural history paradigm that "assess[es] the literary work's relative contributions to social consensus and social reform" rather than a model of "literary criticism [that] ha[s] often focused on a text's aesthetic value" (19). Perhaps Janice A. Radway's *Reading the Romance*, with its methodological commitment to offering "less an account of the way romances as texts were interpreted than of the way romance reading as a form of behavior operated as a complex intervention in the ongoing social life of actual social subjects" is the most radical exemplar and apogee of the critique of aesthetics.[30] We shall have more to say about Radway's work, but for now it is worth observing that, for her, the logical outcome of a critique of "aesthetic achievement" is a methodology that disavows the canon, interpretation, and the text.

Rowe's and Radway's similar critiques of literary criticism, on the grounds of its putative focus on the aesthetic, do not stand alone. Indeed, "a turn to aesthetic questions," writes Donald Pease in *Visionary Compacts*, allowed F. O. Matthiessen to "devise a national consensus" that converted "the conflicting claims" of antebellum political rhetoric into "the achieved art of the American Renaissance."[31] Aesthetics, for Pease, is the stuff of "rarified struggle" (10) as opposed to the real, which comprises "divisive political questions, as well as pre-Civil War cultural context" (10). Whereas Pease's goal is to release the cultural context of canonical texts held in check by Matthiessen's attention to aesthetics, the work of Rowe and Tompkins, as well as that of Cathy N. Davidson, aimed to subvert the notion of the canon itself. Their readings of everything from "The Black Elk Narratives" to Hannah Webster Foster's *The Coquette* to Susan Warner's *The Wide, Wide World* reveal a desire to expand our sense of what counts as literature and the literary. And this is so because of a shared sense that the dismissal of their archive is based on "grounds which have come to seem universal standards of aesthetic judgment" (Tompkins 123). In fact, it is important to keep in mind that the aesthetic has been deployed to keep certain authors in the canon and others out. In challenging traditional and historically decontextualized definitions of "aesthetic judgment," works by women, African Americans, Native Americans, queers, and other previously all but invisible writers have been able to find their place in the critical discourse. Henry Louis Gates's magisterial collection of African American texts from the Schomburg Library is evidence of how critiques of the canon have not only enlarged but also reconstituted the field of American literature.[32] Cathy N. Davidson puts the point this way in her essential *Revolution and the Word*, which helped to make Susanna Rowson's *Charlotte Temple* and

Hannah Foster's *The Coquette* indispensable for an understanding of early American literature: "What we read shapes how we read—a reversal of the usual critical presupposition" and an "imperative toward canonization, toward the creation of a univocal history . . . requires the exclusion of what does not fit into the a priori definition of precisely what is to be defined."[33]

For many of these critics, the turn away from aesthetics has as much to do with an argument about the canon as with a particular claim about literature's relation to culture, that it has no special relation to culture that would enable a text to mount a critique of the social or "redefinition" of it, to use Tompkins's word (xi). Davidson, for example, distinguishes her work from "traditional literary criticism," which she defines this way: "literature is not simply words upon a page but a complex social, political, and material process of cultural production" (viii). For these critics, the ultimate value of literature inheres in what it has to say about the social world, and because the aesthetic (somehow) seems separate from that world, or obstructs our understanding of that world, we must turn away from it.

This critical approach is sometimes described as new historicism, and among its eclectic inspirations are the deconstructive work of Jacques Derrida, Paul de Man, and others who became known as the Yale school, as well as the theoretical works of Michel Foucault and the thought of cultural anthropologists such as Clifford Geertz. It is worth briefly rehearsing the theoretical engines of new historicism because the terms they have given us—terms such as *writing* and *discourse*, for example—are now such a crucial part of our interpretive fabric as to seem almost invisible, perhaps even commonplace. Although this discussion will move us away, for the time being, from the topic of aesthetics, it is a necessary digression because these theories have had an enormous influence on how we define literature and how we practice literary criticism. The question of aesthetics and the status of the literary text are pivotal, even when the term is out of sight.

Let us begin with deconstruction. In his introduction to Paul de Man's *Blindness and Insight*, Wlad Godzich explains "that there is no difference of being between what is within and what is without the frame: they are both of representation."[34] Challenging the distinction between within and without, between signifier and signified, between text and context, is a crucial feature of deconstruction, and Jacques Derrida puts it this (inimitable) way in *Of Grammatology*: "The outside bears with the inside a relationship that is, as usual, anything but simple exteriority. The meaning of the outside was always present within the inside, imprisoned outside the outside, and vice-versa."[35] What this means, according to another Yale school literary critic, Geoffrey Hartman, is "that writing cannot be an antidote to anything except itself, that it questions its own representational claims by a repetition that phantomizes presence."[36] The key term for Derrida is writing, which is understood as a representation that seems to signify something real, but in fact refers only to the absence of the real, only to itself and the fact of its own status as representation. Its repetition merely creates the illusion of presence.

It would seem as if deconstruction, and its close reading of specific texts or, more precisely, specific words in the most canonical of texts (and here we have in mind de Man's reading of Jean Jacques Rousseau and Marcel Proust and Derrida's reading of Saussurean linguistics), has little to do, whether conceptually or methodologically, with new historicism and its disciplinary Luddism. Let us remind ourselves, however, of Foucault's eloquent account of the poet in *The Order of Things*, where he notes: "the poet is he who beneath the named, constantly expected differences, recovers the buried kinships between things, their scattered resemblances. Beneath the established signs, and in spite of them, he hears another, deeper, discourse."[37] What "writing" is for Derrida, "discourse" is for Foucault. In *The Archeology of Knowledge*, Foucault gives literary critics both a definition and a methodology: "The frontiers of a book are never clear-cut: beyond the title, the first lines, and the last full stop, beyond its internal configuration and its autonomous form, it is caught up in a system of references to other books, other texts, other sentences: it is a node within a network. . . . its unity is variable and relative. As soon as one questions that unity, it loses its self-evidence; it indicates itself, it constructs itself, only on the basis of a complex field of discourse." For Foucault, this scattering of unities and understanding of the "interplay of relations within it [the book or any other literary statement or event] and outside it" serves to answer the key question, "how is it that one particular statement appeared rather than another?"[38]

In terms of the aesthetic stakes of this argument, the Foucauldian discursive network is constituted by a variety of texts from a variety of disciplines, leaving open the question of whether or not aesthetic discourse should be granted a certain privileged status by virtue of its beauty (as compared to, say, psychological discourse), self-awareness (relative to, say, ethnographic discourse), or its breadth of referentiality (relative to, say, economic discourse). In large part, the role of the new historicist critic is the reconstruction of this "network," the optimal result being what anthropologist Clifford Geertz famously called the "thick description" of cultural discourse.[39] One might think that critics would be torn between the deconstructive assumption that texts eventuate in "an ultimate impasse of thought engendered by a rhetoric that always insinuates its own textual workings into the truth claims of philosophy" and the Foucauldian impera-tive to challenge the "frontiers of a book" by offering a thickly descrip-tive account of "a complex field of discourse."[40] The fact is that they share some fundamental principles, including a focus on "representation," an insistence on the porousness of discursive boundaries, and a methodology that discovers the fiction, the aporia, that generates the seeming fact. Gil-lian Brown's *Domestic Individualism* makes the theoretical connection quite overtly in her introduction where she discusses how her "deconstruction-ist approach" allows for what we might call great discursive latitude: "in my presentation of the cohabitation of the individual with the economic, material conditions and mental states coalesce." Moreover, in an interpre-tive move that turns the outside inside (and vice versa), she argues that "the individual [himself] shares the definitive principle of domesticity: its withdrawal from the marketplace." In addition, Brown's deconstruc-tive approach begins with an understanding of the self that is "continually under construction, or at least renovation," is dissatisfied with any analysis that produces "a unitary politics" or "totalizing force," and is character-ized by a profound skepticism about binaries, whether it be public/private, male female, person/machine, inside/outside.[41]

What does this mean for the aesthetic? It means what Brodhead said it means: a radically new and productive way of understanding "literary forms in relation to social relations." It does so first by leveling the playing field, in the sense that literature takes its place as one more discourse in the cultural field, which includes economics, psychology, sociology, etc., and, second, it produces the author as one more site where these discursive combinations are seen to operate. This resituation of the literary text—which had for so long been constructed as a unique object untouched by social context and was then being understood as fully imbricated in that context—infused literary criticism with renewed energy and conviction. The explosive impact of deconstruction on literature's "aesthetic dimen-sion" can be found perhaps most provocatively in Walter Benn Michaels's *The Gold Standard and the Logic of Naturalism*, in which he writes, "the only relation literature as such has to culture as such is that it is part of it." The notion of literature as "posit[ing] a space outside the culture in order then to interrogate the relations between that space (here defined as literature) and the culture" is one that Michaels in particular and new historicists more generally worked to dispel. To use one of Michaels's examples, one should not expect to get from "The Yellow Wallpaper" an understanding of Gilman's relation to capitalism because it "seems wrong to think of the culture you live in as the object of your affections: you don't like it or dislike it, you exist in it, and the things you like and dislike exist in it too." What you can get from it, however, is an "*exemplif*[ication] [of] that culture."⁴² A similar claim is made by Wai-chee Dimock in her analysis of Melville's career, *Empire for Liberty*, where she argues: "what each book invokes, affirms, and defends is always the principle of imperial freedom, a principle of authorial license embedded in a technology of control. In that regard, Melville dramatizes the very juncture where the logic of freedom dovetails into the logic of empire . . . where the imperial self of Jacksonian individualism recapitulates the logic of Jacksonian imperialism."⁴³

In one of the most illuminating readings of Melville, Dimock explains how his works repeatedly recapitulate a logic of individualism that is itself a recapitulation of the logic of empire. Melville's literary accomplishment and value, for Dimock, exists primarily in relation to its exemplification of Jacksonian democracy, as his literary production gets absorbed under the rubric of cultural production. But, as we saw in the case of Tompkins, that "substitution" of the literary by the social is not always exact, and we would contend that the latent valorization of the literary that quietly subtends Dimock's analysis is crucial to the power of her argument. Without using the term *aesthetic* and without overtly granting special privilege to Melville's work, the fact is that her readings, time and again, derive value and specificity (separate and apart from the social value she is most interested in illuminating) from the language of aesthetics and the language of Melville's art. We would submit that as much as Melville's novels discursively intersect with "Horace Mann's rhetoric of social cataclysm" (108), Melville's rhetoric is considerably more pleasurable, more stylistically and formally complex than Mann's. Dimock explains, "Melville is not just placating the reader [in *Redburn*]; he is also representing the act of placating, a double operation by which the reader's authority is at once complied with and reexhibited as coercive agency" (90). At one point in her reading of *Moby-Dick*, she does a close reading of the "tautology, 'Ahab is for ever Ahab'" (136), in order to disclose how Ahab occupies the poles both of Manifest Destiny and of Native American doom. She writes: "the instrument of indictment, in both cases, is the very figure of selfhood, a figure that both encloses and excludes: a tautology, finally, within whose confines one always is what one is" (138). It is, of course, Melville's tautology (not reformer Mann's and not historian Francis Parkman's, two other voices comprising the discursive network), which Dimock argues is "as much a social phenomenon as a literary one" (136) that allows her to make this original and illuminating claim. Our observation here is simple. Although Dimock's point is to reveal the analogies between "textual governance" and "social governance," between "authorial sovereignty" and "America's national sovereignty" (7), the strength of the analysis comes, in large measure, from a necessary and at times even stated, though more often not, privileging of Melville's words, style, and forms.

Dimock's argument at once derives its interpretive creativity from the Foucauldian paradigm she is deploying, while it also reveals some of the theoretical pressures a literary critic might encounter when relying on said paradigm.[44] The author, to quote Foucault, is a constructed entity with a variety of functions, not least of which is to serve as "a point where contradictions are resolved, where the incompatible elements can be shown to relate to one another or to cohere around a fundamental and originating contradiction." One should observe here the theoretical kinship between deconstruction and new historicism as the "author-function" becomes the site of the deconstructive aporia. In addition, but unlike deconstruction, the "author-function" enables an evaluative move that allows readers to "speak of an individual's 'profundity' or 'creative' power."[45] For Foucault, we must finally and fully rid ourselves of our interpretive dependence on the author because it is based on a mistaken need for "a principle of unity in writing where any unevenness of production is ascribed to changes caused by evolution, maturation, or outside influence." Thus, at the conclusion of Michaels's *tour de force* reading of Frank Norris, he writes: "the subject of naturalism . . . is typically unable to keep his beliefs lined up with his interests for more than two or three pages at a time, a failure that stems not from inadequate powers of concentration but from the fact that his identity as a subject consists only in the beliefs and desires made available by the naturalist logic—which is not produced by the naturalist subject but rather is the condition of his existence."[46] Similarly, "Melville's authorial practices are," according to Dimock, "neither strictly private nor even strictly literary, for what they adumbrate, in their controlling logic of form, is something like a controlling 'logic of culture'" (7). These analyses accomplish the Foucauldian mandate, which demands that "the subject (and its substitutes) must be stripped of its creative role and analysed as a complex and variable function of discourse."[47]

If literature is one discourse among many, without any exceptional status, and if the author is a function of those discourses, without the pedigree of creativity, it would seem that the category of the aesthetic has been fatally wounded. But that is not exactly true. What has been wounded, and deservedly so, is a particular definition of the aesthetic that links it to a notion of textual or authorial transcendence, not, in other words, a wholesale dismissal of the notion of the aesthetic itself. Thus, even in a work of literary criticism like Claudia Tate's *Domestic Allegories of Political Desire*, which defines itself as "read[ing] these novels [by African American women] against the cultural history of the epoch of their production," she is simultaneously committed to "recovering the[ir] aesthetic value." Tate understands that value as the novels' "ability to gratify a distinct audience of ambitious black Americans who sought to live fully, despite their commonly experienced racial oppression."[48] *Gratification* is a term that also appears in Janice A. Radway's *Reading the Romance* (96), wherein she records the following observation made by one of the women who is talking about the threat men feel when the women around them read romances: it "has little to do with the kinds of books their wives are reading and more to do with the simple fact of the activity itself and its capacity to absorb the participants' entire attention" (91).

It might seem odd to use Radway's account of reading the romance as evidence for the claim that aesthetics has never fully left the critical vocabulary of American literary criticism. Not only does she focus on a genre (popular romance novels) that perhaps more than any other has been dismissed on aesthetic grounds, but she also eschews a reading about "the meaning of romances" to offer a reading of "the meaning of romance *reading* as an activity and a social event" (7). She is writing about books that are, for all intents and purposes, duplicates of one another, stylistically and narratively repetitive. That said, however, she, like Tate, discovers a value in their "ability to gratify," or, as Radway puts it, "the reading experience is valued for the way it makes the reader feel . . . a general sense of emotional well-being and visceral contentment" (70). Moreover, Radway, whose introduction describes a process whereby she realizes the book she is writing is not about "romances as texts" (7), nevertheless ends up with a meditation on the romance and the "narrative technique[s] employed" (205) that create the powerful experience of reading the romance. It is through the "peculiar blend of a deliberately referential language with the signs of 'the literary'" (192) that the reader is transfixed. Radway's use of quotation marks to cordon off "the literary" should not go unnoticed (she does the same thing a page earlier), because it gets at a theoretical difficulty. Radway's method and subject matter are driven by the imperatives of a "culturally oriented scholarship" (3) that works to undo the very cordoning off implicit in that extra set of quotation marks. If the literary really is a manifestation of the social, if popular culture really is literary, why reinforce that separation with a doubling of quotation marks? Is it because the literary is somehow (and this is where the essays in this volume come in) in a different relation to the social, a distinctive relation of the aesthetic to the social that is designated by punctuation if not always by prose?

Like Dimock, Radway's culturally driven analysis is informed by the language of the literary, perhaps nowhere more so than in its final chapter, "Language and Narrative Discourse," a title inspired, perhaps, by structuralist Gerard Genette, though he is not directly referenced, and it turns out that not just any reading experience produces "the feeling of pleasure" (93); rather, it is specific to how "a literary text can be said to operate on the reader" (188). With this formulation about textual "operation[s]," we are back to Tompkins's notion of a text's "cultural work." She writes in her introduction that she "was trying to understand what gave these novels traction in their original setting (i.e., what made them popular, not what made them 'art')" (xv). For Radway, part of the effectiveness of the popular romance's cultural work lay in its usage of literary forms. The romances represent the world here and elsewhere, now and some other time. That is the power and complexity of their artistry. For Tompkins, "non-fictional discourse, when set side by side with contemporary fiction, can be seen to construct the real world in the image of a set of ideals and beliefs in exactly the same way that novels and stories do" (xv). This striking formulation produced a series of readings that, as Tompkins writes in her final chapter, is a "competing attempt [contra Matthiessen] to constitute American literature" (200). She succeeded in reconfiguring the canon.[49] Uncle Tom's Cabin and The Wide, Wide World are required reading for scholars of American literature, not because of their "escape from the formulaic and derivative" but because they "[tap] into a storehouse of commonly held assumptions, reproducing what is already there in a typical and familiar form" (xvi).

But, if these texts are "typical" and "familiar," why read these particular texts and not other typical ones? Why read novels if one can get the same "cultural information" (xvi) from religious tracts? Going back to Foucault, why constitute the discursive network of American sentimentalism through The Wide, Wide World and not one of the hundreds of other sentimental novels written at the time? Is it perhaps because this novel is more typical or more capaciously referential than those others? Does it do a better job, as it were, of "tap[ping] into that storehouse" and might that have something to do with their aesthetic properties? Tompkins is profoundly aware of these questions and attempts to answer them in her final chapter, aptly named, "But is it any good?" Her position is that this question is the wrong one to ask because the term *good* already assumes that everyone knows what is good, and that is precisely what Tompkins is disputing. We agree with Tompkins that the notion of "good" is historically grounded and not universal or transcendent (code words, as we have seen, for the aesthetic). But we think that Tompkins overstates the case, though not necessarily so at the time of writing the book. We do not think that non-fictional discourses construct "the real world in the image of a set of ideals and beliefs in exactly the same way that novels and stories do." Rather, we think of works of art in the way Adorno formulates it in *Aesthetic Theory*: "works of art are after-images or replicas of empirical life, inasmuch as they proffer to the latter what in the outside world is being denied them. . . . Whereas the line separating art from real life should not be fudged, least of all by glorifying the artist, it must be kept in mind that works of art are alive, have a life sui generis. Their life is more than just an outward fate."[50] Rather than Tompkins's "image," we see art as an "after-image." "Exactly the same way" is too limiting because it takes off the interpretive table an entire vocabulary—the vocabulary of the aesthetic—that we might use, once again, in understanding literature.

The Volume

The essays in the present volume are organized into four thematic clusters, followed by an afterword. The essays in part 1, "Aesthetics and the Politics of Freedom," examine aesthetic theory, iconography, form, and public performance in relation to the question of freedom. That relation is essential to an understanding of the eighteenth-century poetry of Phillis Wheatley, the nineteenth-century prose of Harriet Beecher Stowe and Frank J. Webb, the turn-of-the-century poetry of Stephen Crane, and the multiple artistic genres of twenty-first century artist Sekou Sundiata. However, the essays analyze aesthetics from within their historical contexts in order to explain the specific political frameworks and debates that animate the text's aesthetic dimensions. Edward Cahill establishes the dialectic of freedom and constraint that is constitutive of theories of the aesthetic and political analyses of liberty. He then demonstrates how Wheatley embodies this dialectic in her identity as poet and slave as well as in the poetry itself, which is located "within the contested socio-political context of eighteenth-century race slavery without ever becoming reducible to that context." The aesthetic liberty Cahill describes in his essay becomes radicalized in Ivy G. Wilson's account of the "revolutionary aesthetic" he sees at work in the iconographic deployments of writers as diverse as Washington Irving and Ralph Ellison. In this essay, American literature is surveyed for its strategic placement of iconic imagery, particularly George Washington and Toussaint L'Ouverture, in order to illustrate a radical privacy—a space of "innervision . . . that counteracted [African Americans'] depictions in the public imaginary." American literary texts thus enfold within themselves a space for a revolutionary, iconographic aesthetic, one that allows African Americans to see or imagine, in a way that language does not always permit, "themselves as part of the U.S. or, conversely, to fantasize about alternative socialities."

Max Cavitch takes up the question of aesthetics and politics through the lens of Stephen Crane's poetry, and explains how the formal experimentation of free verse has been incorrectly tied to "liberal-progressive accounts of expressivity." In fact, this essay argues that the function of the refrain, and Crane's relentless repetitions that constitute his refrains, are themselves a critique of the position, from within the very structure of free verse, that freedom of form equals freedom of politics. The modernism of Crane's poems thus leads not to a "revolutionary aesthetic" but rather indexes "a paroxysm of the antiaesthetic," which is based not on freedom but convention, not on innervision but its vacuity, not on alternatives but repetition. The last essay in part 1 returns to an analysis of the liberatory politics of the aesthetic. Julie Ellison analyzes the proliferation of institutional spaces that are devoted to the production, through various art forms, of "lyric citizenship," and contextualizes this development in relation to the present moment of Barack Obama's presidency. Through a reading of Sundiata's *51st (dream) state*, as well as texts written primarily by African American academics, creative writers, and public intellectuals, Ellison argues for the renewed presence of an aesthetic dimension in discourse— whether through the language of dreams, magic, or lyric—that represents "political possibility and impossibility, a swinging door between agency and loss." The aesthetic dimension is where hope is alive.

The essays in part 2, "Aesthetics and Sexuality," argue that the embodied pleasures of aesthetic imagining provide the crucial conceptual ground for a redefinition of sociality (see Wilson, Ellison, Bentley, Hale, and Ngai for related claims). The particularities of that redefinition, and the form they take, vary depending upon the historical context in which the text is being produced and read. Judith Butler's deconstructive work on gender, and specifically the radical potentiality she sees in the aesthetic realm, is essential to all these essays as they examine how literature can transform structures of intimacy, sexuality, desire, and beauty. Christopher Castiglia focuses on Nathaniel Hawthorne's *The Marble Faun* in order to delineate how the novel's dense network of friendship becomes a vehicle for Hawthorne to imagine a romanticism that "enhance[s] the possibilities for inventive intimacies." By drawing the connections between Hawthorne's biography (the love letters between him and his "ideal reader," Herman Melville), Schiller's concept of aesthetic as "something akin to the Ideal," and the novel's idealization of the aesthetic in the chapter "An Aesthetic Company," Castiglia unfolds the means by which "the transformative play of aesthetic imagination opens up a space of negotiative and compensatory intimacy." Like Castigilia's, Dorri Beam's essay on Henry James's "A Figure in the Carpet" and Constance Fenimore Woolson's "Miss Grief" is also about intimacy; but the intimacy generated, the "Aesthetic Company" that is kept, takes place less within the pages of each individual story and more across the texts, through characters, and in form. Beam's reading establishes the centrality of gender performance in "Miss Grief" and the parodic confusions those performances entail, which "breed more capacious forms of social and sexual intercourse and more capacious forms of reading." The aesthetic dimension permits Woolson the freedom to write and to parody the conventional sexual and textual relations expected of "the master" toward a potential disciple (the plot of Woolson's story). The two writers are able to forge an intertextual relation with each other that eventuates in an acknowledgment of Woolson's literary value, a recognition that "brings one into relation with the possibilities that unfold." Christopher Looby's essay is concerned with analyzing a set of literary texts from the early twentieth century (late teens to the early thirties) that meditate on a historical transformation that disarticulated erotics from aesthetics. Medical, legal, psychological, and scientific discourses, as we know from Foucault, redefined "various kinds of allied pleasures" as "sexual pathology." Aesthetics, for writers as diverse as Charles Warren Stoddard and H.D., permit a kind of recuperation (both textual and sexual) of uncategorized desire and possibility that "returns us to unmediated sensory pleasure of an elusive kind." As Looby reminds us, at the definitional heart of "aesthetics" is the notion of sense perception, and once that notion of sense perception is restored to our understanding of aesthetics, it makes perfect sense to ask the provocative question that motivates his reading: "what if sexuality is essentially an aesthetic phenomenon?"

The final essay by Wendy Steiner returns us, like Looby's, to an older tradition of aesthetics, one inextricably linked to ideas about beauty. Yet, like
the essays by Castiglia and Beam, Steiner is interested in thinking about
an aesthetic category—such as beauty—as the ground of relation, as the
source of sociality. Nathaniel Hawthorne's short story, "The Birthmark," is
emblematic of the killing effects of the quest for perfection, which is then
traced through twentieth-century texts, such as Christopher Bram's *Father
of Frankenstein*, the writings of Harvard ethicist Michael J. Sandel, and ending with the film musical *Hairspray*. To think of "beauty as an interaction"
is to understand that interaction as ethical or unethical. "The Birthmark"
represents the latter, *Hairspray* the former inasmuch as it makes the case
not for gender unmoored from the constraints of convention (although
that certainly applies to some characters), but rather for a democratizing
ethics of imperfection.

The essays by Cindy Weinstein, Trish Loughran, Jonathan Freedman
and Elisa New—grouped here in part 3, "Aesthetics and the Reading of
Form"—all construe the aesthetic as a matter chiefly of literary form. What
each of them means by form, however, proves to be somewhat different.
Weinstein and Loughran both provide intricate analyses of the ways in
which two of the most difficult and enigmatic of antebellum American
texts, Poe's *The Narrative of Arthur Gordon Pym* (1837–38) and Melville's
Benito Cereno (1855), manipulate narrative form and thus powerfully affect
readerly reception in ways that deeply complicate, if they do not utterly con-
found, critical attempts to extract a stable political meaning from the text.
Without a scrupulous accounting of these formal complexities, Weinstein
and Loughran argue, any attempt to discover the political implications of
the narratives will be fatally compromised. Weinstein outlines the many
ways in which indications of temporality (verb tense, adverbs like *after* and
at length, adjectives like *immediate* and *still*, etc.) are inscrutably woven into
Pym's "narrative fabric" and shows how that narrative fabric is thus so
elaborately overwrought as to be finally indecipherable. This "aesthetics of
temporality," as she calls it, creating the effect of a "dissolution of time,"
is counterposed to the many ways in which, in *Pym*, *spatial* location (and
its affiliated social categories of primitive and advanced as well as racial
categories of black and white) is rendered stable and knowable. Drawing
on the work of anthropologist Johannes Fabian, who has demonstrated that
cultural categories of racial alterity depend upon assignments of temporal
relation (one people being construed as more primitive or more advanced,
for instance, than another), Weinstein further argues that in Poe's tale the

"instability of time" stands in an unsettled relationship to the relative stability of racial categories, although eventually this suspension dissipates as
"the relativity of time is replaced by the reliability of racial terror." The goal
of Weinstein's analysis is not "to save Poe from his politics (or repudiate
him because of them)" but to bear witness to the simultaneity (so to speak)
within *Pym* of a racial logic we might find objectionable and an aesthetics
of temporality that "undercuts that logic by dismantling the temporal pillar
upon which" that racial logic stands.

In Loughran's astute rereading of *Benito Cereno*, the narrative manipulation of time likewise presents a powerful challenge to assured political
judgment. She explicates the details of how Melville ingeniously exploits
the possibilities of narrative art—first implicating the reader of this tricky
narrative in a "disposable" (initial, deluded) reading, then entailing upon
him a "durable" (second, disillusioned) reading. Loughran describes this
double manipulation of the reader not in the interest of making political judgments impossible, but rather to caution against the critical tendency, all too familiar, to recruit a text like this for "presentist" purposes.
Loughran's critique of facile presentism is not offered merely as a defense
of "the historicist turn we have just lived through in the last twenty years or
so in American literary studies," because in fact she wishes to credit Melville with the intention, and the artistic skill, to address an ideal reader who
transcends, in some degree, historical locatedness and limitation. *Benito
Cereno* is famous for the narrative trick it plays, rendering its readers the
dupes (along with the duped captain who narrates it) of a character, Babo,
who is craftily pretending to be a submissive slave when in fact he is a
successful mutineer, a revolutionary. The truth about Babo is eventually
revealed—to Captain Delano and, perforce, to us—so that a second reading of the story will always be a knowing rather than an innocent one.
Acknowledging Melville's powerful conscription of the reader of *Benito
Cereno* into a position of critical reflection on his *own* historical situated-
ness requires, as Loughran shows, scrupulously understanding how the
tale formally dramatizes the structure of "aesthetic reception."

Like Loughran, Jonathan Freedman is interested in the epistemological drama in his text, Henry James's late novel *The Golden Bowl*. Freedman's scrupulous exfoliation of James's emplotment of the calculating
interactions between a small set of players in a game of intimate strategic
manipulation, and his explication of the asymmetries of knowledge among
them, the complexities of motive and interest within them individually,
and the various degrees and vectors of disinterestedness characterizing

their actions, all lead Freedman to credit James with a prescient critique of
the rational actor or game theory model of economic thinking that has held
sway over the field of economics through the course of the twentieth century. It is as if James were writing for a readership to come (as Melville, in
Loughran's account, was anticipating a future reader), a readership attentive enough to the enigmatic intricacies of human social interaction—an
intricacy representable in artful narrative but not reducible, finally, to any
abstract or diagrammatic model—to appreciate his anticipatory critique of
the limits of game theory. *The Golden Bowl*, Freedman writes, "points to the
possibilities of viewing the aesthetic and the literary as conceived of under
the sign of the aesthetic (as autotelic, self-referential, 'difficult'), as providing a form of critical knowledge that may well prove to be useful not only
to our attempts to understand the social at large but also in our attempts
to reckon with the kinds of knowledge made available by the equally autotelic, self-referential and 'difficult' discipline of economics." Freedman
has James exploring the aesthetic dimension within the diegesis of the
novel—the human remainder in social relations that is not reducible to
mathematical modeling or abstract analysis—as well as producing in its
attentive readers an aesthetic education of sorts. The anachronism sustained by Freedman's argument—James providing us with a trenchantly
dramatized critique of the limits of an economic theory that postdated his
own writing career—finds justification in the fact that James was simultaneously a writer who granted to literary art an almost unlimited degree of
autonomy *and* a practicing professional writer deeply and unembarassedly
aware of the financial exigencies of his uncertain existence as a producer
of an artistic commodity for a competitive marketplace.

Elisa New's exquisite attention to the material details of Susan Howe's
poetry may remind us uncannily of the (very different) analysis of materiality provided by Trish Loughran's essay. Loughran, as part of her formalist attention to *Benito Cereno*, parses very delicately the material circumstances of Melville's tale's initial publication in three parts, issued over
three months, in *Putnam's* magazine. New finds that the material details
of Howe's books (cover art, typography, illustrations, etc.) all signify richly
and together make a claim for "poetry's coextensive relation with matter."
What counts as materiality here is various and encompassing: it includes
not only the physical details of a poem's embodiment in print but poetry's
social existence as "a production, a profession, an institution"; the conditions under which a poet makes the poem (desk, chair, light; on sabbatical
in a cabin or in the hushed reading rooms of a great university library) and

the conditions under which a reader encounters it later (in a library, in bed, at a public reading).

Conventionally, a poem's "transcendence of print, paper, and ink" are the assumed conditions of its immortality; "physical aspects of the poetic volume are still meant, in contemporary habits of reading, to evanesce," New observes. The aesthetic or literary dimension, we often assume, resides exactly where the accidental material form of a text is left behind. But Howe's poetic practice turns these ingrained assumptions on their head, insisting instead on "physical density and sensate clamor," refusing to disown or transcend its embodiment. It routinely thematizes its existence as "print, paper, and ink," as well as its rich enmeshment in academic and other institutions as well as literary and intellectual inheritances. To highlight merely one thread in a complex weave of argument and appreciation, New finds that Howe's poem *Pierce-Arrow* has the foundational American pragmatist philosopher Charles Sanders Peirce "at its center." The poem is actually made, in part, from words of Peirce's, quoted words that themselves reflect (as pragmatism does) upon the philosophical mistake of divorcing ideas from their practical purposes, their material effects. Howe's acknowledged debt to Peirce is matched by her explicitly recognized debts to poetic forebears like Jonathan Edwards and Wallace Stevens, both of whom "had the kind of intimate physical relationship with the poetic word that Howe cherishes." Like Weinstein, Loughran, and Freedman, New finds that formalist reading and aesthetic appreciation are, contrary to long-established habits and ideologies, fundamentally circumstanced and located, materialized and embodied, situated and conditioned.

Part 4, the final section of essays in this volume, appears under the heading "Aesthetics and the Question of Theory" and includes contributions from Nancy Bentley, Dorothy J. Hale, Mary Esteve, Eric Lott, and Sianne Ngai. It will be seen immediately that these essays do not dwell, by and large, in the realm of theory as such, but are exercises in practical criticism that nevertheless draw conspicuously and explicitly on certain theoretical resources—Jacques Rancière's idea that aesthetics is the ground of politics (in Bentley's case), various contemporary theories of the novel as well as the "ethical turn" in recent criticism (Hale), questions of aesthetic and ethical value as they were articulated by various mid-twentieth-century American commentators (Esteve), Frankfurt school cultural theory (Lott), and Bruno Latour's social network theory (Ngai). This is an eclectic set of theoretical references, to be sure, but they have in common a desire to connect the aesthetic dimension explicitly to the social and political world, and in that sense they return us in a fashion to the pre-Kantian aesthetic attitudes with which Ed Cahill's essay opened this volume, to the fundamental assumption that aesthetics is always already worldly, embedded in the realm of history, society, and politics.

Whatever value there might be in provisionally suspending our ingrained will to historicize and politicize literature and art—in order to distinguish the aesthetic dimension and thereby bring it more certainly into focus in its at least partial autonomy—none of these contributors wishes, in the end, to separate these matters decisively. Nancy Bentley, in "Warped Conjunctions: Jacques Rancière and African American Twoness," invokes the work of Rancière on the way that sensory experience serves as the space of political existence and uses his arguments to diagnose our current critical situation in American literary and cultural studies, a situation of exhaustion with prevailing modes of ideology critique (we have become, Bentley, suggests, "disenchanted with disenchantment"). But arguments such as Rancière's need to be "illuminated and tested through examples from African American art," a body or tradition of expression that has always been politically invested but has often been equally invested in formal experimentation and extravagance. Bentley works from the inventive formal features of some recent paintings by Kehinde Wiley—the way they violate and reconfigure certain spatial and ornamental conventions of Western representational painting—to show how, by dint of "a kind of displacement or spatial syncopation in the field of rational geometrical space," they contest certain universalizing norms that have been historically associated with (and instrumental in perpetuating) racial hierarchies. Her analysis of Wiley's visual art provides her, then, with tools to bring to bear upon some earlier African American literary works, namely, an early and never completed experimental narrative by W. E. B. Du Bois, as well as *Of One Blood* by Pauline Hopkins and several other fictions by Sutton Griggs and James Corrothers, all of which feature a kind of "aesthetic warping" for which Wiley's paintings provide a retrospective model.

Bentley observes that Rancière attributed to the nineteenth-century novel a new power to "break up and reconfigure" existing normative distributions of sensory entitlement (who gets to go where, who gets to see what, who gets to speak, etc.). Dorothy J. Hale's essay, "Aesthetics and the New Ethics: Theorizing the Novel in the Twenty-first Century," relocates the consideration of novelistic form: she addresses the curious but underexamined conjunction between the "return to ethics" in contemporary literary theory (especially the theory of the novel) and the frequent adversion to novels and novel reading in a good deal of contemporary moral philosophy. Moral philosophers like Martha Nussbaum, for example, find in the novel a special set of ethical virtues, involving the enlargement of our sympathies and the widening of our range of experience; from the literary-critical side, the new ethical criticism finds itself celebrating the aesthetic form of the novel for its capacity to induce readers to realize both their social embeddedness (the limits on their subjective freedom) and, by virtue of that realization, the "subjective potentiality" that is not completely limited by social and material reality. Hale finds that these approaches share common ground in their "ethics of alterity," and she notes that Henry James enjoys a particular contested status at this crossroads between moral philosophy's embrace of the novel and ethical criticism's celebration of the moral value of novelistic form, since each of them finds in James a novelistic practitioner whose art they wish to defend from previous critics who either celebrated him (naively) as a high priest of freedom and consciousness or decried him (crudely) as the great avatar of falsely universalizing bourgeois subjectivity, rather than recognizing in him and in his characters a complex reckoning with "our constitutive sociality."

Mary Esteve examines the fiction of Philip Roth and finds within it a nuanced account of "the relation between aesthetic value or quality and that paradigmatic postwar American feeling, happiness." The theory she brings to bear involves not a critical lens deployed instrumentally to make Roth's work visible in a certain way but a range of social commentators and sociological analysts from the middle of the twentieth century (Howard Mumford Jones, C. Wright Mills, David Riesman, Lionel Trilling, Melvin Tumin, William Whyte) who collectively turned their attention to the question of post–World War II American society and its vaunted pursuit of happiness. They, like Roth, found this pursuit to be in large measure vulgar and materialistic, shallow and self-centered, and they sought to identify means of enabling authentic affective experience to flourish and superior aesthetic encounters to take place. Esteve's account culminates in an interpretation of the engagement in *Goodbye, Columbus* between a young librarian who finds a way to make the library, as a particular institutional piece of a social structure, serve the affective and aesthetic needs of a black boy for whom a book of arts prints is an indescribably valuable inspiration.

The array of aesthetic objects that circulate through Roth's work (Utrillo prints tacked to apartment walls, tasteful Swedish modern furniture, Norman Rockwell images, the middlebrow orchestral music of Mantovani) and the difficulty in assigning aesthetic value to them may prepare us for

Eric Lott's concerted attempt to bring to bear one of the most severely unforgiving instruments of twentieth-century aesthetic judgment (the critique of culture-industry commodification articulated by Max Horkheimer and Theodor Adorno) upon one of the most snobbishly reviled bodies of American popular music, the "Caucasian blues" of Richard and Karen Carpenter. Lott is the author of a prescient 1994 essay titled "The Aesthetic Ante: Pleasure, Pop Culture, and the Middle Passage," in which he argued for the necessity of scrupulous aesthetic analysis of mass-cultural artifacts that might otherwise seem ready-made for ideology critique.[51] Lott finds that, in the sonic forms of their music, the Carpenters "'produced the concept' (à la Althusser) of turn-of-the-seventies Southern California unfreedom" and that, while Adorno might have mounted them as exhibit A in a display of ignoble aesthetic artifacts, they in fact encode, in the very textures of their songs, a powerful negation of the "spurious harmony" they might at a first glance seem to embody.

Sianne Ngai's essay on the poet Juliana Spahr's recent (2007) novel *The Transformation* asks us to think, along with Spahr, about the aesthetics of social formation.[52] What kinds of images or diagrams do we carry around in our heads of the many webs of social relationships in which we find ourselves? In the contemporary period where we are arguably in something called a "network society," a reticulated structure that is in principle resistant to closure, how do we represent that structure to ourselves? This is a practical question, since our behavior within that structure may be largely determined by the picture of it we possess; but it is also an aesthetic question, a matter of appearance and judgment, of the value we place on one kind of organizational matrix versus another. Ngai stages a complex encounter between Spahr's novel, which features a protagonist ("they") who are a triune unit enmeshed in a variety of social and natural networks, and the "actor-network theory" of modern society elaborated by Bruno Latour in *Reassembling the Social*.

A word must be said about the afterword, by Charles Altieri, commissioned for this volume. Astute readers will discover that it is in some ways an unusual afterword, taking (as it does) a skeptical and even contentious approach to the other contributions rather than politely reviewing and synthesizing them as afterwords more often do. We welcome Altieri's demurrals and challenges and hope that, as he is given the final word, the volume as a whole might open up serious debate and lead to further discussion. It might indeed be a useful exercise to reread any of this volume's essays in the light of Altieri's reservations—he holds that these essays by and large deal with materials for which "the aesthetic is not in fact central," mostly because (he claims) works whose fundamental medium is language are not what aesthetic philosophy was created to understand—and he proposes that they could well have made their claims without adverting to the aesthetic at all. Instead of the language of the aesthetic, Altieri proposes that we talk in terms of "imaginative labor to build worlds out of linguistic resources." The essays collected here, Altieri insists, may attend to specific aesthetic properties of particular works of art, but, always with an eye to the social or political utility of those properties; they "build predicates for social use into the very definition of 'aesthetic' from the start." We are reminded here of a comment made to us by a late colleague, Jay Fliegelman, who at one point was meant to take part in this undertaking, before ill health prevented his participation, and who cautioned against subjecting aesthetic pleasure to a political litmus test. As literary and cultural studies was beginning to turn its attention back toward aesthetic questions, Fliegelman observed, aesthetics seemed everywhere to be put on notice that it nevertheless had to serve progressive political and social purposes, and this a priori criterion was itself damaging to the integrity of aesthetic experience. In our email exchanges with Fliegelman we quoted Marcuse's assertion that "the political potential of art lies *only* in its aesthetic dimension," here used as this introduction's epigraph, but Fliegelman objected: "The notion of aesthetics as a staging ground for a future political move still subordinates aesthetics to politics, and implies that aesthetic issues are most important as a site of political potentiality."[53]

We welcomed Fliegelman's contentious resistance then as we welcome Altieri's now. They help point up a fact about academic work in literary and cultural studies—indeed, in the humanities generally—in recent decades: it has become common sense to many of us to agree, with Fredric Jameson, that politics is "the absolute horizon of all reading and all interpretation" (17), that "there is nothing that is not social and historical—indeed, that everything is 'in the last analysis' political" (20). Readers of this collection will see that its overall aim is certainly not to substitute the aesthetic as the "absolute horizon" of interpretation, nor does it insist that "the last analysis" ought to be an aesthetic one. Rather, its purpose is to join in an effort to place aesthetics back on the critical agenda—and not in a fixed subordinate position either, but in a dynamic and unpredictable relationship to the social and political and ideological matters that have dominated our conversations for a good while now. The aesthetic is itself social and historical; it exists within the political horizon of interpretation and often has a powerful role in reshaping that horizon. But the political has its own irreducible aesthetic dimension as well, one that ought not to be characterized pejoratively in all cases and may even constitute an essential element of its capacity to support and extend human flourishing and freedom. Roland Barthes wrote in *Mythologies* that "a little Formalism turns one away from History, but . . . a lot brings one back to it."[54] May we imagine that a candid reckoning with aesthetics would not merely bring us back (predictably) to history and politics, but that the various dimensions of art and life will be understood in the complexity of their dynamic interanimating relationship to one another?

Notes

1. On "organic form," see F. O. Matthiessen, *American Renaissance: Art and Expression in the Age of Emerson and Whitman* (New York: Oxford University Press, 1941); on "romance," see Richard Chase, *The American Novel and Its Tradition* (New York: Doubleday, 1957); on "colloquial style" see Richard Bridgman, *The Colloquial Style in America* (New York: Oxford University Press, 1966).

2. Sacvan Bercovitch and Myra Jehlen, eds., *Ideology and Classic American Literature* (New York: Cambridge University Press, 1986).

3. It should be noted that Poirier was describing what he took to be a recurrent impulse within the texture of American literary style to distance itself from economic, political, and social systems, an impulse he characterized explicitly as an illusion, myth, or fantasy. See Richard Poirier, *A World Elsewhere: The Place of Style in American Literature* (New York: Oxford University Press, 1966).

4. Jane Tompkins, *Sensational Designs: The Cultural Work of American Fiction, 1790–1860* (New York: Oxford University Press, 1986), xv. Further page references will be given in the text.

5. Fredric Jameson, *The Political Unconscious: Narrative as a Socially Symbolic Act* (Ithaca: Cornell University Press, 1981), 9. It would be difficult to underestimate the influence of Jameson's claim for "the political perspective . . . as the absolute horizon of all reading and all interpretation" (17).

6. Our title alludes, of course, to Herbert Marcuse, *The Aesthetic Dimension: Toward a Critique of Marxist Aesthetics* (Boston: Beacon, 1978). Although Marcuse's account takes the value of political revolution as fundamental, he also grants a necessary autonomy to art: "the political potential of art lies only in its own aesthetic dimension," he writes (xii). The aesthetic, according to Marcuse, references something more fundamental than politics, which he calls "humanity as such" (24) or, to list some of his other foundational terms,

human nature, eros, life, subjectivity or inwardness, freedom, happiness, and other basic human qualities or needs that are, so to speak, presocial—and, he claims, embodied in or addressed by the sensuous form of art rather than by its expressed political content.

7. Elizabeth P. Peabody, "Introduction.—The Word 'Aesthetic,'" *Aesthetic Papers* (repr. New York: AMS, 1967), 1. Our understanding of Peabody's strategically flexible use of the term *aesthetic*, as a means of teaching the healthy cultivation of uncertainty and even confusion, owes a great deal to Alison Hills, "Practical Confusion: Aesthetic Perception in Antebellum American Writing," Ph.D. diss., UCLA, 2009.

8. For a beguiling discussion of the varieties of meanings ordinarily attached to the category of the aesthetic, see Leonard Koren, *Which "Aesthetics" Do You Mean? Ten Definitions* (Point Reyes, CA: Imperfect Publishing, 2010). Koren's list includes appearance, style, taste, philosophy of art, thesis or exegesis, artistic, beauty, beautification, cognitive mode, and language.

9. Rita Felski, *Uses of Literature* (Malden, MA: Blackwell, 2008), 4.

10. Paul Ricoeur, *Freud and Philosophy: An Essay on Interpretation*, trans. Denis Savage (New Haven: Yale University Press, 1970), passim.

11. *Scientia cognitionis sensitivae:* quoted in David E. Cooper, ed., *A Companion to Aesthetics* (Malden, MA: Blackwell, 1992), 40. *Scientiam sensitive quid cognoscendi:* quoted in Paul Guyer, *Values of Beauty: Historical Essays in Aesthetics* (Cambridge: Cambridge University Press, 2005), 3.

12. Susan Buck-Morss, "Aesthetics and Anaesthetics: Walter Benjamin's Artwork Essay Reconsidered," *October* 62 (Autumn 1992): 6. The embedded Terry Eagleton quotation is from *The Ideology of the Aesthetic* (Oxford: Blackwell, 1992), 13.

13. Ekbert Faas, *The Genealogy of Aesthetics* (Cambridge: Cambridge University Press, 2002), 1. Richard Shusterman, *Pragmatist Aesthetics: Living Beauty, Rethinking Art*, 2d ed. (Lanham, MD: Rowman and Littlefield, 2000), 263.

14. It is curious that, even among scholars who are once again entertaining the possibility of examining the aesthetic dimension of art and experience, but without abandoning the materialist and historicist approaches that have proven so productive in recent critical history, there has been so little reference made to American pragmatism, which might very well provide valuable theoretical resources for a rematerialized aesthetic criticism. Even at a quick glance, Dewey's *Art as Experience*, for instance, which aggressively reconnects the experience of something designated as an art object with "the human conditions under which it was brought into being and . . . the human consequences it engenders in actual life-experience," would seem to provide a promising model for current explorations. John Dewey, *Art as Experience*, ed. Jo Ann

Boydston and Harriet Furst Simon, intro. Abraham Kaplan, in *John Dewey: The Later Works, 1925–1953* (Carbondale: Southern Illinois University Press, 1987), 10:9. Among the few Americanist critics to derive explicit guidance from pragmatism has been Richard Poirier in such works as *The Renewal of Literature: Emersonian Reflections* (New York: Random House, 1987) and *Poetry and Pragmatism* (Cambridge: Harvard University Press, 1993).

15. See Bruno Latour, "Why Has Critique Run Out of Steam? From Matters of Fact to Matters of Concern," *Critical Inquiry* 30 (2004): 225–48.

16. Sacvan Bercovitch, *The Puritan Origins of the American Self* (Yale University Press, 1975), 186. A 2011 reissue of this book, with a reflective new preface by Bercovitch, has been published by Yale University Press. See also Bercovitch, "The Problem of Ideology in American Literary History," *Critical Inquiry* 12 (1986): 631–53.

17. Russ Castronovo, for example, cites it as such in his entry on "Aesthetics" in Bruce Burgett and Glenn Hendler, eds., *Keywords for American Cultural Studies* (New York: New York University Press, 2007), 11–12.

18. Sacvan Bercovitch, ed., *The American Puritan Imagination: Essays in Revaluation* (Cambridge: Cambridge University Press, 1974). The lead essay in the collection was Norman Grabo's "The Veiled Vision: The Role of Aesthetics in Early American Intellectual History."

19. Sacvan Bercovitch, "Games of Chess: A Model of Literary and Cultural Studies," in Robert Newman, ed., *Centuries' Ends, Narrative Means* (Stanford: Stanford University Press, 1996), 15. Bercovitch's terms here, opposing "aesthetic" or "literary" to "cognitive" analysis, draw upon a deep discursive history, dating from Baumgarten's attempt to distinguish sensory apprehension or perception (the proper realm of aesthetics, he claimed) from cognitive or conceptual analysis (the realm of logic, science, ideas). Thus Hegel wrote that "the beauty of art presents itself to sense, to feeling, to perception, to imagination; its sphere is not that of thought, and the apprehension of its activity and its productions demand another organ than that of the scientific intelligence." G. W. F. Hegel, *Introductory Lectures on Aesthetics*, ed. Michael Inwood, trans. Bernard Bosanquet (New York: Penguin, 1993), 7.

20. Sacvan Bercovitch, "The Function of the Literary in a Time of Cultural Studies," in John Carlos Rowe, ed., *"Culture" and the Problem of the Disciplines* (New York: Columbia University Press, 1998), 69.

21. Sacvan Bercovitch, *The Office of The Scarlet Letter* (Baltimore: Johns Hopkins University Press, 1991).

22. Christopher Castiglia and Russ Castronovo, eds., "Aesthetics and the End(s) of Cultural Studies," *American Literature* 76, no. 3 (2004); Emory Elliott, Louis Freitas Caton, and Jeffrey Rhyne, eds., *Aesthetics in a Multicultural Age*

(New York: Oxford University Press, 2002); Michael Berubé, ed., *The Aesthetics of Cultural Studies* (Malden, MA: Blackwell, 2005); Sharon Marcus and Stephen Best, eds., *Representations* 108 (Fall 2009). To this selective accounting we might add Pamela R. Matthews and David McWhirter, eds., *Aesthetic Subjects* (Minneapolis: University of Minnesota Press, 2003), and John J. Joughin and Simon Malpas, eds., *The New Aestheticism* (Manchester: Manchester University Press, 2003).

23. Sharon Best and Stephen Marcus, "Surface Reading: An Introduction," *Representations* 108 (Fall 2009): 13.

24. Contrast this to Jameson's insistence that "the traditional issues of philosophical aesthetics: the nature and function of art, the specificity of poetic language and of the aesthetic experience, the theory of the beautiful, and so forth . . . themselves need to be radically historicized" (*The Political Unconscious,* 11).

25. Richard H. Brodhead, *Cultures of Letters: Scenes of Reading and Writing in Nineteenth-Century America* (Chicago: University of Chicago Press, 1995), 11.

26. Louis Althusser, "Ideology and Ideological State Apparatuses," in *Lenin and Philosophy and Other Essays* (New York: Monthly Review Press, 2001).

27. For several recent examples of American literary criticism that take up the question of aesthetics, see Castiglia and Castronovo, "Aesthetics and the End(s) of Cultural Studies"; Russ Castronovo, *Beautiful Democracy: Aesthetics and Anarchy in a Global Era* (Chicago: University of Chicago Press, 2007); Bill Brown, *A Sense of Things: The Object Matter of American Literature* (Chicago: University of Chicago Press, 2003); Paul Gilmore, *Aesthetic Materialism: Electricity and American Romanticism* (Stanford: Stanford University Press, 2009); and Theo Davis, *Formalism, Literature, and the Making of American Literature in the Nineteenth Century* (New York: Cambridge University Press, 2007). See also Samuel Otter and Geoffrey Sanborn, eds., *Melville and Aesthetics* (London: Palgrave, 2011).

28. For a reconsideration of new historicism from the perspective of two of its original practitioners, see Catherine Gallagher and Stephen Greenblatt's *Practicing New Historicism* (Chicago: University of Chicago Press, 2000). They write: "no matter how thoroughgoing our skepticism, we have never given up or turned our backs on the deep gratification that draws us in the first place to the study of literature and art. Our project has never been about diminishing or belittling the power of artistic representations, even those with the most problematic entailments, but we never believe that our appreciation of this power necessitates either ignoring the cultural matrix out of which the representations emerge or uncritically endorsing the fantasies that the representations articulate" (9).

29. John Carlos Rowe, *Literary Culture and U.S. Imperialism: From the Revolution to World War II* (New York: Oxford University Press, 2000), 16. Further

page references will be given parenthetically in the text. A critique of "unde-cidability" or "indeterminacy" is often a coded way of distinguishing one's own work from deconstruction. Also see Jonathan Arac's seminal essay on Hawthorne's *The Scarlet Letter,* where he points to the curious fact that "in some current criticism, 'indeterminacy' functions as a closure" (249). Arac, "The Politics of *The Scarlet Letter,*" in Bercovitch and Jehlen, *Ideology and Classic American Literature,* 247–66.

30. Janice A. Radway, *Reading the Romance: Women, Patriarchy, and Popular Literature* (Chapel Hill: University of North Carolina Press, 1991), 7. Further page references will be given parenthetically in the text.

31. Donald E. Pease, *Visionary Compacts: American Renaissance Writings in Cultural Context* (Madison: University of Wisconsin Press, 1987), 256. Further page references will be given parenthetically in the text.

32. Also see Oxford University Press's *Women Writers in English,* which republished, among other texts, Catharine Williams's *Fall River: An Authentic Narrative* and Judith Sargent Murray's *Selected Writings,* as well as Rutgers University Press's American Women Writer series, which republished Maria Cummins's *The Lamplighter,* E. D. E. N. Southworth's *The Hidden Hand,* Constance Fenimore Woolson's short stories, and many other once-forgotten texts.

33. Cathy N. Davidson, *Revolution and the Word: The Rise of the Novel in America,* expanded ed. (New York: Oxford University Press, 2004), 359. Further page references will be given in the text. One often underappreciated feature of Davidson's book is that it presents a comprehensive account of the early American novel, encompassing male writers and canonical figures along with the female authors to whom it helped draw new attention.

34. Wlad Godzich, "Introduction: Caution! Reader at Work!," in Paul de Man, *Blindness and Insight: Essays in the Rhetoric of Contemporary Criticism,* 2d ed. (Minneapolis: University of Minnesota Press, 1983), xxviii.

35. Jacques Derrida, *Of Grammatology,* trans. Gayatri Chakravorty Spivak (Baltimore: Johns Hopkins University Press, 1976), 35.

36. Geoffrey H. Hartman, *Saving the Text: Literature, Derrida, Philosophy* (Baltimore: Johns Hopkins University Press, 1981), 121.

37. Michel Foucault, *The Order of Things: An Archaeology of the Human Sciences* (New York: Vintage, 1970), 49.

38. Michel Foucault, *The Archaeology of Knowledge,* trans. A. M. Sheridan Smith (New York: Pantheon, 1972), 25–26, 32, 30.

39. Clifford Geertz, *The Interpretation of Cultures: Selected Essays* (New York: Basic Books, 1973), 3–30.

40. Christopher Norris, *Deconstruction: Theory and Practice* (New York: Routledge, 1986), 48.

41. Gillian Brown, *Domestic Individualism: Imagining Self in Nineteenth-Century America* (Berkeley: University of California Press, 1990), 8, 9–10, 7, 1, 9. Also see Gregory S. Jay's *America the Scrivener: Deconstruction and the Subject of Literary History* (Ithaca, NY: Cornell University Press, 1990), in which he positions himself vis-à-vis Derrida: "where my argument arrives is at the dissemination of the position of the subject rather than at its disappearance" (x). Poe has been a favorite of deconstructive readings, including Jacques Lacan's famous analysis of "The Purloined Letter." Here is Renza on Poe's "The Oval Portrait": "Such repetitive de-compositions of, first, the woman by the artist, next the portrait by the volume, then this volume by the tale's very narrative, and finally this narrative by the interpretive narrative able to recognize how such verbal circularity figuratively doubles an 'oval portrait,' obviously suggest an endlessly provisional sequence or en abîme of misreading." Louis A. Renza, "Poe's Secret Autobiography," in Walter Benn Michaels and Donald E. Pease, eds., *The American Renaissance Reconsidered* (Baltimore: Johns Hopkins University Press, 1989), 69. On binaries Gillian Brown writes, "I therefore make no attempt to distinguish between classic and feminist or revisionary American literary canons. I have chosen texts that may or may not fit these categories (in some cases previously unread materials) for their various expositions of the problematic of domestic individualism" (7). See Mark Seltzer, *Bodies and Machines* (New York: Routledge, 1992) for a deconstruction of the person/machine paradigm; Michael Warner, *The Letters of the Republic: Publication and the Public Sphere in Eighteenth-Century America* (Cambridge: Harvard University Press, 1992) on the public/private; and Eric J. Sundquist, *To Wake the Nations: Race in the Making of American Literature* (Cambridge: Belknap, 1998) on the black/white.

42. Walter Benn Michaels, *The Gold Standard and the Logic of Naturalism* (Berkeley: University of California Press, 1987), 27, 18, 27.

43. Wai-chee Dimock, *Empire for Liberty: Melville and the Poetics of Individualism* (Princeton: Princeton University Press, 1989), 10. Further page references will be given parenthetically in the text.

44. Single-author texts are especially vulnerable to this potential inconsistency. Such texts automatically grant a kind of privilege to that author, if only to the extent that his or her work most fully encapsulates the paradoxes of a culture. The discursive network, in other words, is built around the author, not quite the other way around. In addition to Dimock, see T. Walter Herbert, *Dearest Beloved: The Hawthornes and the Making of the Middle-Class Family* (Berkeley: University of California Press, 1995), and Michael Paul Rogin, *Subversive Genealogy: The Politics and Art of Herman Melville* (Berkeley: University of California Press, 1985).

45. Michel Foucault, "What Is an Author?" in *Language, Counter-memory, Practice: Selected Essays and Interviews*, ed. Donald F. Bouchard (Ithaca, New York: Cornell University Press, 1977), 128, 127.

46. Michaels, *The Gold Standard*, 177.

47. Foucault, "What Is an Author?" 138.

48. Claudia Tate, *Domestic Allegories of Political Desire: The Black Heroine's Text at the Turn of the Century* (New York: Oxford University Press, 1992), 5, 7, 7.

49. Along with Philip Fisher's reading of *Uncle Tom's Cabin* in *Hard Facts: Setting and Form in the American Novel* (New York: Oxford University Press, 1985), chapter 2; Eric Sundquist's edited collection, *New Essays on Uncle Tom's Cabin* (New York: University of Cambridge Press, 1987); and Elizabeth Ammons's *Norton Critical Edition of Uncle Tom's Cabin* (New York: W. W. Norton, 1994).

50. Theodor W. Adorno, *Aesthetic Theory*, ed. Gretel Adorno and Rolf Tidermann, trans. C. Lenhardt (London: Routledge and Kegan Paul, 1984), 6.

51. Eric Lott, "The Aesthetic Ante: Pleasure, Pop Culture, and the Middle Passage," *Callaloo* 17, no. 2 (1994): 545–55.

52. Elsewhere Ngai has written acutely of the minimal quotient of aesthetic evaluation retained in one of the most ordinary and affectless of phrases in our critical idiom, the judgment that something is "interesting." Sianne Ngai, "Merely Interesting," *Critical Inquiry* 34, no. 4 (Summer 2008): 777–817.

53. Jay Fliegelman, personal communication.

54. Roland Barthes, *Mythologies*, trans. Annette Lavers (New York: Hill and Wang, 1972), 112.

PART 1

Aesthetics and the
Politics of Freedom

[1]

Liberty of the Imagination
in Revolutionary America

EDWARD CAHILL

John Trumbull's *Essay on the Use and Advantages of the Fine Arts* (1770), read at the "Public Commencement in New-Haven," makes one of the earliest American arguments for the moral efficacy of aesthetic pleasure. Borrowing liberally from Henry Home, Lord Kames's *Elements of Criticism* (1762), Trumbull declares that the "elegant entertainments of polite literature . . . ennoble the soul, purify the passions" and give "delicacy and refinement to our manners." Although he laments that the fine arts are "too much undervalued by the [American] public . . . neglected by the youth in our seminaries of science [and] . . . considered as mere matters of trifling amusement," he counters that they are in fact basic to "the common purposes of life" and necessary to the cultivation of virtue. Indeed, he insists that the experience of art and imagination functions as a kind of moral bellwether in a free society: "I appeal to all persons of judgment whether they can rise from reading a fine Poem, viewing any masterly work of Genius, or hearing a harmonious concert of Music, without feeling an openness of heart, and an elevation of mind, without being more sensible of the dignity of human nature, and despising whatever tends to debase and degrade it." There is much to be said about these prospective scenes of aesthetic experience and their purported effects. Although Trumbull takes for granted his audience's experience with a range of artistic forms, his "appeal" suggests that their moral significance comes as a kind of revelation—of something always implicitly known but somehow never before acknowledged. His correlation of aesthetic experience with "openness of heart," "elevation," and "dignity" implies that the nature of virtue is discovered as much in human feelings as in rational discourse. Yet we also hear in the corresponding threat of debasement and degradation the urgency of the present colonial conflict and the stakes of political action. Only six months after the Boston Massacre and at the outset of the crisis that would result five years later in the War for Independence, Trumbull suggests that in aesthetic experience we become "sensible" to the meaning of liberty.[1]

The eighteenth-century correlation of liberty and the fine arts was popularized by Longinus's *On the Sublime* but reiterated by such writers as the Earl of Shaftesbury, David Hume, and Richard Price. "Liberty," writes Longinus, "produces fine Sentiments in Men of Genius, it invigorates their Hopes, excites an honourable Emulation . . . [it is] that copious and fertile Source of all that is beautiful and of all that is great." Trumbull likewise asserts that an "unconquered spirit of freedom" is a necessary condition for the advancement of aesthetic culture; but his claims are also specific to the colonial world he inhabits. America is particularly susceptible to literary achievement, he argues, not only because its citizens "very much excel in the force of natural genius" but also because here education is "diffused through all ranks of people." This invocation of the broad dissemination of learning to a freedom-loving people thus suits the essay's dominant theme of *translatio studii*, the western movement of learning and the fine arts. As Trumbull traces the cyclical achievements of literature and the shifting forces of freedom from the Ancient Greece and Rome of Homer and Virgil across the early modern Britain of Shakespeare and Swift to revolutionary America's "fair prospect" of literary fame, he describes a society whose literary ambitions are bound up in its "late struggles for liberty." Conversely, he argues, "Polite letters at present are much on the decline in Britain," where freedom has been debased and degraded by an oppressive Parliament. Not only are modern British writers "followers in the path of servile imitation" who "fetter the fancy with the rules of method, and damp all the ardour of aspiring invention," but, at the same time, their "men of Genius . . . in contempt of the critic chains, throw off all appearance of order and connection, sport in the wildest sallies of imagination, and adopt the greatest extravagance of humour." In other words, British writers are both too restrained and too free, both devoted to arbitrary rules and unregulated by any rule at all.[2]

The ideal of moderate political liberty implicit in Trumbull's critique derives variously from British traditions of common law, natural law, and Protestant theology. Forged in the violence of seventeenth-century political struggles, "British Liberty" functioned as both a description of the nation's constitutional and representative government and a potent ideological myth that distinguished Britons from less free and enlightened peoples. Central to its conception, however, was the notion that liberty was always bounded by and exercised within authoritative limits. It watched jealously for the abuses of tyranny and the humiliations of "servility," but it also assumed the possibility of its own transgressions in the form of license or "extravagance." Often opposed to the liberty of man in his natural state, British liberty was understood as a creature of society, born of essential human freedom but sustained by a necessary adjustment to the demands of political community. Not only were its limitations rooted in law and thus never arbitrary, they were also consensual, accepted as legitimate by the very persons whose freedom they circumscribed. In the wake of the American Revolution, the idea of liberty evolved into a more abstract and broadly conceived notion of self-determination whose meanings subjected all forms of hierarchy and exclusion to scrutiny. But this challenge to British liberty was soon countered in the 1780s and 1790s by a conservative return to the discourse of authority and constraint. If such an idea of liberty failed to include Africans, Indians, women, or men without property, this is because liberty was understood as a kind of property itself, granted only to individuals thought capable of consenting to its complex and often contradictory demands.[3]

During the revolutionary era, liberty was celebrated, explained, and explored by Anglo-American writers in a variety of literary genres, from poetry and sermons to periodical essays and treatises of political theory. But it also found expression in works of aesthetic theory, including those ideas that informed Trumbull's *Essay*. Such texts as Kames's *Elements*, Francis Hutcheson's *Inquiry Into the Original of Our Ideas of Beauty and Virtue* (1725), Edmund Burke's *Philosophical Enquiry Into the Origin of Our Ideas of the Sublime and Beautiful* (1757), Alexander Gerard's *Essay on Taste* (1759), Thomas Reid's *Inquiry Into the Human Mind* (1764), and Hugh Blair's *Lectures on Rhetoric and Belles Lettres* (1783) were collected in American libraries, taught in American colleges, and redacted or reviewed in American magazines because they offered authoritative discussions of pleasure, association, genius, and taste and taught a rising generation of readers about the virtues of mental gratification and the harmonious order of the imagination.[4] But, as I will argue in this essay, they also offered a nuanced language for articulating and negotiating the problem of liberty. Debates about aesthetic perception cast the liberating fulfillment of mental pleasures against the dissipating slavery of bodily ones. Ideas of imagination, association, genius, and taste turn on distinctions between the autonomous, inventive, individualizing power of the creative mind and restrictions implied by logical relation, the rules of criticism, and the claims of judgment. American writers were particularly sensitive to this homology of aesthetic and political liberty and its implications for both the pleasures of the imagination and matters of national polity.[5] As we shall see, in their critical engagements with aesthetic theory, and in literary texts informed by it, they aimed to delineate the difficult relationship between citizenship and subjectivity and to chart the modes of perception, imagination, and judgment that made liberty in a republic possible.[6]

The language of liberty is most immediately apparent in aesthetic theory's consistent protest against arbitrary and inflexible rules. Joseph Addison introduces his widely read 1712 *Spectator* essays on "The Pleasures of the Imagination" by distinguishing sharply between "Mechanical Rules" and "the very Spirit and soul of fine Writing." Likewise, Kames scoffs at the idea that the classical poets "were entitled to give [the] law to mankind; and that nothing now remains but blind obedience to their arbitrary will." These writers object to what they saw as the sanctity and unthinking quality of such rules, turning instead to aesthetic ideas whose meanings were defined by experience rather than laws of another's making. According to Blair's *Lectures*, extracted in the 1783 *Boston Magazine*, "The rules of criticism are not formed by an induction, a priori . . . [or] a train of abstract reasoning independent of facts and observations." An "Essay on Genius" in Matthew Carey's 1789 *Columbian Magazine* similarly holds that "whoever is, in any degree, possessed of original powers, ought not to cramp and trammel them, by servile imitation, or the rules of mechanical criticism" (347). Throughout this period, all forms of "servility," "slavish imitation," and "blind," "mechanical" pedantry are contrasted against the powerful, dynamic, and autonomous liberty of the imagination. The rejection of rules thus sweeps away the philosophical dogma of the past and, in doing so, invests the empiricism that replaces it with a language of liberty that would define eighteenth-century aesthetic theory's most important claims.[7]

As with most revolutions, however, British aesthetics substitutes one form of authority for another, rejecting arbitrary rules for those derived from experience, nature, or the "universal principles" of the human mind. Addison's project, for example, is precisely "to lay down Rules for the acquirement" of taste; and James Beattie holds that, while to "depart from a mechanical rule, may be consistent with the soundest judgment," the "violation of an essential rule discovers want of sense." If such writers rebuffed both Aristotelian rules and "mechanical critics," that is, they were equally determined to avoid the kind of relativism or subjectivism that deprived society of ordered relations and let loose the unpredictable forces of passion and desire. Thus, although Kames has "taken arms to rescue modern poets from the despotism of modern critics," he assures us that he "would not be understood to justify liberty without any reserve" or endorse an "unbounded license with relation to place and time" (416). Such "liberty" and "license," he warns, would not only result in "faulty" art but also alienated artists and audiences. As David Hume writes, although "to check the sallies of imagination" would likewise lead to "insipid" poetry, poets must nonetheless be "confined by rules of art, discovered to the author, either by genius or observation." In short, aesthetics, like politics, demands both liberty and its constraint.[8]

Such rhetoric was certainly at the heart of the moral question of pleasure. A 1775 *Royal American Magazine* essay, "On Pleasure," for example, warns that, while "it is essential to human nature to be delighted," yet "there should be boundaries fixed beyond which limits [we] should never venture." Likewise, the 1789 *American Moral and Sentimental Magazine* holds that pleasure, in its "boundless fields of licentiousness," exercises an "extravagant dominion" over both men and states. In countless texts of the period, pleasure either confirmed one's essential liberty or led to some form of moral or physical enslavement. Its effects, however, typically depended on whether such pleasure derived from the body or the mind. Addison first gives this distinction significance when, by calling taste a "Faculty of the Soul," he sharply distinguishes mental pleasures from the "Criminal" pleasures of "Vice or Folly." Blair clarifies what is implicit in Addison's claim when he notes that the pleasures of the mind can deter one from those of the body: "He who is so happy as to have acquired a relish for these, has always at hand an innocent and irreproachable amusement for his leisure hours, to save him from the danger of many a pernicious passion." Thus, jeremiads against sensual pleasure, rather than rejecting aesthetics, helped to construct the rhetorical foundation that gave the pleasures of the imagination so much moral authority. In the words of the 1797 *Phila-delphia Minerva*, it is because the "gratifications of sense reside in the lowest regions of our nature" that the pleasures of the mind may be said to "belong to the highest powers and best affections of the soul."[9]

With such assumptions in mind, American critics often figure aesthetic pleasure as a powerful form of liberty. As the 1806 *Literary Tablet* declares, "buoyant on the wings of imagination, [one] travels the unbounded regions of space. . . . [H]ere the mind is not fettered by systematic rules—here the fancy may rove free, and unconfined." But the theory behind such paeans to aesthetic experience is equally grounded in ideas of liberty. In one of the earliest uses of the phrase "liberty of the imagination," Hume's *Treatise of Human Nature* (1739–40) argues that impressions made by sensual percep-tions create "faint images" in the mind called "ideas." Such ideas, when suf-ficiently vivid, can later be called up by the memory in the same order in which the impressions occurred; but the mind's ability "to transpose and change its ideas," to reorder and recombine them at will, is owing to the "lib-erty of the imagination." As Hume argues, in creating ideas from impres-sions, the imagining subject becomes free both from the order in which the impressions originally occurred and from the ordered logic of nature. But this also means that one need neither possess nor even perceive an object to enjoy it. In this way, liberty of the imagination describes a heightened form of independence and possibility, making all the world's pleasures available to anyone capable of enjoying them and carrying one from the material limita-tions of objective reality into the elaborate potential of the creative mind.[10]

For most writers, such liberty is never wholly unregulated because the ideas that produce pleasure or pain are connected by the logic of "associa-tion." According to Kames, associative "trains" of ideas are subject to inalter-able principles of reason (of cause and effect, contiguity, resemblance, hier-archy, etc.). But he also argues that we retain the freedom to engage with the order of ideas presented to our imaginations as we please and to acknowl-edge stricter or looser associations, depending on our will, our "present tone of mind," or the strength of our "discerning faculty." For Kames, then, the logic of association yields a sense of self-affirmation. Because "we are framed by nature to relish order and connexion," he argues, the objective order of the world ratifies the spontaneous impulses of the imagination. Yet, for some critics, association also raises the specter of mental error and the possibility of corrupted imaginations. An 1802 *New England Quarterly* essay warns that "an early false association of ideas" can lead to "absurd antipathies" and even "moral insanities." Likewise, Charles Brockden

Brown's 1807 *Literary Magazine* reprints a popular passage from Reid's *Enquiry*, which cautions that the corruption of one's associations might produce "an affection for deformed objects," such as a "depraved taste" for "cinders or chalk." For these authors, it is paradoxically the freedom of the imagination to pursue such a vast range of ideas that makes everyone, to greater or lesser degrees, what Brown called "the slave of accidental associations." In naming the very logic—or illogic—of imagination and taste, that is, association defined an idea of aesthetic liberty whose potential for failure was, like political liberty, imbedded in the source of its efficacy.[11]

For Kames, the association of ideas implied two distinct, even antithetical types of imagining subjects: the man of *genius*, whose "wit" entertains "a great flow of ideas," and the man of *taste*, whose "accurate judgment" ignores all "slighter relations." Genius and taste were thus often understood as paired categories signaling a dichotomy of aesthetic liberty and constraint. Whereas genius was defined as the capacity to produce excellent or original works of art, taste meant the ability to discern and take pleasure in such excellence. If genius implied the unfettered exercise of the individual imagination and a tendency toward excess and error, taste implied the ordered universality of the mind and the corrective function of judgment. For these reasons, some critics understood genius and taste as complementary powers realized best in combination. According to Gerard, genius "needs the assistance of taste, to guide and moderate its exertions," and taste "serves as a check on mere fancy; it interposes judgment, either approving or condemning; and rejects many things which unassisted genius would have allowed." But for other critics, the distinction between genius and taste produced specifically politicized claims about their relative merits. For example, Joseph Dennie's 1801 *Port-Folio* extract from John Blair Linn's poem, "The Powers of Genius," entitled "taste and genius distinguished," argues that "Taste is confin'd to rules, it moves in chains, / Genius those fetters and those rules disdains." Thus, on the one hand, the greatest philosophical challenge that freedom-loving, rule-breaking genius faced in its comparison with taste was to demonstrate that it obeyed some law, even if it were a law of its own. The fact that it was liberated, rare, and original made it difficult to conceive how its processes could be predictable and virtuous or how its artistic achievements could finally speak a common language, appeal widely, and discern truth as well as beauty. Taste, on the other hand, faced the opposite dilemma. It sought both to define the pleasures of individual perceivers and provide universal principles of pleasure without becoming what Blair calls an imposer of "unnatural shackles and bonds."[12]

One way theorists sought to address the latter problem was to define taste as an autonomous faculty of the imagination, energized in its receptivity to objects and free from the constraints of reason, interest, particularity, and passion. Hutcheson argues that taste is an "internal sense," through which pleasure in beautiful objects or virtuous acts arises just as it does in the external sense from which it is metaphorically derived: immediately, necessarily, and without "Knowledge of Principles, Proportions, Causes, or of the Usefulness of the Object." Although some writers, like Burke and Gerard, question whether taste is a distinct faculty of the mind or a combination of emotional or cognitive responses, most view it as a formidable, independent, even disinterested power. Archibald Alison has such a power in mind when he describes the sensibility by which one responds to objects with pleasure as "freedom of the imagination," which because it involves the free play of association is not unlike Hume's "liberty of the imagination." For the imagination to function "in its fullest perfection," Alison insists, it must be "at liberty" or not preoccupied with any contrary or inhospitable feelings. Given this relative autonomy, taste was widely believed to provide a range of public and private benefits that fostered moderate liberty. It improved morals and manners, facilitated sympathy and social harmony, controlled passions, inhibited luxury, consoled misfortune, encouraged learning, exercised the mind, and even heightened pleasure for its own sake. To enjoy the highest pleasures of taste was akin to bridging the unbridgeable gaps between the sensible and the intellectual and between the individual and the sociopolitical. To cultivate a refined taste through education, practice, and criticism was synonymous with becoming more fully and ideally human.[13]

As this brief summary suggests, aesthetic theory consistently expressed liberty's ineluctable contradictions by giving emotionally palpable form to its extension and limitation. But liberty of the imagination plays more than a merely instrumental or expressive role in American politics, and its metaphors are never reducible to political discourse. If it represents fundamental oppositional but mutually constitutive forces in revolutionary culture, these forces are also discernable in many of that culture's literary texts.[14] Elsewhere I have argued that tensions between freedom and constraint inherent in idealist and materialist theories of the imagination help to explain the formal qualities and thematic concerns of Charles Brockden Brown's novels and that the dialectical opposition of genius and taste gives rise to a highly politicized valorization of the imagination in Federalist-era literary criticism.[15] But the text that perhaps most succinctly exemplifies this rhetorical phenomenon is Phillis Wheatley's lyric, "On Imagination" (1773), whose primary aim is to enact the conflicts at the heart of aesthetic and political liberty. Wheatley's legal status as a slave renders her poem a poignant representation of the aesthetic freedom that was not hers politically: the capacity to navigate what in "On Recollection" (1773) she calls "the unbounded regions of the mind." Yet it also discovers in the language of aesthetic theory a means of representing liberty's acute arcs and unsteady rhythms, voicing the timbre of its invitations and injunctions and thereby registering Trumbull's sense of dignity and debasement in its personal immediacy and historical particularity.[16]

Invoking the idea of imagination in terms of the authority of monarchy and the deferential address of an admiring royal subject, the first lines of the poem are deceptively obsequious:

THY various works, imperial queen, we see,
How bright their forms! how deck'd with pomp by thee!
Thy wond'rous acts in beauteous order stand,
And all attest how potent is thine hand.

By suggesting the grandeur of court, the disciplining "order" of monarchy, and the absolute submission of the subaltern, Wheatley celebrates the "potent" ability of the imagination to command the rational self. The "various" range of its "works" and the brightness of their "forms" describe not only the infinite diversity of sensible impressions and the elaborate trains of associations that await the perceiver but also the abundant artistic output of genius. The speaker's relation to such subjectivity and creativity, however, is complicated by both the assertiveness of her expression and the fact that it is a form of self-submission, more an affirmation of her autonomy than of her subservience. In the next quatrain, then, she demands of the muses "my attempts befriend" and "triumph in my song," thereby claiming both authorship of the poem and authority over its subject. Yet this gesture too is qualified by her description of the act of imagination as both an expansive articulation of self and a loss of individuality:

Now here, now there, the roving *Fancy* flies,
Till some lov'd object strikes her wandr'ing eyes,
Whose silken fetters all the senses bind,
And soft captivity involves the mind.

In replacing imagination with the less conceptual and reliable "*Fancy*," the speaker maintains the poem's third-person address but trades the commanding power of the former for the liberating potential of the latter to rove spontaneously and erratically through trains of associations.[17] The ambiguous status of such imagining is fully realized in its phenomenology of sensuous perception, as the forceful striking of the eye by "some lov'd object" initiates an internal struggle between subjective desire and objective sensation whose outcome is the voluptuous double metaphor of the "silken fetters" of a "soft captivity." As the fetters of aesthetic captivity "bind" and "involve" the mind, they adorn and caress as much as they enslave, leaving the speaking subject quite as "deck'd with pomp" as the queen of imagination herself.[18]

If the metaphor of soft captivity hints at Wheatley's privileged status as a literate and internationally famous slave, it also resonates with the ironic structure of the poem as a whole and thus deserves further attention. Like the "silken reins" of mild government she celebrates in "To the Right Honourable Earl of Dartmouth" (1773), it appears to invoke a conventional ideal of British liberty, a symbol of comity between the beneficent rule of monarchs and the willing consent of free subjects. But the tension implicit in the phrase is perhaps even more complex. Wheatley appears to have borrowed it from Addison's 1713 play, *Cato, A Tragedy*, according to Kenneth Silverman the most quoted Whig literary work in America at the time, an edition of which appeared in Boston in 1767. In a key line from the play, Portius, the more moderate of Cato's sons, offers his wilder brother Marcus cautionary advice about the irresistible power of romantic love: "the Strong, the Brave, the Virtuous, and the Wise / Sink in the soft Captivity together." At the time of this warning, Cato and his sons are threatened with capture and retaliation by Caesar, and thus the "soft Captivity" of love, when not "well tim'd," is not only an explicit threat to a warrior's mental readiness and martial virtue but may also lead to actual physical captivity. Yet because Cato rejects imprisonment as a craven option—he commits suicide instead—soft captivity actually threatens an ultimate self-undoing, both emotionally and physically. Wheatley's use of the phrase, then, suggests the enormous political stakes of figuring liberty of the imagination so stoically and brazenly in terms of its antithesis. It realizes the aesthetic "wandr'ing" of a slave as continuous with capture, oppression, and the imminent prospect of death.[19]

Wheatley's understanding of the reflexivity of aesthetic experience, however, also draws her away from the destructive impossibility of Cato's dilemma toward a more dialectical apprehension of her political status. Insofar as aesthetic pleasure enables unfettered liberty of imagination, it might be read as a dangerous form of self-authorizing individualism, especially for a slave. But since Wheatley's poem emphasizes the imagination's authoritative role as the "ruler" of her "subject-passions," it functions as precisely the kind of Cato-like bracketing of selfhood demanded by elite republican ideals of disinterestedness. As such, her soft captivity also echoes the mode of political submission John Quincy Adams calls "soft compulsion," which Jay Fliegelman describes as oratorical persuasion that "manipulated the passionate springs of human motivation in such a way as to avoid violating human freedom."[20] Wheatley's metaphor thus signals both radical protest and republican consensus, registering her anomalous legal status at the margins of American culture and her rightful place in its very center.[21]

Accordingly, the poem on imagination enacts its powers as it describes them, limning in vigorous neoclassical diction what her imagined citizenship might look like. Indeed, Wheatley defines poetic power in such emphatically spatial and kinetic terms that, as the perception of objects becomes a "mental train" of images, her soft captivity is realized as unfettered mobility:

> We on thy pinions can surpass the wind,
> And leave the rolling universe behind:
> From star to star the mental optics rove,
> Measure the skies, and range the realms above.
> There in one view we grasp the mighty whole,
> Or with new worlds amaze th' unbounded soul.

Such star-roving hyperbolizes both liberty of the imagination and the physical freedom Wheatley lacks as a slave. Just as the "pinions" of the imagination are a technology of the mind whose use implies the autonomous agency of the perceiving subject, her "mental optics"—an allusion to Newton's invention of the reflecting telescope a hundred years earlier—invoke precisely the same inventive powers of imagination Wheatley attributes to Harvard students in her poem "To the University of Cambridge in New England" (1773). This exalted mobility and vision realize in the poem's speaker the highest forms of aesthetic perception, imagination, and judgment. To "grasp the mighty whole" is to take the comprehensive view of an object that most aesthetic philosophers held as necessary to disinterested judgments of taste. To perceive "new worlds [that] amaze th' unbounded soul" is to employ the creative powers of association free from the constraints of objective reality. Such refined and robust powers thus allow her to transcend all natural and political obstacles, even slavery itself: "Though *Winter* frowns to *Fancy's* raptur'd eyes / The fields may flourish, and gay scenes arise; / The frozen deeps may break their iron bands."[22]

At this moment in the poem, the contrary impulses of liberty and constraint seem to have reached an ideal balance. The benign despotism of the autonomous imagination enacts the speaker's sovereignty "o'er the realms of thought" and confirm her in the very agency to which she submits. But as Wheatley's poetic subject travels in her imagination, and the distance between her political and aesthetic liberty increases, their strained homology finally becomes untenable, at which point she removes herself abruptly from the world she has created:

But I reluctant leave the pleasing views,
Which *Fancy* dresses to delight the *Muse*;
Winter austere forbids me to aspire,
And northern tempests damp the rising fire;
They chill the tides of *Fancy's* flowing sea,
Cease then, my song, cease the unequal lay.

The speaker's sudden expulsion from the "pleasing views" of imagination performs the conventional gesture of self-effacement that marks many of the period's poems of sensibility. In the context of Wheatley's slavery, however, the denial of aesthetic liberty produces a more profoundly unsettling effect. The cold north wind—not of objective reality but racial tyranny—reminds the speaker of her enslavement by refusing her poetic aspiration, restricting her liberty, and calling her back from her now-illicit roving. If the violence of this subjugation parallels the bold self-realization it checks, her "reluctant" act of leaving and her departing salute to "delight" and the "rising fire" of imagination give full measure to the injustice of her oppression. Such a moment suggests the very reverse of "soft compulsion": not internalized consent but cruel coercion.[23]

The sudden ceasing of Wheatley's song creates the pathos of the poem whose *peripeteia* juxtaposes the liberating power of imagination against the aching discipline of its constraint. But it is precisely through this pathos that the poem makes its political argument. For the speaker's removal from the "pleasing views" of imagination she has herself created functions simultaneously as punishment and remonstration. It emphasizes the fact of her having already traveled the "realms of thought" of her own free will. As she withdraws rhetorically, her absence and the resulting poetic artifact implicitly pronounce an identity between the capacity for aesthetic judgment and political equality, in this way anticipating Thomas Jefferson's summary rejection of Wheatley's poetry and African intelligence in *Notes on the State of Virginia*.[24] Wheatley calls her lay "unequal" not because her political status renders her unequal to the demands of imagination but because her capacity for aesthetic self-submission claims the rights of political self-determination that her enslavement denies. Such reflexive rhetoric thus gives "On Imagination" a resonance that locates aesthetic theory within the contested sociopolitical context of eighteenth-century race slavery without ever becoming reducible to that context.[25] Conversely, Wheatley's poem apprehends the problem of political liberty in terms of the processes of aesthetic perception without rendering it a mere exercise in philosophical didacticism. By deploying a theoretical vocabulary that foregrounds liberty of the imagination and the politics of aesthetic subjectivity, its most emotionally compelling, structurally significant, and formally complex moments—an ambivalent relation of power, a liberating gesture of self-expansion, and a tragic capitulation—stage dramatic conflicts in which the language of aspiration and agency confronts the forces of law and power.[26]

In this way, "On Imagination" offers itself as a representation of liberty, an affirmation of its importance, and a figuration of its complex truth. Like the imported, reprinted, and redacted aesthetic theory that informs it, its language of liberty of the imagination appeals to the social identities and deeply held beliefs of revolutionary Americans. Like Trumbull's *Essay*, its rhetoric of self-determination implicitly puts the claims of imagination in the service of a politics of colonial resistance, even as it articulates its allegiance to a British cultural heritage. But as a "fine Poem"—as a work of art—it also aims to provoke in its readers morally illuminating feelings of aesthetic pleasure. In Trumbull's words, it invites readers to feel liberty's dignity or to be jealous of its debasement or perhaps to feel something of both—the ironies of liberty inherent in the sensible perception of aesthetic objects and the pleasures of the imagination.

NOTES

1. John Trumbull, *Essay on the Use and Advantages of the Fine Arts* (New Haven, 1770), 3–5.

Studies of Trumbull pay scant, even derogatory attention to the *Essay*. See Alexander Cowie, *John Trumbull: Connecticut Wit* (Chapel Hill: University of North Carolina Press, 1936), 59; and Leon Howard, *The Connecticut Wits* (Chicago: University of Chicago Press, 1943), 45. For a reading that emphasizes the *Essay* as an instance in the "transformation of public discourse," see Christopher Grasso, *A Speaking Aristocracy: Transforming Public Discourse in Eighteenth-Century Connecticut* (Chapel Hill: University of North Carolina Press for the Omohundro Institute of Early American History and Culture, 1999), 288–91.

2. Longinus, *On the Sublime*, trans. William Smith (London, 1739), 103–4. Trumbull, *Essay*, 5, 12, 11. On the eighteenth-century British discourse of "liberty and the arts," see Michael Meehan, *Liberty and Poetics in Eighteenth-Century England* (London: Croom Helm, 1986).

3. My account of political liberty in late eighteenth-century America is indebted to an extensive historiography. Bernard Bailyn and Gordon Wood both describe conceptions of liberty during the colonial crisis in opposition to the "power" of the monarchy and Parliament. See Bernard Bailyn, *Ideological Origins of the American Revolution* (Cambridge: Harvard University Press, 1967), 55–93; and Gordon Wood, *The Creation of the American Republic, 1776–1787* (New York: Norton, 1972), 18–28. Michael Kammen and Eric Foner emphasize the changing meaning of liberty from the mid eighteenth century through the Revolution and the 1780s, including its shifting limitations and exclusions. See Michael Kammen, *Spheres of Liberty: Changing Perceptions of Liberty in American Culture* (Jackson: University Press of Mississippi, 1986), 8–52; and Eric Foner, *The Story of American Freedom* (New York: Norton, 1998), 3–68.

4. On the popularity of aesthetic treatises in eighteenth-century America, see David Lundberg and Henry F. May, "The Enlightened Reader in America," *American Quarterly* 28 (1976): 262–93; and Janice G. Schimmelman, *A Checklist of European Treatises on Art and Aesthetics Available in American Through 1815* (Worcester, MA: American Antiquarian Society, 1983).

5. I use the term *homology*, rather than that of *analogy* or *metaphor*, to suggest a relation between aesthetics and politics based on their shared origins in seventeenth- and early eighteenth-century moral philosophy. For an example, see Thomas Hobbes's *Leviathan* (1651), which begins its account of the modern political state with a discussion of the imagination and the processes of association.

6. Paul Guyer writes that "the central idea to emerge in eighteenth-century aesthetics is the idea of the freedom of the imagination, and it is the attraction of this idea that provided much of the impetus behind the explosion of aesthetic theory in the period." See Paul Guyer, *Values of Beauty: Historical Essays in Aesthetics* (New York: Cambridge University Press, 2005), 25.

7. Joseph Addison and Richard Steele, *The Spectator*, ed. Donald F. Bond (Oxford: Clarendon Press, 1965), 503. Lord Kames, *Elements of Criticism* (Honolulu: University Press of the Pacific, 2002), xiv. "On Criticism and Genius," *Boston Magazine*, December 1783, 57. "Essay on Genius," *Columbian Magazine, or Monthly Miscellany*, September 1789, 347. Monroe Beardsley describes the British tradition of empirical aesthetics as an attempt to "free criticism itself from its own shackles of unexamined, or insufficiently examined, aesthetic theory." See Monroe Beardsley, *Aesthetics from Classical Greece to the Present: A Short History* (New York: Macmillan, 1966), 167. But Walter Jackson Bate notes that early British followers of the French rationalists, like Charles Gildon, believed that the French writers were not blindly following classical rules but using reason to interpret them. See Walter Jackson Bate, *From Classic to Romantic: Premises of Taste in Eighteenth-Century England* (New York: Harper, 1946), 32.

8. Addison and Steele, *The Spectator*, 529. James Beattie, *Elements of Moral Science* (Delmar, NY: Scholars' Facsimiles and Reprints, 1976), 187. Kames, *Elements*, 416. David Hume, *Essays Moral, Political, and Literary*, ed. Eugene F. Miller (Indianapolis: Liberty Fund, 1985), 231. As M. H. Abrams makes clear, the appeal of mechanistic rhetoric in theories of imagination persisted throughout the eighteenth-century, largely in otherwise empirical conceptions of association psychology but even through Coleridge's articulation of the "mechanical fancy." See M. H. Abrams, *The Mirror and the Lamp: Romantic Theory and the Critical Tradition* (New York: Oxford University Press, 1953), 156–70.

9. "On Pleasure," *Royal American Magazine*, March 1775, 184. "Thoughts on Pleasure," *American Moral and Sentimental Magazine*, December 1797, 406. Addison, *The Spectator*, 538–39. Hugh Blair, *Lectures on Rhetoric and Belle Lettres*, ed. Linda Ferreira-Buckley and S. Michael Halloran (Carbondale: Southern Illinois University Press, 2005), 8. "Pleasures, Sensual and Spiritual," *Philadelphia Minerva*, August 1797, 2.

10. "On the Imagination," *Literary Tablet*, June 11, 1806, 78–79. Hume, *A Treatise of Human Nature* (New York: Penguin, 1969), 57.

11. Kames, *Elements*, 3–4. "The Necessity of Regulating the Association of Ideas in Young Minds," *New England Quarterly Magazine*, July 1802, 119. Thomas Reid, "On Taste," *Literary Magazine*, February 1807, 143. Charles Brockden Brown, "On the Standard of Taste," *Literary Magazine*, October 1806, 294. For a comprehensive discussion of the association of ideas, see Martin Kallich, *The Association of Ideas and Critical Theory in Eighteenth-Century England* (The Hague: Mouton, 1970).

12. Kames, *Elements*, 3. Alexander Gerard, *Essay on Taste* (London: A. Millar, A. Kincaid, and J. Bell, 1759), 166–67. Blair, *Lectures*, 22. John Blair Linn, *The Port-Folio*, January 24, 1801, 31.

13. Blair, *Lectures*, 22. Francis Hutcheson, *An Inquiry Into the Original of Our Ideas of Beauty and Virtue*, ed. Wolfgang Leidhold (Indianapolis: Liberty Fund, 2004), 25. Archibald Alison, *Essays on the Nature and Principles of Taste* (Hartford, 1821), 19, 20.

14. Jay Fliegelman describes an "inner dynamic of energy and its containment" in late eighteenth-century American writing. See Jay Fliegelman, *Declaring Independence: Jefferson, Natural Language, and the Culture of Performance* (Stanford: Stanford University Press, 1993), 103.

15. See Edward Cahill, "An Adventurous and Lawless Fancy: Charles Brockden Brown's Aesthetic State," *Early American Literature* 36, no. 1 (2001): 31–70, and "Federalist Criticism and the Fate of Genius," *American Literature*, 76, no. 4 (2004): 687–717.

16. Phillis Wheatley, *The Collected Works of Phillis Wheatley*, ed. John Shields (New York: Oxford University Press, 1988), 62.

17. For most of the eighteenth century, *imagination* and *fancy* were used either interchangeably or with only the slight difference that fancy was somewhat freer and less reliable and comprehensive than imagination. Addison himself used the two terms "promiscuously." On the history of the distinction, see James Engell, *The Creative Imagination: Enlightenment to Romanticism* (Cambridge: Harvard University Press, 1981), 172–83.

18. Wheatley, *Collected Works*, 65.

19. Kenneth Silverman, *A Cultural History of the American Revolution: Painting, Music, Literature, and the Theatre in the Colonies and the United States from the Treaty of Paris to the Inauguration of George Washington, 1763–1789* (New York: Crowell, 1976), 82; Joseph Addison, *Cato, a Tragedy* (London, 1733), 53.

20. Fliegelman, *Declaring Independence*, 37. Fliegelman notes that the phrase derives from Adams's translation of Marcus Manilius, a first-century Roman didactic poet. See John Quincy Adams, *The Memoirs of John Quincy Adams*, ed. Charles Francis Adams (Boston, 1874), 3:442.

21. Peter Coviello sees a similar implication in Wheatley's "To the Right Honourable William, Earl of Dartmouth," whose rhetoric of "the love of freedom" he calls "a defense of the black citizen's very capacity for virtuous republican citizenship." See Peter Coviello, "Agonizing Affection: Affect and Nation in Early America," *Early American Literature* 37, no. 3 (2002): 445.

22. Wheatley, *Collected Works*, 66. Perhaps such emphatic tropes of self-expression even allegorize the volume's publication itself, Wheatley's entrance into the public sphere of the London book trade, or her emancipation in the same year *Poems on Various Subjects* was published. For a useful discussion of Wheatley's public career, see Frank Shuffelton, "On Her Own Footing: Phillis Wheatley in Freedom," in Vincent Carretta and Philip Gould, eds., *Genius in Bondage*, 175–89 (Lexington: University of Kentucky Press, 2001).

23. Wheatley, *Collected Works,* 67, 68.

24. Jefferson calls Wheatley' poetry "beneath the dignity of criticism" and faults her for her insufficient aesthetic power, insisting that Africans express themselves with "the senses only, not the imagination." In the same paragraph, however, he criticizes Ignatius Sancho, the self-educated African intellectual and author of *Letters* (1782), for indulging in excessive aesthetic liberty: "His imagination is wild and extravagant, escapes incessantly from every restraint of reason and taste, and, in the course of its vagaries, leaves a trace of thought as incoherent and eccentric, as is the course of a meteor through the sky." Jefferson, *Notes on the State of Virginia,* ed. William Peden (New York: Norton, 1982), 140.

25. For a discussion of Wheatley, slavery, and the aesthetics of imitation, see Eric Slauter, *The State as a Work of Art: The Cultural Origins of the Constitution* (Chicago: University of Chicago Press, 2009), 179–95.

26. Julie Ellison argues that the sign of "resistance" in Wheatley's poem is her refusal to use the language of sentiment to "testify to her own victimization." See Julie Ellison, *Cato's Tears and the Making of Anglo-American Emotion* (Chicago: University of Chicago Press, 1999), 115. But, in my reading, Wheatley uses the language of aesthetic subjectivity to make a specific argument about the meaning of liberty from the perspective of slavery.

The Writing on the Wall

Revolutionary Aesthetics and Interior Spaces

IVY G. WILSON

At a symbolic moment in Ralph Ellison's *Invisible Man* (1952), the nameless protagonist finds himself glancing at the images on the wall in one of the Brotherhood field offices. They include a map adorned with a heroic Christopher Columbus and a poster, "The Rainbow of America's Future," depicting a romanticized picture of a multicultural U.S. But the most symbolic image on the wall is the portrait of Frederick Douglass. Perhaps more than any other African American, Douglass has been made an icon and lionized equally by both radicals and moderates alike as the embodiment of an American democratic potentiality. As social texts, the three images limn different, if not competing, visions of America; thus when the protagonist later walks into the field office only to find it empty and the Douglass portrait missing, the scene becomes a harbinger of the impending revolution about to erupt on the streets of New York City.

Ellison's use of visual images in *Invisible Man* evinces a wider concern with aesthetics and interior spaces as represented in U.S. literature. In a novel that keenly and self-consciously foregrounds art—from Lucius Brockway's making paint to Mary's cast-iron figurines, from the bronze statue of the college founder to Clifton's paper Sambo dolls—the question of aesthetics is central to the meaning of the story. If, as Lena Hill contends, different episodes of the novel can be seen as museums, many of these should be understood as the private gallery spaces of interior black life.[1]

Thinking about how African Americans conceived of interiority—its possibility, its elusiveness, the dimensions of its conceptual privacy that allowed it even to be imagined—illuminates the necessity of such a space when its physical correlative was often denied, unavailable, or being torn asunder. Here interior spaces are conceptualized in two specific ways. One way is to consider the forms of materiality: rooms, garrets, anterooms, and hideaways that emphasize the relationship between the exterior and the interior. The other way is to conceptualize interior spaces as the imaginative precincts of the mind; the innervision as the domain of the inside. These spaces were especially important for antebellum African Americans—as with, for example, the wooded area where Douglass and his counterparts plan their escape, Henry "Box" Brown shipping himself to freedom in a container, and Harriet Jacobs concealed in a garret—where interiority also signaled a kind of privacy. The dimensionality of these interior spaces, whether physical or psychological, allowed African Americans to imagine representations of themselves that counteracted their depictions in the public imaginary.

The three Brotherhood office images from *Invisible Man* not only accentuate the idea of interiority, they also underscore broader questions about how political dissent is captured in or represented as art. While the removal of Douglass's portrait is meant to intimate a coming revolution in Ellison's mid-twentieth-century U.S., throughout the nineteenth century writers and orators frequently invoked the iconography of George Washington to illuminate contemporary national crises. Washington's image is taken up, in varying degrees and for different ideological purposes, by the poet Phillis Wheatley, the short story writer Washington Irving, and the novelists Herman Melville and Harriet Beecher Stowe. If the image of Washington was conjured to reassess a given crisis through the lens of the American Revolution, then so too was the image of Toussaint L'Ouverture and the Haitian Revolution. L'Ouverture was invoked by the poet John Greenleaf Whittier, the orator Wendell Phillips, the novelist Frank J. Webb, and the writer William Wells Brown, among others. Through the mid nineteenth century, both leaders were reiterated and refashioned again and again, making their iconography an example of a revolutionary aesthetic.

The term *revolutionary aesthetic* is used here to outline two primary definitions. In the most immediate sense, the revolutionary aesthetic suggests the composite cultural production in various art forms that take the historical event of a revolution as their topic, such that, for example, Emanuel Gottlieb Leutze's 1851 painting *Washington Crossing the Delaware* and Robert Colescott's 1975 *George Washington Carver Crossing the Delaware* are both concerned with (re)interpreting the American Revolution. But, equally important, the revolutionary aesthetic is meant to evince an approach to the radical formal stylistics of art that self-consciously erupts former accepted conventions, such that, for example, the base, exaggerated caricaturing of Colescott's oil painting is a profound departure from the luminous romanticism of Leutze's work.

What follows is a consideration of how political subtexts are illustrated through the use of a revolutionary aesthetic that stages questions about the relation between iconography and interiority. Beginning with a reading of Phillis Wheatley and Scipio Moorhead, this essay underscores a particular relationship between interiority, visuality, and political revolution that is heightened further when one considers the various permutations in the iconography of George Washington and Toussaint L'Ouverture from the late eighteenth to mid nineteenth centuries. The permutation of these iconographies traces Washington's image from Wheatley, Irving, Stowe, and Melville as well as a parallel series on L'Ouverture by Phillips, Webb, and James McCune Smith. By examining a number of different simulated portraits of Washington and L'Ouverture, this essay investigates the ways that writers and orators engaged the processes of visualization through literary and oratorical portraiture—a particular concern for African Americans who were preoccupied with the processes of visualization as an operation that allowed them to imagine themselves as part of the U.S. or, conversely, to fantasize about different alternative socialities altogether.

Kindred Spirits: Phillis Wheatley, Visuality, and a Revolutionary Aesthetic

We might do no better in a discussion of revolutionary aesthetic and interior spaces than by beginning with one of the earliest writers in the African American literary canon: Wheatley. Wheatley has too often been at the center of a debate over whether her poetry was too deferential, too imitative, and, alas, too conciliatory about her condition as a slave in the U.S. But Wheatley's poetry itself has been too little studied for its poetics, for its prosody, for its formal conventions as a work of art. Even the poem that has caused the greatest amount of consternation, "On Being Brought from Africa to America" (1773), for its ostensible capitulation to a bifurcated social logic of black/white, Christian/pagan, when visualized, when imagined, presents us with a different picture from what might be registered if we were only listening to the poem.

> Remember, *Christians, Negros,* black as *Cain,*
> May be refin'd, and join th' angelic train.[2]

When restricted to the realm of the sonic, to the world of sound, it may seem as if Wheatley's narrator is making a plaintive gesture to Christians that, although Negroes are black as Cain, someday they may be redeemed. But when we look at the poem as a visual artifact, its sublimated functionality as artifice—a sublimated operation of radicalism, no less, that structurally depends upon an act of envisioning—becomes all the more recognizable, all the more legible. The typographical use of italics, her stylization of the letter, to the atom, if you will, alters the relationship between the poem's visual demarcation and its subsumed political meaning. The prefigured image of the "train" is created precisely by the insertion of a caesura between "Remember" and "Christians," a caesura that fabricates a litany and produces the figurative cars of the "train," "Christians" and "blacks" who are now linked together on an equivalent plane, indeed heading in the same direction on the same itinerary.

To claim such equality between black and white in 1773 would have indeed been radical; but the particular distinction I am drawing here is one that differentiates between the poem's aural resonance and its visual resonance. When these two aspects are considered, the image of the poem yields a different meaning, perhaps even of Wheatley herself. By attending to Wheatley as a poet who self-consciously uses her genre to stylize a form of subversive art, we can better uncover a political aesthetic. But can this be extended to a revolutionary aesthetic? And, given our received image of Wheatley, would we be able to identify it?[3] What would such a revolutionary aesthetic look like? What would it sound like? And, perhaps more important, upon what grounds would we be able to define the criteria for a revolutionary aesthetic?

An early articulation of a revolutionary aesthetic is intimated in "To S.M. a young *African* Painter, on Seeing his Works" (1773). The poem is written as an ekphrasis; that is, a poem about another form of art, most often painting. The opening couplet begins, "To show the lab'ring bosom's deep intent, / And thought in living characters to paint" (*The Poems*, 104).

Ekphrasis usually works in one of two ways: to explain or analyze what is happening in the painting or, alternatively, to derive meaning from the painting to influence a new (literary) work. But it is essential to recognize that there is a visual basis for ekphrasis that is enhanced by things only the mind can see.

Scipio Moorhead, the "S.M." of the poem, was a slave of the Reverend John Moorhead and a fellow Boston artist. The ink drawing upon which the engraved frontispiece of Wheatley's *Poems on Various Subjects, Religious and Moral* (1773) is based is commonly attributed to Moorhead, although the original has been untraced and no other works with his signature have been discovered.[4] Moorhead had been trained as a painter by the reverend's wife, Sarah Moorhead, who was well known in Boston as an art instructor.[5] Although little is known of Moorhead, much of what is known has been filtered through his association with Wheatley; turning to her then might not only tell us about the formation of the early traditions of African American poetry and poetics but yield information about the field of early African American art. Wheatley's decision to note Moorhead's paintings of Aurora and Damon and Pythias, of all his works, suggests that they were versed in Greek and Roman mythology. If her poem "On Imagination," also included in *Poems on Various Subjects*, is an early theory of poetics, then "To S.M. a Young *African* Painter" is more specifically an early history, if not theory, of an African American aesthetics.

Although Wheatley's poem has the appearance of being merely the literary companion to Scipio Moorhead's paintings, the image it generates depicts a different picture altogether. The poem does not describe the paintings themselves; that is, while Wheatley's poem does not offer an interpretation of the scenes, it does take notice of the paintings' animation, their almost genesis-like quality—"When first thy pencil did those beauties give, / And breathing figures learnt from thee to live" (104–5). In the middle of the first large stanza, Wheatley moves beyond the merely radical and into perhaps the revolutionary.

> Still may the painter's and the poet's fire
> To aid thy pencil, and thy verse conspire!
>
> (105)

Wheatley makes a trope of the word *conspire* here, moving the word into a circular orbit within the domain of the poem. The contextual meaning of the word *conspire* as it relates to the dominant theme of the poem reveals that Wheatley is speaking of a shared corporeality between her and Moorhead, the painter and poet "breathing together." This representation of Wheatley and Moorhead might be thought of as a precursor to Asher B. Durand's later painting, *Kindred Spirits* (1849), with its depiction of William Cullen Bryant and Thomas Cole, only in living color.

Wheatley ensconces the more revolutionary impulse of what could be called a proto-black cultural nationalism—an early form of cultural nationalism that (somehow) simultaneously makes overtures to the notion of an elite class of artists and to the black diaspora—by making the express political import of her poem secondary to the ostensible primary one of aesthetics as the alchemy of his pencil and her verse. The common definition of the word *conspire* is to "combine privily for an evil or unlawful purpose; to agree together to do something criminal, illegal, or reprehensible; especially in the form of a plot,"[6] reflecting a deeper connection for Wheatley and Moorhead beyond simply their bond as artists. Her recognition in the second stanza of Damon and Pythias reiterates the sense of communion she feels with Moorhead; in Greek mythology Damon offered himself as collateral for punishment by death as a guarantee that Pythias would return to receive his sentence. Damon and Pythias may have been examples for Wheatley's ideas about loyalty and fidelity and also archetypes for her notions about transposition and transubstantiation, for what could communicate the idea of an interior space more profoundly than the idea of sharing the same psychology and corporeality as someone else? If Wheatley's poem, then, can be said to have a revolutionary subtext, that subtext might best be identified as, after James Baldwin, the fire next time.

The latent revolutionary aesthetic of "To S.M. a Young *African* Painter, on Seeing his Works" is further heightened when one speculates about the publication history of the poem itself. The poem was not listed in the original 1772 proposal for *Poems on Various Subjects,* and one wonders if Wheatley imagined the volume as having a kind of physicality itself, a dimensionality where her own revolutionary aesthetic could be privily secreted between the manuscript pages as an interiorized space only to be later revealed in public at printing.[7]

Head of State

Indeed, one of the earliest examples in the iconography of Washington came from the hand of none other than Wheatley herself. The "Poetical

Essays" section of the *Pennsylvania Magazine: or American Monthly Museum* of April 1776 features Wheatley's poem and letter to Washington.[8] The magazine's editor, Thomas Paine, wrote: "The following LETTER and VERSES, were written by the famous Phillis Wheatley, the African Poetess, and presented to his Excellency Gen. Washington" (Wheatley, *The Poems*, 164). In her accompanying letter, Wheatley wishes his "Excellency all possible success in the great cause [he is] so generously engaged in" (165), an indication of her keen awareness of the American Revolution and its potential significance to the condition of U.S. blacks both free and enslaved. Invoking the muse for inspiration and imploring the "celestial choir" (166) to echo her call, Wheatley exalts Washington as military general as well as his efforts to liberate the American colonies from England.

> Shall I to Washington their praise recite?
> Enough thou know'st them in the fields of fight.
> Thee, first in place and honours,—we demand
> The grace and glory of thy martial band.
> Fam'd for thy valour, for thy virtues more,
> Hear every tongue thy guardian aid implore!
>
> (167)

But Wheatley's poem is actually less a consecration of Washington himself than it is a panegyric on the epochal turn toward "freedom's cause" (166). In the poem, Wheatley mentions Eolus and Columbia, invoking the latter in both its classic sense and as the personification of America. As she had with "To S.M. a Young *African* Painter," Wheatley's use of classical references was a way for her to limn a revolutionary aesthetic, figured here as something embodied by America but not contained by it.[9]

While Wheatley offers her poem in the midst of the American Revolution, when the iconography of Washington as a heroic or national figure is not foregone, Washington Irving's "Rip Van Winkle" furnishes an example of the varied use of literary portraiture in the iconography of Washington. Published in 1819, Irving's tale tells the story of Rip Van Winkle, a quaint villager of the Catskill Mountains, who, after stumbling off and falling asleep under a tree, wakes up twenty years later to find that his wife has died. Unaware that the American Revolution has occurred, Rip piques the chagrin of the villagers when he declares his loyalty to King George III.

If "Rip Van Winkle" subsumes an ostensible uncertainty about the revolution, this uncertainty is translated through Irving's depiction of the village's new aesthetic. The former village inn was replaced by hotel with broken windows mended with old hats and petticoats. On top of a pole, the new flag of the stars and stripes remain strange and incomprehensible to Rip. But it is the portrait hanging on the hotel sign that denotes the shift in political sensibility. Far from an interior space, the placement of the image atop the hotel sign is meant to be inculcated by the public at large. "He recognized on the sign, however, the ruby face of King George, under which he had smoked so many a peaceful pipe, but even this was strangely metamorphosed. The red coat was changed for one of blue and buff, a sword was stuck in the hand of a scepter, the head was decorated with a cocked hat, and underneath was painted in large characters, GENERAL WASHINGTON."[10] The scene depends upon a certain presupposition that attire can be read as a sign of political affiliation; the blue coat replaces the red, the sword the scepter. As an emblem of royalty, the removal of the scepter signals to Rip that the country is no longer under monarchical rule. Irving's story abbreviates the American Revolution by compressing its temporal spatiality, illustrating the transformation from colony to nation as a shift in dress with the metamorphosis of George III into George Washington.[11]

In *Uncle Tom's Cabin; or, Life Among the Lowly* (1852), Stowe takes the experimentation with literary portraiture even further than Irving; where he uses the technique to compress national time, Stowe uses it to imagine a different national temporality. When we are first introduced to Uncle Tom and Aunt Chloe's cabin and made privy to its interior and its contents, we notice something curious about the inventory. Stowe has her narrator ask that we enter the dwelling. "In fact, that corner was the *drawing-room* of the establishment. In the other corner was a bed of much humbler pretensions, and evidently designed for *use*. The wall over the fireplace was adorned with some very brilliant scriptural prints, and a portrait of General Washington, drawn and colored in a manner which would certainly have astonished that hero, if ever he happened to meet with its like."[12] Their cabin is, ostensibly, a proper home—only in miniature. What is the relationship here between the interior and the exterior, between the political and the aesthetic, indeed between the black and the white? For, as Edith Wharton will later announce in *The Decoration of Houses* (1898), "Rooms may be decorated in two ways: by a superficial application of ornament totally independent of structure, or by means of those architectural features which are part of the organism of every house, inside as well as out."[13] The disjunction between the inside of Aunt Chloe's and Uncle Tom's cabin and the outside produces, by Wharton's criteria, an anomaly, an asymmetrical aesthetic—if, in fact, *aesthetic* is the term that one could use to describe the slave quarters. That is, if aesthetic is meant as the strict congruence of style, then Aunt Chloe's and Uncle Tom's cabin is not aesthetic; but, if the term signals the sensory capacities of affect, then their cabin could indeed have an aesthetic insofar as it expresses how they *feel* about their own state relative to the nation.

Perhaps the most conspicuous element about this scene is the description of Washington having been "drawn and colored" and retouched, as it were. Here, the notion that the architectural features of a home should have a complementarity both "inside as well as out" is abrogated, allowing for the imagining of a subversive politics that could be featured inside a black interiority separate from its external housing. It seems precisely here in the recesses of the innervision, in the interior spaces, where the revolution is indeed being imagined. For, like Frederick Douglass, who correlates Madison Washington in his short story "The Heroic Slave" (1853) to Patrick Henry and George Washington, the image of the first president in the "drawing-room" of Aunt Chloe's and Uncle Tom's cabin reinterprets the relationship of race to the birth of the nation, and, in this respect, Stowe advances a revolutionary aesthetic insofar as the scene contests the dominant understanding of art and politics.[14]

The manipulation of the iconography of Washington to reassess the meaning of racialization and nation formation is also depicted in Melville's *Moby-Dick* (1851). In the early pages of the book, after Ishmael has fastened onto the idea of joining a whaling ship, he becomes acquainted with his roommate Queequeg. Simultaneously enthralled and frightened, intrigued and alarmed, Ishmael cannot help but stare at Queequeg; an ocular obsession all the more fixated by Queequeg's fancifully tattooed body that is both an indication of his seeming savagery and a visible sign of stenciled artistry. But when Ishmael stares at Queequeg, he disaggregates the body from the head; for while the body may have the intricate markings of being from another world, Queequeg's head reminds Ishmael of Washington. "It may seem ridiculous, but it reminded me of General Washington's head, as seen in the popular busts of him. It had the same long regularly graded retreating slope from above the brows, which were likewise very projecting, like two long promontories thickly wooded on top. Queequeg was George Washington cannibalistically developed."[15] Ishmael's vision of Queequeg as Washington hovers between an interpretation of the *Pequod* as a ship of state that promotes a radical democratic potentiality of equivalent subjectivity and an illustration of the nascent imperial designs of the early U.S.[16]

Furthermore, the association of Queequeg to Washington illuminates the ideological if not political meanings of interiority when one recalls it is precisely in the privacy of their shared quarters, in the chapter "A Bosom Friend," that has Ishmael fancying an image contoured by a "queer" revolutionary aesthetic.[17] While Stowe racializes Washington to intimate the revolutionary impulse underlining black political thought, even in a seemingly innocuous domesticated household, Melville's depiction signals how the revolutionary aesthetic invoked here is precluded from yielding iconographic portraiture to liken Queequeg as a more permanent figurative head of state by the end of the novel when the *Pequod* is dashed into oblivion and only Ishmael remains.

Stately Portraits; or, The Iconography of Toussaint L'Ouverture

If Stowe and Melville redraw the image of the American Revolution's most iconic figure to illuminate the mid-nineteenth-century slavery crisis as a political predicament endemic to the founding of the U.S., then other nineteenth-century writers and artists reconceptualized the Age of Revolution itself as a historical epoch by portraying Toussaint L'Ouverture as a competing icon. L'Ouverture was the leader of the Haitian Revolution (1791–1804) that liberated the then-colony of St. Domingue from French imperial rule to become the first black republic in the Western Hemisphere. As the slavery debate escalated in the 1850s, the Haitian Revolution was interpreted as a warning sign of what might happen in the U.S. should black slaves decide to revolt. Stowe stages this fear in a conversation between Augustine and Alfred in *Uncle Tom's Cabin*, and Melville does much the same by naming the slave ship the *San Dominick* in *Benito Cereno* (1855). But the reinscription of the Haitian Revolution as a revolution proper, and not simply an insurrection, depended upon a certain shift in its various representations through the iconography of L'Ouverture as a figurehead.

Perhaps the most well-known attempt to depict L'Ouverture specifically as an icon was Wendell Phillips's speech, which he delivered in 1861 on the eve of the Civil War. Phillips opens his speech by proclaiming that he will offer his audiences in Boston and New York a "sketch" of L'Ouverture that is at once a biography and an argument. Phillips contends that, when the record of history is set straight, L'Ouverture will rank above the Greek Phocion, the Roman Marcus Junius Brutus, the French Marquis de Lafayette, and the American George Washington. By comparing him to such figures,

Phillips fashions L'Ouverture as a transhistorical figure, someone who is at once classical and modern.

The oratorical stylistics of his speech might be understood not simply as an example of the structures of classical rhetoric with a subsumed mode of argumentation but perhaps also as a mode of aesthetic embellishment that attempts to artistically portray L'Ouverture. "If I stood here tonight to tell the story of Napoleon, I should take it from the lips of Frenchmen, who find no language rich enough to paint the great captain of the nineteenth century. Were I here to tell you the story of Washington, I should take it from you hearts—you, who think no marble white enough to carve the name of the Father of his Country. I am about to tell you the story of a negro who has hardly one written line."[18] Phillips's speech is almost too conspicuous in its efforts to make an icon of L'Ouverture. The aestheticization of this iconography depends upon a translation of Phillips's verbal cues into the visual, from the oratorical arts into the material arts. L'Ouverture deserves, Phillips implies, language richer than that used to "paint" Napoleon and richer than that to carve Washington's name upon white marble edifices. But Phillips's speech can only have that iconography interiorized in the mind's eye of his audience where the image of L'Ouverture can be envisaged.

While Phillips manipulated the oratorical arts as a proxy for the material arts, James McCune Smith's lecture on L'Ouverture was perceptibly less adorned and more literal in its didactic intention. Twenty years before Phillips delivered his famous speech, McCune Smith delivered a lecture at the Stuyvesant Institute for the benefit of the Colored Orphan Asylum in 1841. A graduate of the local New York African Free School himself, and, later, the University of Glasgow, McCune Smith was one of the foremost African American intellectuals of the nineteenth century. Comparing L'Ouverture to "Leonidas at Thermopyae" or "Bruce at Bannockburn," McCune Smith declares these events to be necessary study for "every American citizen."[19]

> Among the many lessons that may be drawn from this portion of history is one not unconnected with the present occasion. From causes to which I need not give a name, there is gradually creeping into our otherwise prosperous state the incongruous and undermining influence of *caste*. One of the local manifestations of this unrepublican sentiment is, that while 800 children, chiefly of foreign parents, are educated and taught trades at the expense of all the citizens, colored children are excluded from these privileges.[20]

His speech here extends a critique of the latent social formations promulgating the caste system in the U.S. as an antidemocratic or "unrepublican" practice. Slavery was not only unethical, a moral stain against the nation because, among other violations, it promoted a caste system; it was also anathema to the underlying political tenets of a professed democracy. It is only in the last line of Smith's speech that it becomes something less of an anecdote and something more prophetic when he notes L'Ouverture had been taught to read while a slave—a suggestion that there may yet be a L'Ouverture among the ranks at the Colored Orphan Asylum if only they were afforded the opportunity to be educated.

Both McCune Smith and Phillips use oratory as a form of illustration. Their illustrations almost invert the literal definition of iconography as "picture writing" into an aesthetic practice instead of "writing picture" in their attempts to offer a visual biography and narrative of L'Ouverture and the Haitian Revolution. While "picture writing" could be thought of as the didactic use of the visual arts to convey narrative meaning, "writing picture" underscores the use of the expository textures of oratory and narrative that more specifically attempt to craft the visual correlative of an image, an act that is especially perceptible in orations that seek to sketch "character." Manipulating the aesthetic practice of iconography, these writers deployed this history as an allegory for the contemporary crisis of U.S. chattel slavery. U.S. intellectuals, as early as Smith's speech, began depicting L'Ouverture as an exponent of the antislavery movement. The iconography of L'Ouverture compared him to a number of historical figures including Oliver Cromwell, the Duke of Wellington, and, sometimes, Napoleon Bonaparte.

If both McCune Smith and Phillips used the verbal cadences of speech to create auditory reverberations that would linger in the chambers of the mind, then Frank J. Webb used literature to approximate portraiture. Webb was an African American writer whose 1857 novel, *The Garies and Their Friends,* depicts the story of the Garies, a well-to-do interracial family comprising a white husband and his "mulatta" ex-slave-turned-wife, as they leave the South for Philadelphia. In the North, the Garies are situated between Philadelphia's black and white communities, represented in stark terms by the white Stevens family and the black Ellis family. Joining McCune Smith and Phillips in trying to make an icon of L'Ouverture, Webb made particular use of literary portraiture.

While the speeches of McCune Smith and Phillips amounted to a kind of oratorical portraiture, Webb uses literary portraiture to deploy a doubly mediated moment of representation. Like Irving and Stowe, Webb's novel calls attention to paintings and drawings specifically as visual artifacts simulated in narrative fiction. These moments are accentuated by their double mediation, one where readers not only visualize the characters of the story in their own mind but are compelled to see through the eyes of these characters to perceive what they are viewing.

At an important moment in the novel when the Garies are trying to reestablish their lives by resettling in Philadelphia, they rent a home from Mr. Walters, one of the city's most affluent and wealthy African Americans. While walking through the home, Garie halts in the parlor, arrested by an image he sees on the wall.

> "So you, too are attracted by that picture," said Mr. Walters, with a smile. "All white men look at it with interest. A black man in uniform of a general officer is something so unusual that they cannot pass it with a glance. . . . That is Toussaint l'Ouverture and I have every reason to believe it to be the correct likeness. . . . That looks like a man of intelligence. It is entirely different from any likeness I ever saw of him. The portraits generally represent him as a monkey-faced person, with a handkerchief about his head."[21]

Walters's comments to Garie about representation, that he has "every reason to believe it to be the correct likeness," circumscribes portraiture as an aesthetic form whose artistry is tied to its claim about authenticity and accuracy more than its embellishment. It is significant that it is a portrait with its focus on the head and the face, because the image functions to counteract the discourse stemming from contemporary phrenology about blacks as simians or a subspecies, intimated here in Walters's note that portraits of L'Ouverture "generally represent him as a monkey-faced person." But, in suggesting that the portrait "looks like a man of intelligence," Walter's comments also understand aesthetics as a mode of representation that can translate the interior domain and render it externally visible. Here attire designates social position—the uniform as a political emblem works against black caricature.

Equally important to the representation of L'Ouverture imagined in the portrait is its placement in the Walters house itself. The image is properly placed within the spatial logic of the home. The house in which the portrait exists is quite different from the image of George Washington in Aunt Chloe's and Uncle Tom's cabin; indeed, their class positions are altogether different, and, in some respects, the interior and the exterior of the

Walters home have a congruence. As Edgar Allan Poe notes in "The Philosophy of Furniture" (1840), most paintings merely relieved "the expanse of [wall]paper," and most of these paintings were merely "landscapes of an imaginative cast—such as the fairy grottoes of Stanfield, or the lake of the Dismal Swamp of Chapman."[22] Webb accentuates literary portraiture as a political strategy that attempts to contextualize U.S. abolitionism within a larger hemispheric framework of black resistance.

Paint the White House Black

A little more than 150 years after the publication of *Uncle Tom's Cabin*, the image of a colored George Washington that could only be intimated in Stowe's novel was conspicuously rendered on the cover of the *New Yorker* magazine. Drew Friedman's drawing features a portrait of Barack Obama, on the eve of the presidential inauguration, in the likeness of Washington. Taking the image of Washington on the dollar bill as a cue, Friedman represented Obama in three-quarter profile wearing a wig similar to the ones associated with the Founding Fathers.

Appearing on newsstands on the week of the inauguration itself, the *New Yorker* cover was, in some respects, a correction to its earlier iconography of the Obamas, which figuratively placed them outside (at least politically) the nation. The July 21, 2008 cover, titled "The Politics of Fear," featured a Barry Blitt drawing of the Obamas in the Oval Office as subversives—Michelle Obama as an Angela Davis–type black militant and Obama presumably as an Islamacist. *Vanity Fair* riffed the *New Yorker* in August 2008 with a cover of Cindy and John McCain in a similar setting and poses with noticeably less stereotypical, although equally caricatured, appearances. Blitt's drawing, while seemingly meant as satire, invoked, in essence, the wrong series of icons. In drawing Michelle Obama as an Angela Davis figure, Blitt's image resurrected a history of militant black nationalism in the U.S. associated with the Black Panther Party that many Americans would rather forget. Likewise, his representation of Obama as an Islamacist, perhaps most visibly associated in the U.S. with Osama Bin Laden, threatened to castigate the then-presidential nominee as unpatriotic. In both instances, Blitt's drawing associated the Obamas with revolutions that have been interpreted as anathema to the nation.

But the politics of Blitt's drawing were complicated, made especially so because of its focus on iconography. It may have seemed that Blitt was caricaturing the Obamas, but the image might also have been a critique of the innumerable misrepresentations propagated by the Republic right wing. In that respect, the cover was not a caricature at all but, rather, a deeply ironic commentary on right-wing attempts to caricature Obama.[23]

The cover for the January 26, 2009 issue of the *New Yorker*, where Obama is transfigured as Washington, then, is an example of how the semiotics of iconography can underwrite political representation, if not national subjectivity. It not only consecrates Obama as the first black president but likens his election to the (re)birth of the nation and essentially depicts him as a Founding Father immediately after the Revolution. It also harks back to Irving's "Rip Van Winkle," with Obama replacing George W. Bush (as Washington replaced King George III). Indeed, Obama himself invoked a kind of revolutionary aesthetic when developing the particular lexicon that formed the grammar of his political program. Importantly, this lexicon emphasized the word *change,* a necessary prefiguration of any political revolution, especially pronounced during the election when one recalls the discourse about the previous administration being a regime. If Obama's election was indeed an ostensible revolution, then it was one where the aesthetics of idiomatic terms like *hope, progress,* and *change* came together in public as the writing on the wall of a reimagined America.

Notes

1. See Lena Hill, "The Visual Art of *Invisible Man*: Ellison's Portrait of Blackness," *American Literature* 81, no. 4 (2009): 775–803. Hill's essay expands one of the central ideas of Robert Stepto's reading of *Invisible Man*; see *From Behind the Veil: A Study of Afro-American Narrative,* 2d ed. (Urbana: University of Illinois Press, 1991), 177.

2. Phillis Wheatley, *The Poems of Phillis Wheatley,* ed. Julian D. Mason Jr., rev. ed. (Chapel Hill: University of North Carolina Press, 1989), 53.

3. The debate about Wheatley's political views on slavery have a long and contested history in African American and literary criticism. Although generally heralded throughout the nineteenth century, Wheatley began to be increasingly criticized for not rendering an explicit condemnation of slavery in her poetry. James Weldon Johnson wrote that "one looks in vain for some outburst or even complaint against the bondage of her people, for some agonizing cry about her native land." James Weldon Johnson, *The Book of American Negro Poetry* (New York: Harcourt, Brace, 1922), xxvii. This view was extended during

the Black Arts Movement with critics such as Vernon Loggins. Loggins wrote that "she neglected almost entirely her own state of slavery and the miserable oppression of thousands of her race." Vernon Loggins, *The Negro Author* (Port Washington: Kennikat, 1964), 24. More judicious assessments of Wheatley have been offered by Henry Louis Gates Jr., *The Trials of Phillis Wheatley* (New York: Basic Civitas, 2003).

4. Sharon F. Patton, *African-American Art* (New York: Oxford University Press, 1998), 44.

5. Wheatley, *The Poems*, 104n.

6. *OED*, s.v. *conspire*.

7. Wheatley, *The Poems*, 104n.

8. Ibid., 164n.

9. As Thomas J. Steele notes on Wheatley's personification of America as Columbia, "The figure of Columbia, two deities joined into a single new character, thereby serves as an adept unification of two historical figures, George Washington and Phillis Wheatley—the "father of his country" and the mother of black American literature." Thomas J. Steele, "The Figure of Columbia: Phillis Wheatley Plus George Washington," *New England Quarterly* 54, no. 2 (June 1981): 266.

10. Washington Irving, "Rip Van Winkle," in *The Complete Tales of Washington Irving*, ed. Charles Neider (New York: Da Capo, 1998), 12.

11. This scene from Irving's story has been much discussed. See, among others, Jay Fliegelman, *Prodigals and Pilgrims: The American Revolution Against Patriarchal Authority, 1750–1800* (Cambridge: Cambridge University Press, 1982), 124–25; Steven Blakemore, "Family Resemblances: The Texts and Contexts of 'Rip Van Winkle,'" *Early American Literature* 35, no. 2 (2000): 187–212; and Bruce Burgett, "American Nationalism—R.I.P.," *American Literary History* 13, no. 2 (2001): 317.

12. Harriet Beecher Stowe, *Uncle Tom's Cabin; or, Life Among the Lowly* (New York: Penguin, 1981), 68.

13. Edith Wharton, *The Decoration of Houses* (New York: Scribner's, 1897), xix.

14. Importantly, Douglass's story makes use of literary portraiture in depicting Madison Washington. When Listwell, the benevolent white who dedicates himself to abolitionism, sees Madison in the woods, he says that the escaped slave's image was "daguerreotyped" in his mind. Frederick Douglass, *The Heroic Slave*, in *Three Classic African-American Novels*, ed. William L. Andrews (New York: Signet, 2003), 35.

15. Herman Melville, *Moby-Dick; or, The Whale* (New York: Norton, 2002), 55.

16. For a reading of Queequeg cannibalistically developed as an example of Melville's "ruthless democracy" where no man was less than another, see John Stauffer, "Melville, Slavery, and the American Dilemma," in Wyn Kelley, ed., *A Companion to Herman Melville* (New York: Blackwell, 2006), 220; for a reading of the scene as a sign of U.S. burgeoning imperial designs, see Amy Kaplan, *The Anarchy of Empire in the Making of U.S. Culture* (Cambridge: Harvard University Press, 2005), 86.

17. *Queer* is meant here to prefigure the way that Melville explicitly uses the term in the novel as an indication of something being amiss, imbalanced, or unknown, as in Stubb's conversation with Ahab in chapter 29, but also the latent homoeroticism of the novel as with the chapters "A Bosom Friend" and "A Squeeze of the Hand."

18. Wendell Phillips, "Toussaint L'Ouverture," in *Speeches, Lectures, and Letters* (Boston: Lee and Shepard, 1892), 468–94.

19. James McCune Smith, "Lecture on the Haytien Revolutions," in John Stauffer, ed., *The Works of James McCune Smith* (New York: Oxford University Press, 2006), 44, 46.

20. Ibid., 46–47.

21. Frank J. Webb, *The Garies and Their Friends* (New York: AMS, 1971), 122–23.

22. Edgar Allan Poe, "The Philosophy of Furniture," in *The Complete Works of Edgar Allan Poe*, ed. James Albert Harrison (New York: Crowell, 1902), 107–8.

23. If blogs can be used as an index, the majority of comments on the cover did not see it as satire—something that Rachel Sklar noted in her review of the incident, writing that "presumably the *New Yorker* readership is sophisticated enough to get the joke, but still," stating that it would nonetheless anger a great many people. Rachel Sklar, "Yikes! Controversial *New Yorker* Cover Show Muslim, Flag-Burning, Osama-Loving, Fist-Bumping Obama," *Huffington Post*, July 13, 2008. Barry Blitt defended the cover, writing, "I think the idea that the Obamas are branded as unpatriotic (let alone as terrorists) in certain sectors is preposterous. It seemed to me that depicting the concept would show it as the fear-mongering ridiculousness that it is." See "Barry Blitt Defends His *New Yorker* Cover Art of Obama," *Huffington Post*, July 13, 2008. *New Yorker* editor David Remnick reiterated the same sentiment, that it was meant as satire. David Remnick, "It's Satire, Meant to Target 'Distortions and Misconceptions and Prejudices" About Obama," *Huffington Post*, July 13, 2008. In the same week that *Vanity Fair* released its August 2008 issue, it also posted on its Web site the online blog "Politics and Power" where it acknowledged that it was remixing the *New Yorker*. "*Vanity Fair* Covers *The New Yorker*," *Vanity Fair* 22 (July 2008).

[3]

Stephen Crane's Refrain

MAX CAVITCH

Poetry's liberation from the shackles of meter is one of the most important nonevents in late nineteenth-century literary history. It's *important* because it is to this day so commonly invoked, not only to legitimate a particular way of reading poems, as if they were what Theodor Adorno calls "depositions of impulses," but also to celebrate the human subject's liberation from inauthenticity and expressive constipation.[1] It's a *nonevent* because the long and complex history of versification in English poetry is poorly suited to teleological narratives of liberation, despite a lot of early twentieth-century fanfare about breaking "new wood" and "insurgent naked throb[bings] of the instant moment."[2] Yet the perpetuation of such liberation narratives is powerfully motivated and deeply inscribed in our scholarship, our course syllabi, and our anthologies and editions. In the history of poetry in English, Walt Whitman is the foremost symbol of metrical iconoclasm, not least because he is also such a powerful symbol of personal idiosyncrasy asserting itself against many deeply entrenched social and sexual norms. The fictive isomorphism of poetry and person with which Whitman so dearly loved to play, and play off of and against, very understandably tends to get naturalized as the meaning of his achievement: free verse means a free subject.

This is a harder equation to derive from the spare, irrhythmic verses of Stephen Crane, alongside which Whitman's seem reassuringly measured, lushly and extravagantly familiar. Turning from Whitman's poetry to Crane's, one may feel like a figure in one of Crane's poems, searching for erotic opportunities in "the ashes of other men's love."[3] Crane doesn't deny the personal; he combusts it, like a fossil fuel, and lets the residue trail behind on the page, where it congeals into toxic, posthuman landscapes:

Behold, from the land of the farther suns
I returned.
And I was in a reptile-swarming place,
Peopled, otherwise, with grimaces,
Shrouded above in black impenetrableness.
I shrank, loathing,
Sick with it.
And I said to him,
"What is this?"
He made answer slowly,
"Spirit, this is a world;
This was your home."

(P 17)

Like a David Maisel photograph of sewage flows or wasted mines, this untitled poem from *The Black Riders and Other Lines* (1895) conjures a world both industrial and primordial, a world that is uninhabitable, yet for which there is no alternative. And like a Maisel photograph, Crane's poem exploits form as an index of human artistry in relation to a scene of degradation that makes scant place for the human ("This was your home"). Crane's specifically poetic achievement, however, has less to do with aestheticizing visual blight than with figuring the effort to speak from beyond certain conventional limits of the self, the better to articulate the defamiliarized, depersonalized contexts of its communications.

This essay calls to account the sentiment of liberated and liberating free-verse artistry through a reading of Crane's poetry that combines formal analysis (a counting or measurement) and ethical reckoning (a characterization of the lyric subject). More simply put, it is an effort to interpret, in the work of a very untraditional poet, his use of a very traditional poetic device—the refrain—to measure or mark out a timely sense of a depersonalized aesthetics. Timely, that is, not in terms of present critical anxieties about the aesthetic, but rather in terms of a late-nineteenth-century preoccupation, in literature, science, philosophy, and beyond, with the phenomenon of repetition, which is, of course, the precondition for any type of measurement and for any concept of the personal.

As Andrew Ford observes, the word *measure* has never shed its etymological origins in the Greek word *metron*—an evaluative term, Ford reminds us, with moral force.[4] We still say a response is "measured" when it strikes us as proportionate and duly limited. When considering measurement in connection with literature, it's natural to think of poetry, which actively displays, through versification, its competence to measure. Poetry, like Crane's, that departs from conventional versification potentially calls prior evaluations into question, possibly defaces contemporary lineaments of what is called beautiful with disproportionate or excessive markings.

The response to such departures is often disapproving, and we in turn may find ourselves eager to vilify such disapproval as reactionism. A case in point is William Dean Howells's response to the third untitled poem in Crane's *Black Riders*, which he quotes in its entirety, after sharing his own engaged but ultimately disapproving perspective. "I cannot see how the thought in the following lines, which seems to me fresh, and fine and true, would have been any less so if it had been cast in the mould which need not have been broken to secure them the stamp of novelty":

In the desert
I saw a creature, naked, bestial,
Who, squatting upon the ground,
Held his heart in his hands,
And ate of it.
I said, "Is it good, friend?"
"It is bitter—bitter," he answered;
"But I like it
Because it is bitter,
And because it is my heart."

Howells does not say what he takes to be the particular "mould which need not have been broken" in these lines, unless it is the general mould of verses he is prepared to call, as he puts it, "duly rhymed and measured."[5] Instead of vilifying Howells, however, one can simply underscore his own evident sense that something goes unrecognized and unarticulated in his disapproval of Crane's prosodic unruliness, his "free verse," as it would come to be called.

Insofar as anyone any longer remembers the 1890s as a time of important critical statements on prosodic innovation, it's usually in connection with Stéphane Mallarmé's 1897 essay "Crisis of Verse," in which he announces that, with the advent of *vers libre*, the ear has finally been set free from normative versification and "the rigid and childish mechanism of its meter." While acknowledging that "the recollection of strict verses"—in particular, for French poetry, the alexandrine—will continue to haunt prosodic innovators, he nevertheless crows that an unprecedented heterodoxy has taken hold of versification. "For the first time in the literary history of any people," he writes, "anyone with his individual game and ear can compose an instrument, as soon as he breathes, touches, or taps scientifically."[6]

Mallarmé's emphasis on "anyone" seems to suggest that the "crisis of verse," in one of its dimensions at least, is a crisis of democratization. Poetry, it would appear, is for Mallarmé "no longer a specialized activity," as Leo Bersani puts it, suggesting that what Mallarmé refers to as "the 'science' of poetry is equivalent to a kind of self-possession through self-attunement"—a humanistic "science" grounded in the individuated authority of personal feeling.[7] But Mallarmé's essay also reveals itself, in the speculative mobility that Bersani identifies as its hallmark, to be the champion of something like a universalist program for linguistic depersonalization. It goes so far as to anticipate—even to dramatize—"the disappearance of the poet speaking," thereby problematizing a common understanding of the poet's encounter with language "as if," to quote Paul de Man, "it were the expression of a subjective intent with which he could grow familiar . . . a tool that could be made to fit his needs."[8]

De Man is worth briefly citing in this context, and by way of returning to Crane's own problematics, because his interpretation of Mallarméan poetics as an ironization of liberal aesthetics helps clarify the terms of a fin de siècle "crisis of verse" that pertains to poetry in English as well as in French—to Crane as well as his Symbolist contemporaries. One problem, though, with de Man's account is that it is too dismissive of the fact that prosodic experimentation is an index of historical forces to be reckoned with in any account of literary history and the shifting bases of aesthetic judgment. It's true of course that the rhetoric of emergency informing Mallarmé's announcements of unprecedented tamperings with the rules of verse is deeply ironic. But de Man misleads us when he alleges that this irony, while appreciated in Mallarmé's Paris, would have "baffled his foreign audience."⁹ Not at all. The history of metrical variation in English prosody, however it differed from the French, was not so ancient and so eclectic that the contemporary situation of experimental versification was without serious controversy. In English, the term *free verse* often was, and continued for some time to be, a derogatory term. More important, it came to be (and remains) a way of naming certain historical, motivated shifts in the degree and manner of intensity focused on norms of versification.

The question then is: What is the relation between the degree and manner of this intensity in Crane's time and the more or less simultaneous cultural elaboration, corroborated here by the better-known example of Mallarmé, of a counterliberal, post-Kantian aesthetics in which the integrity and dignity of persons is no longer presumed to be the most important measure of artistic value and expressive decorum? Returning to the autocardiophagic creature of Crane's poem "In the desert"—the poem that Howells accused of breaking the mold that need not have been broken—what, if anything, does that poem's form have to do with its figure of depersonalization? The poem is both a literalization and an undoing of the idiomatic phrase "to eat one's heart out." Against a voided background—"the desert"—the creature appears as if out of the blankness of his own annihilation. He has literally become detached from his center, his "heart," and is now perhaps seeking to reintegrate the lost or abandoned self by eating his heart, so to speak, back in. His presentness to the speaker (who sees and hails him) and the phenomenology of taste (he eats his heart and likes it) signify the restoration of the creature's subjectivity. Indeed it may be the speaker's presentness to the creature that is the first sign of this restoration.

Could it also be the last? As the creature eats his heart, reincorporating it in a way that makes personal involvement with others (subjectivity) once again possible, he also destroys the organ, consuming rather than restoring it. The heart makes its appearance on the stage of reintegration only to reveal subjectivity and the suffering that is its index ("I like it / Because it is bitter") to be what Emerson calls "scene-painting and counterfeit."¹⁰ The speaker, and the reader as his representative at the scene of reading, is perhaps being shown nothing more than an illusory glimpse of the interstices of nonconsciousness. The poem, that is, may count most as the description of an interlude in the speaker/reader's own depersonalization, a mere phantasmic break in the nothingness that precedes and follows it. "Eat your heart out" may be the poem's curse upon the reader, the curse of the illusion—the mirage—of individual consciousness.

This reading of the poem's contents makes it rather easy to view its irregular form as another projection of the illusion of individual consciousness. *Free verse* is the term for a complex history of experimental versification that, at least since the eighteenth century, has been notoriously difficult to disengage from liberal-progressive accounts of expressivity. In these accounts, being free from the constraints of traditional forms means being personally free to give more intelligible shape to one's own distinctive voice. From time to time, some canny poet or reader cries out "Hoax!"[11] But antihumanistic readings of metrical and typographical irregularity are rare, and even those recent and contemporary prosodists at the furthest remove from patterns of sentimental expressivism often find it difficult to avoid the self-regard of avant-gardism. How remarkable then to recognize in the irregular form of Crane's "In the desert" what may already be—in what was one of the first volumes of free verse ever published in the U.S.[12]—a kind of immanent critique of free verse as a manifestation of identity and personal freedom.

To pursue the possibility of this critique with Crane is to be driven back again and again on the problematics of repetition. Indeed, it is repetition, the fundamental precondition for all prosody, that links the fin de siècle's intensified focus on norms of versification to contemporaneous moves toward a nonobjectivist depersonalized aesthetics. In the 1880s and 1890s, repetition was at the conceptual heart of existential (Nietzsche) and psychoanalytic (Freud), as well as aesthetic, reorientations of thinking about (and beyond) the human subject. During those same decades, more often associated with literary exhaustion than consequential experimentation, we actually find quite an impressive roster of poets in the U.S., England, France, and elsewhere who, along with Mallarmé and Crane, were doing their best not to flinch from the intuition that any simple equation between free verse and personal freedom was chimerical and that the anxious defense against, or promotion of, the analogy between aesthetic and social forms was symptomatic (one might call it a repetition compulsion) of spiritual, epistemological, and ontological anxieties far less well articulated.[13]

Like many of Crane's poems, "In the desert" contains several words and phrases that recur at least once. In his short, metrically irregular poems, the force of such repetitions is especially strong, though the qualities of that force vary with the specific rhetorical figure constituted by the repetition. "In the desert," with only fifty words unevenly divided into ten lines, exhibits multiple figures, including three I'd like to call by name. These are *ploce* (the repetition of a word after a significant interval—in this case, the two instances of the word "heart"), *epizeuxis* (the repetition of a word two or more times in immediate succession—in this case, the pair "bitter— bitter"), and *anaphora* (the repetition of a word at or near the beginning of successive clauses or sentences—in this case, the trio "I saw" / "I said" / "I like"). I'd maintain that the differentiation of these figures, despite the creeping desuetude of the classical terminology, is helpful inasmuch as it underscores their diversity of effect (a diversity that is often densely concentrated in the device of the refrain, to which I'll come shortly). In the ploce "heart" / "heart," for example, we hear the quoted voice of the creature echoing the principal speaker of the poem, forcing the question of their identity and relation as subjects. Whatever distinct range of symbolic values the heart may have for either subject, they share the same word for it. They conspire, as it were, to stabilize the signifier of those many values, even as the creature's echoing of the principal speaker may augment the reader's sense of its depersonalization, its creaturely subordination.

The epizeuxis "bitter—bitter" is the poem's most dramatic figure of repetition, the creature's vehemence nicely sounded in those explosive tro- chees. At the same time, epizeuxis signals a kind of snag or catch in the flow of meaning, a cognitive stutter, a sensation of being stuck in place. The sensation, depending on how the words are voiced, might be perceived here as either deliberative or defensive. Is the creature testing the word, try- ing it out twice to make sure he has the right one? Does he repeat himself in fear of being misunderstood or disbelieved? Perhaps he is savoring not only the bitterness of his heart but also the word *bitter* itself, as a sign of the pleasure of *articulate* abjection. In his abjection, he has not only been seen by another but is also himself able to correct the other's perception: no, not good, but bitter.

The anaphora "I saw" / "I said" / "I like" helps complicate the scene of recognition and individuation by conflating the subjects of enunciation— the principal speaker ("I saw," "I said") and the creature ("I like")—while also sustaining the contrast between the principal speaker's affective neu- trality and the creature's intensity. It's tempting to treat this poem as an exceedingly compact and austere counterpart to Robert Browning's and W. H. Auden's lyrical readings—in "Caliban Upon Setebos" (1864) and *The Sea and the Mirror* (1944), respectively—of Shakespeare's *The Tempest*, and especially of the creaturely Caliban, whom Browning describes as "a bitter heart that bides its time and bites."[14] For all three poets, the creaturely Cali- ban, or the Caliban-like creature, has a powerfully overdetermined relation to contexts of creation and becoming.

Noting the derivation of *creature* "from the future-active participle of the Latin verb *creare* ('to create')," Julia Lupton observes that "*creature* indicates a made or fashioned thing but with the sense of continued or potential process, action, or emergence built into the future thrust of its active verbal form. . . . The *creatura* is a thing always in the process of undergoing creation; the creature is actively passive or, better, *passionate*, perpetually becoming created, subject to transformation at the behest of the arbitrary commands of an Other." But this Other, too, Lupton argues, following Walter Benjamin, is also *creature*, "is finally both sovereign and subject, mind and matter, tyrant and martyr, but he suffers the two modalities in a wildly disjunct form that refuses to resolve into a reciprocal or homogeneous economy."[15]

The creature stands for the destabilization immanent to identity and for an expressivity that is neither personal nor universal, but always intersubjective. The creature is there to remind us that we are incapable of the authentic production of the same, of reproduction, or simple repetition, but that we are nonetheless constantly falling back on what seem to be the best rhetorical resources—the figures of repetition—enabled by our fictive lives of stable individuation.

In this light, it seems almost inevitable that Edgar Allan Poe would have chosen the refrain as the device on which to base the structure of his most famous poem of creaturely subjection, "The Raven" (1845). And, being Poe, he resolved also to improve upon this ancient and venerable device, to lift it out of what he refers to in "The Philosophy of Composition" (1846) as its "primitive condition." "As commonly used," Poe writes, "the *refrain* . . . depends for its impression upon the force of monotone—both in sound and thought. The pleasure is deduced solely from the sense of identity— of repetition. I resolved to diversify, and so vastly heighten, the effect, by adhering, in general, to the monotone of sound, while I continually varied that of thought: that is to say, I determined to produce continuously novel effects, by the variation *of the application* of the *refrain*—the *refrain* itself remaining, for the most part, unvaried."[16] Poe's aim is to *heap* the refrain (another word for *refrain* is, after all, *burden*) with significance and to insist on instructing the reader (by way of varied "applications") in gradations of that significance through the generation of suspense. As John Hollander puts it, "the ultimate story of modern poetic refrain is 'What is it to mean *this* time around?'"[17]

In other words, every refrain is a little bit refractory. Like other figures of repetition, refrains may substantially allegorize the play of resistance and expectancy in relation to uncertain or unwelcome futures.[18] This helps account for some of the strongly reactionary rhetoric leveled at the opening poem of Crane's 1899 volume, *War Is Kind*:

Do not weep, maiden, for war is kind.
Because your lover threw wild hands toward the sky
And the affrighted steed ran on alone,
Do not weep.
War is kind.

    Hoarse, booming drums of the regiment
    Little souls who thirst for fight,
    These men were born to drill and die
    The unexplained glory flies above them
    Great is the battle-god, great, and his kingdom—
    A field where a thousand corpses lie.

Do not weep, babe, for war is kind.
Because your father tumbled in the yellow trenches,
Raged at his breast, gulped and died,
Do not weep.
War is kind.

    Swift, blazing flag of the regiment
    Eagle with crest of red and gold,
    These men were born to drill and die
    Point for them the virtue of slaughter
    Make plain to them the excellence of killing
    And a field where a thousand corpses lie.

Mother whose heart hung humble as a button
On the bright splendid shroud of your son,
Do not weep.
War is kind.

                                          (*P* 45)

Some contemporary critics, including Willa Cather, hated the idea that Crane's poem might be about imminence rather than retrospection—about the self-perpetuating militarism of modern life, perhaps, or even about what William James referred to as the coming "war against war."[19] Here is part of Cather's remonstration: "Either Mr. Crane is insulting the public or insulting himself, or he has developed a case of atavism and is chattering the primeval nonsense of the apes. His *Black Riders*, uneven as it was, was a casket of polished masterpieces when compared with *War Is Kind*. And it is not kind at all, Mr. Crane, when it provokes such verses as these—it is all that Sherman said it was."[20] One has a sense of irony not simply lost, but anxiously defended against—a sense confirmed by another contemporary reviewer, Rupert Hughes: "It is Mr. Crane's purpose to tell us that war is not kind in a thirty-line Walt Whitmian lyric, so why mislead us? To be ironical is all right, but why drive the iron in so far? We all know that war was brutal, that it killed lovers, husbands and sons, but we never thought of telling the sweethearts, wives and mothers that war, therefore, was kind."[21] To some extent, such reactions against Crane's poem reflect a progressivist spirit of the age, represented importantly not only by William James but also by Jane Addams, who wrote at length in unremitting expectation of humankind's finally "displacing the juvenile propensities to warfare" with the perpetual peace of "cosmopolitan affection."[22] But Crane drove readers to extremes with what they found to be the unbearableness of his irony, encapsulated, of course, in this poem's refrain, "War is kind." The refrain or repetend "War is kind," appearing at the end of the first, third, and fifth stanzas, and also at the end of the initial lines of the first and third stanzas, has a coercive force—not only as part of the refrain against mourning but also as an obscene Orwellian slogan tending to overwrite and override, as Cather suggests, General Sherman's legendary dictum, "war is hell." Repetition solicits remembrance. But more than this, repetition is a figure of truth; it seeks to weary the clamor for persuasion with the self-evidence of iteration. And it may do still more. It may compromise the forces of intellectual and passional resistance by provoking defensiveness and by frustrating hopes for transformative engagement. Under such stress, reading ceases to be experienced as a collaborative field of invention and improvisation, and repetition becomes the rhetorical figure of despair. This is what makes the irony of "War is kind" unbearable to Cather and to many other readers.

This unbearableness has a context and a history. The exquisite sense of dramatic irony in Cather's own fiction, for example, had already found its unsettling counterpart in the work of other nineteenth-century ironists, such as Heinrich Heine, with whom Crane shared a profound disillusionment with religion, a sense of immutable suffering absolutely unredeemed by religious significance, and a tendency to proclaim disillusionment in particularly unsympathetic forms of irony. A dramatic instance of this is the following poem from *War Is Kind*:

A little ink more or less!
It surely can't matter?
Even the sky and the opulent sea,
The plains and the hills, aloof,
Hear the uproar of all these books.
But it is only a little ink more or less.

What?
You define me God with these trinkets?
Can my misery meal on an ordered walking
Of surpliced numbskulls?
And a fanfare of lights?
Or even upon the measured pulpiting
Of the familiar false and true?
Is this God?
Where, then, is hell?
Show me some bastard mushroom
Sprung from a pollution of blood.
It is better.

Where is God?

(*P* 47)

The reiterated insult of "a little ink more or less" conspires with ambiguous
deixis ("these books," "these trinkets") to produce an effect of self-mockery,
repelling sympathy, that is inseparable from the poem's bitter rejection
of religious texts. That is, the poem itself and the book of verse in which
it appears are, like the scripture and dogma on which human misery is
invited by the church to meal, "only a little ink more or less." One might be
disposed to hear a defiant allusion to the poem's own nonmetrical verses
in the contemptuous phrases "ordered walking" and "measured pulpiting."
It's as if the very rhythms of orthodoxy offend the poet, and his response
includes an offense against the regimented patterning of such rhythms.
In their vehement reactions against Crane's formal offenses, then, his
early critics may have been unconsciously acknowledging the difficulty
of responding directly to the substance of what sometimes amounted to
Crane's nihilistic irony.

But measure and order, as we've seen, aren't simply anathema in
Crane's poetics. In fact he had recourse to them in his greatest poem of

cosmic despair, devastating beyond irony, not yet published at the time of his death:

> A man adrift on a slim spar
> A horizon smaller than the rim of a bottle
> Tented waves rearing lashy dark points
> The near whine of froth in circles.
>
> God is cold.
>
> The incessant raise and swing of the sea
> And growl after growl of crest
> The sinkings, green, seething, endless
> The upheaval half-completed.
>
> God is cold.
>
> The seas are in the hollow of The Hand;
> Oceans may be turned to a spray
> Raining down through the stars
> Because of a gesture of pity toward a babe.
> Oceans may become grey ashes,
> Die with a long moan and a roar
> Amid the tumult of the fishes
> And the cries of the ships,
> Because The Hand beckons the mice.
>
> A horizon smaller than a doomed assassin's cap,
> Inky, surging tumults
> A reeling, drunken sky and no sky
> A pale hand sliding from a polished spar.
>
> God is cold.
>
> The puff of a coat imprisoning air.
> A face kissing the water-death
> A weary slow sway of a lost hand
> And the sea, the moving sea, the sea.
>
> God is cold.

(P 83)

The parallelism of clauses, the symmetry of the four shorter strophes around the central longer strophe, and above all the unvarying refrain serve to hem in the ocean's vastness without in any way diminishing its lethalness. Just as the horizon's diminutive rim ("smaller than the rim of a bottle"; "smaller than a doomed assassin's cap") holds in place the sea's seethings and the "lashy dark points" of its waves, so does the diminutive refrain reduce speculation and hope (represented chiefly by the long central strophe, distended by irony and engrossed with conditionals) to the minuscule sentiment of God's deadly indifference: "God is cold."

Like his contemporary Nietzsche (they both died in the summer of 1900, though Crane was little more than half Nietzsche's age), Crane felt acutely the persistent entropic chill of a world from which God was withdrawn. He was far less sanguine than Nietzsche, though, about the potential for reinvesting that once God-afflicted world with thoroughly revalued values. In Nietzsche the sea is one of the scenes of that reinvestment: "at long last," he writes in a famous passage from *The Gay Science*, "our ships may venture out again, venture out to face any danger; all the daring of the lover of knowledge is permitted again; the sea, *our* sea, lies open again."[23] But Crane's sea voyagers—the four men adrift in the short story "The Open Boat," the wrecked sailor in the poem "To the maiden," and the "man adrift on a slim spar"—founder amid waves that are, as Crane puts it, like "dead grey walls / Superlative in vacancy / Upon which nevertheless at fateful time, / Was written / The grim hatred of nature" (*P* 47). As in many other motifs of writing in Crane's work, the uncertain legibility here of the wavewalls (they are "Superlative in vacancy," yet bear the trace of their inscription) also suggests the revelation of historicity ("at fateful time, / Was written").[24] The phrase "at fateful time" (in these lines from "To the maiden," as well as in the poem "God fashioned the ship of the world carefully" [*P*, 5] where the phrase also occurs) means, chiefly, at a consequential, decisive moment. It is fate understood ironically as chance, the fortuitousness upon which history pivots, which is anthropomorphized by Crane's wrecked sailor as "The grim hatred of nature."

The wrecked sailor could easily be taken as one of Crane's recurring figures for the heroically isolated individual, for the imperiled subject that may yet prevail—figures that would include the narrator of his short story "The Open Boat." Daniel Hoffman, in what remains after half a century one of very few readings of the poem "A man adrift," argues for the close relation of the story and the poem as similar narratives of a prevailing subject, a survivor-interpreter. In the poem, Hoffman discovers two clearly differentiated points of view, corresponding to two clearly differentiated subjects: that of the drowning man and that of "another who survives." The refrain, he argues, is "the despairing lament of the dying man betrayed by his God"—until, that is, the final strophe, where it becomes "a judgment made by another who survives to interpret his death to the living."[25] This maneuver grants the reader what may be a more readily satisfying sense of thorough individuation than the text itself supports or than the "fateful time" of its inscription—a time characterized by the emergent historicity of the subject and thus the beginnings of its philosophical deconstruction—is able to bestow upon it.

Indeed, there is no good reason to insist on investing the refrain with the sentiment of personal voice. There never has been. Traditionally, the refrain is precisely the device that interrupts monophonic lyric discourse, either with choral polyphony or with phatic, often subverbal, reassurance. And, no matter how modern and untraditional the poem, a refrain always asserts the disruptive power of the conventional—the power, that is, to disrupt the fiction of the unique voice. In "A man adrift," the refrain "God is cold" doesn't so much consolidate or interpret as interfere with the coalescence of meaning. The poem's grammar suggests as much. None of the four shorter strophes has a nonparticipial verb. They are impression-istic accumulations of detail that suggest a scene just coming into view— a scene repeatedly disrupted and displaced by the simplest of declarative sentences: "God is cold." The scene could be characterized as a scene of pity—thus, "God will not be importuned." Or it could be characterized as a scene of anger—thus, "God will not be denounced." Or we could find pity and anger united in the indecorum of resentment, suggested perhaps by the engrossed and ironic central strophe. Yet this is the only strophe that does *not* evoke the repressive force of the refrain.

It is, however, the only strophe to detour us away from the immedi-ate scene of drowning and thus from its possibly too gratifying aesthetic transvaluation in the surrounding shorter strophes, where a lulling pace is ensured by the absence of enjambment; where frequent sibilance gen-tly—and, of course, ironically—figures the delicacy of fluidic movements; where the impersonal ("A man," "A pale hand," "a coat," "a lost hand") helps ennoble through universalization the pathos of individual helpless-ness; where death's violence is rendered mild and sensuous ("weary slow sway"), even sensual ("kissing the water-death"). Indeed, these may be among the loveliest verses ever written about drowning, verses in the com-pany not only of near contemporaries Whitman (on the death of the gigantic swimmer in "The Sleepers") and Melville (on the death of Billy Budd in "Billy in the Darbies") but also of Shakespeare (on the death of Ophelia in *Hamlet*). What need do such verses have of a refrain, unless it be to check, curb, or reprove that sentiment of beauty? Perhaps the spectatorial relation to suffering is opened to critique in this way: we are at risk for dehumanization in our own sublime detachment from or disinterest in the suffering of the drowning man. Or it may be that the drowning man's own objectification—his own dehumanization—is the extreme toward which the refrain curbs us from tending. Or perhaps it is the uneasy pleasure of reflexiveness as experienced by the poet—or the poet-identified reader—in images that evoke the activity of writing: the sea referred to as "Inky" and the pun on "hand." The antepenultimate line—"A weary slow sway of a lost hand"—is hard not to hear as an allusion to the hand that writes and to handwriting that trails away inconclusively, as inconclusively, as unemphatically, as the poem itself would trail off, exquisitely, without the strong punctuating refrain.

Such speculation on the problematics of enjoyment is not without its own fin de siècle history. Later nineteenth-century elaborations of the socialist critique of the relation between aesthetics and capitalism, for example, percolated through the ersatz socialist world of New York's Art Students' League, in which Crane found his first artistic home and allies and developed his own style of social realism. And around the same time, in its more genteel Boston precincts, the *Atlantic Monthly* (which reviewed but never published Crane's work) complained that "aesthetics is still the vaguest and most fantastic branch of psychology."[26] That was overstating the case, of course. But it makes a good deal of practical and also political sense if, for "most fantastic," we hear "riskiest," and if, for "psychology," we hear "the psychology of freedom." "A man adrift" is a poem about the problematics of enjoyment in that it poses the most basic of existential questions ("Am I alone?") through a figure of extreme attenuation of selfhood: not just the figure of a dying man, but the figure of a subject in the process of relinquishing, or forfeiting, or being confronted with the sheer illusoriness of its differentiation as a subject. That such a process might be experienced as something other than traumatic is a possibility afforded by the terrible beauty of the poem's four short strophes, even as that possibility seems repeatedly to be threatened with repressive closure by the refrain. At the end of the final strophe, the path of what one might characterize as the refrain's strong verticality—its movement from top to bottom of the page, like a heavy thing crashing through the floors of a building—is elegantly crossed by the sibilant, horizontal ploce of the penultimate line: "The sea, the moving sea, the sea." That, within earshot of this juxtaposition, the conventional refrain might sound more like a paroxysm of the antiaesthetic than a reassuringly conventional poetic device is no mean index of the place Crane's poetry ventures to occupy in the history of poetic decorum.

Notes

For their help with this essay I'm very grateful to Virginia Jackson, Matthew Parr, Eliza Richards, Augusta Rohrbach, Bethany Schneider, and especially to Christopher Looby and Cindy Weinstein.

1. Theodor Adorno, *Aesthetic Theory* (Minneapolis: University of Minnesota Press, 1997), 244.

2. See Ezra Pound, "A Pact," *Poetry* 2 (April 1913): 1; and D. H. Lawrence, "Poetry of the Present" (1918), in Vivian de Sola Pinto and Warren Roberts, ed., *The Complete Poems of D. H. Lawrence* (London: Heinemann, 1964), 185.

3. Stephen Crane, *Poems and Literary Remains*, in *The Works of Stephen Crane*, ed. Fredson Bowers (Charlottesville: University Press of Virginia, 1975), 10:62; hereafter cited parenthetically as *P*.

4. Andrew Ford, *The Origins of Criticism: Literary Culture and Poetic Theory in Classical Greece* (Princeton: Princeton University Press, 2002), 18–19.

5. William Dean Howells, "Life and Letters," *Harper's Weekly*, January 25, 1896, 79.

6. Stéphane Mallarmé, "Crisis of Verse," in *Divagations*, trans. Barbara Johnson (Cambridge: Harvard University Press, 2007), 203, 204–5.

7. Leo Bersani, *The Death of Stéphane Mallarmé* (Cambridge: Cambridge University Press, 1982), 37.

8. Mallarmé, "Crisis of Verse," 208; Paul de Man, *Blindness and Insight: Essays in the Rhetoric of Contemporary Criticism*, rev. ed. (Minneapolis: University of Minnesota Press, 1983), 69–70.

9. De Man, *Blindness and Insight*, 5. One notes a further irony here in de Man's echoing of Max Nordau's *Entartung* (Degeneration; 1892): "The whole dispute concerning prosody and the rules of rhyme is, so to speak, an inter-Gallic concern, and is of no consequence to the literature of the world. We have long had everything which the French poets are only now seeking to obtain by barricades and street massacres." Max Nordau, *Degeneration* (New York: Howard Fertig, 1968), 138.

10. Ralph Waldo Emerson, "Experience," in *Essays and Lectures*, ed. Joel Porte (New York: Library of America, 1983), 472.

11. See, for example, de Man's reading of Mallarmé's 1897 poem "A Throw of the Dice" in *Blindness and Insight*, 74.

12. Of course, a great deal of nonmetrical poetry, or free verse, had been published in the U.S. by the time of the publication of *The Black Riders and Other Lines* in 1895. But, unlike earlier volumes of poetry—Emerson's 1846 *Poems*, for example—that mix metrical and nonmetrical verses, *The Black Riders* contains *only* nonmetrical verses.

13. This group of poets included Jules Laforgue, Gustave Kahn, W. E. Henley, John Davidson, Ernest Fenollosa, and W. E. B. Du Bois.

14. Robert Browning, "Caliban upon Setebos; or, Natural Theology in the Island," in *Robert Browning: The Poems*, ed. John Pettigrew, 2 vols. (New Haven: Yale University Press, 1981), 1:809.

15. Julia Reinhard Lupton, "Creature Caliban," *Shakespeare Quarterly* 51, no. 1 (2000): 1, 6. See also Eric L. Santner, *On Creaturely Life: Rilke, Benjamin, Sebald* (Chicago: University of Chicago Press, 2006).

16. Edgar Allan Poe, "The Philosophy of Composition," in *Essays and Reviews*, ed. G. R. Thompson (New York: Library of America, 1984), 17.

17. John Hollander, "Breaking Into Song: Some Notes on Refrain," in Chaviva Hosek and Patricia Parker, eds., *Lyric Poetry: Beyond New Criticism* (Ithaca: Cornell University Press, 1985), 75.

18. Such a stance toward the future might be said to have amounted almost to a generalized cultural condition in the American 1890s, a consequence of such epochal factors as economic depression and widespread unemployment, the mythologizing of the disappearance of the "frontier," the ascendance of the corporate "person" and the failure of antitrust law, the misery of swelling immigrant populations and other urban poor, legislated racism and the terror of lynching, and ambivalence about aggressive imperial expansion. Crane wrote about and reported on many of these phenomena extensively in his fiction and journalism.

19. William James, "The Moral Equivalent of War" (1910), in *Writings: 1902–1910*, ed. Bruce Kuklick (New York: Library of America, 1987), 1281.

20. Willa Cather, review of Stephen Crane's *War Is Kind*, *Leader* (Pittsburgh), June 3, 1899, 6; rpt. in *The World and the Parish: Willa Cather's Articles and Reviews, 1893–1902*, ed. William M. Curtin, 2 vols. (Lincoln: University of Nebraska Press, 1970), 2:700–2.

21. Rupert Hughes, "Mr. Crane's Crazyquilting" (1899), in Stanley Wertheim and Paul Sorrentino, *The Crane Log: A Documentary Life of Stephen Crane, 1871–1900* (New York: Hall, 1994), 385.

22. Jane Addams, *Newer Ideals of Peace* (New York: Macmillan, 1907), 10–11.

23. Friedrich Nietzsche, *The Gay Science* (1887), trans. Walter Kaufmann (New York: Vintage, 1974), 280.

24. For an extensive analysis of motifs of writing in Crane's prose, see Michael Fried, *Realism, Writing, Disfiguration: On Thomas Eakins and Stephen Crane* (Chicago: University of Chicago Press, 1987).

25. Daniel Hoffman, *The Poetry of Stephen Crane* (New York: Columbia University Press, 1957), 97. See also John Blair, "The Posture of a Bohemian in the Poetry of Stephen Crane," *American Literature* 61, no. 2 (1989): 215–29. Blair disputes Hoffman's assertion that the poem expresses Crane's own thorough rejection of God by arguing even more strenuously for the coherence and consistency of the projected persona of the drowning man throughout the poem: "By giving the reader the perceptions of the sailor as he drowns through the sailor's own point of view, Crane puts the reader into the immediacy of the man's physical plight; in the same movement, he gives immediate access to the bitter searching for fault on the man's part. We are privy to the drowning man's denunciation of his God because it is part of his immediate experience as he drowns; yet it is not Crane's experience. . . . There is no hate, no denial in the poem, only an understanding of the emotions, the angst and the denial, of a man isolated in a hopeless situation" (227).

26. "The Philosophy of Enjoyment of Art," *Atlantic Monthly*, June 1896, 844.

[4]

Lyric Citizenship in Post 9/11 Performance

Sekou Sundiata's the 51st (dream) state

JULIE ELLISON

> Civic engagement is in the air, and it's probably in the drinking water.
>
> —Sekou Sundiata, "Thinking Out Loud: Democracy, Imagination, and Peeps of Color"

In June 2004 Sekou Sundiata addressed a national gathering in Pittsburgh, "Diversity Revisited/A Conversation on Diversity in the Arts." Sundiata's speech, "Thinking Out Loud: Democracy, Imagination, and Peeps of Color," makes explicit the fact that he shared the meeting's general impatience with the status quo on multiculturalism and that this impatience propelled his turn to the conjoined forces of democracy and imagination. "Democracy," like "citizenship," is for him not only a feature of political systems or a matter of state but rather a repositioning of the subject: "a humane social practice that . . . brings together the inner need for the freedom to be who you are with the outer need for a social and political and economic ecology . . . for the whole human being."[1] Sundiata's "humane social practice" emerged from his weariness with the politics of protest and the politics of administered diversity in favor of citizenship in a changed key, "new ways of imagining and acting in the world."[2] He urged a shift from diversity to democracy and from color to difference: "When I say 'diversity' I am not talking about a diversity of colors but a democracy of ideas as expressed through different cultures." And he establishes "generous imaginings," differently voiced, as the defining practice of citizens. "Imagination," then, is an epistemological transaction that makes possible "knowledge about the weight and complexity of others": "Democracy: You can't keep it unless you give it away. But you cannot have it, let alone practice it, without a willing and robust imagination because it is through the imagination that we can begin to . . . see the world through eyes other than our own." Sundiata's translational imagination connects "the private realm of the individual mind and the social realm of public life." The imagination is "a necessary and sacred space," a space of "conjuring," but also a space located "within material borders" and "shaped . . . by the material world."[3]

I call this imaginative shift, this change in the construction of a possible or aspirational national subject, "lyric citizenship." This term points to— and, I hope, evokes and describes—new practices or performances of democratic citizenship that are increasingly likely to be mediated by cultural activities. More specifically, these practices are rooted in older histories of poetry, civic culture, and the politics of hope as framed by African American thinkers. Performances that are sociably crafted with a civic intent communicate through a preoccupation with memory and dream as well as through a quest for public agency. They are locally embedded, translocally networked, and collaboratively made. They are lyrical and pragmatic. Their aesthetic of civic engagement arises from and responds to changes in public and counterpublic spheres.

Lyric citizenship, as demonstrated by Sundiata's the 51st (dream) state, marks a shift in the domain of expressive culture and the arts from "the piece"—a work of art, an exhibition, a performance—to "the project," which connects the work and its community of creators, organizers, and sponsors to broader and deeper forms of public participation. This participatory ethos, furthermore, declares the civic—the shared experience of citizenship—as a primary goal. The project foregrounds public narrative as a meaning-making practice that draws on enactments and reenactments of citizen voices. Subsuming "the piece" into "the project" moves us away from other traditional and contemporary notions of the aesthetic. Whereas the piece is set up to generate the space of private consumption or the parallel play of public spectatorship, the project is not only dialogically received but also, in one way or another, publicly made. The publicly engaged cultural project is where the politics of hope, the questioning of genre, and lyrical performance converge.

From Piece to Project: Genres of Engagement

The project involves expanded organizational relationships that flow from the civic purposes of the piece. Through project-specific relationships with scholars and activists, nonprofit organizations, local arts presenters, and university programs, the creative team working on the piece (the performance work itself) nurtures zones of democratic encounter where publics come into being. The aesthetics of the project have a horizontal or spatial dimension, therefore; they also have a defining temporality. The life of the project happens "before," "in," and "after" the "piece." The world of the project may be brief or enduring; it may be characterized by alliances rooted in a broadly shared social vision or by single-issue coalitions or, indeed, by sharp differences in interest and opinion. Whatever the particular variations, the project grows up around the piece as an intentional part of its meaning.

The shift from artistic "piece" to cultural "project" is fundamental to performances of the kind represented by Sundiata's *51st (dream) state*. It is also essential to the efforts of a whole host of organizations. Many of these are performing arts organizations, like the Liz Lerman Dance Exchange, known for its participatory community dance practice, and Amherst's New WORLD Theater and its Project 2050 youth initiative.[4] The model of the participatory cultural project, however, pervades many cultural domains. In performance and other artistic domains, collaborative projects in theater, poetry, public history, public art, education, and cultural tourism are being carried out by arts and presenting organizations, community development sites such as Houston's Project Row Houses and Philadelphia's Village of the Arts and Humanities, museums, libraries, and a growing number of campus-based programs.[5] Collaborations among these organizations have been fostered by national associations committed to such partnerships, including Imagining America: Artists and Scholars in Public Life, the International Coalition of Historic Sites of Conscience, and the much-missed Community Arts Network.

The piece/project relationship is central both to the aesthetics of community-engaged performance and to emerging interpretive and critical approaches to it. Cultural critics have called for altered interpretive practices that are adequate to these undertakings, a set of democratizing interventions motivated by "a critique or undoing of the confinements of academic professionalism."[6] A body of work is forming around this summons. As Suzanne Lacey argues, "new genre public art" (an analogous development in the arena of the visual arts) needs critical strategies that are adequate to participatory, process-intensive works.[7]

I take this distinction between piece and project from an interview with Sekou Sundiata, with whom I collaborated for a number of years. My analysis in this essay of Sundiata's *the 51st (dream) state* aims to open a dialogue between a new, poetry-intensive performance work and scholars of the literary humanities. Until his death in 2007, Sundiata shaped the civic engagement movement in the arts and higher education as a common undertaking of poets and musicians, and new networks taking shape around public cultural institutions, nonprofit organizations, and university programs.

Conceived by Sundiata, a New York poet and theater artist, as a post-9/11 contemplation of America's national identity, its power in the world, and its guiding mythologies, *the 51st (dream) state* was part of a broader initiative, The America Project. As the name makes clear, the relationship between "piece" and "project" was foundational. The America Project had two components. The first was the creation and performance of *the 51st (dream) state*, a multimedia "oratorio" or music theater work in which Sundiata played the central role of the Poet. The second related to public engagement activities organized through the numerous developmental and performance residencies of *the 51st (dream) state*. Part of the "research-to-performance" strategy that Sundiata initiated in 2002, these events surrounded the project, occuring before, during and after the performance itself. They were designed to involve local clusters of campus programs and community organizations, artists, scholars, activists, and interested citizens in dialogues about citizenship.

The residencies took Sundiata and other members of the company to sites all over the country, including, for example, Austin's Free Minds Program (an adaptation of the Clemente Course in the Humanities); the Arab American National Museum in Dearborn, Michigan; the orientation program for first-year students at Lafayette College; Zeiterion Theater in New Bedford, Massachusetts; Aaron Davis Hall (now Harlem Stage); and the Walker Art Center in Minneapolis. Sundiata led numerous "poetry circles" and "citizenship cabarets," conducted interviews, and attended potluck dinners, panels, and forums designed to spark ideas on critical patriotism ("the opposite of uncritical patriotism," as Gladstone Hutchinson of Lafayette College put it).[8] Simultaneously, the project extended to a pedagogical model developed through The America Project course at the New School University, where Sundiata was a faculty member, and elaborated on other

campuses. Some elements of these public or "project" interactions (vid-
eotaped interviews, for example) worked their way into *the 51st (dream)
state*. This work was Sundiata's most fully theorized and most dramatically
realized model of a performance piece located within a project. The project
becomes the vehicle for the social imagination, the medium (in turn) for
the democratic experience of intercultural citizenship.

The model for *the 51st (dream) state* evolved from Sundiata's earlier diasporic collaborations with trombonist Craig Harris in the 1990s.[9] Reading *the 51st (dream) state* in the context of Sundiata and Harris's precursor
works helps us to follow the development of Sundiata's explicit commitment to the imagination—embodied in the project—as an element of civic
engagement. A genealogy of the work enables us to track the change from
theater piece to civic engagement project, effected through Sundiata's performance works of 2000–2002. The origins of *the 51st (dream) state* lie in
these earlier projects, especially *Udu* (2000), which evolved in turn from
The Return of Elijah (1996).[10]

The Return of Elijah began as a collaboration with New WORLD Theater, founded in Amherst in 1979 "as an anti-racist, multiracial project . . .
dedicated to the work of artists of color."[11] Sundiata and Harris conceived
of *Elijah* as a 'time-traveling' adaptation of *The Interesting Life of Olaudah
Equiano or Gustavus Vassa, the African, 1789*. "The form of the work" was
"a hybrid that draws on opera, music theater, and oratorio."[12] *Udu* linked
Africa and America, the eighteenth and twentieth centuries, and ultimately a theater company, a couple of nonprofit organizations, and some
academics. Sundiata and Harris engaged Senegalese percussionists and
contemporary antislavery organizations in a series of interactions that led
to prescient experiments with genre, voice, and time. The tonal and formal consequences of "conversations with history" were at the center of the
experiments that joined what Eleanor Traylor calls "lyric evocation" with
what Angela Davis terms "aesthetic agency."[13]

The turn from piece to project came as *Elijah* was evolving into *Udu*.
Sundiata and Harris began to link their reimagining of Equiano's narrative—rendered orally, instrumentally, and through gesture—to contemporary human rights movements. Both collaborators had responded strongly
to Samuel Cotton's *The Silent Terror: A Journey Into Contemporary African
Slavery* (1999). Cotton, who died in 2004, was a documentary filmmaker
who later organized the Coalition Against Slavery in Mauritania and Sudan
(CASMAS).[14] His book offered a point of engagement for Sundiata and Harris that enabled both the transhistorical and the transnational dimensions

of the work to become more purposeful through specific organizational connections in New York.

This shift to relationship building with activist networks had consequences for the new work, *Udu*. Harris and Sundiata felt that "there was still something missing" from *Elijah*, "something we could feel but could not name." After reading *The Silent Terror*, Sundiata recalled, they knew what it was: "What do we, as artists, have to say about our own life and times? As African Americans, how do we feel and think about slavery that is not our own experience in the west? . . . These new issues challenged the received narrative about slavery . . . in a way that disturbed us deeply. . . . This was a source of our 'trouble in mind' that led to a . . . fundamental change in the work."[15] *Udu* was the generative predecessor of *the 51st (dream) state* because decisions about character, voice, and story were intertwined with finding the work's public purpose. Sundiata and Harris observed that when "we began to work with the new story, we . . . made contact with the author of *Silent Terror* as well as former slaves and other people doing abolitionist work here in the United States. They have agreed to participate in humanities activities linked to performances as the piece travels. The 'piece' has evolved into a project."[16] *Udu* thus yielded Sundiata's model for engaged performance, a "piece" embedded within a "project," and took final form in 2000, a year before the events of 9/11 would provoke Sundiata's The America Project.

The America Project

The 51st (dream) state debuted at Stanford in 2006, eighteen months before Sundiata's death at fifty-eight in July 2007. This work exemplifies the recent turn to the lyric imagination of democracy—a turn begun long before 9/11, and with deep historical roots, but more energetically named and claimed after that date.[17] The show combined the speaking "Poet," a quartet of singers, several instrumentalists, and projected video of a solo dance performance and several interviews, along with still photography and clips from television news or other image sources.

Sundiata began *the 51st (dream) state* and The America Project in a period of intensive creative work in response to the events of 9/11, the "War on Terror," and, later, the devastation of Hurricane Katrina,[18] the "federal flood": "Those events triggered a running commentary, an unsettling conversation with myself to understand what it means to be an American."[19] Imagining, witnessing, dreaming, remembering: these are both The America Project's methods of interpersonal encounter and the content of *the 51st (dream) state*. "I felt that I was in a blind spot right after 9/11 and I was looking for a clearing," Sundiata reflected in an interview, "and I set out then to develop a way to *see*."[20] "America," then, was to be reseen through local ethnographies of national feeling organized by a black artist.

The America Project created multiple intimate expressive publics that were interested—and invested—in *the 51st (dream) state*. Community events—including those organized around reading, performing, and meditating on poetry—had a unique power for those attending them. A poetics of public work grew up around such practices. Gatherings took place in a state capital, a community arts center, someone's home, a small theater, a library, or a classroom.[21] The text du jour might be Suheir Hammad's "First Writing Since," the Declaration of Independence, "Lift Every Voice and Sing," or Robert Frost's "Mending Wall." Each event in the halo of engagement surrounding *the 51st (dream) state* had the potential, at least, for the transitory but unforgettable experience of democratic culture.

Participants in many of these events described a sense of entering what Sharon Cameron has called lyric time. *Lyric time* is Cameron's term for the radically *un*public relationship between "temporal deprivation and immortal recompense" in Emily Dickinson's poems—a temporality that, for Cameron, dramatizes the generic features of the lyric poem.[22] I borrow—and alter—this evocative term for two reasons: its expressive power and its usefulness in both marking and disrupting the affinity of The America Project with lyric poetry. There are important differences between Cameron's use of the term and my application of it to these very different scenes of poetry, even as the quality of lyric is deeply shared between lyric poetry as habitually defined and the lyricism that characterizes *the 51st (dream) state* and The America Project.

Lyric citizenship, in this altered sense, is a term that I propose in order to emphasize the links between publicness, eloquence, empathy, and self that Sundiata's project modeled. Mobilizing the lyric voice for citizenship is a counterintuitive critical move, given the association of the lyric tradition with the inward and the private. Poetry is "of the nature of soliloquy," Mill wrote in one of the most insistently binary constructions of poetry as private and rhetoric ("eloquence") as public. If "eloquence is *heard*, poetry is *over*heard." If eloquence flows from contact with the "outward and everyday world," Mill concluded, then poetry avoids such "intercourse" in "solitude."[23] Nonetheless, lyric citizenship is not an oxymoron.

Asked in Minneapolis, "What do you hope happens here when you leave?" Sundiata replied, the "intersection of art, humanities and public engagement." He added, "I lost interest in making work that would just entertain you . . . I want you to feel implicated."[24] Implication, for Sundiata, should not find its voice in the political discourses of complaint, accusation, or (by itself) ideological critique. Rather, he felt, it should yield a constantly questioned, historically aware, emotionally complex identification with and responsibility for "America," however fraught that position might be. The America Project residencies formed small publics where intersection and implication became a craft. These relatively small gatherings of implicated people supplemented the work's performances and in many cases generated the audiences for them. The project aimed to create places where careful listening could occur—above all, careful listening about race, a specific kind of "implication."

Sundiata's project connected the rise of civic engagement in the cultural sector to the creativity of thinking through race toward an intercultural politics. During a postperformance conversation with community members in Austin, one participant commented: "[I was] struck by . . . [the] indictment that I felt was being made of us along racial lines, and the indictment was made in casting, so that the evolution of the bodies, and the way the music moved and bumped up against things . . . [the ensemble company] became . . . a kind of utopic vision of what the U.S. might be. And I wonder how people have responded to the racialized world that gets projected." Sundiata replied, "I wanted very much . . . to be critical about race," to get past "these cold war terms . . . these black and white terms . . . that's not my experience in New York, in the classroom or traveling this country. It's much deeper and more complicated."[25] Racial formation, then, became inseparable from the experiential aesthetics of democratic engagement. This analysis of race pervaded Sundiata's post-9/11 rereading of his lifelong politics of protest in favor of "a critical citizenship" of intersection and implication. The "multi-arts" logic of the 51st (dream) state and the multiethnic, multiracial cast become metaphors for one another and for the identities, individually and collectively, of the audience.[26]

The unit of Sundiata's public engagements, his principle microgenre throughout the six years of making and touring The America Project, was the story of the "citizenship moment." Narrating the "citizenship moment" was central to his own classroom practice at the New School University and to the residency events that surrounded his performances.

For Sundiata, being implicated in democracy began with the act of finding language adequate to one's first memory of voting or some other crossing of the threshold into history, civics, public identity, or consciousness of the state. He himself recalled the solemnity of folding the flag as a member of the school honor guard. The citizenship moment story, as modeled by Sundiata, is an anecdote told and retold as a way of locating the individual within the group through the reperformance of a breakthrough episode. A discursive occasion, it may be retold later; referenced by the speaker, the performer, and others; or written about. The importance of the word *moment* as the focal point of Sundiata's invitation to narrative participation in these gatherings underscores the lyric turn that The America Project introduced into civic storytelling. Civic ceremonies and texts, songs and anthems, the news—all of them, in one way or another, forms of voice and often forms of eloquence—recur as the focal points of "citizenship moment" stories.

Robin Grice, a graduate student in a class that was actively engaged in Sundiata's 2005 Michigan residency, recalled the story she told in response to the in-class prompt on the first day of the term—"talk about your citizenship moment." She wrote later that this moment marked "the first time I would feel . . . profoundly a part of the world . . . as something that could be shaped, influenced, maybe even owned":

> I'd burst into our family's kitchen singing another anthem of sorts. "Say It Loud I'm Black and I'm Proud" hit Milwaukee in the summer of 1968 and as I marched into the house that evening singing at the top of my lungs, I was terrified . . . *terrified* of the reaction the word "black" might bring from a mother who did not tolerate "profanity" . . . or much of anything else . . . a word could go from "bad" to "good" over night . . . [creating] the feeling of history being made right there in our house. Yes, the transition . . . between the street and domestic space releases the energy bound up in the concealed fusion of private and public within the family.[27]

"Citizenship moment" stories such Grice's form a subset of "public narratives," which have contributed to the recent aestheticizing of non-arts activities. The "public narrative," defined by Marshall Ganz for the 2008 Obama campaign as "the story of self," "the story of us," and "the story of now," is thoroughly grounded in the conviction that the self is social and that personal narratives can be publicly exchanged for the public good.

The Participant Guidelines for Camp Obama Colorado, drafted by Ganz, focus on "Telling Your Story of Self" in a personal/public narrative, developed in small-scale working groups. The organizer's story, according to the guidelines, should connect "self," "us," and "now."[28] The narrative should be ready to take door to door, on the road, to the telephones.

The fact that expressive, value-laden, historically precise personal narratives have entered politics should come as no surprise. The storytelling boom is a medium for the fusion of culture, self, and the social. Personal narratives and "life writing" is everywhere: in radio programs like those produced by the StoryCorps radio project; in Photovoice projects that link image, narrative, and community development; in community theaters where plays are built interactively through oral histories, storytelling, or interviews.[29] The genre of the reflective essay, ubiquitous in compendia of "best practices" in community-based learning, often urges precisely the integration of personal experience, academic reading, and local community engagement. The public narrative, in sum, has become a "relational dramaturgy," in David Scobey's apt phrase, for communities organized around vocalizations of the place- and time-bound intricacy of the individual subject. Sundiata, "called to citizenship in a way I never expected," was also called to stories lyrically remembered and told: "The only way I could really get a hold of it was to understand personal narrative. . . . The deeper you go into personal narrative, you come out the other side into the collective."[30]

Telling the story of a "citizenship moment," the favored practice of The America Project, conveyed dramas of identity and affiliation. The tellers of "citizenship moment" stories sometimes recalled the epiphanic events that launched their careers as political activists, but ideological contest was not what Sundiata was trying to get at with this practice. The expressive power attributed to personal narratives with civic motives blurred the distinction between narrative and lyrical modes. Story acquired atmospheric, associative, metaphoric, and temporal qualities associated with the discontinuous transitions of poetry. The aesthetic entered public narrative through the literary, the poetic, or even the romantic in tropes of song, memory, haunting, night, wandering, and dream. They allowed individuals and groups to negotiate the passage from social and political criticism to experiences, however ephemeral, of transformative implication. These overtly poeticized moments showed what may happen to the political when performed dreamwork becomes part of it.

A Citizen Walks into Citizenship: Reading *the 51st (dream) state*

A key passage in *the 51st (dream) state*, spoken by the Poet as written and played by Sundiata, launches a meditation on the genesis of the work during the apocalyptic, neo-imperial days of the new millennium. The author's own medical crises (a kidney transplant followed by a car accident in which he sustained a broken neck) preceded the national traumas of 9/11 and Hurricane Katrina. Lyrical hope works "against all gravity" for an audience that is "already old" and deeply skeptical:

> A citizen walks into a Citizenship looking for directions as the drama opens in a New American Theater with a view from the 9th Ward that looks out on Speed, an ancient word for a future that is Always Now, a millennium already old and half done. These are the rules to engage this space . . .

> A poet addresses the podium, calibrates her papers and speaks her words into the room where against all gravity they float: *The Scale of Empire.* War she says, but what she means is Wars, but it doesn't seem to matter which one. The audience clears its throat and checks its pockets.[31]

The poet who doubts both the standard discourses of the leftist intellectual and those of the canonical American lyric tries to balance suspicion and hope. This involves altering his or her political language, a process that *the 51st (dream) state* both performs and explains:

> In the early days of the Aftermath
> I was in hiding
> from the lost army of protest
> calling from the 20th century
> for something boisterous and skinny
> on the page

Sundiata's "American feelings" emerged after 9/11 as part of the labor of renegotiating his "strange, hyphenated relation to America" as an African American.[32] "I'm done marching," Sundiata said during a postperformance community conversation in Austin: "I didn't want people to respond in the language of debate, rhetoric, and staking out a position."[33] For most of his "writing life," he felt himself to be "the un-American American" who wrote "from the outside looking in." But in "the aftermath," he mused, "it seems that I'm being forced . . . to invent what it means to be an American again": "What did it mean for me to be making art at this time, what did it mean for me as an African American man to be asking these questions?" In *the 51st (dream) state,* the Poet begins with the physics of writing. Trauma rips open the depths and sends poetry on a search for roots in the body, in craft (of hand and eye) and in the elements of place:

> I began my heresy
> with the scratch and whisper
> of Number 2 lead
> spelling out the opening line
> from instinct to hand to eye
> earth water fire air

The refrain, "Earth, water, fire, air" puts a special emphasis on "air" as the attenuated social space through which voice and music travel. Updated, "air" becomes "airwaves": "America come across the airwaves and empties its soul like a compulsive talker in the passenger seat explaining what it means to be a way of life." Or, in an optative lift,

> Everybody's dreaming a different dream. . . .
> The lines are open. We are in the air!

Sundiata took seriously the word "dream" in his title. Much of *the 51st (dream) state* takes place at night, under the moon, to the tune of the Moonlight Sonata, or in daydream. "Honest language," the Poet reminds us, is neither simple nor straightforward. It embraces the surreal, nocturnal recycling of American tongues—America on the road and on the radio. Being in the air and on the road are equally spaced out conditions and equally American geographies. It takes the suspended animation or parallel play of "quiet hours on the Interstate" to figure out "what a citizen thinks/about citizenship." What a citizen thinks comes down, not to a political proposition, but to the feedback loop of song. Poetry constructs American geography, while American landscapes inhabit the Poet: "If you sing to the mountains / the mountains will sing to the valley in you . . . / If you sing to the highway; the highway will find/ the highway in you."

Unabashedly indulging the romanticism of performed citizenship, the video projection shows a solo black dancer, David Thomson, as the visual manifestation of the Poet's self-making in the dreamlike poise of black-and-white projection. On the multiple projection screens that formed the backdrop of the set, dance introduces a second space of lyrical gesture. Thomson's performance of entranced reflection bespeaks the absorption of a man "thinking out loud" with his body, dancing a pathway through lyric time. This dance is one of many passages in the performance when visible interiority and audible publicness merge.

The race work of *the 51st (dream) state* is inextricable from the conviction that "what's missing and gone is half the story." Lyric citizenship helps to fill in the gaps through performances that often rely on lyric modes, which are spoken, sung, orchestrated, danced, and visualized. Sundiata, like the other writers I discuss in the conclusion, purchases hope through an aesthetic practice with haunted histories. In other words, the uncanny emotions of historical memory mediate the relationship between oppositional negativity and democratic hope. Hospitalized in Brooklyn during 9/11, a kind of hopeful civics of mortality had already come to him as he watched develop, among "all the patients, an absurd and poetic unit of possibility."[34] Thus Sundiata already felt close to the "thin places" of the world.[35]

In *the 51st (dream) state,* the chronically ill body of *Blessing the Boats*, which was Sundiata's one-man show about his kidney transplant, enters public space and time through these "thin places":

I follow horse trails
through secret pathways
indigenous ghost caves
and African Burial Grounds . . .
the Untouchables and Enchanters doo wop
and doo-rag in a spot of starlight
like they don't know they're dead
as if to say See that star, see that light?
This is what we always wanted to be.

Here the broken body meets the broken city, where "what's below the surface, the underlife of the city, history below the ground, animates the city day to day." Buried histories surfaced and the "mineral" life of body and earth commingled.[36] This is Whitman's "The Sleepers" by way of "The Tunnel" section of Hart Crane's *The Bridge*. There Crane, wandering in "interborough fissures of the mind," addresses the specter of Edgar Allan Poe as the subway car is "rivered under streets / and rivers."[37] But it is equally Whitman by way of June Jordan, Sundiata's college creative writing teacher and author of "He's Our Shakespeare: So why is America ambivalent about Whitman?"[38]

In Sundiata's script, the Poet claims imaginative access to a subsurface world, the subterranean burial grounds of Manhattan exposed through Ground Zero. Not narrated in the script, but told many times by Sundiata as one of his public narratives—showing once again that the civic is inseparable from the familial—was the story of his great-grandfather's lynching in South Carolina. He heard this story from his aunts only in late middle age. The lynching occurred at a place that he remembered other children pointing out to him during family visits as haunted or taboo.[39] Patricia Yaeger invites us to consider "geography as ghost story," suggesting that the strangeness of literary topographies reveals the "pressure of what is hidden, encrypted, repressed, or unspoken in global and local histories." Space "possesses a history"—often a racialized history—that is manifest "as a series of folds and pockets, as the dimensional incorporation and exhalation of time."[40]

The 51st (dream) state is set in just such a place. The history of racism "cures" the schoolboy of any facile loyalties to "America, the Beautiful" (W. E. B. Du Bois's sardonic riff on "My Country 'Tis of Thee" is lurking here somewhere),[41] and this is precisely what allows the "beautiful" and the lyrical to enter through tragic "witness" in Lower Manhattan:

> through history's anesthesia
> I came to my feet at the Wall Street station
> and walked towards the door
> like a reluctant witness to the witness stand . . .
>
> And Little Emmett Till came to me
> A face that long ago cured
> my schoolboy faith
> in that lyric . . .
> O beautiful for spacious skies

If the road to critical citizenship is through dreams, *the 51st (dream) state* proposes, dreams come from a "self-critical place" (Sundiata's phrase) and are formed by critical practice.[42]

"Race as a Resource of Hope": Race, Culture, and Dream

In concluding this essay, I shall situate *the 51st (dream) state* in relation to other instances of the poetics of race, culture, family, and dream and, in doing so, suggest that we read *the 51st (dream) state* in the more finite context of writings by a number of black intellectuals and other intellectuals of color, including Robin Kelley, Lani Guinier, Cornel West, Saidiya Hartman, and—not least—Barack Obama. They, too, try out, or try on, arguments for memory, alliance, and hope. The pronounced expressiveness of their writings (in some passages, at least) is bound up with aesthetic sensations specifically associated with the politics of intersection and implication.

The short list of works that form part of this conversation includes Barack Obama's *Dreams from My Father* (1995), Robin Kelley's *Freedom Dreams* and Lani Guinier and Gerald Torres's *The Miner's Canary* (both in 2002), Cornel West's *Democracy Matters* (2004), and Saidiya Hartman's *Lose Your Mother* (2007). In these works, imagination is a metaphor for political possibility and impossibility, a swinging door between agency and loss. It surfaces when these authors shift into an aesthetic register, as imaginative episodes mark shifts in vocation and mood. All these writers introduce the question of hope through the language of magic, tragedy, dream. Their texts suggest that, without the resources of the expressive, the aesthetic, or, indeed, the literary, advocating for hope out loud and in public is scarcely possible.

Some narratives constructed by black intellectuals, then, are preoccupied with the ambivalent condition of hope as a cultural correlative of antiracist politics. We see this in the writings of Cornel West ("I'm a prisoner of hope," a phrase later compacted into the term "tragicomic hope") and in those of Lani Guinier (who understands "race as a resource of hope and racism as an enduring curse").[43] If race is a signifier of hope, then the scene of signifying with others, the public performance of surmise, is what connects being "implicated" in racism to the condition of hopefulness. In *the 51st (dream) state,* the vocalists (all women) take charge of the music that moves toward this historically informed affective possibility. They specify the particulars of citizen imaginings to Sinatra's refrain from "The House I Live In": "That's America to me." And at the end they get the last word, a song structured around "what if" questions and statements beginning with "suppose." "America, the Beautiful" resurfaces only to be gently sidelined in favor of its sequel, a "beautiful question" marking the mortal threshold of hope:

What if we are Life / or Liberty
and the Pursuit of something new?

And suppose the beautiful answer
asks the more beautiful question,

Why don't we get our hopes up too high?
Why don't we get our hopes up too high?
High!

The word *imagination* is a key signifier for Guinier and Gerald Torres, as it is for Sundiata, but its meaning in these two texts is not identical. Their theory of political race—"a ridiculously optimistic exercise of our imagination"—requires a magical realism informed by Gabriel Garciá Márquez and Augusto Boal. Guinier and Torres yoke political optimism to a surreal aesthetic, an "emancipating faith in the unseen and the unknown." And that aesthetic supports the rituals of engagement, the formation of zones of purposeful enchantment where "individuals . . . share their stories and construct relationships that reinforce a more systemic and critical social understanding."[44] While Guinier and Torres may be in conversation with Sundiata, however, theirs is a different way of thinking through the relationship between the aesthetic and the political. They do not, for example, foreground the transformations of language performed by the inward- and outward-looking citizen of Sundiata's projects.

The literary enters these writings in the form of a politically necessary moment or episode, a conversion to hope by way of the nocturnal, magical, or radiant. Robin Kelley reads the repetitive, accusatory analysis of power as the dead end of professional academic habits of critique. He accepts the fact that "we [on the left] don't know what to build, only what to knock down," but believes that there are alternative discourses, including— significantly—those revealed by women within the family: "I inherited my mother's belief that the map to a new world is in the imagination . . . rather than in the desolation that surrounds us."[45] The everyday labors of democracy are inseparable from altered states of consciousness illuminated by the conjured past and the sense of being haunted—again, familial emotions. "It was as if I had conjured her up," Saidiya Hartman says of the archival phantasm of an ancestor."[46]

Barack Obama's breakthrough moments, in *Dreams from My Father*, likewise turn on poetic and aesthetic experiences he describes as "haunted," "luminous," and liminal. Obama discovered the public power of memory through the "sacred stories" of the Chicagoans he met as a political organizer. He characterizes them as tellers of "stories full of terror and wonder, studded with events that still haunted or inspired them." Their narratives were full of "poetry," allegorized as "a luminous world always present beneath the surface." The eloquence of citizens, saturated with memory, led him toward hope. And hope materialized in church, through ekphrasis and allusion. Barack Obama heard third-hand about George Watts's late Victorian allegorical painting of Hope as a blindfolded woman. This happened during the sermon by Jeremiah Wright that yielded the signature phrase "audacity of hope."[47]

Temporal slippage is central to these texts, especially the phenomenon that Saidiya Hartman, in her book on a yearlong pursuit of the presence and absence of slavery in Ghana, calls "tumbling the barricade between *then* and *now.*"[48] Like Nikhil Singh in his rereading of Du Bois, Hartman is looking back in order tentatively to look ahead to a way of "thinking and feeling beyond" what it currently means to be a cultural critic of the nation-state.[49] Hartman's *Lose Your Mother* is a report on her quest for traces of the history of transatlantic slavery. Her book is a public narrative in the form of a detective story or perhaps a ghost story. "To what end," Hartman asks, "does one conjure the ghost of slavery, if not to incite the hopes of transforming the present?" Living in "the future created" by slavery induces the "ongoing crisis of citizenship" out of which she writes: "To believe, as I do, that the enslaved are our contemporaries is . . . to acknowledge that they accompany our every effort . . . to imagine a free territory, a new commons. . . . It is a glimpse of possibility, an opening, a solicitation without any guarantee of duration before it flickers and then is extinguished."[50] The civic imagination does many things in these works. It is an element of social movements. It is a metaphor for political possibility and impossibility. It is a rhetoric of persuasion. It is a trope for surmise, reflection, and sympathy. Likewise the word *public* changes from object to experience, raising questions about whether *public* is a location, a value, a story line, a politics, a keyword, an identity, or (I would argue) all of the above.

What we see in these writings and performances is not the aestheticization of blackness, though the association of blackness with specific expressive styles—with otherness, exoticism, disinhibition, or cool—is an inescapable part of their cultural context. Rather, what we discern are two implied or explicit claims. The first claim is that the works of black intellectuals in the U.S. provide a model of "implication"—of resistance, negotiation, historical study, hope, and rhetorical extravagance—that speaks to the political and cultural conditions of the last decade. These texts show that hope is not politically naive, conceptually weak, or historically unmoored.

The second claim that undergirds these writings is that artistic creativity, or something very like it, is fundamental to the individual's capacity to entertain political hope. This is why revisiting the resources of the idea of the lyric matters. Sundiata and other creators of public cultural projects claim that imagination is a necessary part of democratic engagement. We can enter into the social labors of a multiracial, antiracist political culture *only* by passing through an aesthetically rich, memory-plagued, powerfully figurative and ultimately hopeful encounter with our own histories and the history of America. The moment of lyric citizenship may turn out to have been a phenomenon of a decade or two and one that involved a relatively modest number of artists, scholars, educators, political figures, cultural organizers, and active citizens. In the stricken economy of the postelection environment, the future of the interlocking discourses of race, hope, imagination, and democracy remains unclear. But it is far too soon to dismiss the staying power of artful counterpublics.

Notes

I am indebted to Maurine Knighton and Ann Rosenthal for providing access to Sekou Sundiata's unpublished work in many forms and to David Scobey for his generous comments on this essay.

1. Hosted by the August Wilson African American Cultural Center of Greater Pittsburgh and supported by the Association of Performing Arts Presenters, this was a breakaway meeting from a larger national convention for "fifty regional and national leaders in the arts who have a history of applying successful diversity efforts." As George Sanchez has argued, there is ample reason to challenge the reductive effects of managed and marketed diversity, and Sundiata's response to this challenge was to articulate a theory and practice of engaged intercultural performance. See George Sanchez, "Crossing Figueroa: The Tangled Web of Diversity and Democracy," *Foreseeable Futures* no. 4 (Imagining America, Syracuse, New York): 17.

2. Sundiata's The America Project was in conversation with recent mediations of the progressive tradition of Addams and Dewey; with a nondoctrinaire, loosely "counter-hegemonic" arts and culture network resonating with the "cultural front" of the thirties as framed by Michael Denning in *The*

Cultural Front: The Laboring of American Culture in the Twentieth Century (New York: Verso, 1998).

3. Sekou Sundiata, "Thinking Out Loud: Democracy, Imagination, and Peeps of Color," in *Diversity Revisited/A Reflection: A Summary of Diversity Revisited/A Conversation on Diversity in the Arts*, Report on Diversity Revisited Conference, June 8–9, 2004 (Pittsburgh: African American Cultural Center of Greater Pittsburgh, 2004), 8–9.

4. The principles and strategies of community-engaged theater are manifest in the mission of MAPP International, which produced The America Project and *the 51st (dream) state*. This approach to a wide range of performance practices is also embodied in the work of, for example, Rennie Harris Puremovement, Detroit's Matrix Theater Company, Cornerstone Theater in Los Angeles, Appalshop, the August Wilson Center for African American Culture, and many other sites.

5. Examples include the Center for Diversity and Democracy at the University of Southern California, the Simpson Center for the Humanities at the University of Washington, the Center for the Humanities and the Public Sphere at the University of Florida, the Institute on Culture, Ethnicity and the Modern Experience at Rutgers-Newark, the Harward Center for Community Partnerships at Bates College, the Arts of Citizenship Program at the University of Michigan, and the Cultures and Communities Program at the University of Wisconsin-Milwaukee.

6. David Scobey, "Across: The Heterogeneity of Civic Education," in Michael B. Smith, Rebecca S. Nowacek, and Jeffrey L. Bernstein, eds., *Citizenship Across the Curriculum* (Bloomington: Indiana University Press, 2010).

7. Suzanne Lacey, "Introduction," in *Mapping the Terrain: New Genre Public Art* (Seattle: Bay, 1994),19–46.

8. Gladstone Hutchinson, "The Art of Dialogue on Difficult Issues: Critical Patriotism as a Theme for New Student Orientation," unpublished paper presented at the National Conference on Students in Transition, November 6–8, 2005, Costa Mesa, California.

9. Amiri Baraka, "Baraka Eulogizes Sundiata," at the memorial service held at the New School University, New York, August 22, 2007. http://www.seeingblack.com/article_254.shtml (accessed September 25, 2009). Baraka recalled meeting the young poet at an important transnational event in Dar es Salaam, Tanzania at the Sixth Pan African Congress in 1974. Sundiata was in his mid twenties, "finding his way through the maze of Pan African political unity, struggle & polemic."

10. Roberta Uno and Lucy Mae San Pablo Burns, eds., *The Color of Theater* (New York: Continuum, 2005), 5–6. This book, rooted in the practice of the New WORLD Theater at the University of Massachusetts, Amherst (at this

writing closed due to university budget cuts), reflects the critical framework of *the 51st (dream) state*, then in its earliest phase of development.

11. Roberta Uno, "Introduction: The Color of Theater," in Uno and Burns, *The Color of Theater*, 7.

12. Talvin Wilks, "Elijah's Journey: Introduction to *Elijah*," in Uno and Burns, *The Color of Theater*, 386. Sekou Sundiata, "Afterword on *Udu*, formerly *Elijah*," ibid., 421–23.

13. Joni L. Jones, "Conversations with History: Sekou Sundiata, Craig Harris, and *Elijah*," in Uno and Burns, *The Color of Theater*, 409–19. Jones draws usefully on Eleanor Traylor, "Two Afro-American Contributions to Dramatic Form," in Errol Hill, ed., *The Theater of Black Americans* (New York: Applause, 1987), 53, and on Angela Davis, *Blues Legacies and Black Feminism* (New York: Random House, 1999), 164.

14. Samuel Cotton, *The Silent Terror: A Journey Into Contemporary African Slavery* (New York: Writers and Readers, 1999).

15. Sundiata, "Afterword on *Udu*," 422.

16. Ibid.

17. *The Crisis*, special issue on *Black Patriotism* 108, no. 6 (November/December, 2001) http://www.thecrisismagazine.com/issues/2001/01_11–12.htm (accessed September 25, 2009). See also Hutchinson, "The Art of Dialogue."

18. Carol Bebelle, "The Vision Has Its Time: Culture and Civic Engagement in Postdisaster New Orleans" in Amy Koritz and George Sanchez, eds., *Civic Engagement in the Wake of Katrina* (Ann Arbor: University of Michigan Press, 2009), 89–90.

19. Sekou Sundiata, "Disintegrating General Public: Waking Up in the 51st (dream) state," address, Bucknell College 2007 America Project Kickoff Program, February 4–8, 2007, 79–80.

20. *Finding the 51st Dream State* (DVD documentary), 2009. Stanley Nelson, Firelight Media, director; Ann Rosenthal, MAPP International Productions, producer and publisher Packaged with excerpts from the script, The America Project course curriculum, and a DVD video of the full performance of *the 51st (dream) state*, recorded live at the Brooklyn Academy of Music in November 2006.

21. The residencies yielded all four of the participant interview segments projected onto the multisectioned video screen at the rear of the stage during the performance. Two interviews highlight key organizers of Sundiata's Michigan residency. Ismael Ahmed was then executive director of ACCESS (Arab Community Center for Economic and Social Services). Ahmed's interview is paired with that of Anan Ameri, director of the Arab American National Museum in Dearborn, Michigan. A second set of interviews was shot in Amherst at the New World Theater. Kiku Uno talks about the family's internment during

World War II, and Uday Joshi speaks of being mistaken for an Arab on the subway traveling from one university campus to another after 9/11.

22. Sharon Cameron, *Lyric Time: Dickinson and the Limits of Genre* (Baltimore: Johns Hopkins University Press, 1981), 3–4.

23. John Stuart Mill, "Thoughts on Poetry and Its Varieties," in *The Collected Works of John Stuart Mill*, ed. John M. Robson, 33 vols. (Toronto: University of Toronto Press, 1963–1991), 1:348–49.

24. Sekou Sundiata, community conversation, March 2007 (archival DVD), The America Project 2006–2007 residency, Austin, Texas. Produced by Evan Carton, director, Humanities Institute, University of Texas. A community dialogue participant in Austin pointed to the "theology of organizing" that was her version of democratic "implication": "I was raised in a religious home, and if you do not participate, you're not part of the world . . . watching . . . doesn't help anybody, it doesn't help you, you're missing out [on] the sense of community . . . that's what I feel citizenship is, it's action, it's awareness . . . to be able to really connect . . . I was able to do that after your performance. It just kind of came together for me. It was very moving. I can't tell you." See also Mark R. Warren, *Dry Bones Rattling: Community Building to Revitalize American Democracy* (Princeton: Princeton University Press, 2001), on "a theology of organizing" (chapter 2, passim), and specifically on "the 'soft arts' of relational organizing," 68.

25. Sundiata, community conversation. Sundiata continued: "by the time Cornel West says the whole nation has become niggerized, there's something very potent about that. So people responded to that . . . piece, 'Nigga please.' No matter what you do with that word it is so historically charged . . . that it may have all these other resonances . . . but it never loses that specificity which to me is a great place to enter a conversation."

26. The multi-arts character of Sundiata's work is explicit in the name of the producer of *Blessing the Boats, the 51st (dream) state,* and *Finding the 51st dream state,* formerly MultiArts Projects and Productions (MAPP), now MAPP International Productions, New York, New York.

27. Grice still didn't think that she had told a true "citizenship story"—one like Sundiata's, with "America" in the middle. Then she found one in the act of writing: "suddenly . . . the action of memory continues into the writing process": "It was second grade and Mrs. Maxwell, a stern, unsmiling black woman . . . had us stand and make a circle in the middle of the room. For what now feels like the entire school day she drilled us on the lyrics to the national anthem." Grice understands this moment as part of the ambivalent, lyrical pedagogy of national implication: "Her goal was not just to teach us the words, but . . . to teach us to be citizens. And it would no doubt take a book or two to

sort out the mental gymnastics it took for black people like her . . . to get to that place." "Citizen Robin," unpublished paper (2005).

28. Obama-Biden Campaign, Camp Obama Colorado Participant Guidelines 2008. *Self* is printed in quotes (Telling Your Story of "Self") in the original document. Thanks to Harry Boyte, codirector of the Center for Democracy and Citizenship, Augsburg College, and codirector of the Civic Engagement subcommittee of Urban Policy Committee of the Obama-Biden Campaign, for providing a copy. The guidelines, principally authored by Marshall Ganz, include a literary template: "A *plot* begins with an unexpected *challenge* that confronts a *character* with an urgent need to pay attention, to make a *choice* for which s/he is unprepared. The choice yields an outcome—and the *outcome* teaches a *moral*. Because we can empathetically identify with the *character*, we can 'feel' the *moral*" (13–19). See also Marshall Ganz, "Why Stories Matter: The Art and Craft of Social Change," *Sojourners Magazine* (March 2009).

29. StoryCorps is an independent nonprofit best known for weekly broadcasts on National Public Radio's Weekend Edition and for its touring Mobile-Booth recording studio: http://www.storycorps.org/ (accessed September 25, 2009). For examples of Photovoice methodology, see Caroline C. Wang, Susan Morrel-Samuels, Peter M. Hutchison, Lee Bell, and Robert M. Pestronk, "Field Action Report: Flint Photovoice: Community Building Among Youths, Adults, and Policymakers," *American Journal of Public Health* 94, no. 6 (June 2004): 911–13. For an example of the participatory coauthorship of plays that is characteristic of many community-based theaters, see Roadside Theater's "Community Residency Methodology," http://www.roadside.org/methodology.html. (accessed September 25, 2009.) For a definitive recent investigation of "life writing," see Sidonie Smith and Julia Watson, *Reading Autobiography: A Guide for Interpreting Life Narratives*, 2d ed. (Minneapolis: University of Minnesota Press, 2010).

30. Sundiata, community conversation.

31. Sekou Sundiata, *the 51st (dream) state,* unpublished script quoted with permission of Maurine Knighton.

32. Sundiata, *Finding the 51st Dream State.*

33. Such rhetoric, however, was reperformed by Sundiata as a voice that the culture can't shake. Sundiata's signature riff, repeated with variations in several works over many years, was the delusional and spooky outpouring of the character "Space," a street corner apparition from the days of Black Power in New York City.

34. Sekou Sundiata, National Public Radio Fresh Air, from WHYY, "Performance Poet Sekou Sundiata," March 25, 2005. http://www.npr.org/templates/story/story.php?storyId=4561097 (accessed September 29, 2009).

35. Sundiata, community conversation.

36. Sundiata, *the 51st (dream) state*.

37. Walt Whitman, "The Sleepers," http://www.whitmanarchive.org/published/LG/1871/poems/102 (accessed October 9, 2009). Hart Crane, *The Complete Poems and Selected Letters and Prose of Hart Crane*, ed. Brom Weber (New York: Liveright, 1966), 108–12.

38. June Jordan, "He's Our Shakespeare: So Why Is America Ambivalent About Whitman?" Poetry Media Service: A Service of Poetry Foundation. http://www.poetryfoundation.org/programs/media.syndicate.html?id=6 (accessed April 2, 2011. Excerpted from "For the Sake of People's Poetry: Walt Whitman and the Rest of Us," in *Some of Us Did Not Die: New and Selected Essays* (New York: Basic/Civitas Books, 2002), 242–56.

39. Barbara Palmer, Stanford Report, http://news-service.stanford.edu/news/2006/ may 3/sekou-050306.html (accessed March 2, 2011.

40. Quoted in Julie Ellison, *Cato's Tears and the Making of Anglo-American Emotion* (Chicago: University of Chicago Press, 1999), 156.

41. W. E. B. Du Bois, "My Country 'Tis of Thee," in W. E. B. Du Bois, *Creative Writings*, ed. Herbert Aptheker (White Plains, NY: Kraus-Thomson, 1985). From Du Bois's headnote: "Arise, gracefully remove your hat, and tilt your head. Then sing as follows, powerfully and with deep unction. They'll hardly note the little changes and their feelings and your conscience will thus be saved."

42. "This is what I came to find out is what I loved about America—the democratic tradition: the abolitionists, the labor movement, the women's movement, the suffrage movement," which yielded "a body of ideas and knowledge and music and culture that comes out of that self-critical place." *Finding the 51st dream state. The 51st (dream) state* works against the amnesiac epistemological habits of "infantile citizenship" as construed by Lauren Berlant in "The Theory of Infantile Citizenship," *The Queen of America Goes to Washington City* (Durham: Duke University Press, 1997), 408–9.

43. Cornel West, Commencement address at Wesleyan University, Middletown, Connecticut, May 30, 1993. http://www.humanity.org/voices/commencements/speeches/index.php?page=west_at_wesleyan (accessed September 25, 2009). Nikhil Singh, *Black Is a Country: Race and the Unfinished Struggle for Democracy* (Cambridge: Harvard University Press, 2004).

44. Lani Guinier and Gerald Torres, *The Miner's Canary: Enlisting Race, Resisting Power, Transforming Democracy* (Cambridge: Harvard University Press, 2002), 20.

45. Robin Kelley, *Freedom Dreams: The Black Radical Imagination* (New York: Beacon, 2003), 2.

46. Saidiya Hartman, *Lose Your Mother: A Journey Along the Atlantic Slave Route* (New York: Farrar, Straus, and Giroux, 2007), 16.

47. Barack Obama, *Dreams from My Father: A Story of Race and Inheritance* (New York: Three Rivers, 1995), 190–91.

48. Hartman, *Lose Your Mother,* 15.

49. Singh, *Black Is a Country,* 224.

50. Hartman, *Lose Your Mother,* 170, 133, 169.

PART 2

Aesthetics and the Representation of Sexuality

[5]

Aesthetics Beyond the Actual

The Marble Faun and Romantic Sociality

CHRISTOPHER CASTIGLIA

> The true mystery in the world is the visible, not the invisible.
>
> —Oscar Wilde, *The Picture of Dorian Gray*

> It must be a very dear and intimate reality for which people will be content to give up a dream.
>
> —Nathaniel Hawthorne, *The Marble Faun*

No one seems capable of saying or writing a sentence these days without throwing in the word *actually* for no apparent reason. Actually is the new like. This change in idiom might seem insignificant, but it marks a worrisome displacement, a shift from approximation to dead certainty, from coy affection to self-evident empiricism, from the surprising to the reassuring, from aesthetics to facts. Sure, *actually* may satisfy the psychic cravings of an age so inundated with virtuality as to starve for the real. At the same time, however, we've evolved into a culture of open secrets in which half-truths are told to the public, not expecting the public to buy them, but rather to invite the pleasures of figuring out the "actual" behind the smoke and mirrors, a phenomenon we might think of as the Woodward and Bernsteining of America. Watergate was the context for the intellectual movement that would become new historicism, which naturalized *as* criticism the impulse to reveal the ideological humbug lurking behind surface obfuscation. Criticism as a mode of advocacy (of "liking") or of metaphorical inventiveness (of imagining what the world might be "like" if unfettered from the actual) was replaced by *critique,* the revelatory regime of discerning the truth (if only an ideological and not a Kantian variety) beneath illusion.

Given this critical genealogy, we might speculate that new historicism is the logical outgrowth not only of Watergate but of late nineteenth-century realism, which was itself a response to the aesthetic counteractuality of romanticism. If Marx can be called the first significant antiaesthetic historicist of the postromantic period, his heirs, through and beyond Terry Eagleton and Fredric Jameson, have persistently yoked imperatives to "always historicize" to an acute skepticism about the ideological interpellations of aesthetic formations and affects, located, with unfailing consistency, in the "magical narratives" of the romantic era.[1] This distrust of the play of surfaces is a shortcoming in social criticism because in order to imagine a society operating under more just conditions, one must be capable of imagining a social world unmoored from the binding imperative of precedent and set adrift in the speculative potential of the as-yet-only-imagined. This work of inventive imagination transforms aesthetic speculation into world-making transformation, a process Judith Butler implies when she reminds us that fantasy is not unreal but "not-yet-real," or a discredited version of "the real."[2] If one's lifestyle and aspirations run counter to the imperatives of normative convention, they will become discredited as whimsy, day-dreaming, ivory-towerism, delusion, and all the other terms used to neutralize the imaginative power of those who want something they haven't seen—or seen often—except in the mind's eye.

This is the transformative power Oscar Wilde implied in his aesthetic manifesto, "The Decay of Lying" (1889), in which the art of untruth—what we might call counteractuality—becomes a romantic act of defiance. For the essay's protagonist, Vivian, arguably a stand-in for Wilde himself, the prime menace of late nineteenth-century realism is its relentless production of "evidence in support of a lie."[3] The realist, Vivian contends, by presenting a biased and soul-consuming concoction as an empirical and natural inevitability, fosters "a morbid and unhealthy faculty of truth-telling, begins to verify all statements made in his presence, has no hesitation in contradicting people who are much younger than himself, and often ends by writing novels which are so lifelike that no one can possibly believe in their probability" (8). Vivian attributes realism's fact fetish to the "crude commercialism of America, its materialising spirit, its indifference to the poetical side of things, and its lack of imagination and of high unattainable ideals," all of which, he claims, arises from "that country having adopted for its national hero a man who, according to his own confession, was incapable of telling a lie, and it is not too much to say that the story of George

Washington and the cherry-tree has done more harm, and in a shorter space of time, than any other moral tale in the whole of literature" (25–26).

Of course, Mason Locke Weems's spurious 1800 account of Washington and the cherry tree was not the only aesthetic production of nineteenth-century America, as Wilde well knew, nor was Wilde's the only articulation of the romantic imagination as a counterforce to crass materialism. "Like Emerson," Vivian proclaims, signaling the roots of his counteractual theory in antebellum aesthetics, "I write over the door of my library the word 'Whim'" (3). Fashioning his own aesthetic transcendence, Vivian imagines whim "breaking from the prison-house of realism" (27). For Wilde's Artist, however, transcendent aestheticism is no transparent metaphysics, but a deliberate process that releases experience from binding precedent, generating alternatives whose appeal arises from the pleasures that "whim" encourages and that "reality" seeks to curtail. Turning superficial artifice threateningly serious, Wilde claims that while Art "begins with abstract decoration, with purely imaginative and pleasurable work dealing with what is unreal and non-existent," soon enough "Life becomes fascinated with this new wonder, and asks to be admitted into the charmed circle. Art takes life as part of her rough material, recreates it, and refashions it in fresh forms, is absolutely indifferent to fact, invents, imagines, dreams, and keeps between herself and reality the impenetrable barrier of beautiful style, of decorative or ideal treatment" (20). Dissatisfied with the mortifying imperatives of reality, Art reveals a greater truth in "things that are lovely and that never happen," or in "things that are not and that should be" (51). Responding pleasurably to art, one not only disavows what is natural and hence inevitable, moreover, but also joins a "charmed circle," a sub- or counterculture. Pleasure then becomes the affective adhesive binding individual aesthetic experience to collective social relations—made *of* the "rough materials" of reality but not bound to its purportedly inherent values—that prove more hospitable to those "whose sorrows were more terrible than any sorrow man has ever felt, whose joys were keener than lover's joys, who had the rage of the Titans and the calm of the gods, who had monstrous and marvellous sins, monstrous and marvellous virtues" (20). Although "reality" ultimately "gets the upper hand, and drives Art out into the wilderness" (20), the transformative power of invention—what Wilde expresses simply as "romanticism"—can never be fully contained or silenced. "Life goes faster than Realism," Vivian asserts, "but Romanticism is always in front of Life" (53). When romance, "with her temper of wonder, will return to the land," Vivian predicts, the "very aspect of the world will change to our startled eyes" (51).

Realists of our own age, as I've already suggested, have continued the skepticism and disregard of the world-transformative potential of romantic aesthetics, accusing writers like Hawthorne, Melville, and Poe of ignoring the "real" ideological struggles of their day. More disturbing, however, are those who have taken up the recent "return" to aesthetics, but have ignored Wilde and his aphoristic, pleasure-seeking, and counteractual followers, as if "queer style" played no role in nineteenth-century aestheticism. The "straightening" of aesthetic theory suggests an uneasiness with what Michel Foucault has claimed is most disturbing in homosexuality, not sex "itself," but the values that structure the subcultures generated and maintained through Wildean aesthetics: "everything," as Foucault writes, "that can be troubling in affection, tenderness, friendship, fidelity, camaraderie, and companionship, things our rather sanitized society can't allow a place for without fearing the formation of new alliances and the tying together of unforeseen lines of force." Foucault makes explicit what Wilde leaves implicit: that the work of aesthetic transformation, undertaken by queers (those possessed of "monstrous and marvelous vices"), is ultimately "a way of life," a social ascesis, an ethics.[4] It's not that friendship is itself a substitute for social struggle or that sociality can replace socialism, but without strong social bonds struggle is less sustainable, pleasurable, or inventive. To return "queer style" to aesthetic theory is, therefore, to conceive it not as an escape from but as a powerful engagement with social aspiration (the aspiration to be social) and collaborative invention. That work, as Wilde shows, demands that we develop the skills not only of critique—of discovering and analyzing the actual—but of creation, of the powers to imagine what has not-yet-been, what's been left untried or banished from the thinkable to the interior states of fantasy, daydreaming, reverie, and, as Wilde would have it, art.

While we have not previously considered the antebellum United States as a hothouse of queer aesthetics, Wilde's Vivian saw himself working within romanticism, from which he drew his inspiration for how "abstract decoration" and "whimsy," "unreal and non-existent," can transform realist morality into counteractual sociability. In order to move from realist critique to inventive reconstruction, we must revisit, as Wilde did, romanticism's visionary promise of a more generous, radically expansive intimacy: not intimacy judged by the criteria of institutions (abstracted character, mutual knowledge, self-sacrifice, and longevity), but intimacy judged by its relation to aesthetics.[5] That promise is perhaps most evident, as the following discussion of *The Marble Faun* will show, in Nathaniel Hawthorne's aesthetic experimentation and his fantasy, no less serious for being fantasy, of social relations released from the internal confines of consciousness through the aesthetic imagination.

What makes *The Marble Faun* exemplify romanticism's social aesthetics is not, as is often asserted, its location outside the United States. It is certainly true that its Italian setting—redolent with ruined antiquity, robust superstitions, and mystic Catholicism—indexes, sometimes in an orientalist register, Hawthorne's characteristically romantic features, providing what Henry James yearned for in Hawthorne's work: a "crepuscular realm of the writer's own reverie" distinct from "the vulgar, many-coloured world of actuality."[6] Releasing Americans from the "iron rule" of the Protestant work ethic that demanded "an object and a purpose in life" and that turned all humans into "parts of a complicated scheme of progress, which can only result in our arrival at a colder and drearier region than we were born in" (215), Italy, however, is more a frame of mind than a geopolitical locale.[7] That "foreign" fantasy, where "progress" gives way to unpredictable countertemporal reversals of modernity and antiquity, and where superstition, myth, and belief challenge clear-sighted pragmatism, is exemplified by Hawthorne's young count, Donatello, who evokes for the Americans the mythic faun of the title. A "lawless thing" who possesses "an indefinable character" (11) and who "has nothing to do with time" (12), Donatello, at once "evanescent and visionary" (4), enacts "no strict obedience to conventional rules" (12). Little wonder that all the Americans, yearning to mix "the Real and the Fantastic" (417), fall in love first with Rome and then with Donatello.

More significant than its Italian setting, however, are two additional features that have been less often noted: the novel's focus on same-sex friendship and its attachment of those friendships to aesthetic theory. *The Marble Faun* is the first of Hawthorne's romances to emphasize same-sex friendship rather than heterosexual romance. While the love between Donatello and Miriam is an important plot element, it receives less narrative attention than the friendships between Miriam and Hilda or between Kenyon and Donatello. "We taste one intellectual pleasure twice, and with double the result," Hawthorne writes, "when we taste it with a friend" (296), and if this is true of "intellectual pleasures" in general, it proves truest, in *The Marble Faun*, of the pleasures of romanticism. Hawthorne frees his characters from "all customary responsibilities for what they thought and said" (12), not to make them transcendental individualists, or even solitary aesthetes, but to enhance the possibilities for inventive intimacies. As Hawthorne seemed to realize, it is not simply, as Foucault speculated, that friendship generates new social ethics, but that those ethics must first be invented through critical romanticism, though acts of inscription and interpretation, for friendship to flourish. We might call such a readiness for inventive friendship romanticism's *intimation*.

Hawthorne raises this possibility from the opening of *The Marble Faun*, which begins, as do his other romances, with an instructive preface. Unlike his earlier prefaces, "addressed nominally to the Public at large," Hawthorne offers *The Marble Faun* to "a character with whom he felt entitled to use far greater freedom." "He [the author] meant it for that one congenial friend—more comprehensive of his purpose, more appreciative of his successes, more indulgent of his short-comings, and, in all respects, closer and kinder than a brother—that all-sympathising critic, in short, whom an author never actually meets, but to whom he implicitly makes his appeal, whenever he is conscious of having done his best" (xxiii). Friendship relies, for Hawthorne, on appreciative reading, on a sensibility unusually attuned to intimacy and to aesthetics. But pause on *actually* in this opening: Hawthorne uses the word to lift sociability—friendship—from the realm of everyday proximity (someone one *actually* meets) to that of fantasy, the projection of an author's aesthetic and intimate aspirations. Despite his reference to the "actual," then, friendship, for Hawthorne, is profoundly counteractual.

At first, Hawthorne represents his ideal reader as an unattainable ideal, not surprisingly so given what the sculptor Kenyon says within the romance about attainable intimacy between men: "'between man and man," Kenyon states, "there is always an insuperable gulf. They can never quite grasp each other's hands; and therefore man never derives any intimate help, any heart-sustenance, from his brother man'" (258). Kenyon assumes that, because there are gaps—moments of absence, mystery, or autonomy—in men's friendships, intimacy will necessarily fail. Rather than seeing an "insuperable gulf" as the opportunity for inventive fantasy, Kenyon reads it only as grievous loss. Imagining his Ideal Reader as separated from the author by temporal and spatial "gulfs," Hawthorne seems to set up interpretive intimacy as a similarly disappointing exercise in "heart-sustenance," a failure constitutive of the "actual." But Hawthorne is not Kenyon. Although he begins by lamenting, "I never personally encountered, nor corresponded through the Post, with this Representative Essence of all delightful and desirable qualities which a Reader can possess," he soon back-pedals, proclaiming that he "never therefore concluded him to be merely a mythic character" but instead maintained "always a sturdy faith in his actual existence" (xxiii–xxiv). "Actual" now signifies a *potential* proximity, a like-ness, a hopeful mediation between fantasy and faith, presence and potential, and necessary to the generation of art. His faith is not necessarily divorced from experience, moreover, as "that friend of friends, that unseen brother of the soul," actually "did once exist for me and (in spite of the infinite chances against a letter's reaching its destination, without a definite address) duly received the scrolls which I flung upon whatever wind was blowing, in the faith that they would find him out" (xxiv).

Hawthorne's ideal reader, we might speculate, was Herman Melville, with whom, between 1850 and 1851, Hawthorne walked the Berkshire woods, talking about what Melville characterized as "possible and impossible matters."[8] Although the two men occasionally visited one another, their intimacy seems to have grown primarily, as Hawthorne's preface suggests, through letters that, layering textual mediations, describe the men's interpretations of each other's literary productions. Melville first charmed Hawthorne by reviewing with superlative praise his *Mosses from an Old Manse*. Melville in turn received Hawthorne's praise for *Moby-Dick*. As is always the case in epistolary relationships, distance and silence are as important to the interpretive inventions comprising intimacy as are the proximate grasps of the hand privileged by Kenyon. While he found Hawthorne's letter of praise "joy-giving and exultation-breeding" (240), Melville assured his often shy friend that he required no reply to his own letter, claiming, "Possibly, if you do answer it, and direct it to Herman Melville, you will missend it—for the very fingers that now guide this pen are not precisely the same that just took it up and put it on this paper" (241). Understanding that he changes himself in the act of reading and writing, Melville dismisses the fiction of full disclosure or even correspondence, in both senses of the word. Instead, Melville apparently enjoys that the two men's "divine magnanimities are spontaneous and instantaneous" (240), like inspiration itself, and ephemeral ("The Gentle Reader," Hawthorne notes in his preface, "is apt to be extremely short-lived" [xxiv]). Instantaneous and ephemeral, an unlikely investment in the future, intimacy is situated firmly in the present (the sensation aroused by Hawthorne's praise, Melville claims, is no pledge of future satisfactions, but brings instead present satisfaction, rendering the author "Content"[240], both fictional and gratified). Characterized by ephemerality, spontaneity, immediacy, and contingency, this friendship falls beyond the pale of the institutional virtues (permanence, futurity, disclosure, and commitment) that characterize conventional intimacy, but their distance from convention made the relationship more, not less, "actual," for, as Melville notes, "truth is ever incoherent" (241).

Out of the spaces of incoherence—of what Kenyon calls "insuperable gulfs"—Hawthorne and his Ideal Reader generated an occasion for "ineffable socialities" (240), romantic and collective self- and mutual inventions ("Lord," Melville asks Hawthorne, "when shall we be done changing?" [241]) that transform, as Wilde predicts aesthetics will, monstrous sins into marvelous virtues ("I have written a wicked book," Melville claims of *Moby-Dick*, "but I feel spotless as the lamb" [240]). It was arguably this tense proximity of presence and absence, embodiment and inscription, precedent and fantasy, sending and missing, revelation and concealment that generated for the two men what Melville called "ontological heroics" (238) or what we might call aesthetics beyond the actual.

Not surprisingly, given this experience with Melville, *The Marble Faun* centers on the relationship between same-sex intimacy and aesthetics, a connection that sets *The Marble Faun* apart from Hawthorne's earlier texts. The novel turns on the moment when the pure and virtuous, hopelessly uptight Anglo-Saxon Hilda becomes a secret witness to a murder and, as a result, severs her close friendship with the woman she believes to be the murderer, Miriam. The mysterious, passionate, and Semitic Miriam has been stalked, throughout the novel, by a man known simply as The Model, who appears to hold the tormented artist in his power. One night, as Miriam and the simple but loyal Donatello (who has fallen in love with Miriam) gaze upon Rome from on high, they are confronted by The Model. Without a word, Donatello surmises the whole "mystery" and, lifting up Miriam's foe, hurls him to his death. Witnessing this scene, Hilda resolves to sever her friendship with Miriam, an agonizing break for both women. As Hawthorne writes, Miriam's "'crime lay merely in a glance'" (421).

Yet "glancing" suggests not only witnessing but also the art of viewing, an inherently aesthetic endeavor, and in *The Marble Faun* there are aesthetic as well as legal crimes. Two artists, Miriam and Hilda, represent two opposing perspectives on aesthetics, both of which have debilitating effects on the women's friendship. For Miriam, art is pure invention, generated entirely from within some dark, mysterious, largely inaccessible unconscious. Given that the "meaning" of Miriam's work is inaccessible, even to the artist, viewers must supply their own affectively charged meaning to her creations. Miriam's aesthetic shapes her sociability as well. Just as her emotional depth generates unconventional art, so it makes for unconventional manners. "Miriam had great apparent freedom of intercourse," Hawthorne writes; "her manners were so far from evincing shyness, that it seemed easy to become acquainted with her, and not difficult to develop a casual acquaintance into intimacy" (17). Yet just as viewers find it impossible to discern meaning without supplying it themselves, held at bay by the unconventional aesthetics of the work, so her acquaintances find Miriam's apparent friendliness deceptive: "By some subtle quality," Hawthorne reports, "she kept people at a distance, without so much as letting them know that they were excluded from her inner circle" (17), so eventually people "recognize[d] the impossibility of getting nearer to Miriam, and gruffly acquiesced" (17). Just as Miriam's art demands sympathy of comprehension from the viewer that it simultaneously frustrates, so Miriam both "demands friendship, love, and intimate communion, but is forced to pine in empty forms, a hunger of heart, which finds only shades to feed upon" (100–1).

Unlike Miriam, who paints to express deep emotional turmoil, Hilda is a copyist infatuated by the surfaces that, for her, are the locus of meaning. The effect of Hilda's focus on surfaces was "to make her appear like an inhabitant of picture-land, a partly ideal creature, not to be handled, nor even approached too closely" (54). While her simplicity invites everyone to consider themselves her friend, "a subtle attribute of reserve . . . insensibly kept those at a distance who were not suited to her sphere" (54). Believing that none of her work's meaning generates within her, Hilda also believes that viewers take meaning purely from the work's formal "genius." While Miriam's art is "'too nervous, too passionate, too full of agitation'" (103), Hilda, "working entirely from the outside, and seeking only to reproduce the surface," can only "leave out that indefinable nothing, that inestimable something, that constitutes the life and soul through which the picture gets its immortality" (51). Having lost "the impulse of original design" (48) by viewing the Master's work "with his own eyes" (49), Hilda became "but a finer instrument, a more exquisitely effective piece of mechanism" (51), or, as Hawthorne more caustically calls her ilk, "Guido machines or Raphaelic machines" (51). When, after viewing the murder, Hilda's "capacity of emotion was choked up with a horrible experience" (303), she can no longer copy and loses her capacity for art making. Having moved toward Miriam's domain of suffering interiority, Hilda becomes a "melancholy girl" grown "sadly critical" (308). Caught between her aesthetic dedication to pure form—"'The Old Masters will not set me free'" (302), she laments—

and her critical uncertainty as to "whether the pictorial art be not altogether a delusion" (303), Hilda is both emotionally and imaginatively paralyzed.

The differences between the women's aesthetics become most evident in their diverging interpretations of Guido's portrait of Beatrice Cenci, which Hilda is copying. Hilda reports that while she was painting the "fallen angel, fallen, and yet sinless," she occasionally felt "as if she were trying to escape from my gaze." Because Hilda perceives that Beatrice, like Miriam, is forever isolated by her unappeasable sorrow, she yearns to help her subject, but believes that "nothing can be done to help or comfort her, neither does she ask help or comfort, knowing the helplessness of her case better than we do" (56). Because she can see only surfaces, empathy—and hence comfort—is impossible for Hilda. She has given so much autonomy to the visual object for the production of meaning that she can imagine no agency for herself, only for the painted object, which yearns to escape observation. Miriam, on the contrary, takes meaning making back to the viewer, challenging her friend's description of Beatrice as "sinless" by asserting, "'This is not so plain to me'" (56). If Beatrice is an autonomous person, as Hilda suggests, she is also, for Miriam, possessed of interiority—"'if I could only get within her consciousness'" (57), Miriam exclaims—although Miriam is separated from Beatrice as much by inscrutable inwardness as Hilda is by impenetrable superficiality.

As their debate over Beatrice's sin demonstrates, differences in aesthetic theory generate divergent ethical systems as well. Miriam, believing that interiority dictates meaning, also believes that emotions are mitigating factors that suspend ethical categories of right and wrong. Hilda, however, believes in ethical objectivity. "But there is, I believe, only one right and one wrong," she declares, "and I do not understand (and may God keep me from ever understanding) how two things so totally unlike can be mistaken for one another; nor how two moral foes—as Right and Wrong surely are— can work together in the same deed" (347). Where each woman locates "meaning," in other words—either in the surface or in the interior—determines her faith in an objective and discernible moral order; for the former, interpretation of laws plays no role, their meaning being self-evident; for the latter, interpretation is everything, since truth is inaccessible and unpredictable.

These ethical-aesthetic beliefs reflect two predominant aesthetic theories of the eighteenth century. Like Hilda, who draws a rigid sense of moral order from her superficial appreciation of classics, the third Earl of Shaftesbury argued that the aesthetic senses take pleasure in finding in external objects an order and harmony that is also the order and harmony of morality. The aesthetic senses thus become, for Shaftesbury, a way to perceive the orderly morality inscribed by God. In this view of aesthetics, an external law becomes internalized through the sensory perception of a beauty that is always already the same as that law.[9] In contrast, Shaftesbury's heir, Francis Hutcheson, divorced sensory pleasure from both cognition and will, and thereby established the aesthetic and ethical theory embodied by Miriam. Not only does aesthetic appreciation internalize external law, it negates the need for self-analysis (Miriam repeatedly asks others to interpret her to herself) and from action (Miriam is inexplicably paralyzed when confronted by The Model, or indeed with any difficulty requiring resolute action). Our pleasures are not to be analyzed or acted upon, for Hutcheson, but simply *experienced*. No longer connected to a divine order, Hutcheson's aesthetic experiences were less law bound, but they were similarly less *social*, preserved in the realm of the senses.[10]

Both these accounts constitute what Kant would describe as "negative" freedoms: freedom from competing claims for morality in Shaftesbury's case and from the need to analyze or act in Hutcheson's. But what both ultimately entail is a freedom from *relationality*, either between spectator and artwork in the generation of "meaning" or between persons in the generation of intimacy. Things outside the subject never *change* the subject: whether interiority is ordered by divine law or disordered by pleasurable passions, interiority remains inviolable, beyond the transformative "grasp" of other persons or of external objects. As the rupture in Hilda and Miriam's friendship demonstrates, these ethical-aesthetic viewpoints threaten intimacy. Not only does Hilda's ethical system lead her to judge Miriam without compassion and Miriam's prevent her from understanding the moral turmoil her actions have generated for Hilda, both women's aesthetic visions prevent the mutual understanding that would revise and correct those extremes. While Miriam's overreliance on her own unconscious makes her overly self-dependent, her emotions never teach her anything she doesn't already know. Hence, "all her romantic fantasies aimed at this self-same dreary termination" (29). Miriam's imagination, like her conscience, seems stuck in a dreadful rut, returning compulsively "to run on these stones of bloodshed, in which woman's hand was crimsoned by the stain" (38), leaving her, as she begins, alone to "brood, brood, brood" (254). When Kenyon asks, "'With all your activity of mind . . . so fertile in plans as I have known you—can you imagine no method of bringing your resources into play?'" (254), the answer is unwaveringly no, for, claiming that there "is never a new group now-a-days; never, even, so much as a new attitude" (110), Miriam refuses herself the intimate nonconformity that would release her from guilt and shame. At the other end of the spectrum, but with similar results, Hilda's complete denial of interiority gives her the impression "of being utterly sufficient to herself!" (107).

What Hilda and Miriam need, then, is a new aesthetic theory that combines rather than separates, imagines rather than judges, and acknowledges that relationships with others who maintain an alterity to our moral orders might transform, rather than confirm, our interior conceptions of truth and beauty. That theory came in the form of Friedrich von Schiller's 1794 "Letters Upon the Aesthetic Education of Man," a text central to the emergence of European—and subsequently American—romanticism. Schiller argued that the human subject is compelled simultaneously from two directions: on the one hand, pulled toward a particularizing sensuality by instinctual corporeal urges, on the other pulled by extrinsic laws that attempt to impose abstract systems onto sensuous urges. The subject is thus caught between savagery and barbarism, hedonism and totalitarianism, particularity and universalism. Unlike many Enlightenment thinkers who favored the abstract, universalizing side of these pairings, Schiller saw the need for both, particularly in an age that "far from giving us freedom, only develops, as it advances, new necessities; the fetters of the physical close more tightly around us, so that the fear of loss quenches even the ardent impulse toward improvement, and the maxims of passive obedience are held to be the highest wisdom of life."[11] In a culture of law, Schiller contends, "concrete individual life is extinguished, in order that the abstract whole may continue its miserable life, and the state remains for ever a stranger to its citizens, because feeling does not discover it anywhere" (20). Here "concrete life" is more unpredictable and fantastic than either facts or abstractions, a middle ground akin to what both Wilde and Hawthorne characterized as both romanticism and intimacy.

Accordingly, Schiller contends, the only hope is to open up "a middle state" (64) clear of the imperatives both of sense and sensibility, that being the space opened in the mind by aesthetic experiences. In aesthetics' neutral space, the competing forces of the psyche can adjust themselves, the universal asserting its influence through the abstraction of form, the sensual infusing that form with affective life.

> Man raised on the wings of imagination leaves the narrow limits of the present, in which mere animality is enclosed, in order to strive on to an unlimited future. But while the limitless is unfolded to his dazed

imagination, his heart has not ceased to live in the separate, and to serve the moment. The impulse towards the absolute seizes him suddenly in the midst of his animality, and as in this cloddish condition all his efforts aim only at the material and temporal, and are limited by his individuality, he is only led by that demand of the reason to extend his individuality into the infinite, instead of to abstract from it. He will be led to seek instead of form an inexhaustible matter, instead of the unchangeable an everlasting change and an absolute securing of his temporal existence.

(87–88)

What is important for Schiller is that *both* happen simultaneously, so that the psyche, in its moments of aesthetic contemplation, achieves corrective harmony.

Schiller's optimistic claim that "in the aesthetic state the most slavish tool is a free citizen" (110) might represent the illusory suturing of social divisions that, as mentioned earlier, materialist critics have claimed is endemic to aesthetics. Indeed, Schiller's aesthetic liminality is pointedly asocial, as "a disposition of mind that removes all limitation from the totality of human nature must also remove it from every social expression of the same," becoming, in its abstraction, "the foundation of the possibility of all" (76). I want to claim something more for Schiller, however, akin to what Judith Butler calls the force of fantasy, a force social history has notoriously neglected, but one that aesthetics has accounted for with remarkable sophistication. From the negative freedom of aesthetic space Schiller conceived a theory of the imagination or what he called *play*, the active enlargement of "free judgment" beyond the detached realm of art to the materiality of "a sociable character," while also preserving, against public opinion, the "Egotism" (15) that allows imagination to flourish in defiance of common sense. Imaginative play, for Schiller, is transformative, moving beyond detached and evacuated equilibrium to a manifestation *in materiality* of the social principles developed in playful imaginings.

Nevertheless, in claiming that "a state of mind which comprises the whole of humanity in itself must of necessity include in itself also— necessarily and potentially—every separate expression of it" (76), Schiller renders *unnecessary* intimation, an aesthetics of intimate possibility, where the forces of sensuality and moral rigor or of projection and alterity might meet not as opposing halves of a self-contained consciousness but as two persons, two *friends*, whose interactions would open the interpretive play that constitutes, in the sphere of the social, what Schiller could conceive only intrasubjectively. Here we can return to *The Marble Faun*, in which

Hawthorne imagines a social version of Schillerian aesthetics in which the transformative play of aesthetic imagination opens up a space of negotiable and compensatory intimacy. Artists in particular, "not wholly confined within the sordid compass of practical life" (122), move, as would Schiller's, to "the Beautiful," the contemplation of which partakes of "something akin to the Ideal" (122). Yet Hawthorne is careful to keep these artists from moving fully into ideality, maintaining romantic aesthetics, rather, as a mix of "the Real and the Fantastic" (417). Combining ideal form and bountiful delight, Hawthorne imagines an aesthetic play in line with Schiller's, but with a pointedly social cast. As Hawthorne states of artists, "In every other clime, they are isolated strangers; in this Land of Art, they are free citizens" (118). In a chapter tellingly titled "An Aesthetic Company," when artists gather, "a cheerful and airy gossip began to be heard. The atmosphere ceased to be precisely that of common life; a faint, mellow tinge, such as we see in pictures, mingled itself with the lamplight" (122). In the midst of such social gatherings, Hawthorne continues, "the imagination is not debarred from lending its assistance, even while we have the reality before our eyes, and helping the weakness of human senses to do justice to so grand an object. It requires both faith and fancy." Combining faith and fancy, the two components of fantasy, this company becomes "conscious of a social warmth from each other's presence and contiguity" (118), an "aesthetic company" that is ideal and embodied, proximate and fantastic.

The intimacy of these artists, importantly, does not rely on sameness of outlook, longevity of commitment, or reciprocal knowledge. Not bound even by "any large stock of mutual affection," this group partakes of "jealousies and petty animosities" (118) as much as anything. Such differences and contestations are essential to aesthetic intimacy. What Hawthorne says of aesthetically inviting artworks—that their charm "lay partly in their very imperfection; for this is suggestive, and sets the imagination at work; whereas, the finished picture, if a good one, leaves the spectator nothing to do, and, if bad, confuses, stupefies, disenchants, and disheartens him" (123)—is equally true of intimacies, which rest as much on fantasy as on realism, on obscurity as on revelation. The autonomous alterity of "others" may be, finally, their keenest appeal.

In these terms, the ideal artist and friend in the romance is neither Hilda nor Miriam but the sculptor Kenyon, who articulates principles of aesthetic intimacy closest to Schiller's. Kenyon first discovers his aesthetics, appropriately, when he attempts to sculpt his friend, Donatello, but encounters frustrating difficulty, not in "hitting the likeness," but in making "this genial and kindly type of countenance the index of the mind within" (244). "So evanescent a show of character" demands that Kenyon reach "beyond his consciousness" (245). Kenyon must move beyond Hilda's faith in form and Miriam's reliance on consciousness to something more interactive, the play of subjectivity and materiality that generates the middle ground of aesthetic imagination. "There is a singular effect, oftentimes," Hawthorne writes of Kenyon's aesthetic process, "when out of the midst of engrossing thought and deep absorption, we suddenly look up and catch a glimpse of external objects. We seem, at such moments, to look farther and deeper into them, than by any premeditated observation; it is as if they met our eyes alive; and with all their hidden meaning on the surface, but grew again inanimate and inscrutable the instant that they became aware of our glances" (293). Meaning shifts, in Kenyon's aesthetic, from the object's surface to the viewer's imagination ("There is always the necessity of helping out the painter's art with your own resources of sensibility and imagination," Hawthorne writes, to the extent that "you will be apt to fancy that the loftier merits of the picture were of your own dreaming, not of his creating" [303]), without surrendering the power of the object to *transform* the viewer by inviting a more fantastic ordering of experience. This process, in which the object becomes more fantastic than its material form, yet retains a transformative solidity that forbids full possession and transforms the viewer's consciousness, becomes most strikingly evident when Kenyon stumbles upon a half-buried statue. The "magical" (381) effect of the discovery diverts Kenyon from his obsessive search for the vanished Hilda without enabling the cathexis of possessive desire onto the statue's always half-obscured female figure.

Consciousness without full comprehension, revelation that turns out to be (partial) projection, the mixture of materiality and invention: these are the elements of romantic aesthetics that also enable a nonpossessive, non-judgmental, and mutually transformative intimacy. Just as Kenyon's aesthetics combine Hilda's formalism with Miriam's hypersubjectivity, so his ethics combines Hilda's rigid categories of right and wrong with Miriam's mitigating emotionalism. He tells Hilda, "'you do not know (for you could never learn it from your own heart, which is all purity and rectitude) what a mixture of good there may be in things evil; and how the greatest criminal, if you look at his conduct from his own point of view, or from any side-point, may seem not so unquestionably guilty'" (346). Translating objective moral categories into negotiated social contracts, he warns Hilda, "'when a human being has chosen a friend out of all the world, it is only some faithlessness between themselves, rendering true intercourse impossible, that can justify either friend in severing the bond'" (187). Hilda seems to learn this lesson, albeit too late, musing, "'Methinks, it is this that makes the Catholics so delight in the worship of saints; they can bring up all the little worldly wants and whims, the individualities and human weaknesses, not as things to be repented of, but to be humoured by the canonized humanity to which they pray'" (413).

Kenyon's lesson is ultimately aimed not at Hilda, but at the reader of *The Marble Faun*, however, as Hawthorne makes clear in his famously vexing postscript to the narrative, which seems to affirm his sculptor's views on both aesthetics and intimacy. Reporting his readers' dissatisfaction with the narrative holes left in *The Marble Faun* by its cryptic conclusion, Hawthorne confesses of the third-person narrator: "he was himself troubled with a curiosity similar to that which he has just deprecated on the part of his readers, and once took occasion to cross-examine his friends, Hilda and the sculptor, and to pry into several dark recesses of the story, with which they had heretofore imperfectly acquainted him" (418). His "friends," however, provide all the clarity "of a London fog," and Hawthorne is just as glad, for clarification is the death of imaginative intimacy, as he suggests by invoking, once again, his ideal reader, who "would not thank us for one of those minute elucidations, which are so tedious, and, after all, so unsatisfactory in clearing up the romantic mysteries of a story" (410). The "sagacity, by which he is distinguished," Hawthorne continues, "will long ago have taught him that any narrative of human action and adventure—whether we call it history or romance—is certain to be a fragile handiwork, more easily rent than mended. The actual experience of even the most ordinary life is full of events that never explain themselves, either as regards their origin or their tendency" (410). Such a gap invites collaborative invention, friendship's mutually transformative interpretations, the experiential truth of "actual experience." As Hilda learns too late, nobody "'ought to read poetry, or look at pictures or statues, who cannot find a great deal more in them than the poet or artist has expressed. Their highest merit is suggestiveness'" (342).

What's true of art is truer of intimacy. While Miriam and Hilda are torn apart by their inability to transform through mutual exchange, the friendship between Donatello and Kenyon changes both men, aesthetically and morally. By the novel's end, Donatello has become "seasoned" by sin and Kenyon has come to see the need for optimism (his final call to Hilda to guide him home). Again, same-sex intimacy—and the resemblance of the two men to Hawthorne and Melville is suggestive—leads from extreme self-containment or world-weariness to a middling position that allows for imagination (Donatello refuses to supply the "truth" of his mythic background among the fauns, while Kenyon, in the final "interview" with the author, helps him to keep things foggy). Intimacy is powerful because it is suggestive, gap ridden, incomplete. It is powerful because it makes beauty both interpretive and material (a collage-work of intimacy). It flourishes on the mysterious, the marvelous, the mythical—Schiller's ideal aesthetic realm was, not surprisingly, Greece—in defiance of the pedantic plausibilities of the actual.

The relationship of imaginative aesthetics to visionary intimacy was brought home to Hawthorne by his Gentle Reader, who was also, happily, an Exuberant Writer. In June 1851 Melville wrote to Hawthorne from nearby Pittsfield, "I am told, my fellow-man, that there is an aristocracy of the brain. Some men have boldly advocated and asserted it. Schiller seems to have done so, though I don't know much about him." Melville knew enough to suggest that Schiller might help generate "ruthless democracy," in which movement beyond the plausible, the conventional, and the actual is possible.[12]

Postscript: The Return of the Marble Faun

Over a hundred years after Hawthorne published his romance, the Marble Faun returned, this time in the modern-day centers of the counteractual, Hollywood and New York. In 1975 Albert and David Maysles released *Grey Gardens,* soon to become a cult classic. The documentary film examines the lives of Big Edith and Little Edie Bouvier Beale, the eccentric aunt and cousin of Jacqueline Kennedy Onassis, who lived in a dilapidated East Hampton manion. The documentary—and the 2006 musical adapted from it—depicts a surprisingly Hawthornesque intimate aesthetic. Although the two inhabitants of Grey Gardens bear a surface similarity—of musical ambition, of paternal disapproval, of domestic eccentricity, even of name—each maintains a fantasy life that allows her, despite constant and lifelong proximity, to assert periodic autonomy. As Little Edie's eccentric outfits comprising incongruous household items demonstrate, moreover, their intimate combinations of familiarity and strangeness draw from an aesthetic combination of materiality and fantasy that produces aesthetic responses no less startling than those produced by the two women's relationship. Grey

Gardens, in other words, is, in relation to its suprising intimations, a remarkably queer place of nearly impossible to define intimacies, of fantastic aesthetic creation, and of resistant counterculturalism (as Edie sings in the musical, East Hampton "is a mean, nasty Republican town!").

Its queerness became even more evident when the Marble Faun made one last appearance, this time in a taxi cab in Queens, New York.[13] When a cabbie asked a young filmmaker in his cab if she knew *Grey Gardens*, which she did, he informed her, "I'm the Marble Faun." A teenage runaway, Jerry Torre entered Grey Gardens one afternoon when, in response to his knock at the door, Little Edie answered and exclaimed, "Oh my God—the Marble Faun has arrived!" Torre became the Beales's caretaker, developing a particularly affectionate relationship with Big Edith (captured in the musical by the number "Jerry Likes My Corn"). Appreciating the mixure of the real and the fantastic Hawthorne placed at the heart of romance, as well as of the generously social intimations it enables, Torre claimed that the Beales "showed me a life where you could be yourself, explore, take chances." When not engaged repairing Grey Gardens or helping Big Edith mix cocktails, Torre was a regular at Manhattan's gay bars, especially the Anvil, where he danced on the bar in a jockstrap and where he escorted cousin Jackie when she asked him to take her clubbing. In 1977 he was voted Mr. Club Baths. After Big Edith died and Little Edie decamped from Grey Gardens to start a brief career as a cabaret performer and fashion designer, Torre, appropriately enough, opened an East Village art-moving company and, in a wonderful twist of fate, took up sculpting. Asked in 2006 about his plans for the future, he claimed, "I want to attend The Arts Students League, here in NY, to be taught the ins and outs of stone-carving." He bought a copy of *The Marble Faun* on Amazon.com but claimed never to have read it. If he had, he might have been startled by his own transformation from sculpture to artist and how closely the unpredictable and fantastic intimacy he created with the Beales reproduces Wildean aesthetic sociality. The cult following of both the documentary and musical suggests a continuing hunger for an aesthetics beyond the actual, which, as Hawthorne, Wilde, and the inmates of Grey Gardens all understood, romanticism is uniquely able to provide.

Notes

1. In "A 'Hive of Subtlety': Aesthetics and the End(s) of Cultural Studies," Russ Castronovo and I discuss the convention of opposing aesthetics and social

criticism. That tradition stems from Marx's claim in *The Eighteenth Brumaire* that performativity and poetics are counterrevolutionary to Roland Barthes's claim that "Revolution excludes myth" to Terry Eagleton's sustained analysis of how the major chords of aesthetic theory give voice to bourgeois ideology to Fredric Jameson's declaration that what looks like political engagement in aesthetics is only an "epistemological repression" that prevents sociality from coming into focus. Christopher Castiglia and Russ Castronovo, "A 'Hive of Subtlety': Aesthetics and the End(s) of Cultural Studies," *American Literature* 76, no. 3 (September 2004): 423–35. See Roland Barthes, *Mythologies*, trans. Annette Lavers (New York: Hill and Wang, 1972), 146; Terry Eagleton, *The Ideology of the Aesthetic* (Oxford: Blackwell, 1990); and Fredric Jameson, "Marx's Purloined Letter," *Ghostly Demarcations: A Symposium on Jacques Derrida's "Specters of Marx,"* ed. Michael Sprinker (London: Verso, 1993), 52–53.

2. Judith Butler, "The Force of Fantasy: Mapplethorpe, Feminism, and Discursive Excess," *The Judith Butler Reader*, ed. Sara Salih (Oxford: Blackwell, 1990), 183–203. The "real," for Butler, is "a set of exclusionary and constitutive principles which confer on a given indication the force of an ontological indicator" (186). For Butler, fantasy need not be "equated with what is not real, but rather with what is not *yet* real" or "what belongs to a different version of the real" (185). For a fuller discussion of the implications of Butler's argument for Romantic aesthetics, see my *Interior States: Institutional Consciousness and the Inner Life of Democracy in the Antebellum United States* (Durham, North Carolina: Duke University Press, 2008), 213–15.

3. Oscar Wilde, "The Decay of Lying," *Intentions* (London: Methuen, 1927), 4. Further page references will be given parenthetically in the text.

4. Michel Foucault, "Friendship as a Way of Life," in *Ethics: Subjectivity and Truth*, ed. Paul Rabinow, trans. Robert Hurley and others (New York: New Press, 1997), 136, 138.

5. For a fuller discussion of the relationship of queer intimacy to institutional intimacy, see my "Alienated Affections: Hawthorne and Melville's Trans-Intimate Relationship," in Jana L. Argersinger and Leland S. Person, eds., *Hawthorne and Melville: Writing a Relationship* (Athens: University of Georgia Press, 2008), 321–44.

6. Henry James, *Hawthorne* (New York: Cornell University Press, 1956), 105. Further page references will appear parenthetically in the body of the essay.

7. Nathaniel Hawthorne, *The Marble Faun; or, The Romance of Monte Beni* (New York: Modern Library, 2002), 215. Further page references will appear parenthetically in the text. Hawthorne imagined that in Italy the world "had been set afloat, as it were, for a moment," relieving his characters "of all customary responsibilities for what they thought and said" (12). For Hawthorne, Italy was

a "floating world," bringing forth what is most speculatively nonconforming in "the texture of all our lives" (4). Hawthorne draws on similar language to describe Italy as Wilde used to describe that other "floating world," Japan, which, according to Wilde, "was a pure invention" of and for Wilde's British readers.

8. Quoted in Sidney P. Moss, "Hawthorne and Melville: An Inquiry Into Their Art and the Mystery of Their Friendship," in James C. Wilson, ed., *The Hawthorne and Melville Friendship: An Annotated Bibliography, Biographical and Critical Essays, and Correspondence Between the Two* (Jefferson, NC: McFarland, 1991), 179. Further page references to exchanges between Hawthorne and Melville will be given parenthetically in the text and will refer to this collection.

9. Shaftesbury, Third Earl of (Anthony Ashley Cooper), *Characteristics of Men, Manners, Opinions, Times* (Cambridge: Cambridge University Press, 2000).

10. Francis Hutcheson, *An Inquiry Concerning Beauty, Order, Harmony, Design* (Whitefish, MO: Kessinger, 2003).

11. Friedrich Schiller, "Letters Upon the Aesthetic Education of Man," *Aesthetical and Philosophical Essays*, ed. Nathan Haskell Dole (Boston: Wyman-Fogg, 1902), 1–16. Further page references will be given parenthetically in the text.

12. Wilson, *The Hawthorne and Melville Friendship*, 234.

13. The facts of Jerry Torre's "return" and of his life at Grey Gardens come from Adam Green, "The Marble Faun," *New Yorker*, March 6, 2006, http://www.newyorker.com/archive/2006/03/06/060306ta_talk_green (accessed April 9, 2011).

[6]

Henry James, Constance Fenimore Woolson, and the Figure in the Carpet

DORRI BEAM

The troubled, even catastrophic, history of Constance Fenimore Woolson's and Henry James's literary and personal friendship has led a notable critical afterlife, epitomizing male homosexual panic in Eve Kosofsky Sedgwick's account and emblematizing James's egregious professional misogyny in numerous feminist accounts. Despite the odds, I want to propose that another history lies between James and Woolson in the less charted terrain of their fiction, and in so doing I wish to suggest the ways that the aesthetic domain opens onto and sometimes extends the terrain for social relations. While Woolson's first and best-known artist story, "Miss Grief," has become the touchstone for assessing her bitter sense of gendered exclusion from the literary field and the attentions of its strikingly James-like guardians, "Miss Grief" also inaugurates a dialogue with James that he reciprocates in his own portraits of artists, especially in his 1896 tale, "The Figure in the Carpet," a title he adapts from "Miss Grief." "The Figure in the Carpet" and "Miss Grief" are about literary relations, and they forge a literary relation. That is, in both theme and form the stories mediate and recast registers of literary relation—between authors, between readers and the text, and between the social and aesthetic domains.

Furthermore, "The Figure in the Carpet" gives us both an alternative record of James's recognition of Woolson and the opportunity to come to Woolson's curious story on new terms, terms that James helps *us* to recognize. *Recognition* is a term that resonates, within and between these stories, with sexual, social, and formal implications. Both tales feature the quest of an unnamed first-person narrator, a bachelor writer, who seeks to unlock a text of genius—Miss Grief's in Woolson and the great novelist Vereker's in James. But various ambitious strategies or narrow formalist presumptions on the part of the narrators are the object of derisive irony and propel the frequently overlooked comedy of the stories. Within the farce, however, lies a less lofty but more urgent desire that reading and interpretation be forms of generative mutual relation.

Woolson's historical legacy for much of the twentieth century has been to be remembered as the woman writer who pined for validation from Henry James, despite the acknowledged centrality of the friendship to both authors' lives. More recently, she figures importantly in Sedgwick's seminal essay "The Beast in the Closet" as the figure behind James's May Bartram who waited patiently for some acknowledgment of love or erotic intimacy from James but may have fathomed more than he about her victimization by homosexual panic.[1] Sedgwick corrects Leon Edel's profile of Woolson as merely a love-sick minor author for whom James couldn't have harbored serious regard, and burgeoning studies of Woolson reveal that she was as much of a critical success as James when she introduced herself to him in 1880, at the start of the "middle years" of his career.[2] Whatever feelings James may have harbored for or withheld from Woolson may never be known, as he burned his entire correspondence with her after her 1894 suicide. Certainly, the four letters from Woolson that escaped that fate reveal her frustration with James as an interlocutor, one who often failed to engage her critical responses to his writing (there is "no allusion to anything I have said," she exclaims after sending a detailed response to *The Portrait of a Lady*).[3] And though James included her as the only American author besides Emerson in his *Partial Portraits* (1888) of authors, the compliment was mixed, for he used the occasion to minoritize her writing as "feminine," "essentially conservative," and "private."[4] When he proposes that Woolson's writing speaks only for, to, or about women, James risks not recognizing the affinities I argue he does ultimately acknowledge, affinities formed across and through shifting, not static, differentials of gender and sexuality.[5]

"Miss Grief," which has by now been widely anthologized, often sets the tone for studies of Woolson's relation to James.[6] The story diverges from

Woolson's customary regionalist mode to offer instead an artist study set in Rome, where, in the same year, Woolson introduced herself to James. "Miss Grief" involves an odd, unpublished middle-aged woman seeking the critical opinion of a bachelor who is the darling of the literary establishment. While the story is often taken as a representation of Woolson's initial encounters with James, careful critics have warned that it was almost certainly written and submitted to *Harper's* before the authors' first meeting. As Anne E. Boyd rephrases the relation of story to event, "In 'Miss Grief' Woolson essentially sends Miss Crief [the character's actual pen name], a partial representative of herself, ahead to encounter the derision she anticipated she herself might also face for being forward and unconventional."[7]

The literary politics of recognition have had currency for our own recent recovery of women authors and the kind of critical attention we give them, and it has not gone unnoticed that such politics are the very theme of "Miss Grief." Briefly, the bachelor writer, an American, narrates the story of how the woman, also an American, repeatedly calls on him at his apartments in Rome to introduce herself. The narrator mishears the butler's pronunciation of her name, Miss Crief, as Miss Grief. Eventually he is home and out of boredom admits the woman. She has read every word of his writing and has chosen him to read and evaluate her own creative work. When she recites his best work in a way that illuminates the core of his meaning, he is compelled to agree to her request. He finds to his surprise that he is passionately enthusiastic about the "genius" of "Armor," a drama; at the same time, it seems riddled with error that he hopes to correct. One of the amusing surprises of the story comes as Miss Crief, whom he continues to call Miss Grief and who has seemed an utterly unresisting soul, flatly refuses to change her writing in any way. In vain, he tries to correct the work himself, but it is "like taking out one especial figure in a carpet": the work loses the elusive texture of her genius and becomes his.[8] He half-heartedly seeks a publisher for her work in its original form, but the publishers confirm his sense that the work is "unavailable for publication" (118). At the conclusion he learns that Miss Crief is dying, from actual starvation and a malaise that seems related to his long silence about the possible publication of her work. By the wasting woman's bed, he tells her, falsely, that he has procured a publisher for her drama and she dies contented. He never shows "Armor" to another person, instead planning to go to the grave with it himself.

"Miss Grief" like "The Figure in the Carpet" is a riddle and a wry ruse that fingers the knitting of the aesthetic and social domains. James' parodic treatment of textual approaches that reify and decontextualize the aesthetic, its form or content, highlight retroactively what may be an unexpected corresponding parody in Woolson. Feminist critics have offered important insight into the story, but, ultimately taking the story at face value as an earnest expression of female victimization by the literary market, they have failed to come to terms with Woolson's figure in the carpet. Linda Grasso claims that Woolson (and her contemporary, Mary Freeman) "decry the waste of the sacrificed female self; they underscore the deadly effects man-made institutions and aesthetic standards have had on the writing woman's sense of self and literary productivity."[9] These authors want the "revenge" gained by "telling the woman's story," she asserts.[10] However, "Miss Grief" does not really tell the woman's story; the bachelor writer does, and the reader must grapple with this filter. In an intriguing reading, Paul Crumbley suggests that Woolson connects "failed female health to the inadequate circulation of a print record that embodies the experiences of real women."[11] As Crumbley himself points out, however, we do not know enough about Miss Grief's texts (just as we know even less about James's Vereker's texts) to assess their content or manner: we don't know and can't assume that her print record, if published, would "embody the experiences of real women." Woolson is up to something far more complicated than a complaint about the injuries or the self-division the literary field inflicts on women writers. Though, as this story is indeed eager to point out, "print conventions constrain literary representation," it would be a mistake not to extend to Woolson's story some recent poststructuralist insights, which understand, to borrow Judith Butler's phrasing, that the scene of constraint is also the scene of improvisation.[12] Indeed, we might well ask, with the wondering narrator, what is the nature of Grief's "little pantomime. Comedy? Or was it tragedy?" (105).

Boyd seems right about Miss Crief's surrogacy as a character who will reconnoiter the territory James may have represented for Woolson and psychically test the waters or take the heat prior to Woolson's own arrival on the scene, but a critical sense of the nature of this relation remains to be articulated. Miss Crief is not exactly a representative of Woolson's self, but an impersonation of a type, the social persona that Woolson understands to be imposed on the woman artist. This is where the story gets, not earnest, but funny. Woolson, I believe, is camping up her woman artist. Her bachelor narrator fears the mysterious caller will be trying to sell him something: an intaglio because she knows his "fancy for oddities" (104) or, when he sees the flat box she carries, old lace. When she finally tells him it is a manuscript she wishes him to read, he exclaims to himself, "An authoress! This is worse than old lace" (107). It is a display of misogyny, to be sure, but we should not mistake Woolson's comedic tone here. In short, Woolson's intriguing story takes a form that seems a bit at odds with its apparent social thematics.

Indeed, there is something ludicrously hyperbolized about many of Woolson's portraits of women artists. Ettie of "The Street of the Hyacinth," for example, arrives in Rome as a young woman from the Midwest intent on becoming a visual artist; she has already subjected herself to the privation and sacrifice of which she learned by reading "the lives of all—almost all—artists"; she has removed to Rome and now is keen to take the next step in her self-fashioned artist's life.[13] So utterly literal and single-minded is she in her quest for artistic achievement that she fails to notice the subtleties of either social or artistic conventions. Her hair is severely styled in the last generation's do; she takes no hints from the narrator about her outrageous demands on his time. She is the tactless American innocent abroad, made garish by her unbounded artistic, rather than social, ambition. Similarly, Miss Grief—for really it is "Miss Grief," and not Miss Crief, we come to know through the narrator's perspective—is utterly in earnest, so earnest that she is unable to assume any kind of persona or surface effect. Her dress is always the same, nondescript and black, sometimes abjectly damp. She attempted to practice cigar smoking, she tells the narrator blankly, but was unsuccessful (suppressed sniggering from the narrator). She is thus not clearly legible as a gender invert, as has been argued by some who attempt to locate an identifiably lesbian subtext.[14] The shabbily clad foot that is exposed to the narrator's vision when she falls asleep while he reads her manuscripts seems to indicate that her character partakes more of a feminine grotesque—a vulnerable, graphic, unaestheticized female body.

In the passage that seems the grain of James's own interest in a "figure in the carpet," the narrator describes the form Miss Grief's aesthetic appreciation takes, which seems a significant component of the persona Woolson develops. Admiring her choice of scenes from his work, he "had always felt a wondering annoyance" that the public "had never noticed the higher purpose of this little shaft, aimed not at the balconies and lighted windows of society, but straight up toward the distant stars" (106). (James's celebrated author, Vereker, will disclose the existence of his own "little point," long unnoticed, to the eager critic-narrator.)[15] But the "riddle" here will not concern the little shaft, as in James's story, but the mystery of the form Miss Grief's genius as a reader and a writer takes. When Miss Grief arrives at the key passage,

> her very voice changed, and took, although always sweetly, the different tones required, while no point of meaning, however small, no breath of delicate emphasis which I had meant, but which the dull types could not give, escaped appreciative and full, almost overfull, recognition which startled me. For she had understood me—understood me almost better than I had understood myself. It seemed to me that while I had labored to interpret partially a psychological riddle, she, coming after, had comprehended its bearings better than I had, although confining herself strictly to my own words and emphasis.
>
> (106)

The figure of Grief's reading, rather than a figure of her text, is the focus.

While James' story maintains an eroticized (and facetious) emphasis on the reader's and critic's reading as "penetration," the term he repeats in his preface to the New York Edition, it would not be accurate to say that Miss Grief penetrates the narrator's meaning here. Rather, she inhabits and embodies his text—breathing his very emphases, inhabiting his words and their luminescent sense. Moreover, she is not reading from the text; she has internalized and is reciting it. It is perhaps because she so thoroughly embodies the text that she cannot also intellectualize or find words outside of it to describe it. She also recites her own work, refusing to "read" it to the narrator, who wishes to use reading to gain the distance and distinction necessary for critique. "I worked hard," the narrator exclaims: "the perspiration stood in beads upon my forehead as I struggled with her— what shall I call it—obstinacy? But it was not exactly obstinacy. She simply could not see the faults of her own work," he says (113). Sure enough, when he allows her to recite the story, the strong passages are stronger and the "faults, which seemed nothing to her, were made by her earnestness to seem nothing to me, at least for that moment" (113). Again we see that Woolson's women artists are inveterately "earnest": they are utterly devoid of a critical sense of themselves or their art.

The earnestness of the artists should not be confused with Woolson's own tone, which is as ironic as James's; however, critics have taken the story straight and labored to assign some inherent or natural expression of gender or sexuality to the form of Grief's genius. Grief's transcendence of textuality, the way she conveys an intelligence in the tones of her voice or in the appearance of her handwriting, tempts critics to identify her portrayal as an articulation of feminine difference, as, for instance, "an unrecorded, nonhierarchical, and thus feminine language."[16] Others have sought to attribute her excesses to "a lesbian imagination."[17] And yet it seems to me that Woolson's story does not buy the dichotomy—"the tensions," as Elaine Showalter assesses the story, "between male and female literary culture" or between a feminine and masculine imagination—it seems to pose.[18] Woolson is mocking, sometimes savagely, suppositions about the woman writer as naive, natural, and unselfconscious. If there is a personal retort to James, it may be to his assessment in the *Nation* in 1878 of a fellow regionalist, Julia Constance Fletcher, like Woolson known for her "scenery fiction" (as James calls it). Though he praised Fletcher's writing, James also found it "irremediably feminine."[19] When the narrator finds Grief's errors to be an essential quality of her work, the figure he cannot remove, Woolson sardonically takes irremediableness as the very essence of femininity. The mystification and excess of Grief's genius are parodic, and, as in "The Figure in the Carpet," mock certain textual approaches. Neither story accepts that an inherent textual essence is to be divined and isolated by critics within or outside of the stories. Woolson's hyperbole in drawing the earnestness and "originality" of Miss Grief actually works to denaturalize those concepts because parody, as a form of copying, is the process of exposing the natural and the original as imitable and transferable, not inherent.

The story is thus not a self-expression of Woolson's own professional experience, and it is not a plausible tableau of her anticipated encounter with James. Instead, the role Grief plays is one that allows Woolson to allegorize and expose the gendered relations of power she experiences. But "Miss Grief" suggests that the ways by which Woolson understood her gender are mediated by her professional role, her status as a woman author. Thus we cannot simply extrapolate from taxonomies of femininity in the sociohistorical field. In Woolson's text the woman writer is not just a theme; she takes a form in dynamic relation to the content Woolson is working out, a form that troubles literary and social convention and opens up the whole parodic dimension of the text. We cannot understand Woolson's treatment of gender and literature without also recognizing and attending to the comedic tone, the parodic treatment, and the narrative voice to understand how the content is being shaped and how we are to interact with it. Using the insights of theories of camp and drag, we might see that, through the figure of Miss Grief, Woolson explores a sense of the unreality and illegibility of a woman who writes, and it is through this figure, I argue, that she deterritorializes sexual and social norms.[20] She uses this figure to wedge open a site of nonheteronormative gender complexity.

To recognize Woolson's parody is to open one's self to its implications. Frank Kermode suggests that one step toward the greater analytic appreciation James seems to call for in "The Figure in the Carpet" is to understand that Vereker's secret, "the thing for the critic to find," is "not the subject, but the treatment," and indeed attention to the interplay of form and content in Woolson's story is essential to its interpretation.[21] But both stories' internal emphases on readers rather than texts help us to see that the figure in the carpet is not an autonomous formal entity and "a thing to find" but a function of reading, an interdependence of text and reader. Woolson in particular helps us to see the importance of reading as an encounter by her story's focus on the dynamic of interaction between reader and writer, but such a dynamic is ultimately the basis for James's figure in the carpet as well.

Woolson does give us an unexpectedly concrete suggestion about a more identifiable figure in the carpet, though commentators have overlooked it. Woolson has the narrator descend from his impressionistic evaluations of Miss Grief's work to furnish us with a strikingly detailed account of the plot of her prose story: "but here was the trouble: through the whole narrative moved another character, a physician of tender heart and exquisite mercy, who practiced murder as a fine art, and was regarded (by the author) as a second Messiah! This was monstrous." Will Miss Grief "cut him out"? "Certainly not," she replies (116). After the story is rejected because the publisher also cannot stand the doctor, the narrator secretly tries to "improve" the story himself, but "that apparently gentle 'doctor' would not out: he was so closely interwoven with every part of the tale that to take him out was like taking out one especial figure in a carpet that is impossible unless you unravel the whole" (118–19).

As the story concludes, a strange overlap between the egregious doctor and the narrator emerges to complicate the identified figure in the carpet. The narrator acts the heroic doctor to Grief's text: he "amended, altered, left out, put in, pieced, condensed, lengthened" (118). He labors to "'improve' Miss Grief"; he attempts to "cut" out the errors, but his surgery fails (119, 116). He avoids Grief until Aunt Martha more or less accuses him of murder as a fine art: "And as to who has racked and stabbed her, I say you, *you*—YOU literary men!" (119–20). He returns to Grief's apartment to buy her wine and "tell her—a romance invented for the occasion," and she dies contented that the drama will be published, according to his fabricated account (121). She has asked him to be her executor and to bury her other unpublished works with her. Like the doctor, then, he assists her death—both literally and literarily. And Woolson overlays the scene with suggestions that the wine-wielding narrator is a false messiah, as Miss Grief plays the worshipful, intellectual Mary to her aunt's housekeeping, world-weary Martha. Woolson seems to raise the possibility that the figure in the carpet has to do with the narrator himself. Take him out and the fabric of Miss Grief's text is lost.

On this view, it is not that the narrator "ruins Miss Crief's chance of public recognition and literary success."[22] Something is built into the system of literary production that determines the dialectical position these two characters occupy. The story seems to posit familiar dichotomies (with gender wittily reversed) between genius and conventionality, poles embodied by the main characters. The distance Woolson creates between Miss Grief and convention is, again, not borne out of her earnest or essential sense of women's greater genius but out of her perception of the position women occupy in the literary field. To be a genius is to be set apart, to escape definition, but Woolson exaggerates this distance and correlates it to a segregation of women writers that is both literary and social. Woolson overlaps Grief's ingenious lack of conventionality with her gendered lack of entry into the inner circle of literary enterprise and access to "recognition."

Certainly the bachelor is an essential figure in the text *we* read. It is in the dissonance between the debonair bachelor narrators and the unwitting gall of the woman artist that much of Woolson's humor resides. Her women artists assume that they can enter the literary market and the lives of its guardians without fanfare, on the basis of the work in the case of Miss Grief, and simply by following the plan in the case of Ettie. They assume the right simply to "be" artists. Their guilelessness is made particularly vivid through the perspective of the polished narrators who themselves are startled out of convention and sometimes out of their patronizing attitudes by the encounter. We understand something the narrators do not about the hilarity of the women's earnestness and what it exposes not just about the narrators' contrasting insincerity but also about the mutual constitution of their roles.

One striking structural similarity James's "The Figure in the Carpet" bears to "Miss Grief" is that the narrator never understands he too is already part of the figure in the carpet he seeks. Evoking one of Vereker's analogues for the figure in the carpet, Jonathan Auerbach has argued, "Like a string of pearls linked together by an invisible thread," the narrator, "together with his fellow detectives, make up the very configuration they would solve. The riddle involves social relations."[23] The narrator reductively seeks a single key, an element of composition, without realizing, as Auerbach argues, that "James' riddle is to be lived, not solved, its clues experienced, not communicated."[24] Rather than suggesting that "experience" is something to be brought to the text, I would qualify Auerbach's emphasis to suggest that, read together, the stories emphasize the "social relations" and the "experience" of a specific activity: reading. Both narrators misrecognize their role as readers. Woolson's narrator wishes not so much to find the figure in the carpet as to "fix" and overcome it, but it is only a version of the same kind of criticism or reading that James's narrator vainly strives to perform. James's narrator seeks to penetrate the text and access the secret of its essence. But form is not autonomous, intrinsic, and organic, a thing apart waiting for James's narrator to discover it, and it is not a container into which Woolson's narrator might pour Miss Grief or her texts. Rather, to use an insight of feminist critic Ellen Rooney, to which I will return, form is both the enabling condition and the product of reading.[25] The text has a form, but it is only viable, it only takes shape, via a reader's apprehension and involvement with it. The narrators, however, misrecognize their roles and cannot see themselves. They can see in the text neither their projections onto it nor their unwitting involvement in its reading. As in James, the farce in "Miss Grief" happens at the expense of the reader who cannot discriminate between the narrator's approach to a text and a more viable one. Such near misses lead to much of the sexual comedy both stories proffer when the narrators fail to gauge the extent of their involvement.

Ultimately, the narrator takes Miss Grief's earnestness earnestly and to his great exasperation. It is worth tracking backward to one of the story's antecedents to understand the features of the narrator's encounter with Grief, especially her blank obtuseness and failure to yield despite all of his ostensibly charitable perseverance, for the encounter can be productively compared to that in Herman Melville's "Bartleby, the Scrivener." As in "Bartleby" the bachelor narrator tells the story of the arrival and ultimately the betrayal of a mysterious being, vaguely Christ-like.[26] As with "Bartleby," the reader is treated to a story about the advent of something new and puzzling in the mundane, conventional world of business-as-usual. The narrator, meanwhile, must figure out how to relate to the unfamiliar and nonnormative. In "Bartleby" the narrator functions as a kind of straight man who keeps coming back, asking the irrational Bartleby to be rational. This is the case with "Miss Grief" as well; the narrator keeps returning to the utterly earnest writer, asking her to be, in effect, self-critical, canny, and conventional—to pitch and alter her writing for the literary market. The comedy turns on the narrators' misrecognition of a process of encounter that calls preconceived "norms" into question.

We might say that the "straight man" cannot see what is happening, but the queerness of the figure brings him out, as it were, to keep repeating the encounter. This dynamic is observable in "The Figure in the Carpet" as well: Eric Savoy has argued much the same of a "circuit of refusal and renewed perseveration" undergone by James's narrator in his pursuit of the enigmatic textual figure and explicitly places the "embarrassments" of these encounters under the sign of homosexual panic and the closet.[27] As my discussion already suggests, in both "Miss Grief" and "The Figure in the Carpet" a system of sometimes oblique double entendre charges the terms of intimacy and personal relation in ways that task and complexify these as metaphors for reading and interpretation.

As many commentators on James have observed, marriage provides a kind of veiled allegory for the critical act of reading or interpretation. But when the narrator thinks he can get at the secret he seeks by marrying Gwendolyn, his strategy highlights what Frank Kermode humorously identifies as a mistaken kind of penetration the narrator presumes to bring to the text. On the other hand, Gwendolyn's and rival critic Corvick's apparent possession of the secret is made to seem enigmatically related to the event of their engagement and marriage. Gwendolyn asserts that the secret is not something to be told, it is her "life," and Kermode finds a more viable basis for critical perspective here—it is "a quality pervading the life of the subject, like marriage."[28]

It cannot be said, however, that the bachelor narrator's own "engagement" with the figure in the carpet is devoid of "life" or human dimension, for it takes shape in his encounters with the author Vereker. These encounters, registered in "unnarrated dialogue, dramatic moments when significance is construed jointly," can be read in terms of "James' concept of union."[29] In what Auerbach dubs the "groping process of give-and-take," the exchange of "metaphors for the artist's life and passion" (the "little point" [364], "a complex figure in a Persian carpet" [374], "the very string . . . that my pearls are strung on" [374]), the secret that precipitates the quest "assumes life" in the dialogue between Vereker and the narrator.[30] As Savoy points out in the only essay to explicitly address the homoerotic basis of the narrator's "engagement" with Vereker, these metaphors verge on the campy as they dance around the homoerotic relation the narrator cannot acknowledge. It is not that the narrator overlooks the figure in the carpet, it is that he has failed to recognize his constitutive involvement with it, which may be a function not only of his critical blindness but of the social regime that stigmatizes such recognition.

James' story allows us to discern Woolson's own network of pun and innuendo, which curiously interweaves sexual with literary interaction. Woolson's story has been included in Susan Koppelman's excellent collection of "lesbian stories," but I would argue that the basis for a queer reading lies in Woolson's queering of categories rather than in a categorizable "lesbian" subtext. Woolson works to queer the typical intercourse between woman writer and male critic and gatekeeper. In fact it is the confusion between literary and sexual relations in the treatment of women authors that Woolson seems particularly interested in critiquing. In her own string of puns, running through the text, Woolson probes the confusion the author-as-woman creates in the codes and mores of the literary profession, a confusion that ultimately exposes and troubles its normative heterosexism. The narrator, for example, does not know whether to woo her, filiate himself to her, or critique her; he is perpetually confused in his address to her. Woolson plays on the literary standards the narrator represents to show how Miss Grief's purported lack of "convention" is both a literary characteristic and a social effect her presence generates.

When he first meets Grief again after reading her work, the narrator considers that he "ought to go do down on [his] knees before her and entreat her to take her proper place of supremacy" as a towering genius (111). But he recoils as he suddenly associates such an act of deference to a woman with a marriage proposal ("one does not go down on one's knees, combustively, as it were, before a woman over fifty" [111]), and here her sexual maturity makes her no more an appropriate object of such attention than her femininity makes her a proper object of professional deference. Woolson thus plays on contexts of "reception" for Miss Grief, revealing indeed how social relations, rather than literary qualities, determine them. To some extent, Grief's presence unmans the narrator: "I did not quite know what to do, but, putting myself in her place, I decided to praise the drama; and praise it I did. I do not know when I have used so many adjectives," he reflects (111). "Putting [him]self in her place" unleashes what he calls a "verbal Niagara" that would seem more associated with feminine fluidity and talk (111). He claims to assert himself here as "an anti-hysteric" (111) against her tears, but his own floods seem more to reveal his inability to relocate himself in a social identity that was so smugly secure prior to Grief's presence in his bachelor-parlor. The fluidity of a space that is both dining room and library, in which the bachelor enjoys an ease of movement between domestic and professional occupation, is queered by Grief, who has already, so the narrator avers, "sacrificed her womanly claims by her persistent attacks upon my door" (104). Miss Grief's presence, the woman in the bachelor's digs, uncomfortably exposes the sexual indeterminacies in the bachelor's status and the performativity of his own masculine and heterosexual presumptions.

The narrator's confused overtures continue to determine the character of his intercourse with Grief, and, as James also must have appreciated, Woolson significantly overlaps sexual and readerly relations. The "romance" (as he calls his tale about the publication of her drama), wine, and flowers he shares with her at her sickbed suggest that he continues to confuse the nature of his obligation to her. (One wonders, in a story where near misses provide salient confusions [Crief/Grief, Aaronna/Erroneous] whether the title of her drama, "Armor," might also provide a little fun when, upon perusing the title page, the narrator muses, "Grief certainly needs armor" (109). Is the near-homonym *amour* hovering, to feed the chain of suggestions about the narrator's attitude toward her?) But Grief, as the narrator repeats, remains "unavailable": by emphasizing both this term and the term *unaccepted* and attaching them to Grief's person rather than her texts in the closing epithet, "my poor, dead, 'unavailable,' unaccepted 'Miss Grief,'" the narrator unwittingly elaborates the conceit (123). The narrator's misrecognition of his relation to Grief, his continued adherence to the chivalric rituals of courtship in an overrecognition of her sex and an underrecognition of her vocation, is foiled by her intractable lack of fit into his codes and mores—her irremediableness. When he admits that he cannot "'improve' Miss Grief" (119), it completes this chain of double entendre: the nature of their literary intercourse, despite the narrator's heterosexist presuppositions, has indeed been queered by its failure to be fruitful and multiply Miss Grief's texts through publication. Nor has their relation succeeded in attaching her to a social or literary convention.

And yet perhaps the strange bond they achieve, farcical as it is, embodies some kind of qualified redemption—or rather the mutual recognition so elusive in the world the text delineates. To return briefly to the analogy with "Bartleby," some kind of bond is already in place, it is what the narrator saw but didn't see in the figure in the carpet. Aunt Martha suggests that "literary men" like the narrator are "vampires"—that they "take [Grief's] ideas and fatten on them," but the obverse relation obtains when he fills her with the publishing "romance" he invents and the wine of his praise

(120). She claims to finally know what it is "to be fully happy. . . . Yes, I am happy" (121). She says to him, "You had success—but I had the greater power. Tell me: did I not have it?" "Yes, Aaronna," he responds, and she states with contentment, "It is all in the past now. But I am satisfied" (122). The narrator recognizes her work or shares his own, the romance invented for the occasion, and the gesture sustains and satisfies her. She is "full" and "satisfied," not drained. It is perhaps a return on "the appreciative and full, almost overfull, recognition" of his work she had given him in their first meeting (106). Recognition, attention, notice: these terms subtly lace their encounters and trigger moments of communion and reciprocity. Grief may even be aware of or unconcerned with the falsity of his final "romance," for she herself inaugurates it: "Tell me," she prompts for the first of three times in the final scene, "I *know* you have good news [of the drama]" (120). The "romance" is not coauthored exactly, but mutually generated here, shaped by the needs of the listener who inaugurates its telling. A figure for reading that is echoed in James's account of the exchange of metaphors between novelist and critic, the "romance" does not clearly distinguish what is the author's and what is the reader's share, and their mutual involvement generates new versions of intimacy. And this "romance" occurs outside the heteronormative frame in which the narrator continues to cast their relation. Comically, they fill and suffuse each other—the narrator with the wine of his praise or his romance and Miss Grief with the suffusing intelligence of her recitation—in a relation that seems nonnormative because physiologically interchangeable and mutual.

What James's story responds to and allows us to fathom in Woolson's is the irony of a confusion of the sexual and the textual that is both risible and generative. Both stories call for literary reading and interpretation to be more capacious and dynamic, but maintain that such engagement has a significant social dimension, making sexual and textual desires ineluctably entwined. While the narrators' confusion between the two types of intercourse remains both ludicrous and tragic, within the textual frisson taking place in the narrators' blind spots, the discursive confusions exfoliate more capacious forms of social and sexual intercourse and more capacious forms of reading. Our full recognition of one is connected to the other, just as the narrators' misrecognition of the terms of both their sexual and literary engagement are also linked.

A connection unrecognized, disavowed, or undernourished has been the refrain of studies of James and Woolson. Either James fails to recognize, at least until after her death, that his homosexual panic stunts their intimacy and diminishes both lives, in Sedgwick's reading, or James fails to acknowledge Woolson's literary achievement or even entertain her critical responses in his writing about and to her. My aim is not to refute either of these perspectives. Woolson's story, and James's too, has already delineated for us the deeply vexed terrain of gender, sexuality, and literary endeavor on which their relationship would have proceeded. But I wish to suggest that through "The Figure in the Carpet," James does allude to something Woolson has said after all. In doing so, he acknowledges Woolson's work— her literary value, her formal performance, and the social terrain her story traverses and alters. He recognizes, and allows us to recognize, her parody and her poses and the demands they make on the reader; indeed, he allows us to see how her treatment of the subject, the form her story takes, makes a challenging appeal to the reader that is in fact the point. James's recognition of Woolson is neither closeted nor panicked. Nor does he play the master; instead, in "The Figure in the Carpet," he has allowed Woolson's story to recognize him, and his response meets her on the terrain of the gender and sexual complexities she has opened up.

If, through gender parody like Woolson's, we "grasp one of the mechanisms by which reality is reproduced and altered in the course of that reproduction," James allows us to see how "reading" is a form of recognizing that performance, where recognition brings one into relation with the possibilities that unfold.[31] By recognition, I mean something more provisional and less totalizing than identification with or of another, or the imposition of normative categorical legibility, though these are risks. Judith Butler's *Undoing Gender* asserts that the act of recognition is a way of doing justice, a gesture of inclusion that extends "reality" and the norm. It is a form of acknowledgment and openness to the other that enables a "life," a life open to gender complexity and unprescribed intimacies. For James and Woolson, the aesthetic medium allows for a play of recognition, recognition of sexualities and between gendered positions that were undoubtedly more intractable in person.

Given the dreary chronicles of his reception of women writers, it is perhaps embarrassing to lean on James for his insights, and it is always a possibility that James didn't see the figure in the carpet, the form of his engagement with Woolson, in his own "The Figure in the Carpet." We do well, then, to consider the parables of reading these stories offer and ask how we might better prepare ourselves to recognize the kind of challenges Woolson's story represents to our own ways of reading and mechanisms for literary inclusion and political critique. In a recent essay that calls on political criticism to examine its reliance on social themes or theoretical motifs and to reinvest in form, Ellen Rooney describes her interest in form in a way that resonates with "the figure in the carpet" in the stories by James and Woolson. Rooney insists that form is not the thing that is the purported delight of conservative defenders of literary value and the canon who exclude attention to social content or historical context. Form is, for Rooney, as I believe the figure in the carpet is for James and Woolson, a figure not for an isolatable textual feature but for reading itself; it is both the enabling condition and the product of reading. In the "most fundamental sense," then, form "is not 'given.'" It "emerges under pressure of a reading."[32] In "Miss Grief" Woolson does not simply articulate the experiences of the woman writer, she subjects that category to an analytic and a parodic form that troubles rather than reflects other "given" forms of gender and literary convention. Woolson's figure of the woman writer involves us in a dynamic that reinvents the grounds for our recognition of her, as it did for James.

Notes

1. Eve Kosofsky Sedgwick, "The Beast in the Closet: James and the Writing of Homosexual Panic," in *Epistemology of the Closet* (Berkeley: University of California Press, 2008 [1990]), 213–52.

2. Leon Edel, *Henry James: The Middle Years: 1882–1895* (Philadelphia: Lippincott, 1962). Studies treating the Woolson-James relationship include Sharon Dean, "Constance Fenimore Woolson and Henry James: The Literary Relationship," *Massachusetts Studies in English* 7, no. 3 (1980): 1–9; Cheryl B. Torsney, "The Traditions of Gender: Constance Fenimore Woolson and Henry James," in Shirley Marchalonis, ed., *Patrons and Protégées: Gender, Friendship, and Writing in Nineteenth-Century America* (New Brunswick, NJ: Rutgers University Press, 1988), 161–83; Victoria Coulson, "Teacups and Love Letters: Constance Fenimore Woolson and Henry James," *Henry James Review* 26, no. 1 (2005): 82–98; Lyndall Gordon, *A Private Life of Henry James: Two Women and His Art* (New York: Norton, 1998); Anne E. Boyd, "Anticipating James, Anticipating Grief: Constance Fenimore Woolson's 'Miss Grief,'" in Victoria Brehm, ed., *Constance Fenimore Woolson's Nineteenth Century: Essays* (Detroit: Wayne State University Press, 2001), 191–206.

3. Letter from Woolson to James, August 30, 1882, in *The Letters of Henry James*, ed. Leon Edel (Cambridge: Belknap, 1974–80), 3:542. Boyd, "Anticipating

James," Coulson, "Teacups," and Gordon, *A Private Life,* usefully analyze Woolson's correspondence.

4. Henry James, "Miss Woolson," in *Partial Portraits* (New York: Haskell House, 1968 [1888]), 178–79. Lyndall Gordon calls the portrait "a calculated betrayal; it carried an armoury of stings in its velvet glove" (*A Private Life,* 213). Coulson, in "Teacups," concurs and argues that in "turning the discretion of Woolson's prose against itself" and feminizing it, James disingenuously associates a literary style he himself employed with a perceived inherent femininity (93).

5. I use the term *minoritize* as cognate with Sedgwick's, in *Epistemology of the Closet,* where she refers to the "minoritizing view" of those who understand homosexuality as relevant to only a small segment of the population (1). She reveals how minoritizing views paradoxically coexist with "universalizing views" to create our contemporary inchoate understanding of homosexuality as simultaneously an issue for a few and an issue of "determinative importance in the lives of people across the spectrum of sexualities" (1). We might say James risks "feminine panic" when he proposes that Woolson's subjects and techniques have nothing to do with his own artistic expression, with masculine identities, or with his own treatment of gender and sexuality. My essay implicitly maintains that such a limited view of homosexuality, as constitutive of the lives and work of only a distinct community, would diminish both James's and Woolson's stories. Of course, it also draws on a strategically minoritizing view by focusing on Woolson's negotiations with the category of the woman writer and both writers' engagement with queer sexualities.

6. Notably, in Victoria Brehm and Sharon L. Dean, eds., *Constance Fenimore Woolson: Selected Stories and Travel Narratives* (Knoxville: University of Tennessee Press, 2004); Susan Koppelman, ed., *Two Friends and Other Nineteenth-Century Lesbian Stories by American Women Writers* (New York: Meridian, 1994); Joan Myers Weimar, ed., *Women Artists, Women Exiles: "Miss Grief" and Other Stories* (New Brunswick, NJ: Rutgers University Press, 1988). *The Heath Anthology of American Literature* and *The Norton Anthology of American Literature* include "Miss Grief."

7. Boyd, "Anticipating James," 200.

8. Constance Fenimore Woolson, "Miss Grief," in Koppelman, *Two Friends,* 118–19. All further page references are to this edition and will be given parenthetically within the text.

9. Linda Grasso, "'Thwarted Life, Mighty Hunger, Unfinished Work': The Legacy of Nineteenth-Century Women Writing in America," *ATQ* 8, no. 2 (June 1994): 97–118, quot. 99.

10. Ibid., 99.

11. Paul Crumbley, "Haunting the House of Print: The Circulation of Dis-embodied Texts in 'Collected by a Valetudinarian' and 'Miss Grief'" in Robert McClure Smith and Ellen Weinauer, eds., *American Culture, Canons, and the Case of Elizabeth Stoddard* (Tuscaloosa: University Press of Alabama, 2003), 83–104, quot. 83.

12. Ibid., 84. I refer to Judith Butler's work in *Undoing Gender* (New York: Routledge, 2004) as well as to her earlier *Gender Trouble: Feminism and the Subversion of Identity* (New York: Routledge, 1990).

13. Constance Fenimore Woolson, "The Street of the Hyacinth," in Weimer, ed., *Women Artists, Women Exiles*, 174.

14. See Kristin M. Comment, "Lesbian 'Impossibilities' of Miss Grief's 'Armor'," in Brehm, *Constance Fenimore Woolson's Nineteenth Century*, 207–24.

15. Henry James, "The Figure in the Carpet," in *The Figure in the Carpet and Other Stories* (New York: Penguin, 1986), 355–400, quot. 364.

16. Cheryl B. Torsney, *Constance Fenimore Woolson: The Grief of Artistry* (Athens: University of Georgia Press, 1989), 113.

17. Koppelman, *Two Friends*, 102.

18. Elaine Showalter, "Introduction," in Elaine Showalter, ed., *Scribbling Women: Short Stories by Nineteenth-Century American Women* (New Brunswick, NJ: Rutgers University Press, 1997), xxxvi.

19. Woolson seems interested in irremediableness as a suggested quality of the feminine, rather than in its specific content. The review is generally positive but regrets the "slightness of subject" and "an unbusiness-like way of telling the story." Henry James, review of Fletcher's *Mirage*, in Leon Edel, ed., *Literary Criticism: Essays on Literature, American Writers, English Writers* (New York: Library of America, 1984), 275. For a discussion of Woolson's "scenery fiction," see Katherine Swett, "Corrine Silenced: Improper Places in the Narra-tive Form of Constance Fenimore Woolson's *East Angels*" in Brehm, *Constance Fenimore Woolson's Nineteenth Century*, 161–71.

20. See especially David Bergman, ed., *Camp Grounds: Style and Homo-sexuality* (Amherst: University of Massachusetts Press, 1993); Esther Newton, *Mother Camp: Female Impersonators in America* (Chicago: University of Chicago Press, 1979), and Butler, *Gender Trouble*, 163ff.

21. James, "The Figure in the Carpet," 366. Frank Kermode, "Introduction," in James, *The Figure in the Carpet*, 28.

22. Grasso,"'Thwarted Life,'" 97.

23. Jonathan Auerbach, *The Romance of Failure: First Person Fictions of Poe, Hawthorne, and James* (New York: Oxford University Press, 1989), 150.

24. Ibid.

25. Ellen Rooney, "Form and Contentment," *MLQ: Modern Language Quar-terly* 61, no. 1 (2000): 17–40.

26. Herman Melville, "Bartleby, The Scrivener," in *The Piazza Tales and Other Prose Pieces, 1839–1860*, ed. Harrison Hayford, Alma A. MacDougall, and G. Thomas Tanselle (Evanston: Northwestern University Press and the Newberry Library, 1987), 13–45. See Grasso, "'Thwarted Life,'" and Torsney, *Constance Fenimore Woolson*, for readings of the Christological reference in "Miss Grief."

27. Eric Savoy, "Embarrassments: Figure in the Closet," *Henry James Review* 20, no. 3 (1999): 227-36 quot. 230.

28. Kermode, "Introduction," 28.

29. Auerbach, *The Romance of Failure*, 157.

30. Ibid.; James, "The Figure in the Carpet," 364, 374.

31. Butler, *Undoing Gender*, 218.

32. Rooney, "Form and Contentment," 37.

[7]
Sexuality's Aesthetic Dimension

Kant and the Autobiography of an Androgyne

CHRISTOPHER LOOBY

"I happen to be an aesthete," averred the self-described sexual invert or "fairie" who wrote under the pseudonym Earl Lind, in his incomparable *Autobiography of an Androgyne* (1918).[1] But, despite the rhetoric of mere accident, there appears to be a good deal more than a coincidental relationship between the aesthetic proclivities and the sexual tastes of the pseudonymous author to whom I will henceforth refer, in deference to his own stated preference, as "Pussie."[2] Pussie tells us early on in his tale that, in the provincial community where he spent his early years, he "was probably more a prey to sensual imaginations than any other boy" (47). This is in fact how he thinks of what we might (somewhat anachronistically) call his "sexuality" or what he referred to as his style of "sensual practices" (75): it is a matter of "sensual imaginations," a specific configuration of sensuality, guided and driven by a particularly vivid imagination—which makes it, in effect, a variety of aesthetic experience. Later theorists might distinguish, say, mere "aesthetic" appreciation of the beauty of a male body from sexual desire for that body. Pussie couldn't tell the difference. Erotic desire and aesthetic admiration were one. He had a very specific—nearly exclusive—taste for performing fellatio on handsome rough young (preferably Irish or

Italian) men of the working classes, and he understood this to be an aesthetic preference, a desirable encounter with a supremely beautiful object.

The identification of erotic desire with aesthetic attraction only seems strained or counterintuitive to those of us born after the historical invention of sexuality as a distinct category of experience and personhood; since that time the supposed verity of sexuality's existence as a separate and integral aspect of ourselves has been widely inculcated, and the distinction between erotic interest and aesthetic admiration solidified, but the alliance or identification of sexual and aesthetic interests was common sense in the West for many centuries. Since the modern invention of the categories of homosexual and heterosexual it has been in the interest of advocates of heterosexual normativity to claim that (innocent) aesthetic appreciation of male beauty can be confidently distinguished from (guilty) sexual attraction to that beauty. But under an earlier dispensation, before "homosexuals" and "heterosexuals" were routinely sorted out, there was relatively little reason to distinguish between one kind of sensory receptivity and another. And there was plenty of reason, in fact, for advocates of desensualizing moral regimes (like that of the small-town Connecticut bourgeois Protestant environment in which Pussie was raised) to treat all sensual pleasures as deeply connected to one another, potentially involving one another in causal chains.[3] This is all quite evident throughout Pussie's story because he writes on the cusp of this large historical change, the advent of sexuality as such: he was well-versed in the discourses of medico-legal diagnosis, which were growing in authority in his lifetime, and he employed their descriptive language and categories in his tale (including their discernment of a specifically "sexual" impulse or instinct), to some degree assuming a pathological identity prescribed by those discourses, but, at the same time, he routinely and preferentially characterized his erotic life in aesthetic terms.

"Estheticism and homosexuality are often linked together," he wrote in an appendix to his text, in which he discussed "The Case of Oscar Wilde," who was, he claimed, "the most extreme esthete (extravagant feeder on beauty wherever it is to be found, like the author) the world has ever seen" (206). This internally discordant analysis of Wilde—and of Pussie himself—is telling in several respects. On the one hand, Pussie treats "estheticism" and "homosexuality" as distinct entities that may often be contingently "linked" but are not the same; on the other hand, however, he describes Wilde's aestheticism as a fundamental and capacious attribute, a matter of seeking beauty "wherever it is to be found," in male bodies or art objects or delicious food and drink. This account of the relationship between Wilde's (and his own) aestheticism and homosexuality vacillates between distinguishing (but linking) them, on the one hand, and treating them as versions of the same thing on the other. This vacillation is itself a textual trace of the historical precipitation of sexuality as such out of a more comprehensive regime of sensory protocols and structures of taste.[4]

Pussie's tale incorporates an interesting account of its own formal accretion over a period of years, as he reflects here and there on how the narrative document had been written up to a certain time in his life (at that point in the text), but had failed to find a willing publisher, only to be extended again up to another present moment.[5] He sought a publisher for many years without success, until finding it possible in 1918 to issue it under the guise of a case study offered to a limited professional public by the press of *The Medico-Legal Journal*, with the imprimatur of that journal's editor, Dr. Alfred W. Herzog. It is possible to detect within it, then, textual traces of the history of sexuality that had transpired over the course of Pussie's life, as sexual typologies were invented, elaborated, and promulgated, with, among other results, one view of Wilde (that his fundamental aestheticism included various kinds of allied pleasures) giving way to another view (that his aestheticism was one telling symptom of his fundamental sexual pathology).

Pussie candidly details some of his presumably many encounters with the academic and professional discourses that gradually came to frame his sexual experience and identity: around 1892, during his college years, he "came across two articles in a journal of anthropology which treated of eunuchs" (65), for instance, and in 1896 he "read Krafft-Ebing's 'Psychopathia Sexualis,' besides a number of articles on inversion which had been published in American and European journals," to be followed shortly thereafter by reading Havelock Ellis's *Sexual Inversion* (116). It appears that this kind of reading introduced Pussie to the idea that sexuality or sexual desire constituted a separate aspect of himself, distinct from his aesthetic pursuits; but his prior assumption that his fundamental aestheticism—the fact that he had "a nature peculiarly susceptible to sensuality" (55), that he possessed a "delirious imagination" (58), that his "mind and body have . . . always been hypersensitive to all stimuli and impressions" (83)—was the source and ground of his "sensual practices" survived not only as a relic of an earlier experiential and intellectual regime but as a counterdiscourse to the emergent disciplinary medico-legal and sexological discourses with which he had become familiar. This contention between emergent sexualizing academic and medico-legal discourses, on the one hand, and residual aesthetic frameworks for understanding bodily pleasure, on the other, will be seen, as I will show below, in a wide variety of early twentieth-century American writings.

Pussie characteristically thought of his own attraction to fellatio (and any other form of erotic attraction) as an aesthetic instinct, and he thought of sexual distaste under this description as well. Remembering his dutiful attempt to school himself in heterosexual practices as an adolescent, he conceded that "after months of effort, feminine beauty proved powerless to attract me in the least, while male beauty was constantly increasing its sway over me" (49).[6] The unalterable fact of this attraction to male beauty eventually led him to argue, quite boldly, that "the instincts of the normal man and of the invert are on a par morally and esthetically" (32). "In general, throughout my life," he writes, "whenever I have encountered virum [men] who appeared to me as exceptionally beautiful, a strong desire has immediately arisen membrum virile in ore recipere" (81).[7] What makes it clear that Pussie's self-understanding of his supposed "mere sexual attraction" (79) is fundamentally aesthetic in its substance—even disinterested in a Kantian way, so to speak—is that he expressly disavows any interest in orgasm, in what we might tend to believe would be his own sexual pleasure. "With me the satisfaction was practically all mental," he claims. "I found it exclusively in the body of my associate, not at all in my own" (86).[8] He took satisfaction in witnessing his partner's physical arousal and climax, but he was an unselfish assistant and disinterested admirer, so to speak—in fact, he was disappointed and ashamed if he discovered evidence of his own orgasm at any time (via nocturnal emission, for instance) and he never wished to come when he sucked someone off. During his "fairie apprenticeship" he ejaculated while fellating his partner about once in every ten episodes, he ruefully admits, but "it was accompanied by such horrible feelings and thoughts that I used my will power to prevent it" (82).[9] Even when his intimate associates treated him violently, as they often did, he says he "was so fascinated by the savagery and beauty of my tormentors that I experienced a species of mental satisfaction, being willing to suffer death if only I could contribute to their pleasure" (114). There would be clinical descriptions today for this attitude (some form of masochism, presumably), and moralizing frameworks (internalized homophobia), as well as labels in queer argot for this particular style of pleasure (a stone femme oral sub bottom, perhaps), but it is unnecessary to redescribe it in such terms when Pussie was so eloquent in his presentation of it as a matter of disinterested aesthetic appreciation. The "charm of masculine beauty" (119) held him in thrall, so that "in my sexual life, my pudenda were practically non-existent" (159).[10]

It may seem facetious to characterize the organization of Pussie's sexual life in Kantian terms. Probably the Prussian philosopher had something quite else in mind—not the willful suppression of one's own orgasm—when he argued that the essence of aesthetic judgment was its disinterestedness and purposelessness. Kant insisted that in determining an ideal of beauty it was necessary that "no sensory charm is allowed to be mixed into the satisfaction in its object."[11] My argument here is not, of course, that Pussie was a good Kantian in his sex life (whatever that might mean), but that his understanding of his own relationship to intimate bodily experience was largely organized by aesthetic categories. He appears to have been thoroughly familiar with ancient Greek concepts of the beautiful that were, as he says of Greek literature generally, "suffused with pederasty" (*Female-Impersonators* 27n).[12] The general Platonic idea of gradually ascending to an ideal posture of aesthetic admiration through the hands-on experience of pederastic pleasure doubtless lingered in his mind, consequentially, even as Pussie became familiar, in his "university course in æsthetics" (*Female-Impersonators* 17), with later theorists like Kant who divorced aesthetic judgment from bodily interest. It would not be surprising to discover that Pussie's reading had familiarized him with other aesthetic philosophers, perhaps including American contemporaries like George Santayana, who in his meditations on "the relations of sex with our æsthetic susceptibility" explicitly rejected Kantian criteria of disinterestedness and universality as requirements of valid aesthetic judgment. Santayana held that "sex is not the only object of sexual passion," because this passion was never completely exhausted by its orientation toward specifically sexual objects of interest, but needed other beautiful and attractive objects on which to spend its attention; indeed, as Santayana argued, "the whole sentimental side of our æsthetic sensibility—without which it would be perceptive and mathematical rather than æsthetic—is due to our sexual organization remotely stirred."[13] While Pussie clearly had access to intellectual resources (ancient and modern) that justified his conflation of erotic and aesthetic interest and experience, there nevertheless is a constant (Kantian) pressure in his self-narrative to describe his gratification in sexual experience as strictly "mental satisfaction" (114), to emphasize his "non-sensual, wifely love" (173; cf. 78) for the young men he adoringly fellated.

One can't help wondering if, when Pussie (presumably) read Kant's Third Critique in college, he lingered over §17, Kant's discussion of "the ideal of beauty." Here, as Whitney Davis has discussed in *Queer Beauty: Sexuality and Aesthetics from Winckelmann to Freud and Beyond*, Kant elaborates on the claim that the ideal of beauty is universally valid because it is the product of a generalization of multiple singular aesthetic judgments— indeed, in principle, the product of all of the aesthetic judgments of everyone. Kant asks his readers to follow him in a thought experiment in which "someone has seen a thousand grown men" and can recall their images and shapes to mind as well as compare them to one another by means of a quasi-optical superimposition in the imagination of those thousand retained images. This imaginary superimposition will yield, Kant says, an average or standard to constitute the ideal of "a beautiful man" (118). As Davis argues, properly speaking the universal aesthetic standard of "a beautiful man" would be fully produced only by extending this thought experiment exponentially: a thousand men would each collate a thousand images, then their resultant standards would be collated with the products of each other's collations, ad infinitum.[14]

It seems noteworthy that Pussie claims to have had, before the age of seven, "more than one thousand" experiences of fellatio with his boyhood friends and playmates (38) and in adulthood to have had "800 intimates" (38; cf. 22, 78) with whom he had an average of two encounters apiece, yielding a count of approximately 1,600 sexual experiences (84, 85, 107).[15] Throughout this sexual career he was plainly collating his observations of various male physiques as well as specific genital conformations, noting the "variety" that existed in both cases (78) and producing for himself an aesthetic ideal of the male body in general and its genitalia in particular. Just as Kant's thought experiment produces an ideal male body that excludes the extremes of disproportion and anomaly, so Pussie's collation of his experiences takes careful account of "anatomical peculiarities" of the male genitalia (he specifically mentions monorchidism, "pronounced varicocele," and phimosis) that needed to be ruled out of the aesthetic standard (108). Was this a burlesque of Kant's thought experiment? Was Pussie traducing Kant's exposition, which takes the male body as its exemplary experimental object-image, but only to strip it of anything like erotic interest? I would like to think so.

Toward his own body Pussie took a "disinterested" aesthetic attitude as well, careful of his hygiene and exacting in his routine depilation: "I removed all the growth of hair on my body and limbs by means of a safety

razor so that they were as glabrous as statuary" (105–6). His assimilation
of his own body to the aesthetic ideal of cold marble sculpture took the
extreme form, in *The Female-Impersonators*, of his modeling for nude pho-
tographs (reproduced therein) of himself in poses imitative of classical
sculpture, including the ancient Greek "Hermaphroditos" (facing the title
page). Pussie understood not only his own taste for certain pleasures as
aesthetic matters, but others' distaste as well; those who did not share his
own fondness for fellatio—who may in fact have been disgusted by it—
regarded the act as "highly unaesthetic" (112). He is not unaware that many
of those who rejected his kind of pleasure did so consciously on moral
or religious or hygienic grounds; but he was insistent that this disgust
involved a large element of aesthetic judgment.[16]

There is plenty of evidence all around us, even today, that dissident sexualities have at least a contingent relationship to aesthetic pursuits and
aesthetic experience, and probably something more than that. The fashion and beauty industries are well populated with gay and lesbian profes-
sionals; and the NEA under Republican administrations has told us (if we
didn't scandalously know already) that the worlds of high art and avant
garde artistic practice have been arenas for challenging norms of sexuality and sexual expression. Pussie did not fail to note that "the male dress-
maker and milliner, and the dilettante" were likely to exhibit the effeminate
behavior that typified the androgyne (22) and that two of his "girl-boy playmates" in childhood had grown up to be "an organist and an orchestra-
leader by profession when they became adult" (39), thus recognizing the
affinity between aesthetically creative forms of labor in the useful arts, as
well as the professionally organized fine arts, and nonnormative sexual
identifications. This relationship between art (broadly construed) and nonnormative sexuality can be explained sociologically, to be sure: in a reflexive
fashion, at least since the eighteenth century, the increasingly differentiated social world of self-conscious aesthetic "bohemia" has, by virtue of
its professed devotion to traducing bourgeois norms, attracted sexual as
well as artistic heretics; since it has served as an available haven for these
purposeful reprobates it has naturally attracted more of the same. Something similar could be said of the everyday world of consumer pleasure
typified by the fashion and beauty industries, interior decoration, floristry,
and so forth: they have functioned as social sectors where gender-deviant

and sexually dissident individuals were mostly tolerated and sometimes valued (precisely for their supposed aesthetic inclinations), and so they have continued to attract queer aspirants to their ranks. Driving this contingent and self-sustaining process of social formation may be a phenomenon Harold Beaver identified some time ago: people with socially disparaged (and often punished) sexual tastes have had to learn, by necessity, skills of social dissimulation and disguise as well as observational skills of detection and coded communication that well prepare them for artistic pursuits in which such creative and critical skills are professionally elaborated and rewarded.[17]

Given the confidence with which Pussie detailed the multiple relationships between sexuality and aesthetics, it comes as no real surprise that in a large number of other early twentieth-century American autobiographies, autobiographical fictions, long fictions, and novels the two phenomena—aesthetics and sexuality—are often explicitly linked, either in an historically contingent manner or, in some cases, with a strong suspicion of an intrinsic connection. In the remainder of this essay I will describe a broader archive of early twentieth-century texts that exhibit this concern for the configuration of sexual nonnormativity and aesthetic undertakings.[18] In doing so, I have in mind not only the value of outlining a broader archive to contextualize what might otherwise seem to be Pussie's idiosyncratic account but also the fact that in contemporary queer studies (as in other fields of inquiry) there is at least the beginning of an "aesthetic turn," a swerve away from ideological critique and theoretical deconstruction. There is not space in the present essay to address the current critical situation in very great detail, and in any case I want to focus on presenting the historical archive because I note that even in as refreshing and congenial an account as David Halperin's *What Do Gay Men Want? An Essay on Sex, Risk, and Subjectivity*, which champions the search for alternatives to the medical and psychological discourses that currently frame much discussion of homosexuality, and specifically adverts to *aesthetic* discourse as an alternative, the author strays far afield to find usable intellectual resources—Halperin enlists French novelists Jean Genet (who has at least been widely translated into English) and Marcel Jouhandeau (who thus far has not) as chief among the textual resources, "aesthetic in inspiration," that he contends will aid us in resisting the "intellectual monoculture of psychology."[19] There are plenty of other models of aesthetic resistance in American literature emerging with the sexualizing of psychology and other disciplinary discourses.

Charles Warren Stoddard's *For the Pleasure of His Company* (1903) is roughly contemporaneous with the initial composition of *Autobiography of an Androgyne*, and it ratifies (by virtue of its setting in bohemian and sexually renegade late nineteenth-century San Francisco) Pussie's suggestive claim that erotic culture during his years of sexual activity was much more liberal west of Kansas City.[20] Stoddard's protagonist, Paul Clitheroe, is a poet, actor, and dreamer, whose unspecified and somewhat changeable erotic nonconformity goes hand in hand with his restless aesthetic experimentation. He is at various times a poet, reviewer, editorial assistant, stage actor, and aspiring novelist—and a well-known and active member of several circles of bohemian artists and intellectuals in San Francisco proper as well as across the bay in Oakland. He has intense and intimate (presumably sexual) relations with several men, but his deepest friendship is a nonsexual one with a young woman named Miss Juno (although she prefers to be called Jack by her close friends). The very ground of their relationship is their mutual ambition to write novels: they encourage each other in this artistic endeavor, although, as it happens, their relationship deteriorates precipitately when Paul discovers that Jack's formal conception of her contemplated novel is extraordinarily conventional in its heterosexual romantic plotting. Stoddard's novel is largely autobiographical, and this relationship (and vexed contrast) between two novelists and their variant conceptions of queer novelistic form was drawn from Stoddard's friendship with Julia "Dudee" Fletcher, who published (under the pseudonym George Fleming) a host of widely successful novels including *Kismet* (1877), the insipidity of which Paul Clitheroe (and presumably a disenchanted Charles Warren Stoddard) would have certainly disparaged. The central point here, however, is that within the diegesis of Stoddard's novel the mutual pursuit of aesthetic accomplishment becomes, at least for a time, the basis of an experimental relationship outside of heteronormative definitions between an effeminate young man and a similarly gendernonconforming young woman (which ostensibly mirrored Stoddard's own friendship with Fletcher). Stoddard later redoubled this depicted implication of sexuality and aesthetics by rehearsing it in his own experimental novel—which, in its daring formal contortions, as well as its explicit disavowal of compulsory heterosexual romance, constituted a critique of the sexual and gender norms finally endorsed and embodied by Miss Juno's fictional novel and by the real popular novels of Fletcher/Fleming.[21]

⁂

In Blair Niles's *Strange Brother* (1931) the young protagonist, Mark Thornton, a midwesterner transplanted to New York City, living in a settlement
house in Italian East Harlem and teaching art to poor children in the
neighborhood, has a literary avocation (he reads widely, writes poetry, and
collects in a notebook what he considers to be pro-homosexual passages
from ancient and modern literature to include in an anthology on *Manly
Love*, an undertaking he began as a personal therapeutic project, but one
that he hopes eventually to publish for social benefit).[22] But he is centrally
a visual artist, and his various modes of drawing and painting are given
detailed description. His artistic practice in the present time of the narrative is divided between two styles that have different correspondences
to the conflicting dimensions of his erotic life. On the one hand, he is
an exacting scientific illustrator, producing pictures for publication as an
assistant to a (straight) naturalist named Philip Crane whom he admires
abjectly and with whom he is, frustratingly, deeply infatuated. His social
interactions with this scientist, and with Crane's cousin June Westbrook
and their sophisticated Manhattan coterie, introduce him to a world of
"progressive" social thought, including new "tolerant" sexological theories
like those articulated by Philip's friend Irwin Hesse, a Viennese labora-
tory scientist who is investigating the endocrine system and its role in the
production of sexual characteristics (including hermaphrodism and inversion). Hesse is in fact about to leave New York to attend the International
Sex Reform Congress in Vienna, and he has hopes that his researches will
eventually lead to the elimination of sexual abnormality; Mark is gratified
to think that his psychic deformity and homosexual urges might someday
have a medical cure. June Westbrook, too, hopes that "psychoanalysts and
physiologists" might successfully address the problem of what her cousin
Philip calls "degenerates" (54–55). Mark himself is led to read Forel, Ellis,
Hirschfeld, Ulrichs, and other sexological and homosexualist theorists
and investigators—books that had been left with Mark by Hesse to be forwarded to Vienna (299).

Tellingly, the "fine accurate line drawings of soldier ants and female ants
and worker ants which Mark was doing for Phil," which include a "detailed
drawing of a *gynandromorph*, with its head, female; its thorax and legs male
on the left and female on the right," a style of illustration associated in this
novel with the scientific approach to sexual abnormality, have their precursors in some "grotesquely decorative studies of beetles and grasshoppers
and butterflies" (72) that hang on Mark's wall and that date from childhood
visits to his grandfather's farm (where he had an intensely remembered

friendship with a pretty boy named Luis). Even June cannot help ruefully contrasting these "decoratively grotesque grasshoppers" that Mark exhibits for his own eyes (and that constitute what he would have called an "outlet" for his fantasies) with the constrained scientific illustrations of ants he now draws for Philip (232).

On his own time nowadays, Mark produces picturesque "impressions of New York life," including skyscrapers, tenements and fire escapes, bridges and ferries, as well as "studies of Italian boys and of Harlem types" like tap dancers, prize fighters, and musicians (72)—including many sketches of a handsome eighteen-year-old neighborhood fruit vendor named Rico with whom he has an ambiguously friendly acquaintance.[23] Mark's interest in Rico is principally aesthetic, but this aesthetic interest shades impercep-tibly into the sensual: "Rico's dark Sicilian beauty satisfied his love of the exotic. He liked to see the dimples come in Rico's olive cheeks, and he liked the warm eager light in Rico's black eyes, and the tumbled black hair which Rico never troubled to cover with a hat. Most of all he liked the unthinking animal happiness of Rico" (83–84). *Strange Brother* is unsat-isfactory in all kinds of ways, but its delicate narrative of the wary attrac-tion between Mark and Rico (and its refusal to comment omnisciently on what really was going on between them) is impressive. We learn that Rico favored Mark with discounted prices on fruit and that after Mark made a purchase Rico "stared after him as he disappeared down the street" (86). We learn too that Mark "often engaged Rico to pose for his class" (86) and that Rico, obviously, consented to be employed for this aesthetic pur-pose. Mark's friend June exclaims over Rico, "What a beautiful boy!" (231), and a fairie acquaintance of Mark's named Lilly-Marie congratulates Mark conspiratorially, after meeting Rico, "You've got good taste. . . . He's good looking . . . your Rico" (285). Lilly-Marie assumes what Mark apparently cannot imagine, that Rico is an eligible sexual partner and might welcome Mark's erotic attention; as historian George Chauncey has explained, in early twentieth-century New York City it was normal for young men in Italian and other ethnic immigrant communities to engage sexually with fairies and other submissive sexual partners (Pussie would have been able to advise Mark on the protocols).[24]

Eventually Rico turns on Mark viciously (he saw Mark take Lilly-Marie back to his room) and threatens him with blackmail ("I've been watching," Rico says, "And I saw who came home with you last night" [314, 315]), send-ing Mark into despair and precipitating his sudden suicide. But Niles leaves it permanently unclear what Rico's motives were. To Mark's protestation, "I thought you liked me!" Rico replies, "Liked you? There wasn't anybody else in the world for me. But you didn't see me. I wasn't on the map for you. And I thought it was because you weren't that kind, even though I'd always had a suspicion that you were. And I told myself that I'd been wrong to believe that" (315). Rico—who gazed at Mark down the street—feels that he watched and saw Mark, but that Mark never saw him; is his complaint that Mark saw him (condescendingly) as a picturesque subject but not (affectionately, desiringly) as an erotic object? Did Rico understand his posing for Mark's art class as part of a failed seduction? He evidently understood (or thought he did) that Mark's aesthetic interest in him was continuous with sexual desire for him, and now feels rejected—having seen what he mistakenly believes to be Mark's preference for someone like Lilly-Marie.

Strange Brother allegorizes the genetic continuity between aesthetic interest and erotic attraction, collating one style of visual art (scientific illustration) with one form of impossible desire (frustrated attachment to a straight man, Philip) and another visual style (picturesque illustration) with another form of what only seems to be impossible desire (unconfessed attraction to Rico). In the case of Rico, it is exactly Mark's failure to connect his aesthetic interest with his erotic desire that produces the tragedy: in this rather overwrought melodrama, had Mark been less of a disinterested Kantian in his framing of Rico as an aesthetic object—had he been equipped, like Pussie, to think of his aesthetic and erotic interests as interchangeable or mutually sustaining—things might have turned out much differently.

The framing of erotic questions in aesthetic terms finds further exploration in one of H.D.'s novels. Like Stoddard's *For the Pleasure of His Company*, H.D.'s *Paint It Today* (written in 1921, published in 1992) is a roman à clef, derived and adapted from her friendships and associations with a coterie of modernist artists—especially her difficult relationship with the poet Ezra Pound, to whom she had been engaged as a young woman (he is called Raymond in the novel); the British novelist to whom she was later married, Richard Aldington (called Basil here); as well as two female lovers, Frances Josepha Gregg (thinly disguised as Josepha) and Annie Winifred Ellerman, better known as the novelist Bryher (who is called Althea).[25] H.D. herself is called Margaret in the novel or, more familiarly, Midget. As *Paint It Today*'s modern editor, Cassandra Laity, makes clear in her edition, this is a text that knows about the long historical trajectory of the nexus of sexuality and aesthetics and deploys that knowledge in overt and covert—and self-reflexive—ways. For example, at a moment when Midget is reflecting on the failure of her marriage to Basil, she remembers the "jesting half-banter" of a letter Basil had written her, in which he addressed her as "sister of Charmides" (58) because she did not return his affection as he would have liked. "Sister of Charmides. Basil had read her the Wilde poem under the shadow of the extraordinarily bad statue of Verlaine in the Luxumbourg [*sic*] gardens. Charmides, it seems, was a youth in Greece, who fell in love with a statue" (59). As Laity's note to this passage details (leaving the obvious homoerotic associations of Verlaine and Wilde aside), the Roman poet Lucian told a story about a young man who fell in love with a statue of Aphrodite. Basil's deeply self-aware and arch gesture here— choosing the Verlaine statue as the place to read to Midget a Wilde poem "in which 'statue-love' . . . encodes transgressive (homoerotic) desire" (as Laity puts it, 94*n*41)—conflates sexual desire and aesthetic attachment vividly, making of this conflation an accusation against Midget's wayward attractions. "H.D.'s references to Midget as 'sister of Charmides' refer both to her homoerotic desires and to her coalescence of eroticism with 'cold' aesthetic passion," as Laity observes (94–95*n*41). It is true enough that H.D. is orchestrating this multilayered set of associations from queer artistic history, as Laity argues. But it should not go unnoticed that H.D. is depicting a scene in which her characters (presumably based here on her real self and her former husband) themselves are manipulating these associations; that is, it is not just H.D. making reference to a figure's characteristic "coalescence" of eroticism and aestheticism, it is H.D. giving us an account of the way two persons living through the breakdown of their marriage because of the errant erotic interests of at least one of them (Midget) together negotiate this passage by means of the deployment of aesthetic categories and artistic references. "She knew that she did not feel as he wanted her to feel, with warmth and depth and warm intensity. She knew that if she felt at all it was not with warm but with cold intensity. She did not feel for Basil with that intensity. She was forever conscious of the fact. But the comradeship was perfect. At one time she had believed that he would accept from her that comradeship and from the world what else it had to give him, but he had changed so since his years in France" (59). It is Basil at the time who orchestrates the scene, bringing Verlaine and Wilde and a loaded reference to misdirected passion to bear upon his frustrated personal relationship with Midget; it is Midget who later remembers Basil's wicked orchestration of this conjuncture and who tops him (so to speak) twice—by first exercising her aesthetic judgment (the Verlaine statue is "extraordinarily bad," how could Basil have had the bad taste to make his scene *there*) and by expressing her willingness to form an unusual experimental relationship of "comradeship" with him (smuggling in her own allusion to Whitman, at a guess) and to allow him whatever other relationships he wished in his life (as she wished to be permitted to have relations with women in hers). *He* had changed and rejected this creative ethical possibility, she holds.

Basil had changed because of World War I, his years of wartime military service, and his injury in a poison gas attack; now he finds Midget's tepid affection for him insufficient and leaves her. But in this novel there is a palpable sense of other relevant historical changes directly involving the formation and consolidation of sexual categories. In Midget's childhood her family does not approve of her intense friendship with Josepha, whom they consider "not a good influence," "unwholesome," "not normal" (9)—vague rubrics signifying suspicious disapproval not yet articulated to named deviant categories. Midget and Josepha themselves feel a solidarity with each other (and a difference from others) that remains indistinct, but slowly begins to include a sense of themselves as part of a class of people that includes others like them, which is nascently both a community of the sexually alike and a group of the aesthetically superior: "She and Josepha and such as she and Josepha were separated, irreparably, from the masses of their country people" (20).

Counterposed to these intimations of sexological and psychological taxonomization and diagnosis transpiring in the time of the diegesis, *Paint It Today* offers several alternative aesthetic protocols that evade identification as such. The lyrical opening paragraphs of the novel will serve to illustrate: "A portrait, a painting? You cannot paint today as you painted yesterday. You cannot paint tomorrow as you paint today. A portrait, a painting? Do not paint it of yesterday's rapt and rigid formula nor of yesterday's day-after-tomorrow criss-cross—jagged, geometric, prismatic. Do not paint yesterday's day-after-tomorrow destructiveness nor yesterday's fair convention. But how and as you will—*paint it today*" (3). Throughout the novel the act of writing is likened to the art of painting. Here there is an initial distinction proposed between a more traditional style of representation or realist portrait painting (which aims at a visual likeness to the subject and assigns a certain fixity to that subject) and a more abstract or painterly style that does not aim to be a copy of the original subject (or conspire in its fixing), but draws attention to itself as a painting and to the process of its own making. *Paint It Today* is self-consciously modernist or antitraditional in style and method; the author is here identifying herself with the artistic avant-garde, whose impulse is toward radical change, stylistic experimentation,

and she is allying this artistic movement with the question of subjectifica-
tion and social taxonomization. H.D. is plainly referencing one specific
avant-garde school of painting, cubism ("criss-cross—jagged, geometric,
prismatic"), and its experiments in the optical fragmentation of human
figures, and she is implying that this style, while new, is also already old
hat: "yesterday's day-after-tomorrow destructiveness." The principled modernist devotion to making it new (through aesthetic deformation) involves,
here, a corollary dedication to reconceiving or reformatting the human
subject indefinitely—finding again and again what is a short while later
in the novel called "the door to another world, another state of emotional
life or being" (12).

Midget herself is an aspiring experimental writer who adduces painterly
analogues for her attempt to break aesthetic boundaries. There is an elaborate system of floral symbolism in *Paint It Today*, and H.D. would appear
to understand that floriculture generally and the genre of popular literature denominated "the language of flowers" had a longstanding evocative
relationship to transgressive female sexuality in general and specifically
lesbian sexual intimacy as well.[26] Thus her reflections on her literary ambitions, routinely taking various forms of flower painting as appropriate analogues, encode (to echo Cassandra Laity) transgressive homoerotic desire,
but in addition encode a will to transcend the regime of sexual categoriza-
tion altogether: "She, Midget, did not wish to be an eastern flower-painter.
She did not wish to be an exact and over-*précieuse* western, a scientific
describer of detail of vein and leaf of flowers, dead or living, nor did she
wish to press flowers and fern fronds and threads of pink and purple sea-
weed between the pages of her book. Yet she wanted to combine all these
qualities in her writing and to add still another quality to these three. She
wished to embody, as this other quality, the fragrance of the flowers" (17).
The distinction proposed here between two styles of flower painting (one
scientifically exacting and "western," the other presumably more romantic
and atmospheric, i.e., "eastern") will recall Mark Thornton's two styles of
painting and their correlations with his divided sexual impulses. Midget,
standing in for H.D., however, tries to imagine a third possibility, one not
tied to reductive binary sexual identifications (in Mark's case, pathological scientific specimen or despised fairie), but opening onto improvisatory
sensual freedom. The fragrance of flowers—a vivid sensory experience—
cannot be conveyed by sculpture, or music, or any form of painting, H.D.
goes on to concede. But writing, she hopes, can "at least attempt to express
something" (17) like fragrance; that is, it can aim to pursue a utopian

aesthetic practice that returns us to unmediated sensory pleasure of an elusive kind, a kind absolutely not susceptible of scientific description.

My discussion has highlighted three novels, the obscure turn-of-the-century experimental novel *For the Pleasure of His Company* (1903), the successful middlebrow "progressive" novel *Strange Brother* (1931), and the posthumously published modernist novella *Paint It Today* (1912, 1992). The vicissitudes of the aesthetic in these novels of erotic experimentation and transgression have many other counterparts in early twentieth-century American writing. In Edward Prime-Stevenson's *Imre: A Memorandum* (1906) the two main characters understand their "aesthetic" predilections as telling symptoms of their homosexuality. Throughout *Imre* these shared aesthetic dispositions stand in marked contrast to another ground on which their secretive relationship is built, their mutual schooling in modern sexological theory and their common (failed) experiences with medical "cures."[27] Henry Blake Fuller's protagonist in *Bertram Cope's Year* (1919) is a graduate student in literature with a flair for dramatic singing, while older gay men in the novel are opera buffs and antique collectors, and Bertram's best friend is a flamboyantly effeminate musical theater queen.[28] The care with which Fuller excludes all specific reference to sexological categories in favor of characterization based in aesthetic interest and artistic bent has to be the result of a deliberate decision to demote the latter's importance. Glenway Wescott's main character's conflicted alienation from his family in *The Babe's Bed* (1930)—alienation at once from the stifling norms of marital respectability, domestic intimacy, and obligatory reproduction that make them all miserable—seems to have everything to do with his unspecified artistic vocation.[29] The man and woman whose (platonic) friendship is at the heart of Dawn Powell's *Come Back to Sorrento* (1932) form their bond through a shared sense of aesthetic superiority and exclusiveness; they improvise a miniature bohemian enclave for themselves in a provincial midwestern village.[30] The Greenwich Village bohemians in Charles Henri Ford's and Parker Tyler's *The Young and Evil* (1933) find that avant-garde artistic endeavor and sexual experimentation feed each other in various (sometimes sinister) ways. This novel (like Stoddard's and H.D.'s a roman à clef based on the authors' own lives in avant-garde circles) features a speech on artistic freedom by one of the protagonists, Karel, at a "symposium" (the word seems to bear a weight of Platonic implication here), during which we are asked to imagine why two members of the audience, while listening to Karel talk about the bearing of politics on "our personal lives," might campily ask each other "where Karel's feather fan was."[31] In Richard Meeker's *Better Angel* (1933), one of the earliest programmatically "affirmative" treatments of homosexuality, the protagonist Kurt Gray is (of course) a musical composer, who in the course of events reads "the new psychology—Brill, Jung, Freud, Ellis, Carpenter," but they provide him with distinctly less valuable sustenance than do Wedekind, Cellini, Michelangelo, Shakespeare, Shelley, and, most importantly, Plato. "The high idealism of the Phaedrus and the Symposium had captured him and engulfed him as a flood."[32] Frankie, the tomboyish protagonist of Carson McCullers's 1946 novel *The Member of the Wedding*, not only imagines a future of professional creativity for herself—her present penchant for writing "shows" may lead her to Hollywood, she imagines—but she would essentially like to redesign the world to allow for erotic variety. She and her friend John Henry and her nurse Berenice often play a game of overweening aesthetic ambition called "criticize the Creator" in which Frankie usually "plan[s] it so that people could instantly change back and forth from boys to girls, which ever way they felt like and wanted," while Berenice insists that "the law of human sex was exactly right just as it was and could in no way be improved."[33] Such fictions as these by Prime-Stevenson, Fuller, Wescott, Powell, Ford and Tyler, Meeker, and McCullers, along with the novels by Stoddard, Niles, and H.D. discussed at greater length previously, recognize a sociohistorical fact (the affinity of queer persons for artistic activity in the era of the emergence and consolidation of gendered sexual identities), but they also seem to be exploring the possibility of an intrinsic relationship between sex and aesthetics. What if sexuality is essentially—they ask—an aesthetic phenomenon?

The etymological meaning of *aesthesis* has to do with sense perception. Although aesthetic experience since Kant has been frequently and authoritatively described as a fundamentally disinterested (or disembodied) mode of experience, there has recently been a turn back to understanding aesthetic experience as radically embodied, rooted in and pertaining to the senses,[34] having to do with the social organization of sensory experience and sensual pleasure, and best understood in terms like those proposed (for instance) by Jacques Rancière, whose phrase "the distribution of the sensible" attempts to get at the socially organized inequality of access to sensory experience and pleasure.[35] It is also the case that recent work in the history and theory of sexuality has sometimes adverted to the category of the aesthetic, often through the new (old) perspective of sense experience. Leo Bersani in *Homos* argues that sexual identity derives from "the wish to repeat pleasurable stimulations of the body."[36] Tim Dean in *Beyond Sexuality* holds that sexuality involves more than just genitals or even bodies, but a whole set of protocols of aesthetic taste.[37] And Michel Foucault in his late work routinely spoke of sexuality in terms of an "aesthetics of existence" or aesthetic self-fashioning.[38] It seems intuitively right—maybe even obvious—that sexual experience, because it ineluctably has a sensory dimension, can be described in terms of aesthetic experience. It is less obvious, perhaps, that sexuality as such (the modern organization and consolidation of a range of sensory and psychic phenomena into a fictive unity called "sexuality") is a product of the historical emergence of a sphere of aesthetic autonomy in the late eighteenth and early nineteenth centuries.[39] And it is still less obvious that when, in the early twentieth century, sexualities were systematically defined and hardened into "homo" and "hetero" versions, the aesthetic dimension of this process—the ways in which sexuality, originally (let us posit for the moment) an aesthetic phenomenon, used artistic means to consolidate itself while at the same time using aesthetic categories and artistic means to resist the psychologization of sexuality performed by medico-legal discourses and institutions—came under curious critical scrutiny by literary artists themselves. These self-narratives and novels dramatize not only the ways in which the consolidation of a new sexual system took aesthetic form, but the ways in which aesthetic means could be deployed to resist the disciplinary effects and undercut the coercive social power of the normative sexual system.

Notes

1. Ralph Werther [Earl Lind], *Autobiography of an Androgyne*, ed. Scott Herring (New Brunswick, NJ: Rutgers University Press, 2008 [1918]), 27. Further page references will be given parenthetically within the text.

2. "A strange young ruffian one day passed me on the street, and addressed me jocularly: 'Hello Pussie!' I cannot express how much it pleased me, and I longed to be called 'Pussie' always" (34). The moniker "Ralph Werther," the author says, was patterned on what he had inferred was Oscar Wilde's practice in phonetically altering his given name to produce "Escal Vigor," the title of a novel by Georges Eekhoud that Pussie believed (erroneously) was written

in fact by Wilde. "I have myself built a pseudonym on my baptismal name in similar fashion" (30), he stated, enjoying the associations with the celebrated painter and with Goethe's hero along with the affiliation with Wilde and the invocation of Eekhoud's daring homoerotic novel (34). Lind (also a pseud-onym) used "Ralph Werther" as his pseudonym when he published a sequel to *Autobiography of an Androgyne* in 1922 under the title *The Female-Impersonators*. He elsewhere refers to himself as Raphael Werther, Jennie June (34), and Baby (26) as well as Pussie.

3. Pussie refers to the "Puritan circle" in which he was raised, in which he was "never vouchsafed the least sex knowledge" and therefore tried vainly to resist his venereal impulses rather than moderate them healthfully. "I believe my health and happiness were tremendously impaired by my ultra-puritan views which made me obstinate before Nature's behests." *The Female-Impersonators* (New York: Medico-Legal Journal, 1922; repr. New York: Arno, 1975), 56, 61, 71.

4. In *The Female-Impersonators*, which even more fully reflects Pussie's absorption and endorsement of medico-legal discourses (he had meanwhile joined the editorial staff of the *Medico-Legal Journal*), he more decidedly favors the notion that sexuality is primary and inborn and that aestheticism is "a con-sequence" (17) of that basic sexual disposition.

5. As Pussie explains in his preface to *Autobiography of an Androgyne*, he wrote up his life in 1899 down to that date (when he was age twenty-five); it drew on the diaries he had been keeping since age fourteen (cf. 153). Subse-quently he added to the narrative periodically, as well as inserting material in what was already written; as a result, "parts of some pages were written in different years," and the whole waited eighteen years to see print (17). At numerous places it incorporates what purport to be unedited transcriptions from his diary and letters (e.g., 52–53). The text's formal incorporation of its own distended time of composition, and the witness it bears to the changes in the discursive construction of sexuality over that period of time, are among its invaluable features.

6. At age thirty-three, after his voluntary surgical castration, Pussie attempted sexual intercourse with a woman for the first time, his positive aversion to the act having somewhat abated at that point; but he felt no positive desire for women either, and the "scientific experiment" was a failure (189).

7. The editor of the edition from which I cite provides an interpolated brack-eted translation of Pussie's coy Latin phrase: "[to perform oral sex on them]" (81). It seems dubious to me to substitute a fussy contemporary locution that is distinctly less direct and raunchy than a more literal translation would be: "take the cock into my mouth."

8. In the sequel to *Autobiography of an Androgyne*, Pussie mentions that he had taken a "university course in æsthetics," in which the professor seemed to suggest something about "the notorious frequency of homosexuality among æsthetes." Pussie also speculates that Kant had been what he calls an "anaphrodite," someone coldly indifferent to all sexual experience (*The Female-Impersonators*, 17, 14*n*). Here again he claims that for those like himself, the "ultra-androgynes," sexuality is informed by a kind of Kantian aesthetic disinterestedness: "the individual's genitalia [are] entirely divorced—as a rule—from the sexual life" (20).

9. Pussie makes it clear repeatedly that he did not like being penetrated anally, but again he has a (distorted) Kantian rationale for enduring and even relishing the experience occasionally: "I later enjoyed it somewhat only because I enjoyed witnessing all kinds of amorous conduct on the part of ultra-virile young men. I had a craze to see them sexually excited" (85).

10. Pussie's inadvertent orgasms, he reports, were "always prompt and complete" but somehow "disagreeable" (108).

11. Immanuel Kant, *Critique of the Power of Judgment*, ed. Paul Guyer, trans. Paul Guyer and Eric Matthews (Cambridge: Cambridge University Press, 2000), 120. Further page references will be given parenthetically in the text.

12. "I read Greek six years in 'prep' and university. My observation is that androgyne scholars have a penchant for that language and drift into teaching it. Prior to the twentieth century, the Greek and Latin masterpieces—in all 'preps' and colleges read unexpurgated because the sexually full-fledged have not generally understood the homosexual inscriptions—were the only publications affording androgynes an inkling of the secrets of their sex life" (*The Female-Impersonators*, 27*n*).

13. George Santayana, *The Sense of Beauty: Being the Outline of Aesthetic Theory* (New York: Scribner's, 1896; repr. Dover, 1955), 37, 40, 38.

14. Here I refer to chapter 1, "Queer Beauty: Winckelmann and Kant on the Vicissitudes of the Ideal," in *Queer Beauty: Seuality and Aesthetics from Wincklemann to Freud and Beyond* (New York: Columbia University Press, 2010), 23–50. As Davis argues, Kant's protocols for making collective (hence valid) aesthetic judgments were remotely derived from Winckelmann but suppressed the homoerotic context that was integral to Winckelmann's aesthetics (see esp. 39–41).

15. Pussie also keeps tabs on the specific favorite subcategory of sex with soldiers: he engaged in "flirtation with at least two thousand professional soldiers, only about four hundred of whom, however, went to extremes" (101).

16. In *The Female-Impersonators* he continues to characterize strong aversion (on the part of normal men) to same-sex sexual acts in such terms: "Do they

not offend the *æsthetic* sense of the majority of mankind?" (51). Cf. 23, "those who dare to offend his æsthetic sense."

17. Harold Beaver, "Homosexual Signs (*In Memory of Roland Barthes*)," *Critical Inquiry* 8, no. 1 (Autumn 1981): 99–119.

18. I have previously discussed a number of these texts from the perspective of the history and generic form of the novel; see "The Gay Novel in the United States 1900–1950," in John T. Matthews, ed., *A Companion to the Modern American Novel 1900–1950* (Chichester: Wiley-Blackwell, 2009), 414–36.

19. David Halperin, *What Do Gay Men Want? An Essay on Sex, Risk, and Subjectivity* (Ann Arbor: University of Michigan Press, 2007), 105

20. Charles Warren Stoddard, *For the Pleasure of His Company: A Tale of the Misty City, Thrice Told* (San Francisco: Robertson, 1903). To be precise, Pussie claimed that, having traveled extensively in the United States and in Western Europe and having "explored the Underworld in many cities of both continents," he found that "in America's smaller cities west of the meridian of Kansas City, the sexual Underworld is more bold and wields more political power than anywhere else in the United States or Europe" (*Female-Impersonators*, 6).

21. Stoddard's spiritual autobiography, *A Troubled Heart and How It Was Comforted at Last* (Notre Dame: Ave Maria, 1885), relates the story of his conversion to the Roman Catholic faith, and candidly presents his spiritual regeneration (which he found to be in no way incompatible with his adventurous and largely pederastic sexual relations—not, of course, detailed therein) as grounded in the seductive aesthetic appeal of the Catholic mass. For Stoddard's life see Roger Austen, *Genteel Pagan: The Double Life of Charles Warren Stoddard*, ed. John W. Crowley (Amherst: University of Massachusetts Press, 1995).

22. Blair Niles, *Strange Brother* (New York: Liveright, 1931). Page references will be given parenthetically in the text.

23. For an incisive account of the "picturesque" and its relationship to ethnic and racial difference, among other matters, in the late nineteenth and early twentieth centuries, see Kendall Johnson, *Henry James and the Visual* (Cambridge: Cambridge University Press, 2007).

24. George Chauncey, *Gay New York: Gender, Urban Culture, and the Making of the Gay Male World, 1890–1940* (New York: Basic, 1994), 75–86.

25. H.D., *Paint It Today*, ed. Cassandra Laity (New York: New York University Pres, 1992).

26. See Dorri Beam, *Style, Gender, and Fantasy in Nineteenth-Century American Women's Writing* (Cambridge: Cambrudge University Press, 2010) on the flower imagery in "highly-wrought" fiction by nineteenth-century American women, esp. chapter 1, "Florid Fantasies: Fuller, Stephens, and the 'other' language of flowers" (37–81); also Paula Bennett, "Critical Clitoridectomy: Female

Sexual Imagery and Feminist Psychoanalytic Theory," *Signs* 18, no. 2 (1993): 235–59.

27. Edward Prime-Stevenson, *Imre: A Memorandum*, ed. James J. Gifford (Peterborough: Broadview, 2003 [1906]).

28. Henry Blake Fuller, *Bertram Cope's Year*, ed. Joseph Dimuro (Peterborough: Broadview, 2010 [1919]).

29. Glenway Wescott, *The Babe's Bed* (Paris: Harrison, 1930).

30. Dawn Powell, *Come Back to Sorrento*, in *Novels 1930–1942* (New York: Library of America, 2001), 204–369.

31. Charles Henri Ford and Parker Tyler, *The Young and Evil*, ed. Steven Watson (New York: Gay Presses of New York, 1988 [1933]), 119.

32. Richard Meeker [Forman Brown], *Better Angel* (Boston: Alyson, 1987, 1990 [1933]), 84–85.

33. Carson McCullers, *The Member of the Wedding*, in *Complete Novels* (New York: Library of America, 2001), 547.

34. See, for example, Peter Osborne, ed., *From an Aesthetic Point of View: Philosophy, Art and the Senses* (London: Serpent's Tail, 2000).

35. Jacques Rancière, *The Politics of Aesthetics*, trans. Gabriel Rockhill (London: Continuum, 2004), 7–45.

36. Leo Bersani, *Homos* (Cambridge: Harvard University Press, 1995), 60.

37. Tim Dean, *Beyond Sexuality* (Chicago: University of Chicago Press, 2000), 277.

38. See Halperin, *What Do Gay Men Want?* 8.

39. I have addressed this general historical transition speculatively in "Strange Sensations: Sex and Aesthetics in 'The Counterpane,'" in Samuel Otter and Geoffrey Sanborn, eds., *Melville and Aesthetics* (London: Palgrave, 2011), 65–84. Rancière calls this the "aesthetic regime of the arts," which he dates to the beginning of the nineteenth century and associates with Schiller's notion of the "aesthetic state" (*The Politics of Aesthetics*, 23–24).

[8]

From Hawthorne to *Hairspray*

American Anxieties About Beauty

WENDY STEINER

In the arts of the New World one can discover almost any Old World topos in aesthetics. The English beauty fable *Frankenstein* finds a New England counterpart in Hawthorne's "The Birthmark," and the paradoxes of Baudelaire and Wilde echo in Warhol's "Beauty is shoe" and the camp and glamour of Hollywood cinema. But if beauty is too universal a category to respect national borders, we might still note how beauty anxieties play out in the American context, and that is the limited goal of this paper.

Venus in Exile describes the marginalized status of beauty in twentieth-century modernism and notes signs of its becoming once more a central concern in the arts.[1] The current "return to beauty," however, is not a revival of nineteenth-century clichés, despite the pink nudes and classical columns of a few nostalgists. What seems to be capturing artists' attention is not a formal notion of beauty as a property of objects, but, instead, beauty as an interaction. In the experience of beauty, perceivers discover value in something beyond them and, at the same time, observe themselves moved by that value. Their ability to be so moved reveals to them their affinity for this value, their participation in it. 'I find this beautiful' implies 'I am someone capable of finding this beautiful.' People feel gratitude, admiration, awe—and occasionally dismay—toward artists and artworks that show them as worthy connoisseurs. It is a great pleasure to learn something about who we are through what we value.

The correspondence of subject and object in the experience of beauty has often been noted in the history of aesthetics. In "An Essay on Criticism," for example, Alexander Pope describes the true product of the imagination, "wit," as

Something, whose Truth convinc'd at Sight we find,
That gives us back the Image of our Mind.[2]

Immanuel Kant's notion of "judgment" involves a similar mirroring of self in other: "Because the subject has this possibility within him, while outside [him] there is also the possibility that nature will harmonize with it, judgment finds itself referred to something that is both in the subject himself and outside him."[3] We are easily seduced by this offering of "the Image of our Mind," as Bob Dylan clearly realized in writing "Lay Lady Lay": "Whatever colors you have in your mind / I'll show them to you and you'll see them shine."[4]

The mirror of beauty has a checkered past as a symbol. "Snow White" warns about the destructive narcissism real mirrors may promote, but when art is the mirror, we see our image through something beyond ourselves. In this interchange, beauty is an experience of communication, mutuality, and shared power. In his 1996 novel, *Father of Frankenstein* (aka *Gods and Monsters*), Christopher Bram spells out the ethical import of this mirroring. He pictures the real-life Hollywood director James Whale as a young English art student posing for one of his school chums. "What I don't like is I sit and you draw," Whale says. "Not fair, John. Not democratic." Obligingly, John undresses too, and both men pose as well as draw each other. "Whale is relieved, pleased. They have corrected the balance of things, made themselves equals. One of the joys of art is that it introduces a new hierarchy into the world."[5]

This encounter marks the beginning of Whale's experience as a homosexual, which sadly never again lives up to its early promise. The trauma of World War I and the homophobia of the day thwart empathy and equality in art and love alike. Rejecting avant-garde coldness, Whale gives up painting and immigrates to Hollywood to become a director. His masterpiece is *Show Boat*, a milestone in the treatment of racism in American film. But by the end of his life, this achievement has been overshadowed by his

Frankenstein movies. In 1950s California—where high art is still equated with esoteric abstraction and the movies with mindless entertainment—Whale is seen as the eccentric old queen who made the *Frankenstein* flicks. This was the era before cultural studies; there was no analysis of camp yet and no grasp of the gender issues worked through in popular art. But Christopher Bram, an American novelist writing in the 1990s, is in a very different place from his protagonist. He poses the issues of gender and, via *Show Boat*, racial equality through a meditation on the interactive possibilities of beauty.

In doing so, Bram was taking his place in an American tradition from Nathaniel Hawthorne's classic tale, "The Birthmark," to twenty-first-century debates on bioengineering. "The Birthmark" presents in the starkest terms possible the danger of misunderstanding beauty as static, formal perfection rather than an empathetic interaction between equals. When the President's Council on Bioethics embarked on its inquiries on January 17, 2002, it devoted a full session to this story. As the council saw it, Hawthorne's protagonist was a proto-bioengineer obsessed with beauty. The connection between aesthetics and ethics in "The Birthmark" was tailor-made for policymakers seeking guidance from art.

This use of a literary text looks like a philistine error only through the lens of late nineteenth-century aestheticism and the twentieth-century avant-garde. These movements militantly separated art from life and aesthetics from morality, a move reflecting the growing modernist preoccupation with virtuality, semiosis, and eventually *différance*. Previous eras, including Hawthorne's, had operated through a religious metaphysics in which art had a self-evident relation to morality. Creativity was a moral act in which the artist became analogous to God. As Pope John Paul II observed, artists feel "the pathos with which God at the dawn of creation looked upon the work of his hands. . . . The human craftsman mirrors the image of God as Creator."[6]

This pathos in creators presumably arises from their realization that their creations are flawed—in the case of God's handiwork, fatally flawed. But human artists, scientists, and engineers should not think they can do any better, as a host of cautionary myths warn—Babel, Icarus, Prometheus, Faust, Golem, *Frankenstein*. Next to the works of God and Nature, human creations are paltry and imperfect. Philip Roth's alter ego Zuckerman suffered greatly for the discrepancy. He was so depressed by negative reviews of his novels that he resolved to become an obstetrician: "When the baby appears they don't start shouting, 'You call that a baby? That's not a baby!'"[7]

But in fact the gods and Mother Nature have perennially been subject to the same bad reviews, and medical science has arisen to perfect their ill-formed artworks. Bioengineering is the latest critic to exclaim, "You call that a baby?"[8] But bioethicists are all too aware that as soon as one takes over the author function, whether of novels or babies, the possibility of failure arises. If Zuckerman had decided to study bioengineering instead of obstetrics—a choice unavailable in the early 1980s when *The Anatomy Lesson* was written—he would have opened himself to the very criticism he was seeking to escape. In the perennial analogy between human and divine creativity, the issues of artistry, beauty, and perfectibility are unavoidably connected.

"You call that a baby?" is more or less the response of Hawthorne's protagonist Aylmer to his wife Georgiana, despite the fact that she is the most beautiful woman anyone in the neighborhood has ever seen. Among her many charms is a birthmark, which resembles a rosy little hand "printed" on her cheek. Aylmer loves Georgiana dearly, but he finds the mark an intolerable defect in her beauty and marshals all his arcane scientific knowledge to the task of removing it. Hawthorne explains in one of his notebooks (as paraphrased by Edward H. Davidson) that Aylmer is making a logical error: "the very nature of beauty is its being flawed, and that which, in this life, is most pure and ethereal is so only in its imperfection."[9] Beauty is different from perfection; to equate them is a formalist error with dire ethical consequences. Indeed, the very concept of perfection implies absoluteness, an independence from context, contingent social norms, and relationality that "ethics" implies.

The explanation for Aylmer's category error, according to the narrator, is his one-sided intellectualism, which lacks the counterbalance of emotion. For Aylmer, beauty is as abstract and formal as the flawless corpse he makes by "perfecting" Georgiana. This separation of reason from emotion was a defining concern of romantic aesthetics. In his 1795 *Aesthetic Education of Man*, Schiller pictured the Greeks as integrated beings akin to "all-unifying Nature," whereas "Moderns" model themselves on "all-dividing Intellect."[10] Schiller considered Kant a genius, "but will such a mind, dissolved as it were into pure intellect and pure contemplation, ever be capable of exchanging the rigorous bonds of logic for the free movement of the poetic faculty, or of grasping the concrete individuality of things with a sense innocent of preconceptions and faithful to the object?"[11] The answer was an emphatic "no."

However, for Hawthorne, the opposite extreme—grasping only the concrete individuality of things—is just as problematic. He contrasts Aylmer to his lab assistant Aminadab on this score: "With his vast strength, his shaggy hair, his smoky aspect, and the indescribable earthiness that incrusted him, he seemed to represent man's physical nature; while Aylmer's slender figure, and pale, intellectual face, were no less apt a type of the spiritual element."[12] Aminadab has no trouble appreciating Georgiana's beauty despite the mark on her cheek: "If she were my wife," he says, "I'd never part with that birth-mark" (770). Had Aylmer been able to see with Aminadab's eyes, he would have loved Georgiana as she was and lived his life a happy man. Yet, at the same time, Aminadab is described as repellent—gross, vulgar, and quite likely prurient in his attraction to Georgiana. Despite Hawthorne's obvious disapproval of Aylmer's perfectionism, he is equally disapproving of Aminadab's "harsh, uncouth, misshapen tones" (772).

The story seems to snag on this contradiction: to embrace a beauty distinct from perfection, one must have at least a touch of brute physicality, but a brute, ipso facto, is unworthy of beauty.[13] A vast fairy-tale heritage underscores this dilemma. Whenever a Beauty and a Beast cross paths, the Beauty remains endangered or oppressed until the Beast changes into a Prince, leaving his vulgar physicality behind. The conventions of literary romance perpetuate this body-spirit opposition. Even when a hero fails, for him to have been a hero in the first place—a Gawain, a Redcrosse Knight, a Gatsby—he must have possessed unusual refinement and a willingness to sacrifice all for his ideal. His failure reflects the imperfection of the human condition, but Aylmer is an absolutist in this respect. Even Georgiana celebrates her husband's uncompromising nobility: "Her heart exulted, while it trembled, at his honorable love, so pure and lofty that it would accept nothing less than perfection, nor miserably make itself contented with an earthlier nature than he had dreamed of. She felt how much more precious was such a sentiment, than that meaner kind which would have borne with the imperfection for her sake, and have been guilty of treason to holy love, by degrading its perfect idea to the level of the actual" (777). "Holy love" and "perfect beauty" are oxymorons in "The Birthmark"; the first term in each annihilates the second, and yet Hawthorne offers no way out of this contradiction.

Aminadab is not alone in finding Georgiana's beauty unspoiled by the birthmark. As Judith Fetterley points out, "To those who love Georgiana, her birthmark is evidence of her beauty; to those who envy or hate her, it is an object of disgust . . . Clearly, the birthmark takes on its character from the eye of the beholder."[14] Beauty as Hawthorne presents it is the product of an interaction. Among the opinions the narrator reports is that "some fairy, at her birth-hour, had laid her tiny hand upon the infant's cheek" or that the mark is an ornament, a "charm," as Georgiana herself describes it (765, 764). The double meaning of *charm* echoes ominously in this word choice—a charm against what?—as do the dangers princesses are wont to encounter when fairy presents are taken away from them.

Georgiana's mark, her imperfection, keeps her alive, or more accurately, it is the condition of being alive. Living entails bearing a mark, and therefore embodied beauty can never be perfect, without spot or blemish. Disappearing when Georgiana blushes, the little red imprint is also tied to her emotionality and even her sexuality. The mark "was the fatal flaw of humanity which Nature, in one shape or another, stamps ineffaceably on all her productions, either to imply that they are temporary and finite, or that their perfection must be wrought by toil and pain. The crimson hand expressed the ineludible gripe in which mortality clutches the highest and purest of earthly mould, degrading them into kindred with the lowest, and even with the very brutes, like whom their visible frames return to dust" (780). The narrator's claim is that beauty is not apart from life, nor immune to brutishness. Georgiana and Aminadab are part of the same continuum. In responding to her mark with revulsion, Aylmer has "rejected the best that earth could offer" (780). His desire for perfection in life is a logical contradiction. But as we have seen, Hawthorne presents it as a romance inevitability, unavoidable as long as the grail of the hero-creator is the formal perfection of his creation.

Hawthorne both perpetuates this convention and satirizes it. He describes Aylmer's error not through the high-flown symbolism of sin and pride, but through the secular metaphor of patent violation. The medieval alchemists Aylmer has studied, Paracelsus and Albertus Magnus, have "imagined themselves, to have acquired from the investigation of nature a power above nature, and from physics a sway over the spiritual world" (774). But Aylmer's experiments have shown him that it is no easy matter to rival Nature's creativity. For Nature protects her methods: "our great creative Mother . . . is yet severely careful to keep her own secrets. . . . She permits us indeed, to mar, but seldom to mend, and, like a jealous patentee, on no account to make" (769). The creation of life—in Georgiana's case, a beautiful woman—is evidently guarded by a top-secret patent. Aylmer has given up on trying to "make" a living being himself,[15] but even trying to "mend" or perfect Mother Nature's inventions requires access to her secret formula. The birthmark is a symbolic patent or copyright mark, a stamp of the inventor's hand, and Aylmer's attempt to remove it amounts to intellectual property theft. Nature, not he, is Georgiana's author.

As Greek hubris and Judeo-Christian original sin sink to the bathos of patent infringement, a somewhat prurient pun sets in. Etymologically, the word *patent* means "open" (a reference to the "open letters" announcing ownership of an invention). But "our great creative Mother, while she amuses us with apparently working in the broadest sunshine . . . in spite of her pretended openness, shows us nothing but results" (769). The vaunted openness of Nature's female creativity is thus a lie, a tease; her "patents" are closed, allowing no penetration. Fetterley remarks upon "the undercurrent of jealousy, hostility, and frustration toward a specifically female force" in this tale and, like Roth, locates "the source of this attitude in man's jealousy of woman's having something he does not and his rage at being excluded from participating in it."[16] The "closed opening" of the patent pun suggests that Aylmer wishes to penetrate Nature in order to father his creation, his own wife. Obvious but unspoken is the fact that Aylmer could have had legal access to "Nature's formula" simply by having a child with Georgiana. But, of course, the resulting creation would have been as imperfect as its mother. We might note, by the way, that Aylmer's own appearance is never mentioned. The female gendering of beauty is taken for granted; the equivalent male virtue is uncompromising perfectionism.

The undercurrent of narcissism and incest running through the patent pun becomes explicit in Aylmer's evocation of the Pygmalion myth. He tells Georgiana that "even Pygmalion, when his sculptured woman assumed life, felt not greater ecstasy than mine will be" (768). The jump from past to future tense here is jarring; Aylmer is unceremoniously appropriating Pygmalion's ecstasy across a gulf of millennia. It is a doomed attempt. Pygmalion's Galatea started out a statue and ended up the living wife of her artist-creator, whereas the opposite is Georgiana's fate: she goes from living wife to lifeless "artwork." The narrator hints at this reverse symmetry by noting "the marble paleness of Georgiana's cheek" (779) at the moment she drinks Aylmer's potion.

Galatea and Georgiana have some other disturbing correspondences. Pygmalion created his sculpture because he was disgusted with living women, whom he believed were all prostitutes. Aylmer's revulsion at Georgiana's birthmark seems similarly extreme, suggesting that he shares with Pygmalion a disgust at female sexuality. But Pygmalion's purity turns out to be hypocritical. According to Ovid, his innocent statue raises his lust; he caresses Galatea's marble limbs and in his longing calls upon the gods to let him unite with her in marriage. Aylmer, too, despite his high-toned rhetoric, seeks the "ecstasy" Pygmalion experienced, though he will not leave his satisfaction to the will of the gods or nature. Moreover, both creators, in longing for a mate whom they have brought into being, engage in symbolic incest, seeking marriage to what amounts to their offspring.[17] Across the ages, Aylmer appropriates not Pygmalion's ecstasy but his misogyny, incest, and narcissism, and the result is the death of his loving wife.

As Hawthorne presents it, then, the equation of beauty with formal perfection is a terrible threat to women as well as to the perfectionists who purport to love them. It has become a very expensive error by our day. The Harvard ethicist Michael J. Sandel reports that, in Internet auctions, the eggs of fashion models fetch starting bids of $15,000 to $150,000.[18] Alarmed, he entitled his 2007 meditation on genetic engineering *The Case Against Perfection.* Sandel had been a member of the President's Council on Bioethics, which spent several hours interpreting Hawthorne's story.[19] The medical ethicist William F. May provided an overview of the tale, relating Aylmer to parents considering the bioengineering of their child. "On the one hand parents need to accept the child as he is. . . . On the other hand parents must also encourage the well-being of the child. They must promote excellence."[20] The chairman of the council, Leon R. Kass, M.D., labeled these two positions—unconditional love and the striving toward perfection—as "savoring" and "saving" and criticized Hawthorne for disapproving so strongly of saving.

Professor Sandel, however, saw "The Birthmark" as "a parable of the folly of perfectionism, the aspiration to perfect what nature has given us. It is a parable of the folly of despising the given." And yet, "it is not so clear in this story whether this birth-mark really is a defect we should take seriously or not. It seems trivial, [and] if it is trivial then it is not a test of perfectionism or of the given at all. That test could only come if this was really a serious defect." Sandel observed that Hawthorne's intent would have been clearer if Georgiana had been unable to walk properly because one of her legs was shorter than the other, and the other council members agreed. But they were missing the crucial fact that it was Georgiana's beauty rather than her physiological functions that were at issue. When beauty is equated with perfection, no flaw is trivial.

However, the councilors did put their finger on the interactive problems in Aylmer's perfectionist aesthetics: his objectification of his creation, the absoluteness of his control, the godlike authority he took on as creator. Dr. Robert P. George, professor of jurisprudence at Princeton, insisted that the story was about the need for unconditional belief in "human worth and dignity." Professor Stephen Carter of the Yale Law School claimed that the really terrifying aspect of the story was "the obsessive control of one individual over another; the obsessiveness about this characteristic is a problem for us or ought to be equally repulsive whether the treatment succeeds or not."

Professor Carter identified Georgiana's awe toward Aylmer with the mystique continuing to surround science today. "The confidence that the world can be changed or that we can be changed, something can be changed for the better through the life of pure mind, in effect through the life divorced from other concerns, is seduction." This statement might remind us of Schiller's worry over the separation of intellect from emotion, but here the concern is couched in the language of seduction and fall. Indeed, such biblical language ran through the meeting. Dr. Hurlbut stated that with new scientific possibilities opened by DNA research, "The question is what do we do in this situation where there is a sense of imperfection? How do we respond to a world where you cannot, metaphorically speaking, un-bite the apple?"

Chairman Kass suggested that the seductive promises of science were probably irresistible:

A question, I suppose, is whether one could really, in fact, love something wholeheartedly in an idealized sense if it were not perfect, and is[n't] mortality for at least some people a sufficient blemish. . . . What kinds of deaths are not premature when the desire to live knows no bounds? . . . There is something in the culture at large and something in medicine today, however modestly practiced, that almost says, "Look, we will never stop until we can deal with mortality as such." . . . That remains a deep question for us as we look at various kinds of efforts to improve this or to fix that. What are the limits and to what extent do we have to accept the given both as given and as perhaps perfectible?

No answer was immediately forthcoming, and, in the years that followed, Professor Sandel encountered a wide range of opinions on these issues, which he summarized in The Case Against Perfection (26–27). People fear the possibility that we could engineer perfect beings, because "some element of unpredictability seem[s] to make a moral difference" (3), because cloning a child seems to violate its right to autonomy, because making people ideal raises "questions about the moral status of nature" (2). Genetic engineering represents "a kind of hyper-agency," he reports, "a Promethean aspiration to remake nature" (26).

Many of the arguments in this list reveal the connection between perfection and one-sided power and agency, and, without explicitly describing beauty and excellence as interactive appreciation, Sandel was laying the grounds for this idea. Bioengineering, as he describes it, stands or falls on connoisseurship, and connoisseurship depends on power sharing. A clone's beauty may be flawless, but if we do not value that beauty the cloning is not justified—and what Sandel discovered is that we will not value it. A perfect creation, totally determined by its bioengineer, would be valued only as an expression of its creator's skill: "The bionic athlete would not be an agent. . . . 'His' achievements would be those of his inventor" (26). This self-aggrandizing creativity could not provide an ethical justification for bioengineering. The agency of the creation must be respected.

Evidently, this is so even when creators perfect themselves. If athletes could take drugs and have cloned parts, Sandel says, games would perhaps be interesting spectacles, but we would not *admire* the athletes. Respect, admiration, and appreciation come in response, paradoxically, to "the display of natural talents and gifts that are no doing of the athlete who possesses them" (28), however much the athlete may have cultivated those gifts. Sandel goes so far as to claim that complete control gives us "nothing to affirm or behold outside our own will" (100). The bioengineer or the athlete or beauty who engineers herself is the equivalent of a Pygmalion, in love with nothing but the exteriorization of himself. But no one else values him in that way or would condone the genetic alteration of life in order to further such a goal.

Thus, Sandel concludes that the wonder of extraordinary beauty and talent lies in their accidentality. For a creation to have value, indeterminacy and risk must enter its creation. Sandel's central claim is that we must defend a belief in what he calls the "giftedness" of life: that "our talents and powers are not wholly our own doing, nor even fully ours. . . . It is, in part, a religious sensibility. But its resonance reaches beyond religion" (27). Beauty need not be attributable to God, he claims; it is attributable instead to accident. In "giftedness," where creativity and appreciation are inextricably linked, beauty is beyond any single agent's control.

In "The Birthmark" it was the creator Aylmer who wanted to exert a control so complete that it destroyed the beauty it sought to perfect. In our day the danger is that the Georgianas of the world will take over this male perfectionism and, in the process, bring about their own destruction. According to a recent *New York Times* headline: "Study Suggests That a Need for Physical Perfection May Reveal Emotional Flaws."[21] Evidently, scientists have discovered that women who elect plastic surgery are three times as likely as others to commit suicide or die of substance abuse. As one of the researchers states, "it is our responsibility to ascertain that a patient is a stable person with realistic expectations who wants breast augmentation for the right reasons." He does not specify what those right reasons might be, but we may surmise that perfection is not among them.[22]

Feminism told this story of women's self-subversion long before the researchers, but despite persistent warnings against the "temptation to be a beautiful object,"[23] and the exposure of the impure motives of cosmetic surgeons like Thomas Pynchon's Dr. Schoenmacher in the novel *V.*, there is not a woman in America—perhaps not anywhere—who does not feel pressure to improve or perfect her appearance. Bioengineering, we might say, is Us. And the reason is obvious: the social pressure for formal perfection has been unrelenting in our culture, especially for those not blessed with Georgiana's minimally flawed beauty.

Beauty perfectionism has a special relevance in political systems based on equality. As Sandel points out, the "giftedness" of beauty is "an uncomfortable fact for democratic societies" (28). Of course, the uneven distribution of beauty was a concern long before egalitarian governments arose. "Cinderella" and "Snow White" are testimony to these anxieties. In "The Ugly Duckling" the inequality is corrected when the duckling grows up to become a swan far more beautiful than the ducks who formerly mocked him. Democratic values do not seem to have been much served by this reversal, though revenge is always sweet.

But American popular culture is now embarked on a more radical solution: dropping the equation of beauty with formal perfection and embracing beauty as interaction. In the television show *Ugly Betty*, for example, the heroine is short and plump and wears glasses and dental braces, but she possesses social virtues that are recognized as a superior beauty—gutsiness, humility, humor, kindness—and potentially available to anyone. Similarly, the early twenty-first-century ad campaigns for Nike, Dove, and Chicken of the Sea feature ordinary-looking models appearing to be having a wonderful time. These campaigns promote (and profit from) the idea that women's beauty lies in their capacity for pleasure, self-realization, and human connection rather than in their having a size 0 body.

The musical *Hairspray* makes the link between egalitarian beauty and interaction explicit, presenting formal beauty as downright un-American.

Interactive beauty, in contrast, has the power to create a democratic utopia. Velma Von Tussle, the would-be seductress played in the 1988 film by Deborah Harry and in the 2007 remake by Michele Pfeiffer, is bad through and through—repressive, power-hungry, and totally self-serving in the use of her fading charms. As the producer of a teen dance show on television, Velma acts out her "lookism" and its frightening correlate, racism, in 1960s Baltimore. She herself is a former beauty contestant who slept with judges in the vain hope of receiving the crown, and she stands about the TV set in provocative poses, directing the teenage girls in the show to dance like conformist automata. Her idea of beauty is the frozen perfection of a sculpted Galatea, and the girls' identical, inflexible helmets of hair symbolize this corpselike, regimented beauty. Take away the "spray" and you have the liberationist *Hair,* a musical for which *Hairspray* might be considered the prequel.

The heroine Tracy Turnblad sports the same lacquered hair as the other girls until her liberationist triumph at the end, at which point her flip relaxes into a flow. But, from the beginning, she is more concerned with dancing than hairdos. She exhibits the brilliance and originality of a "natural," dancing like the black teenagers who are limited to the segregated version of the TV show. Velma at first prevents the plump Tracy from appearing on the show, and Tracy understands this lookism as equivalent to the racism that keeps the black teenagers off the regular show. Tracy dances with anyone, black or white, as long as he is a good dancer, and good dancers want to dance with the short, fat Tracy, regardless of the "flaws" in her appearance. The camera shows her and her partners thrilled with each other, inspiring each other to greater and greater virtuosity.

Tracy's mother Edna is a victim of the beauty anxieties enforced by Velma's fascism. For decades Edna has been too ashamed to go out of her house because of her weight, remaining hidden away inside, "closeted." The absurdity of Edna's self-imposed house arrest covers an outrage—an exclusion that must be corrected—and Tracy teaches her mother the joy of coming out. Through this pun, *Hairspray* adds homophobia to racism and lookism as infringements of equality and freedom brought on by the beauty police epitomized by Velma.

The role of Edna Turnblad calls for a male actor in drag: Divine in the original film and John Travolta in the remake.[24] Cross-dressing thus creates a double identity for "Edna" as both a female character suffering from her lack of conventional beauty and a male actor who comically simulates that formal failure. The brave black woman played by Queen Latifah encourages

Tracy and Edna's liberation as well as the black dancers', showing how magnificent a queen-sized woman can be—actor and character both—if she carries herself with pride and instills a corresponding pride in those around her. The actor's name, Queen, is another conjunction of gender, race, and beauty emancipation.

In the comedy of their double identity, Divine and Travolta play into some very conventional heterosexual assumptions, for example, that a closeted fat woman is about as ridiculous as a male actor cross-dressing to look like her. Like Dustin Hoffman's Tootsie, Travolta's Edna is as ugly and ungainly as we might expect a woman played by a man to be. This is a very different meaning from the more typical situation, in which professional female impersonators style themselves as feminine beauties—the Hollywood star, the exotic seductress, the porn queen. Their virtuosity lies in the astonishing seamlessness of the imitation, as in Breffni McKenna's role as Tinker in Neil Jordan's *The Crying Game* or Toni Cantó's Lola in Pedro Almodóvar's *All About My Mother*. To make huge efforts in order to look like an ugly woman is to spoof the aspiration to female beauty as such, and the cuddling that goes on between Travolta's ungainly Edna and her sensitive fey husband (played by Christopher Walken) is an oddly touching affirmation of domestic love, oblivious to such superficialities as fashion, physical appearance, and perhaps even biological sex.

Judith Butler has argued that Divine's appearance in *Hairspray* "implicitly suggests that gender is a kind of persistent impersonation that passes as the real." Butler continues: "Her/his performance destabilizes the very distinctions between the natural and the artificial, depth and surface, inner and outer through which discourse about genders almost always operates. . . . Does being female constitute a 'natural fact' or a cultural performance, or is 'naturalness' constituted through discursively constrained performative acts that produce the body through and within the categories of sex?"[25] The fact that Edna is played by a man, however, does not necessarily suggest that gender is a performance lacking a basis in the real. Such is certainly the case for Velma, whose approach to femininity is based on hypocrisy and artifice. But she is the villain of the piece, whereas Tracy and Edna are unequivocally coded as authentic and genuine. When it comes to gender, in fact, *Hairspray* is far more concerned with the equal opportunity to express one's nature rather than any split between gender and nature. The first thing Edna does after she "comes out" is to go shopping for new clothes. Tracy, despite her independence, is as interested in hair and boys as the other girls in the film. For Velma, the idea of fat women dressing up, or of men finding them more attractive than her, is absurd. The natural order of things, as far as she is concerned, assigns a monopoly on these pleasures to the beautiful, and, when she discovers that nature does not subscribe to this order, she enforces it through other means.

For better or worse, *Hairspray* is far more essentialist in its view of gender than its puns and cross-dressing would suggest. If clothes, hair, and flirtation are elements of a performance, all women in the show seem eager to perform. The musical shows nothing arbitrary or unnatural about their behavior, or, to put it differently, this is not gender performance but, on the contrary, gender expression, and the point is that all women should have equal access to it. What *Hairspray* attacks is unequal access to natural expression: black dancers not permitted to dance because of racism; pubescent girls not allowed to have fun because of puritanical parents (the case of Tracy's best friend); women not allowed to behave like women because of prejudice against the fat or the "ugly."

Admittedly, Divine and Travolta do literally perform femininity in enacting Edna. But, rather than equating gender with performance, this fact suggests a parallel between victims of beauty perfectionism (women) and victims of "gender perfectionism" (gays, cross-dressers). Coercive social mores and the rigid binaries embedded in the literary romance (as in "The Birthmark") value only formally beautiful women and straight men, and that leaves a lot of people "less equal."

The symbolic antidote to this injustice is Tracy's dancing. It is presented as a natural talent, Sandel's "gift," for, within the racial assumptions of the community, it is an unaccountable accident: Tracy has "rhythm" even though she is white. Her dancing stirs the admiration of the cutest boy on the TV show, also a puzzling development given that he could have had his pick of the pretty girl dancers. He admires Tracy's talent and spirit and eventually comes to love her, gaining a sense of social justice in the process. Tracy's dancing thus creates connection, empathy, and equality. It is her beauty, and a thoroughly interactive beauty at that. In the triumphant climax of *Hairspray*, Tracy's dancing leads to the end of racial segregation in Baltimore. Thus, if Sandel sees the unequal distribution of formal beauty as "an uncomfortable fact for democratic societies" (28), *Hairspray* finds interactive beauty an unequivocal democratic blessing. To trade form for interaction is to shake off the coercion and *un*naturalness of perfectionism.

Hairspray might seem a banal ending to an essay on beauty in American culture. It is a commercial product, after all, and its invocation of pop culture as the solution to racial injustice is simplistic in the extreme. But, if we resist learning the value of an interactive notion of beauty from a blockbuster musical, we should remember how useful our elitism is to the forces of perfectionism. They choose to present the "case against perfection" as the case *for* Aminadab, and few of us feel comfortable making such a case. But here we might borrow something from the Old World *Frankenstein*, a work in which the alternative to the death-dealing perfectionist is not a vulgar brute, but the less extreme and far more lovable characters of Henry Clerval and Elizabeth, Frankenstein's best friend and his fiancée, respectively. Their hearts thrill to the world's imperfect beauty. If *Hairspray* transports Elizabeth and Henry to Baltimore, fat or in drag, maybe we can see through to the "naturals" beneath and join with them in a dance of ethical beauty.

Notes

1. Wendy Steiner, *Venus in Exile: The Rejection of Beauty in Twentieth-Century Art* (Chicago: University of Chicago Press, 2001).

2. Alexander Pope, *An Essay on Criticism* (London: W. Lewis, 1711), 19.

3. Immanuel Kant, *Critique of Judgment*, trans. Werner S. Pluhar and Mary J. Gregor (Indianapolis: Hackett, 1987), 229.

4. Bob Dylan, "Lay Lady Lay," *Nashville Skyline* (Columbia Records, 1969).

5. Christopher Bram, *Father of Frankenstein* (New York: Dutton, 1995), 11; also published as *Gods and Monsters*, after the 1998 film.

6. "Letter to Artists" (1999), quoted in Michael Novak, "Beauty Is Truth: The Changing of the Tides," in *Frederick Hart: Changing Tides* (Manchester, VT: Hudson Hills, 2005), 1.

7. Philip Roth, *The Anatomy Lesson* (Toronto: Collins, 1983), 103.

8. Just as people perennially confuse "art" with "good art," they will soon be in a position to confuse "baby" with "good baby." For a discussion of the use of the category, art, as an honorific, see Wendy Steiner, *The Scandal of Pleasure: Art in an Age of Fundamentalism* (Chicago: University of Chicago Press, 1995), chapter 1.

9. Edward H. Davidson, Headnote to "The Birthmark," in Perry Miller and Jean C. Sisk, eds., *Major Writers of America*, shorter ed. (New York: Harcourt, Brace and World, 1966), 389.

10. Friedrich von Schiller, "From *On the Aesthetic Education of Man*," in Vincent B. Leitch, William E. Cain, Laurie A. Finke, and Barbara E. Johnson, eds., *Norton Anthology of Theory and Criticism* (New York: Norton, 2001), 575.

11. Ibid., 579.

12. Nathaniel Hawthorne, "The Birthmark," in *Tales and Sketches*, ed. Roy Harvey Pearce (New York: Library of America, 1982), 770. Further page references to Hawthorne's tale will be given parenthetically within the text.

13. The President's Council on Bioethics revealed their confusion on just this issue. According to Professor Meilaender, "I do not know whether . . . the animal nature is to be more trusted than the spirit or whether the animal nature divorced from the spirit perhaps. I mean, whether really we need the two together." January 17, 2002 (session 2): http://bioethics.georgetown.edu/pcbe/transcripts/jan02/jan17session2.html (accessed April 10, 2011).

14. Judith Fetterley, *The Resisting Reader: A Feminist Approach to American Fiction* (Bloomington: Indiana University Press, 1978), 31.

15. Mary E. Rucker writes, "As he unabashedly tells Georgiana, he has engaged in 'thought which might almost have enlightened me to create a being less perfect than yourself.' While he does not attempt the homunculus, he is confident that he can correct nature's imperfection." "Science and Art in Hawthorne's 'The Birth-Mark,'" *Nineteenth-Century Literature* 41, no. 4 (March 1987): 455.

16. Fetterley, *The Resisting Reader*, 27, 28.

17. Pygmalion's incestuousness is a critical commonplace (Montaigne, for example, mentions it in his *Essais* and Sir James Fraser does so in *The Golden Bough*). Arnold Silver writes that, in Shaw's treatment of the myth, he "knew that in longing for the union between Eliza and Higgins we ignore the secret appeal of the Pygmalion legend. . . . For after all the sculptor would be committing incest in marrying the woman he fathered parthenogenically," quoted in Jean Reynolds, *Pygmalion's Wordplay: The Postmodern Shaw* (Gainesville: University of Florida Press, 1999), 140.

18. Michael J. Sandel, *The Case Against Perfection: Ethics in the Age of Genetic Engineering* (Cambridge: Harvard University Press, 2007), 72. Further page references will be given parenthetically within the text. Note the echo of Benjamin's "The Work of Art in the Age of Mechanical Reproduction," evoking a parallel between the technological reproduction of artworks and of people.

19. Though the council was concerned about bioengineered children rather than cosmetically perfected wives, Hawthorne's tale encompasses "creations" of either sort, as its subtheme of incest suggests.

20. See note 13 for the current Web location of the transcript of this hearing. Further quotations from the several speakers at the hearing all refer to this transcript.

21. Natasha Singer, "Study Suggests That a Need for Physical Perfection May Reveal Emotional Flaws," *New York Times*, August 12, 2007, http://www.nytimes.com/2007/08/16/fashion/16sside2.html?_r=1&scp=1&sq=Study%20Suggests%20That%20a%20Need%20for%20Physical%20Perfection&st=cse (accessed April 10, 2011).

22. It is interesting that scientists are telling this as a story of mental imbalance among women, given the commercial motives fanning the craze for cosmetic enhancements. Maureen Dowd reports that they "have become so common that you can now get 'frequent flier' cards for wrinkles—racking up rewards every time a dermatologist or a plastic surgeon sticks a needle in your face. . . . Medicis Pharmaceuticals, the maker of Restylane, an anti-wrinkle skin filler, is offering a rewards program 'to encourage injections every six months by offering gifts that escalate in value with each subsequent appointment." Maureen Dowd, "Frozen Mermaids, Scary Sirens," *New York Times*, March 3, 2005, http://www.nytimes.com/2005/03/03/opinion/03dowd.html?scp=2&sq =Frozen+Mermaids%2C+Scary+Sirens&st=nyt (accessed April 10, 2011).

23. Dana Densmore, "On the Temptation to Be a Beautiful Object," *No More Fun and Games: A Journal of Female Liberation* (February 1969): 43–47.

24. The casting of John Travolta in the film of course lent a special irony to the role, because of the dance role in *Saturday Night Fever* that made him a star.

25. Judith Butler, "From *Gender Trouble*," in Leitch, *Norton Anthology*, 2489.

PART 3

Aesthetics and the Reading of Form

[9]

When Is Now?

Poe's Aesthetics of Temporality

CINDY WEINSTEIN

Time is an essential component in the narrative of *The Narrative of Arthur Gordon Pym*. Augustus's watch stops and his father's chronometer disappears. The passage of days, hours, and minutes occupies much narrative space and anxious speculation. The narrative assumes the form of a log with months and dates demarcated. But time's presence runs even deeper. Adverbs designating the passage of time, for example *after* and *at length*, are a constitutive feature of *Pym*'s narrative fabric, as are adjectives that convey an experience of time, such as *immediate* and *still*. As much as Pym's is a journey in space, his is also a journey in and through time. In an analysis of how anthropological discourse deploys the markers of time, such as tenses and adverbs, to produce the subjects of its study as colonized others separate in time, Johannes Fabian provides a valuable template for understanding *Pym*, which contains pages of material plagiarized from antebellum exploration narratives. By reading key anthropological texts, Fabian foregrounds the central but unstudied role time plays in the imperial/epistemological conquest of space and argues that "time [was required] to accommodate the schemes of a one-way history: progress, development, modernity (and their negative mirror images: stagnation, underdevelopment, tradition)": "In short, *geopolitics* has its ideological foundations in *chronopolitics.*"[1] Another way of putting this is to say that "chronopolitics" posits a static temporality—the past or then—against which progress—the present or now—measures itself. There must be a zero degree, an origin, in order for the story of progress to tell itself.

On the one hand, *Pym* tells the story of the Tsalalian culture far removed in space and stuck in an originary moment of time that, upon contact with the modern (white) world, must be destroyed because of its savage and primitive (black) nature. On the other hand, the temporal complexities of Poe's narrative constantly undermine the "one-way history" that is essential to the imperial project. *Pym*'s chronopolitics, then, are not as ideologically straightforward and consistent as Fabian's analysis might lead us to believe, and there are two reasons why: because the "now" of *Pym* is constantly shifting and because *Pym*, for all of its borrowings from travel narratives, is a fiction and a self-conscious work of art that aims to amuse, baffle, and frighten the reader. Inasmuch as there is a chronopolitics at work in *Pym*, there is also what I shall call an aesthetics of temporality. The two are in tension and pull the text in quite different directions, with the chronopolitics offering a stable sense of past and present in order to make an argument about the necessity of racial hierarchy and domination and the aesthetics subverting that stability in order to have the desired effect on the reader.

What follows is a close reading of *Pym* that combines narrative theory, history of science, and Poe's racial politics. With Fabian's analysis in mind, I begin by identifying the uses to which time in *Pym* is put and then read those uses in a dialectic relation with "wider" contexts. First, my analysis foregrounds and theorizes *Pym*'s colliding tenses through the vocabulary provided by Gerard Genette, specifically the temporal "anachronies" of prolepsis and analepsis.[2] The temporal chaos of the narrative—its shifting dates, unknowable o'clocks, and warping sentences—is both caused by and reflected in the text, which fails to keep track of its time-keeping devices, in particular the run-down watch and the lost chronometer.[3] The missing chronometer leads to my reading's second framework, which is the history of science, particularly John Harrison's 1735 discovery of the chronometer and the measurement of longitude. Longitude, which is the conversion of time into space, gave explorers a sure sense of where they were and consequently made exploration safer and more profitable. Calculating longitude, however, depends upon keeping track of time, which is a dicey proposition in *Pym*. The third step in my reading is an examination of Poe's perturbations of time in relation to his representations of race. I argue that *Pym*'s quick descent into a temporal freefall works against Poe's notion of time as a reliable demarcation of the differences between civilization and savagery, present and past, white and black. The text attempts to recover, but not wholly successfully, its sense of now by locating its then in the alleged clarity of racial difference (the "perfectly white wool of the Arctic bear" and "the jet black complexions" of the Tsalalians) with which *Pym* concludes.[4]

"The Sentence Had Passed"

Critics have observed that *Pym* is a strange tale for Poe to have written because of its length. Unlike "The Black Cat," for example, thirty minutes (Poe's ideal duration for achieving the greatest effect on his reader) is not enough time, even for the speediest reader, to get through *Pym*, which means that Poe's own text goes against his statement that a reader can sustain a high degree of excitement within "the limit of a single sitting." Perhaps Poe was right about the limitations of the reader (and himself as a writer of lengthy works), and this is why antebellum reviewers complained about the "tough stories in this book [being] told in a loose and slip-shod style" or criticized "the faulty construction and poorness of style."[5] Poe was encouraged by friends at Harper and Brothers to write something longer than usual in order to attract new readers and make some much-needed money, but he succeeded in neither. He did not want to write such a long story and he inflicted his own sense of artistic integrity, compromised by economic necessity, upon his reader. Even readers who acknowledged its accomplished style were more interested in contesting the preface's claims that "the public were not at all disposed to receive it as fable" (56) and establishing what was and was not true.

Because the preface purposefully confuses the two (Poe poses as Pym's editor, urging Pym to publish his narrative as true, and Pym decides to publish it in the "*Southern Messenger under the garb of fiction*" [56]), readers of *Pym*, then and now, have tried to separate the ridiculous from the possible. Burton R. Pollin's magisterial edition meticulously examines Poe's claims. For example, when Pym and Augustus take a joyride on the Ariel, and Pym states, "we should be out of sight of land before daybreak" (60), Pollin remarks, "In terms of time, distance, and rates of speed, more realistically interpreted than Poe perhaps intended, a boat of this size, running off the wind in this weather, at a probable five knots, in about three hours would hit Monomy Point at the southeast corner of Cape Cod, where he would still see the land" (220). Regarding such inconsistencies, antebellum reviewers responded as if personally attacked (and the preface certainly gave them reason) and lambasted the text's "gross improbabilities and preternatural adventures." Poe was also attacked for his "evident ignorance in all nautical matters," including his description of the stowage on the Grampus: "No Yankee captain of a whaler ever packed his oil casks in such a careless manner."[6]

But what does that mean? We could follow this approach and quote the preface where Pym informs us that he "kept no journal during a great portion of the time in which he was absent" (55) and therefore he could not possibly know the lines of latitude and longitude until his return, then making them up. But he made the whole thing up, which leads us to conclude, in the words of the New York Review, "the work is all a fiction"—which Poe has already told us.[7] A more fruitful approach concedes the fictionality of Pym and considers how Poe utilizes the markers of time in his fiction (markers that usually help to produce the illusion of reality in that fiction) to create in the reader's mind a profoundly disorienting experience of narrative time. Poe-time runs according to a logic that invokes the conventional passage of time and undercuts the reader's ability to follow its passage. The instability of time establishes Poe as its arbiter and the reader as the amused/bemused/confused victim of his temporal shenanigans. Now is when I, Poe, say it is.

The dissolution of time, or conventional measurements of time, is literalized in the early section of Pym when Augustus gives the narrator a watch, which soon stops working. Despite informing us that "the watch . . . was run down, and there were, consequently, no means of determining how long I had slept" (70–71), the narrator, nevertheless, writes "for the last fourteen or fifteen hours I had no water—nor had I slept during that time" (78). Although the narrator has confessed that there is simply no way he or the reader can know this, the narrative overloads itself with phrases, such as "in about an hour" (70) or "for some minutes" (76), that say just the opposite. Interspersed among these denominations of time, other temporal markers appear, such as "quickly" (89) and "momentary" (81). And if a sentence does not insist on noting through hours or adverbs the passage of time, words such as "next" (77), "before" (78), "at last" (78), "then" (76), "presently" (77) and "now" (77) register the narrative's hold on sequence.

But to put Pym into a sequence, on the order of Genette's example in Narrative Discourse, is to get lost amidst the false distinctions of hours and minutes, between then and now, finding oneself searching for a present moment against which to measure the narrator's retrospective and anticipatory or, to use Genette's terms, analeptic and proleptic statements. Such terms are useful for thinking about the preface, which appears first in the story but is written at some point, unknown, but certainly after the first two installments of the narrative have appeared under Poe's name in the *Southern Literary Messenger*. The preface fulfills the requirements of analepsis in that it recounts a set of events in the past leading up to the present in which Pym is writing. Yet it is also an example of prolepsis in that its final paragraph is a series of sentences containing the words, "it will be seen at once," "it will be also be understood," and "it will be unnecessary to point out" (56)—anticipatory phrases that are the hallmark of prolepsis. According to Genette, one begins to understand how a text works by mapping these kinds of temporal relations between narrative and story.

I use the word *map* because throughout *Narrative Discourse* Genette relies on spatial metaphors to describe the temporal operations of narrative. He speaks of "narrative information that has its degrees" (162), and describes "the Proustian scene as a 'magnetic pole'" (111). In the chapter "Order," he writes, "pinpointing and measuring these narrative *anachronies* . . . implicitly assume the existence of a kind of zero degree that would be a condition of perfect temporal correspondence between narrative and story" (35–36). In the chapter "Mood," Genette characterizes narrative as "keep[ing] a greater or lesser *distance* from what it tells" (163) and reminds us that this "common and convenient spatial metaphor . . . is not to be taken literally" (162). However, he continues to use the metaphor of the "degree zero" as he strives to locate "a reference point for a rigorous comparison of real durations" (86, 87). In defining narrative speed, he writes, "we mean the relationship between a temporal dimension and a spatial dimension (so many meters per second, so many seconds per meter)" (87). The zero degree is thus necessary to structure the oppositions between before and after, then and now, Pym and Poe.

There is a longitudinal rhetoric and logic to Genette's assumption of "the existence of a kind of zero degree." His search for a way to measure "real durations" is, bizarre as the analogy might seem, narrative theory's equivalent of the scientific desire for a chronometer. Historian of science Dava Sobel tells the story of John Harrison, the English clockmaker who invented a chronometer that could keep track of time at sea. This invention was so important to English imperial ambitions that the British Parliament passed "The Longitude Act of 1714," which would reward millions of dollars in today's valuation to the person who invented a clock that could determine longitude. The difficulty lay in constructing an instrument that would be immune to the climate changes, alterations in atmospheric pressure, and a ship's vacillations. What was needed was a chronometer that would not only mark the passage of time aboard ship but also maintain the time of the ship's point of origination. For every hour that the ship has traveled from the home port, that ship has traveled fifteen degrees of longitude. Without knowing home port time, ships did not know where they were, which often had terrible consequences. Sobel describes one "miserable history [that] relates quintessential horror stories of death by scurvy and thirst, of ghosts in the rigging . . . of drowned corpses fouling the beaches."[8]

Without knowing their longitude, which is only possible with a chronometer, a shipwreck like this, with all its gothic terrors, awaits Pym and company. Indeed, Sobel's story sounds an awful lot like chapter 10 of *Pym*, in which the narrator describes "twenty-five or thirty human bodies . . . scattered about between the counter and the galley, in the last and most loathsome state of putrefaction" (124). The potential for gothic effect is heightened by the absence of a chronometer (Sobel would not put it quite this way, but Poe might), and Poe is certainly aware of the fact and importance of chronometers (a chronometer appears in "The Unparalleled Adventure of One Hans Pfaall"). Harrison had built a functioning chronometer as early as 1770, which means that the navigators aboard the Grampus would have had access to one. Third, and most importantly, Poe tells us in chapter 4 that Augustus's father had a chronometer: "the first mate, eyeing [Augustus's father] with an expression of fiendish derision, and deliberately searching his pockets, from which he presently drew forth a large wallet and a chronometer" (85). The chronometer is one of two timepieces aboard the ship, the other being the watch that Augustus puts in Pym's hiding place and which frequently runs down. It is the chronometer, however, that is the important instrument for measuring time, and it mysteriously disappears from the narrative. What the mate has done with the chronometer is never explained, but his fate is: in reaction to Pym's disguise as Rogers's corpse, the mate "fell back, stone dead" (112). Was the chronometer with him when he fell stone dead? Did it break? If not, where did it go?

The chronometer momentarily appears in *Pym* only to vanish, and with it the degree zero, the Greenwich meridian against which time can be told and against which the narrative can support its sense of now, its hold on the past, and its grip on the future. Pym admits as much in his account of falling asleep, passing out, and realizing that his watch has run down. Yet these confessions of temporal uncertainty keep company or compete with attestations of temporal certitude. The reader shuttles between these positions, struggling to keep track of what has happened and when, even though to figure that out, which the narrative demands we at least try to do, is pointless according to the narrator's admissions that he has no idea what time it is. This is a source of humor in a footnote to chapter 18 that follows the words "this morning" (166). The narrator writes, "the terms *morning* and *evening*, which I have made use of to avoid confusion in my narrative, as far as possible, must not, of course, be taken in their ordinary sense. For a long time past we had no night at all, the daylight being continual. The dates throughout are according to nautical time, and the bearings must be understood as per compass" (167). With this, a wedge is driven between the dates on the page and their signification. We think we know what "morning" means, but perhaps not. Morning does not necessarily signify the sun rising, or having risen, because it has never set.

Lest we think that calendrical dates are real, the footnote continues: "I would also remark, in this place, that I cannot, in the first portion of what is here written, pretend to strict accuracy in respect to dates, or latitudes and longitudes, having kept no regular journal until after the period of which this first portion treats" (167). We have seen this language of "the first portion" before, and that is in the preface, where Pym talks about Poe "draw[ing] up, in his own words, a narrative of the earlier portion of my adventures, from facts afforded by myself" (56). The question arises, to what "first portion" does this footnote refer? Indeed, this footnote is a miniaturized version of what repeatedly happens in *Pym*, as the reader, under the direction of a narrator who constantly uses temporal markers that promise sequence but do not deliver, struggles less to keep track of what happened than when it happened. In the first chapter of *Pym*, which the narrator "relate[s] . . . by way of introduction to a longer and more momentous narrative" (57), Augustus drinks too much and passes out. Pym temporarily manages until he too passes out, only to wake up and find himself and Augustus rescued. The narrative then shifts to an explanation of what happened during the time of lapsed consciousness. Although the narrator retrospectively presents this account, he has received it from someone else (perhaps Augustus, but it is not clear) who retrospectively narrates the rescue. We are taken into a past about which Pym could not have known, and he states, "the mystery of our being in existence was now soon explained" (61).

When is this now? It is not the now of the narrator's present, with which he concludes the opening paragraph of chapter 1: "when I now think of [my adventures], it appears to me a thousand wonders that I am alive to-day" (57). Rather it is the now of a narrative that is embedded within a narrative that is embedded within a narrative. To clarify: the first *now* is Pym's present, as he recalls his adventures. When he speaks of this now, he speaks in the present tense: "when I now think of them, it appears to me . . . " (57). The second *now* is in the past as Pym narrates the troubles aboard the Ariel: "I now boomed along before the wind, shipping heavy seas occasionally" (60). This is in the past tense. The third *now* is Pym coming out of his swoon and listening to the account. He writes that he "was told" (61) of what happened during the time he had passed out, and the fact that he and Augustus are alive "was now soon explained" (61). Even this *now* is not quite now, however, because the word *soon* implies a later. As if this were not complicated enough, embedded within this *now soon* is another: "In the meantime, Henderson [the person leading the rescue] had again put off from the ship, although the wind was now blowing almost a hurricane" (62). The past tense is no longer a simple past, but rather the pluperfect: "he had not been gone many minutes" (62–63).

The levels of retrospective narrative accrete so intensely that the analepses produce what Genette calls "narrative interference" (50). The narrative's time frames become almost impossible to separate, leading to "redundancy or collision" (50), as phrases such as the following demonstrate: "as I said before" (60), "which it will be remembered" (61), or "the period of time just mentioned" (63). The narrative is strewn with evidence of colliding temporalities: "I have already spoken" (99), "many years elapsed before I was aware of this fact" (94), and my favorite, "shortly afterward we could perceive a sensible diminution in the force of the wind, when, now for the first time since the latter part of the evening before, Augustus spoke" (117).

The Narrative of Arthur Gordon Pym. Of Nantucket. Comprising the Details of a Mutiny and Atrocious Butchery. On board the American Brig Grampus, on her way to the South Seas, in the Month of June, 1827. With an account of the recapture of the vessel by the survivers; their shipwreck and subsequent horrible sufferings from Famine; their deliverance by means of the British Schooner Jane Guy; the brief cruise of this latter vessel in the Antarctic Ocean; her capture, and the massacre of her crew among a group of islands in the Eighty-Fourth Parallel of Southern Latitude; Together with the Incredible Adventures and Discoveries Still Farther South to which that Distressing Calamity Gave Rise.

Poe is very interested in length, whether the length of a poem, the length of time one can breathe while buried alive, or the length of time a reader's attention can be sustained. *At length* is one of Poe's favorite phrases and topics. Interestingly, the term is temporal (how long does something take to happen) and spatial (how long is that sentence). Indeed, length is a topic to which the narrative often gravitates. This is the case because length is both a condition of writing imposed upon Poe by Harper and Brothers and it is a condition that he can impose upon his reader. If nothing else, he controls how long Pym lasts. Therefore, length is not only a theme of the story (how long can Pym survive without water? How long before the match goes out?) but a formal concern as well. If the experience of time varies from individual to individual, and if time must nevertheless be subjected to standardized representation, Poe produces an ironic version of time's zero degree, one that refuses to stay in place. Poe's time is simultaneously relativistic, because it is subject to individual experience, and arbitrary, because it is subject to individual whim—Poe's whim.

Perhaps most whimsical is the length of the full title.[9] Its lengthiness is a parody of lengthy titles and was something upon which reviewers remarked: "what say you, reader to that for a title page?"[10] What lengthens the work is not only the series of events narrated and passages from other accounts of exploration Poe copies but also the unnecessary and repetitive words that do little except lengthen the sentences. Thus, Poe writes about "two or three violent quarrels" (88), "twenty-five or thirty human bodies" (124), "twelve or fifteen miles" (131). But there are other signs of lengthening. In one paragraph alone, "at length" appears twice, in addition to "afterward," "shortly afterward," "now," "we lost no time," and "after a short delay" (118–19). Adverbs, especially those designating time and speed, appear throughout, especially "repeatedly" (95), "frequently" (93), and "immediately" (96). In one especially self-conscious moment, Pym confesses, "in far less time than I have taken to tell it, we found ourselves masters of the brig" (113). When he describes the scene of the survivors drawing straws to see who will be cannibalized, Pym writes, "let me run over this portion of my narrative with as much haste as the nature of the events to be spoken of will permit" (134). In disclosing how long it took to consume Parker's body, Pym writes, "we devoured the rest of the body piecemeal, during the four ever memorable days of the seventeenth, eighteenth, nineteenth, and twentieth of the month" (135).

Time (and *Pym*) are getting stretched out here to make the reader squirm and to increase the length of the story. It is as if there is some ideal word count that will make *Pym* a novel, and Poe keeps grasping for it, and there is always the sense that more is needed. Pym explains, "I am at a loss to give a distinct idea of the nature of this liquid, and cannot do so without many words" (171), and he prefaces his description of the Jane Guy being surrounded by Too-wit and "the black-skin warriors" (187) with this familiar phrase: "in less time than I have taken to tell it" (186). At length elongates the chapters and is part of an overall pattern of language that warps the reader's experience of time: time stands still, slows down, moves fast.[11]

I want to focus on one particular phrase from this parodically loquacious title: June 1827. This would be ten years before the first two installments of Pym appeared in the January and February 1837 issues of the Southern Literary Messenger and eleven years prior to Harper and Brothers' publication of the full text in 1838 in which the preface first appeared. How do these dates match up with the following claims in the preface? First, Pym informs us that the note is written "upon my return to the United States a few months ago" (55). Second, he tells us that he was urged to begin the writing process "at once" (55). Third, the preface is dated July 1838. Thus, the words "a few months ago" indicate that he returned to the U.S. around April 1838, which is impossible because the first two installments were published in 1837. What if we allow that "a few months ago" refers to the three months before January 1837, which means that he returned to the U.S. around October 1836? Thus, his journey took nine years. It is worth recalling that the journal entries in chapter 25 conclude on March 22, 1828, with the famous image of the "shrouded human figure" (206). The narrative ends with an additional note that asserts the "late sudden and distressing death of Mr. Pym" (207) and the admission of "the loss of two or three final chapters (for there were but two or three)" (207). If the journey took nine years, which is confirmed in chapter 10, and the account of it that we read covers less than two years, it is difficult to imagine the additional seven years could be covered in two or three chapters. Difficult, but not impossible.

What is impossible to know is what time frame Pym is referring to when he includes phrases such as "we two have since very frequently talked the matter over" (64) or "since my return home" (158) or "I have since frequently examined my conduct" (66). Since returning home, Pym has done many things, including dying. Thus, when he reflects upon his adventures aboard the Ariel, he remarks, "when I now think of them, it appears to me a thousand wonders that I am alive to-day" (57). According to the concluding note of the narrative, however, he is not alive today. Or rather, he was alive on the day he was writing it, but now he is dead. When does this sentence stop making sense? When does that now stop being present and become past? Indeed, two crucial dates are missing from a text that is full of them: the date of Pym's return and the date of his death.

But there is even more to say about this ambiguity. When Pym says "we two have since very frequently talked the matter over" (64), he is referring to himself and Augustus, who, according to the narrative, dies on July 31, 1826. Since when?

Like the words *now* and *present, since* implies a temporal present against which the reader can separate past from present, but the narrative keeps changing when that present is. According to the *Oxford English Dictionary, since,* as an adverb, refers to "some or any time, between then and now; subsequently, later." In *Pym, since* is accompanied by a verb in the perfect tense whose action takes place in the past and its effects continue into the present. What happens to those effects when the persons referred to as experiencing those effects into the present die? What happens when the present keeps changing?

The answer to this question is that there is no stable point against which *since* makes sense. There is no home port, no ground zero. What there is is a wholly individualized experience of time in which the present is perpetually relative. Put another way, the individualized experience, which is one of perpetual relativity, becomes the ground zero for telling time. The zero degree—both the Greenwich meridian and the present tense of Poe's story—have been arbitrarily designated. And if anyone is to do the designating, it will be Poe. When is now is when Poe says it is. Poe asserts his power by creating a standard of time that is in a state of constant deviation. If we return to *Pym*—both the text and the time line of its production—we can see how this works.

A funny thing happens when the first two installments from the *Southern Literary Messenger* are published by Harper and Brothers in 1838.[12] They are identical except in three places. Installment number 1 recounts the Ariel episode and the concluding paragraph of part 1 reads, "during the three or four months immediately succeeding the period of the Ariel's disaster" (*SLM* 17). The paragraph in the 1838 edition, however, begins with: "about eighteen months after the period of the Ariel's disaster" (65). A difference of fourteen or fifteen months. Also the length of the installments differs from the length of the chapters. Installment number 1 includes Pym and Augustus's "scheme of deception," which enables them to get on the Grampus against the wishes of Pym's grandfather. The installment concludes, "vessels enough would be met with by which a letter might be sent home explaining the adventure to my parents" (*SLM* 17). In the Harper and Brothers edition the conclusion to installment 1 is the final sentence of the third paragraph in chapter 2.[13]

There is no evidence to suggest that these differences from magazine to book are typesetter errors, and common sense indicates "three or four months" and "eighteen months" look so dissimilar it is impossible to imagine a typesetter confusing them. Poe's correspondence with Harper and Brothers suggests nothing about these alterations. A similar change appears if we look at the February 1837 installment in relation to the 1838 edition. Installment number 2 begins, "The middle of April at length arrived, and every thing had been matured" (*SLM* 109). In the Harper publication, the paragraph reads, "The middle of June at length arrived, and everything had been matured" (67). A difference of about two months. When Pym explains in the 1837 version that "the brig put to sea, as I had supposed, in about an hour after he had left the watch [which was on the twentieth of April]" (*SLM* 115), he maintains the consistency of the change by stating in the 1838 edition that the brig put to sea "on the twentieth of June" (84).

But consistency is not quite the right word. On the one hand, in changing April to June, Poe also changes April 20th to June 20th, but, on the other hand, why bother changing April to June? Similarly, why the change from "three or four months" to "about eighteen months?" The changes change nothing. It is completely unimportant whether they wait three months, four months, or eighteen months. It is also utterly irrelevant whether the brig leaves in April or June, the 15th or 20th. One could say the same about Pym's statement that "when I had in some degree satisfied my thirst, Augustus produced from his pocket three or four boiled potatoes" (83). Three or four? What does it matter? Or Pym's description of his dog's behavior: "I first observed an alteration in his conduct while rubbing in the phosphorous on the paper in my last attempt. . . . Soon afterward, it will be remembered, I threw myself on the mattress, and fell into a species of lethargy. Presently I became aware of a singular hissing sound. . . . Presently I relapsed into my stupor from which I was again awakened in a similar manner. This was repeated three or four times" (81). Three or four, presently or afterward, first or again. It is the language of sequence that not only calls attention to its absolute meaninglessness but actually makes the sequence meaningless. All these words do is make the story longer and stop the reader in her tracks as she wonders about the significance of these numerical possibilities.[14]

As assertions of Poe's power, however, they signify a great deal. In a story about extreme states of powerlessness, Poe preserves himself. The details of Poe's composition of *Pym* provide a counternarrative to the story of decomposition that he tells in *Pym*. What is so fascinating about Poe's assumption of authority in *Pym* is that the form it takes is an emptying out or decomposing of some of the fundamental assumptions the reader makes about narrative, especially tense. Roland Barthes observes that "when the novelist relates that the Marchioness went out at five o'clock," such past tense (or preterite) statements "have the stability and outline of an algebra . . . which [makes] reality neither mysterious nor absurd; it is clear, almost familiar, repeatedly gathered up and contained in the hand of a creator; it is subjected to the ingenious pressure of his freedom." Poe's math is profoundly mysterious, often absurd. Poe's expressions of ingenuity and freedom are found in the blurring of temporal outlines and the reader's resulting perplexity. Poe's hands are not unlike those of a magician, but of a different sort than Barthes imagines. Poe is uninterested in the "reassuring effect" that accompanies a narrative told in the past which "escapes the terror of an expression without laws."[15] He is continually bringing the reader back to an experience of "reading zero degree." Reading and stopping time. Reading and going nowhere. Indeed, even the most careful reader has difficulty figuring out where things have gone when Poe's hands are opened and nothing is there.

Writing Zero Degree: Latitude and Race

Thus far, my analysis of *Pym* has focused on the text's refusal to keep its temporal markers consistent, propelling the reader into a zone of confusion, where "now" keeps changing. The text's zero degree—its narrative Greenwich meridian—does not stay put as Poe decides when now is and now may change, depending upon the quantity of liquor consumed, the degree of fatigue, or the rotation of the earth. That is not to say Poe does not "assume the existence of a kind of zero degree" (36), to return to Genette. And that "kind" is the zero degree of latitude or the equator.

Unlike longitude, whose calculation is embedded in the complexities of time, latitude is a spatial construction that is comparatively easy to compute. This scientific principle applies to the narrative of *Pym* as well, where Pym's experience of space is more easily narrated than his sense of time. When writing of his stowage aboard the Grampus, Pym writes: "in this space I found myself comfortably situated for the present" (99), despite being sandwiched "between the oil-casks and the upper deck" (99). Though trapped in space, he is relatively comfortable. One cannot say the same of Pym's experience of being trapped in time. Why?

The answer is that, in *Pym*, the experience of space is made coherent by the putative clarity of racial categories. Images of black and white pervade the chapters with Captain Guy, the Liverpool merchant/explorer who, while sailing southward, "has purchased five hundred seal-skins and some ivory" (156). In their travels, they see "a gigantic creature of the race of the Arctic bear [whose] wool was perfectly white" (165). They encounter a group of savages, whose "complexion [was] a jet black. . . . They were clothed in skins of an unknown black animal. . . . [and] the bottoms of the canoes were full of black stones" (168). Finally, "nothing worth mentioning occurred during the next twenty-four hours, except that, in examining the ground to the eastward of the third chasm, we found two triangular holes of great depth, and also with black granite sides" (196). Race in *Pym* enables a degree of precision—"the exact situation of this islet" (165–66)—an exact zero degree that eludes temporal assignations.

Thus, while *Pym* delights in unraveling what the reader might have thought were the stable categories of past, present, and future, certain "laws of nature" remain operational (even if only to show that those laws are being broken) and necessary, the most significant being the racial distinctions between black and white. That Poe, the "average racist," to use Terence Whalen's designation, believes these laws help ensure the survival and prosperity of whites is clear; that their representation in his texts is more complex and self-aware is also true. Maurice S. Lee states the conundrum this way: "the problem is that such acute self-consciousness fails to raise Poe's moral conscience."[16] Where is here is far less problematic for Poe than when is now. Racial certainty organizes the here, and not the now, which is to say that the lines of latitude in *Pym* are anchored by racial taxonomies, whereas the coordinates of longitude are subject to the relativity of time.

The first line of latitude to appear—35/30—is interpretively rich. Pym writes, in chapter 4, after the mutineers cut adrift: "This event happened, however, in latitude 35 degrees 30 minutes north, longitude 61 degree twenty minutes west, and consequently at no very great distance from the Bermuda Islands" (88). Poe does not use the Mason-Dixon Line's 36 degrees latitude (but retains its thirty minutes) or the actual latitudinal designation of the Bermuda Islands, which is 32 degrees twenty minutes. No, he chooses 35. This numerical alteration could indicate a questioning of the latitudinal (and racist) logic inherent in the 1820 Missouri Compromise, similar to his skepticism about arbitrary longitudinal designations. This is not, however, the case. Poe might be willing to fictionalize the Mason-Dixon Line and change its latitude from 36 to 35, but he is not willing to dispute the underlying fictions of the Missouri Compromise that separated blacks and whites into slaves and free persons on the basis of a made-up line of latitude and an alleged sense of white superiority.

Racial hierarchy and the power of whiteness, though threatened in *Pym*, are nevertheless the zero degree against which the chaos of Tsalal can be measured: 35/30 provides Pym and Augustus with a kind of Mason-Dixon Line, an entrance into a dreamscape of the South, where "a singular ledge of rock . . . bear[s] a strong resemblance to corded bales of cotton" (165), where white men are threatened by wild black men. Although Pym will be buried alive here, there is an explanation for his experiences, and this gives the text a much surer sense of the causes and effects of Pym's vulnerabilities. That is, as Pym enters a *Benito Cereno*–like world in which nothing is what it seems—"the islanders for whom we entertained such inordinate feelings of esteem, were among the most barbarous, subtle, and bloodthirsty wretches that ever contaminated the face of the globe" (180)—the reason for the gap between seeing and understanding is straightforward. It is race.

Race appears early on in *Pym* through the hybrid figure of Peters and the black cook, but it assumes center stage in the text's second half, about which Whalen observes: "a break in the style and purpose of the narrative coincides with Pym's rescue by the British Schooner *Jane Guy*."[17] It also coincides with their crossing the Equator—latitude zero—which Pym describes in chapter 12: "At noon the sun appeared to be nearly vertical, and we had no doubt that we had been driven down by the long succession of northward and northwesterly winds into the near vicinity of the equator" (140). In addition to a "break in the style and purpose," there is also a break from north to south, from white to black, and from longitude to latitude. This break happens at the center of the text (the narrative's equator, as it were) and provides *Pym* with its zero degree—race. The latitudinal certainty of the equator (35/30 is one degree off) gives Pym's narrative the stable point of reference that Poe's temporal aesthetics have been working so hard (and successfully) to unmoor.

I do not mean to imply that Poe's narrative experimentation ends with the crossing of the equator. Later chapters contain phrases such as "which I mentioned before" (188) or "during the six or seven days immediately following" (191). Yet, as formally chaotic as those final chapters may be, the chaos is a product of what Poe imagines to be the natural and necessary differences between black and white. The undoing of these differences represents a comforting, familiar chaos. White men are buried alive. Hiero-glyphs need deciphering. Whatever chaos there is can be explained in terms of black and white. Unlike narrative time, which flows along the unstable axis of longitude, racial difference and its "laws of nature" operate according to the axis of the equator. In other words, those laws regarding the natural-ness of racial difference, arbitrary and relativistic as we know them to be, provide the text with a zero degree, even as those laws get broken.

Latitude is therefore aligned with space, and space is aligned with a certitude about race, which ironically leads Poe into a kind of comfort zone where the relativity of time is replaced by the reliability of racial terror. For example, Nu-Nu, Pym's island captive, is "violently affected with convulsions" upon seeing a "white handkerchief" (204) and Pym, upon seeing "a large black bird of the bittern species" is "so much startled that [he] could do nothing" (188). Both are made prostrate by the other's presence. Based on these similar responses, one could say that Poe col-lapses racial difference (white and black react the same to the terrifying presence of one another) to demonstrate a progressive perspective about the similarities between races or one could say that the collapse of racial difference engenders such horror (white and black are terrified by the presence of one another) to argue a racist position about the incontrovert-ible oppositionality between the races. Fright can be counted on because of essential differences between black and white that ought to be pre-served. When they are not, there is terror, and there is nothing relative about this.

Poe's racial politics have received extensive analysis, though as Jared Gardner observes: "[the] resurgence of interest of late in Poe's thoughts on slavery [is] somewhat curious in that Poe's opinions on the subject have long been quite visible: he supported slavery both as a southerner and as an individual." The first approach to the question of Poe and race is per-haps best represented by John Carlos Rowe, who argues that Poe's racism is evident in both content and form. The second takes Poe's racism as its departure point and reads the text against the grain. Dana D. Nelson con-tends, "while on one level Pym is a racist text, on another the text provides a reading that counters racist colonial ideology, and the racialist, scientific knowledge structure." Teresa Goddu similarly reads Pym as "deploy[ing] and reinforc[ing] social stereotypes," while nevertheless "reveal[ing] race to be a social invention." On this view, Poe's racism is somewhat less baleful because the text "point[s] out that [racial fantasy] is merely a representa-tion." At least he knows he is a racist.[18]

That *Pym* "transgresses" the color line "instead of policing it," according to Goddu, has been taken as a sign that his representations of race run counter to his personal politics (87); that is, his inability to police the line makes him someone who does not fully believe in it or someone who understands its arbitrariness. But just because Poe via *Pym* might voice a constructivist's view of race does not mean that he thinks the line is bogus (because arbitrary) or that it should be crossed. That the line is transgressed is certainly true. The hybrid Peters both rescues Pym *and* has the "merriment . . . of a demon" (87). Whiteness, like the "white ashy shower" and the "white birds" (205) at *Pym*'s end can terrify as much as blackness. These representations, however, need not be unconscious admissions of ideological complexity (and therefore a resistant racism), but might simply be Poe's observation that white and black are sometimes proximate. "Whiteness," Pym writes, "is no longer transparent" (204). Nevertheless, the desirability of pure whiteness remains, either in its negative articulation ("living inhumation" is "the blackness of darkness" [182]) or its positive (the Arctic bear's wool "was perfectly white" [165]). White's perfection becomes marred as liquid whiteness comes to possess "a milky consistency and hue" and "a fine white resemble[s] ashes" (204). Crossing the zero degree of the equator is entering a state (of mind, of place, of color) with its own experience of disorientation, but, unlike the unending relativity of the temporal variety, this confusion is binary, locatable, and color-coded. Poe's works, as Toni Morrison observes, are constituted by an "Africanist" presence that is a "haunting . . . that moves the hearts and texts of American literature with fear and longing."[19] Following Morrison's claim, Gardner argues that Poe requires this haunting because "racial difference [is] the condition—the ground—for an American writing" (141). The ground zero we might say.

Rather than trying to save Poe from his politics (or repudiate him because of them), I have been proposing an approach that allows us to see how *Pym*'s "chronopolitics" are embedded in an authorial and national will to power that pulls the text in antipodal directions. One subtends a logic of slavery by representing the conquering of space and (black) people who inhabit it as the result of a natural superiority grounded in race. The other undercuts that logic by dismantling the temporal pillar upon which that understanding of space rests. Poe's aesthetics of temporality, in other words, replicates and enforces the arbitrary assertion of power, but at the same time problematizes it. Ironically, Poe's "narrative interferences" interfere with the racist logic of *Pym*'s final episodes. Poe tries to retrieve and deploy the category of time as an instrument of conquest and hierarchy in his account of Nu-Nu's brutality. The episodes with the Tsalalians, described as "savages" (196), capture the temporal certainty that, according to Fabian, is essential to imperialism.[20] Indeed, there is one especially powerful moment when *Pym* finds its narrative zero degree and the disorientation of relativity has been temporarily suspended. In what is perhaps *Pym*'s shortest sentence, Nu-nu's teeth are described: "These were black" (205). There is no need for more length. Racial clarity has replaced temporal uncertainty. The vicissitudes of "now" are anchored in space, made coherent by racial categories. Poe's experiment with narrative temporality has at last, or at length, come to an end.

Until we read the note with which the story concludes—yet again. This note informs us that Pym has died, creating a gap in the narrative "of two or three final chapters (for there were but two or three)" (207). The chaos and crisis are back. Unlike the figure of "the perfect whiteness of the snow" (206)—the perfection of racial purity—the numbers are relative. Is it two or three? That question gets asked not once but twice. The South would go to war for this figure of whiteness, and Poe would undoubtedly have supported it. The perfection or racial purity of that figure of white holds things in check for just a moment, disclosing Poe's historical and geographical past as an antebellum Southerner, but then his conviction of temporal disturbance and relativity asserts itself, revealing his future canonization as an American (post)modernist before his time. Two or three; his "now" is both.

Notes

I would like to thank the editors at *Poe Studies*, where a longer version of this essay first appeared, for their generosity. Special thanks go to Geoffrey Sanborn and Scott Peeples for their terrifically helpful readings.

1. Johannes Fabian, *Time and the Other: How Anthropology Makes Its Object* (New York: Columbia University Press, 1983), 144.

2. Gerard Genette, *Narrative Discourse: An Essay in Method*, trans. Jane E. Lewin, foreword by Jonathan Culler (Ithaca: Cornell University Press, 1980), 40.

3. Pollin notes that Augustus's father's "chronometer" is more likely a pocket watch because a chronometer with its "balance wheel, escapement, and gear train" (243) would not fit in a pocket. This is, however, another case where *Pym* as fiction runs counter to *Pym* as fact. It is a fact that a chronometer does not fit into one's pocket; however, Poe uses the word *chronometer* in order to

establish the importance of tracking latitude and longitude on board the Grampus, and the subsequent importance of losing that device. *Collected Writings of Edgar Allan Poe*, vol. 1: *The Imaginary Voyages*, ed. Burton R. Pollin (New York: Gordian, 1981), 243, note 4.3B. Scott Peeples's analysis of *Pym* correctly notes, "Regardless of Poe's intentions, however, to read such an error-laden text—assuming one notices the errors—is to be constantly reminded of its fictional nature, no matter how much nautical (and botanical and zoological) detail Poe includes to convince us that the story is 'real.'" Peeples, *Edgar Allan Poe Revisited* (New York: Twayne, 1998), 61. Similarly, J. Gerald Kennedy maintains, "even the simplest declarative sentence . . . refers not to a pure, immanent fact but to what the speaker or writer wishes his audience to construe as a fact," which leads him to conclude that "any textual distinction between truth and fiction must remain intractably problematic. J. Gerald Kennedy, *Poe, Death, and the Life of Writing* (New Haven: Yale University Press, 1987), 150–51.

4. Pollin, *Collected Writings of Edgar Allan Poe*, 165, 168. All further quotations from *Pym* will be from this edition, incorporated parenthetically into the text. My reading of Poe's relation to language is influenced by Sam Worley's work on *Pym* as a critical reflection of pro-slavery discourse, which upholds "the vision of a social hierarchy that manifested itself in varying degrees of linguistic authority." Worley, *"The Narrative of Arthur Gordon Pym* and the Ideology of Slavery," *ESQ* 40, no. 3 (1994): 222. Whereas Worley uses Poe's self-conscious suspicion about language's transparency to argue for Poe's covert critique of the pro-slavery position, I maintain that his assertions of "linguistic authority" actually and ironically get in the way of the text's racist vision.

5. Epigraph from *Collected Works of Edgar Allan Poe*, vol. 1: *Tales and Sketches, 1831–1842*, ed. T. O. Mabbott (Cambridge: Belknap, 1969, 1978), 684. Quotations taken from *Edgar Allan Poe: Essays and Reviews*, ed. G. R. Thompson (New York: Library of America, 1984), 15; I. M. Walker, ed., *Edgar Allan Poe: The Critical Heritage* (London: Routledge and Kegan Paul, 1986), 93, 96.

6. Walker, *Edgar Allan Poe*, 91, quoted in J. Don Vann, "Three More Contemporary Reviews of Pym," *Poe Studies* 9, no. 2 (June 1976): 43; Walker, *Edgar Allan Poe*, 97.

7. Walker, *Edgar Allan Poe*, 98.

8. Dava Sobel, *Longitude: The True Story of a Lone Genius Who Solved the Greatest Scientific Problem of His Time* (New York: Penguin, 1995), 14.

9. Here is another case where Poe calls attention to the fictional status of his text, even as he invokes the verisimilitude of the travel narrative. It is one thing—and acceptable—for Benjamin Morrell to have a title page that exceeds the length of some paragraphs; it is another thing altogether (which I am calling parodic) for Poe to have this kind of title page. Morrell's title, upon which

Poe based his, is *A Narrative of Four Voyages, to the South Sea, North and South Pacific Ocean, Chinese Sea, Ethiopic and Southern Atlantic Ocean, Indian and Antarctic Ocean. From the Year 1822 to 1831. Comprising Critical Surveys of Coasts and Islands, with Sailing Directions. And an Account of Some New and Valuable Discoveries, Including the Massacre Islands, where Thirteen of the Author's Crew were Massacred and Eaten by Cannibals. To which is Prefixed a Brief Sketch of the Author's Early Life.*

10. Walker, *Edgar Allan Poe*, 94.

11. Of course, plagiarizing from other texts is another fundamental way in which Poe lengthens *Pym*. For an excellent account of Poe's "defense of plagiarism" (213) as authorial mastery, see Meredith McGill, *American Literature and the Culture of Reprinting: 1834–1853* (Philadelphia: University of Pennsylvania Press, 2003), especially 204–17. My reading of *Pym*'s self-conscious lengthening develops Richard Kopley's claim that *Pym* is "striking [in] its economy." Kopley, "The 'Very Profound Under-Current' of *Arthur Gordon Pym*," in Joel Meyerson, ed., *Studies in the American Renaissance 1987* (Charlottesville: University of Virginia Press, 1987), 157. Its economy is indeed striking by virtue of its relentless profusion of sameness in the guise of difference. Rather than interpreting the novel as "dense with language conveying multiple meanings" (157), which has been the quite fruitful allegorical approach taken by Kopley and others, I read *Pym* as creating the illusion of a text "dense with language" conveying multiple meanings; in other words, it is just dense with words.

12. The citations from the *Southern Literary Messenger* installments are taken from the "Making of America" Web site. http://www.hti.umich.edu. Page references will be provided parenthetically within the text. Also see Pollin, *Collected Writings of Edgar Allan Poe*, 211–14. Pollin bases his edition on the 1838 Harper and Brothers text, but he provides a list of *Southern Literary Messenger* variants as well as a discussion of changes, throughout the "Notes and Comments" section, reflected in the Harper version.

13. Here I am going over points made in Pollin's edition, but with the goal of demonstrating how Poe's authorial mastery of time in the context of the material production of *Pym* is replicated in the narrative technique of *Pym*. Pollin remarks upon "this gross discrepancy of narrative time" (*Collected Writings of Edgar Allan Poe*, 216), which I read in the context of Poe's desire to assert his authorial power.

14. Louis Renza makes a similar point: "as allegories of their process of misreading, his tales never quite exist." Louis A. Renza, "Poe's Secret Autobiography," in Walter Benn Michaels and Donald E. Pease, eds., *The American Renaissance Reconsidered* (Baltimore: Johns Hopkins University Press, 1985), 70. There is an impressive body of criticism on *Pym* that takes a deconstructive

approach, for example, John T. Irwin, *American Hieroglyphics: The Symbol of the Egyptian Hieroglyphics in the American Renaissance* (New Haven: Yale University Press, 1980); and John Carlos Rowe, *Through the Custom House: Nineteenth-Century American Fiction and Modern Theory* (Baltimore: Johns Hopkins University Press, 1982). Richard Kopley takes a different approach to Poe's use of allegory, and offers two readings in essays from the 1980s that do not take the deconstructive approach (Poe's allegory is an allegory of reading), but rather see Poe's allegory as having a psychological referent as well as a biblical one. For the more psychologically inflected reading (*Pym* as an allegory of the deaths of Poe's brother and mother), see "The Hidden Journey of *Arthur Gordon Pym*," in Joel Myerson, ed., *Studies of the American Renaissance 1982* (Boston: Twayne, 1982), 29–51. *Pym* as biblical allegory can be found in Kopley, "The 'Very Profound Under-Current' of *Arthur Gordon Pym*": "Even as the Tsalal landslide . . . allegorically represents the destruction of Jerusalem as prophesied in Isaiah, so, too, does Pym's imaging the 'human figure' in the Tsalal chasm . . . allegorically represent John of Patmos' first seeing Christ in Revelation" (156).

15. Roland Barthes, *Writing Degree Zero*, trans. Annette Lavers and Colin Smith (New York: Hill and Wang, 1968), 31, 32.

16. Maurice S. Lee, *Slavery, Philosophy, and American Literature, 1830–1860* (Cambridge: Cambridge University Press, 2005), 46. For an excellent overview (and critique) of how literary critics have discussed, ignored, and/or simplified the question of Poe and race, see Terence Whalen, *Edgar Allan Poe and the Masses: The Political Economy of Literature in Antebellum America* (Princeton: Princeton University Press, 1999), chapter 5, "Average Racism: Poe, Slavery, and the Wages of Literary Nationalism" (111–46). My reading of *Pym* has been guided by Whalen's historically rigorous and deeply sensible approach: "the case of Poe demonstrates the importance of race in determining what literature is—the form and meaning of its sentences, the form and meaning of its silences" (146).

17. Whalen, *Poe and the Masses*, 160.

18. Jared Gardner, *Master Plots: Race and the Founding of an American Literature* (Baltimore: Johns Hopkins University Press, 1998), 129; John Carlos Rowe, *Literary Culture and U.S. Imperialism: From the Revolution to World War II* (Oxford: Oxford University Press, 2000), 70, and "Poe, Antebellum Slavery, and Modern Criticism," in Richard Kopley, ed., *Poe's "Pym": Critical Explorations* (Durham: Duke University Press, 1992), 117; Dana D. Nelson, *The Word in Black and White: Reading "Race" in American Literature, 1638–1867* (Oxford: Oxford University Press, 1993), 29; Teresa A. Goddu, *Gothic America: Narrative, History, and Nation* (New York: Columbia University Press, 1997), 86. Further references to Gardner and Goddu will be given parenthetically within the text.

19. Toni Morrison, *Playing in the Dark: Whiteness and the Literary Imagination* (New York: Vintage, 1993), 33; Gardner, *Master Plots*, 141.

20. The temporal remoteness and fixity (and decimation) of the black Tsalalians would seem to be predicted in Poe's 1837 *New York Review* notice of John L. Stephens's *Incidents of Travel in Egypt, Arabia Petraea and the Holy Land,* where Poe writes about Egypt, "it, however, was distinctly foretold that this country of kings should no longer have one of its own—that it should be laid waste by the hand of strangers—that it should be a base kingdom, the basest of the base—that it should *never* again exalt itself among the nations—that it should be a desolation surrounded by desolation. Two thousand years have now afforded their testimony to the infallibility of the Divine word, and the evidence is still accumulative. 'Its past and present degeneracy bears not a more remote resemblance to the former greatness and pride of its power, than the frailty of its mud-walled fabrics now bears to the stability of its imperishable pyramids'" (Thompson, *Edgar Allan Poe,* 926).

[10]

Reading in the Present Tense

Benito Cereno and the Time of Reading

TRISH LOUGHRAN

When the "I" seeks to give an account of itself, it can start with itself, but it will find that this self is already implicated in a social temporality that exceeds its own capacities for narration; indeed, when the "I" seeks to give an account of itself, an account that must include the conditions of its own emergence, it must, as a matter of necessity, become a social theorist.

—Judith Butler, *Giving an Account of Oneself*

If I could only be certain that in my uneasiness my senses did not deceive me, then—

—Captain Amasa Delano, in Herman Melville, *Benito Cereno* (1855)

If you can squeeze Melville into oct. it would be great.

—George W. Curtis, editor, writing to Joshua Dix, publisher (September 7, 1855)

The Posthistoricist Present

This is an essay, in part, about the historical moment in which Herman Melville's *Benito Cereno* was composed and then consumed by historical readers. It began as an experiment in which I wondered whether I could both make use of the skills I had amassed as a historicist—in particular my knowledge of the local book cultures of the eighteenth and nineteenth centuries—even as I joined that knowledge to a different set of questions about the (potentially) less historically grounded practice of *reading*. I wanted to consider the extent to which reading is an experience that can in fact be historicized, in order to see if reading a story like, say, *Benito Cereno* in 1855, at the site of production, looked and felt remotely like reading it in 2009, at the furthest-most point of its (then) (ongoing) reception. The question I wanted to pose was something like this: how is the (historical) time of reading related to (aesthetic) reading time?

This question focuses on two seemingly opposed aspects of literary texts: first, the historically fixed facts of textual production and consumption (bookmaking and book buying) and second, the somewhat less moored act of aesthetic reception—in other words, the always potentially transhistorical experience of reading. Nineteenth-century American literature turns out to be a good place to ask this question, in large part because so many of its authors seem to have responded to the precarious conditions of antebellum book production by trying to reach a historically unmoored reader, an ideal reader who very often seems to bear little or no relation to the actual, embodied readers walking around streets and bookstores and libraries in the 1830s, '40s, and '50s. And one way these authors address this historically unmoored (or ideal) reader is, I would argue, by crafting what I want to call present-time reading experiences—authoring texts that are not so much syntactically posed in the present tense but that experimentally organize themselves around the reader's own phenomenological "reading time" (the actual moment when the act of reading is taking place, whenever that moment might be). In this sense, aesthetic reception is cultivated as a refuge from the vagaries of more materialist forms of consumption: real editors, real readers, real publishers, and all the complicated limitations that such readers pose.

Benito Cereno is both exemplary and exceptional in this regard. Here, Melville uses a now famous twist toward the end of his narrative to knowingly craft two radically different versions of the same text in one: one (almost disposable) version of the text that is to be consumed just once (upon first reading) and another (more historically durable) version that is assigned a memory and meaning after the fact of (a first, or flawed) reading, which is intended to be understood retroactively as a *mis*reading. This double reading has, I think, a local purpose for Melville, but it also has a clear pedagogical purpose. As he writes in *Pierre*: "If a man be told a thing wholly new, then—during the time of its first announcement to him—it is entirely impossible for him to comprehend it. For—absurd as it may seem," he says (now shifting not just to the plural but reorienting his claim to include both a speaker and those spoken to), "things new it is impossible to make [men] comprehend."[1] Insisting not on one but on two (or more) readings, Melville seeks to create, as it were, his own ideal reader, someone who will be forced to bear a double relation to the story over time—first by misreading it (alongside Captain Delano) and then by disavowing that first reading every time the story is read thereafter.

Whether the story's ideal reader has come to be embodied in the form of a real reader remains to be seen, but in this essay I will consider the long historical reception of *Benito Cereno* first as a theoretical problem across time (giving special attention to a remarkable number of what I call presentist or present-tense readings of the text) and then as a more local matter in Melville's own moment. I start with the presentist reception of the novella for two reasons: first, because *Benito Cereno* has generated, over time, a remarkably high number of historically unhinged readings (made further remarkable given the content of the story, which is so historically specific) and, second, because critical presentism has become one of the signal gestures of our own contemporary practice in American studies (and for this reason the story seems to have something to tell us about ourselves). Thus we might say that the essay you are now holding in your hands (or reading on your screen) is not exempt from the presentist gesture it describes, but it is going to try to think about it and theorize it as something that has a distinct origin, in this case, in the story itself and, maybe more to the point, in the world in which Melville lived—and wrote. In the end, this essay is an experiment in how to think about aesthetic reception in ways that are both theoretical and materialist at once.

Reading Melville in the Present Tense

Melville has, of course, been expertly appropriated to every critical moment his corpus has endured. If you visit JSTOR or Project Muse, you will find archived there all the obligatory critical gestures, each in their calendrical carrel: *Benito Cereno*, in particular, has been avidly dissected by old historicists, by formalists, by poststructuralists, by multiculturalists, and by new historicists (each of whom, in their own way, was reading the story in the present tense, accommodating it to the critical preoccupations of their own moment). But *Benito Cereno* has also been appropriated in a far more striking way for particular moments—and indeed, in a totally inverse way that resonates quite peculiarly with the historicist turn we have just lived through in the last thirty years or so in American literary studies. As grounded as the text might seem to be in a certain set of historical practices and assumptions, *Benito Cereno* has routinely lent itself for over a century to numerous readings that rely on an almost total evacuation of its actual historical content, often producing highly allegorical, transhistorical, and, most of all, very presentist readings—readings in which the specific scene, setting, and content of the tale are replaced by some other scene, setting, and content.

Take, for example, the case of Carl Schmitt. Schmitt, a central figure in the work of Giorgio Agamben, was a twentieth-century German political theorist who has been called both the Crown Jurist of the Third Reich and (because of his ongoing popularity with contemporary neoconservatives) the Éminence Grise of the Bush-Cheney White House.[2] Like many Germans in the 1930s, however, Schmitt was also an avid reader of Herman Melville, and by far the text he fixated on most acutely, both privately (in correspondences with friends) and professionally, in his university teaching, was *Benito Cereno*. Numerous letters and anecdotes indicate that Schmitt saw the story not so much as a story about the United States in the 1850s (as it has for some decades been assumed to be in American studies) or even about the hemispheric effects of the global slave trade in the eighteenth and nineteenth centuries (as it is increasingly understood to be) but as an allegory for life under Hitler in the twentieth century. Indeed, according to Tracy Strong, Melville's eighty-four-year-old story was "widely read and discussed in terms of the contemporary political situation" in Germany upon its appearance in German translation in 1939.[3] Schmitt himself thought the story "very current" when he first read it (apparently in English) in the 1930s. He so identified with what he called "the situation" on board the *San Dominick* that on several occasions he actually wrote letters to friends in which he signed off as "Benito Cereno" or (even more abjectly) "your Benito Cereno." In one such letter, circulated after World War II (when Schmitt was under investigation for his implication in Nazi war crimes), he announced: "I am the last conscious representative of the *jus publicum Europaeum* (the European public order) . . . and I'm experiencing its end just as Benito Cereno experienced the pirate ship's journey." Using the story to help explain his behavior throughout the war, Schmitt concedes that "my book [*Leviathan*, written during the 1930s] contains shrill anti-Semitic tones" and worries that "the uninitiated reader . . . who does not know that I wrote this book in the role of Benito Cereno will think I am a racist and consider me complicit in the murder of Jews."[4]

One of the most interesting things about Schmitt's seizure of *Benito Cereno* for his own contemporary experience of German history—and indeed, for highly biographical and self-interested purposes—is the mythic and ahistorical character of his fantasy. On one hand, he believes he has come to the end of some part of history: somewhat astonishingly (having witnessed the Holocaust), he claims himself to be the only survivor of a fading formation that he nostalgically calls "the European public order." On the other hand, his unique experience has been foreshadowed, many years before, in the figure of Benito Cereno, whom Schmitt treats as the very archetype of passive subjection—or abjection. Schmitt's reading is thus both timely and timeless, but it's important to realize that both these effects are generated, in some sense, by the story itself, which appears to have taught Schmitt something about how to endure a historical crisis by urging people to find multiple interpretations for what they've read. When Schmitt describes, for example, his book's anti-Semitism, he takes a page from Melville by suggesting that this reading of his work should be dispatched to the dustbin of disposable readings while a new (more durable) postwar reading should be substituted in its place: only "the uninitiated reader," he insists, "will think I am a racist." By signing this defense with the name Benito Cereno, he hopes to show that he never really was complicit at all in Nazi ideology—that he was, like Cereno, an unwilling participant in someone else's masquerade.

Schmitt's appropriation of the story is remarkable, but he's hardly alone. Schmitt saw *Benito Cereno* as a story about the Third Reich, but other prominent readers throughout the twentieth century made the same move, appropriating Melville for their own historical present in much the same way that Schmitt did in the 1930s and '40s. The best-known example may be C. L. R. James, who deftly braves the contradiction of his own critical position (which I would describe as historically presentist) by opening *Mariners, Renegades and Castaways* (1952) with a syntactically unsettling use of the present tense: "one evening over a hundred years ago," he writes, "an American whaling-vessel is out at sea on its way to the whaling-grounds."[5] Unlike Schmitt, who opportunistically plucks the story out of time and reinserts it into his own, James wants to establish a dialectical relation with Melville's world. More often than not, however, James simply posits Melville as a man *out* of time (or before his time)—someone exceptional and miraculous (rather than fated and historical). Indeed, "the miracle of Herman Melville," James writes, "is . . . that a hundred years ago . . . he painted a picture of the world in which we live. . . . His characters are instantly recognizable by us who have lived through the last twenty years and particularly the last ten" (3). *Benito*

Cereno in particular "seems as if it was written not even after World War I but after World War II" (110).

I could go on to accumulate several more examples of this kind of appropriation of *Benito Cereno*, but the basic structure of this kind of reading is already evident in the two interpretations just cited.[6] I've chosen Schmitt and James not because I want to flatten them out—they are clearly very different—but because they serve to demonstrate just how flattening presentism as a practice can be. As we see here, the presentist gesture actually enables these two totally different readers to treat the story as if it were an empty container, a structure with no political or historical content of its own—even though each of them probably thought the story very political and very historical, in some sense.

The prevalence of this kind of reading in the early twentieth century would not be all that remarkable if *Benito Cereno* weren't in the midst of a presentist renaissance even as I write. Since the year 2001 (at least), *Benito Cereno* has been repeatedly read as a story that can teach *us* something about *our* historical present. Most notably, it has been persistently linked to discussions of global terrorism by critics working in a wide variety of fields. Lindsay Waters, for example, put the case rather bluntly in the spring of 2002, just after the events of 9/11, when he referred to Babo's slave revolt as a "hijacking," connecting Babo and Mohammad Atta with that one powerful word. The situation Americans are facing today, Waters wrote, "is exactly like Melville's *Benito Cereno*. We need energy now in the form of petroleum. We needed it then in the form of slaves."[7]

Sheer as this conflation is, its most basic premise has been repeated by a number of different scholars since 2001. The popular political theorist Benjamin Barber, for example, argues that "the myth of innocence captured by Melville has persisted down into and through the twentieth century and right into this new millennium, where it colors and helps explain the Bush administration's new preventive war doctrine."[8] Andy Doolen, a literary critic whose work focuses on the period before 1820, agrees: he sees *Benito Cereno* as "a prophetic tale of American obtuseness" and insists that "the same racial ideology that prohibited Delano from seeing either the slave rebel's humanity or his true intentions would come to justify U.S. military and economic intervention in foreign places like Nicaragua, Cuba, the Philippines, Mexico, and Haiti."[9] Likewise, Andrew Delbanco, who, in his recent prize-winning cultural biography of Melville takes a break from a more conventional kind of historical biography to note that "in our time of terror and torture, *Benito Cereno* has emerged as the most salient of

Melville's works; a tale of desperate men in the grip of a vengeful fury that those whom they hate cannot begin to understand. . . . It is a tale that most Americans could not—*and still cannot*—bear to hear."[10] All these post-9/11 readings make a powerful presentist claim for *Benito Cereno*. Waters insists that the situation on the *San Dominick* is "exactly like" our present day situation. Barber believes that the story can "help explain" President Bush's foreign policy in the "new millennium." Doolen thinks "the same" racial ideology in play in 1855 is still alive and well today. And Delbanco believes we "still" have not learned the very political lesson that Melville is out to teach.

As in the earlier examples, there is something both universalizing and particularizing in each of these more recent readings, as if they are trying to be both presentist and historicist at once. But the thing that interests me the most about them is that they almost all attach and indeed *invest* themselves in the figure of Delano and in his very powerful and particular penchant for misreading. Unlike someone like Schmitt (who identifies almost entirely with the figure of Benito Cereno), all four of the post-9/11 readings align themselves (or contemporary Americans more generally) *after the fact of reading the whole story* with the perception of Melville's spectacularly obtuse captain. Lindsay Waters, for example, calls Delano "a typical American male not just of the nineteenth century but of today" and concludes that "he is my compatriot."[11] Delbanco is less cagey. He overtly disidentifies with Delano at several points in his reading—"Delano's stupidity is staggering," he says—but he also sometimes aligns himself with the "not undistrustful" captain, as when he repeatedly points out that "we [as readers] feel [Delano's] relief" with him when the slave revolt is revealed. This collapse of critic into reader ("*we* feel his relief") and of reader in turn into character (not only a critical commonplace but I would argue a necessary effect of this narration the first time through) allows a number of anachronisms to slip into Delbanco's rhetoric. In fact, in channeling Delano's diegetic point of view, the chapter channels his historical consciousness in peculiarly unfiltered ways, using the word *Negro* without historicizing quotation marks and remarking on one occasion on Cereno's "hot Spanish petulance."[12] The critic thus focalizes, as Melville once did. But to what end?

Moments like these suggest some of the pitfalls of presentism, a practice that at its best establishes a dense continuum across time and at its worst simply collapses two moments without attending to the process that animates the moments in between.[13] The more contemporary ones are simply more telling because they are ours and (for a time at least) they

are now. In conflating the contemporary American experience of terrorism with Delano's perceptual experience of the slave revolt, these readings
circumnavigate timelines both grand and minor (matters of both history
and what we might call more local reading time). The most basic thing
we can say is that they collapse two time frames. In doing so, they expose
something about how readers inhabit both time and history. Here's the
rub, however. To the extent that they maintain a focus on the unenlight-
ened Delano (in Waters's words, "a typical American male not just of the
nineteenth century but of today"), they wind up in the end doing one of
two problematic things. If, as scholars, we sustain an interest in what we
might call the durability of the disposable reading (insisting that the story
is somehow "about" willful innocence as opposed to something else), then
we are either actively identifying with Delano and hence refusing to read
the story dialectically (by positing a reader who refuses to be changed by
his reading) *or* we are actively dividing the labor of enlightenment from the
fruits of innocence, disidentifying both with Delano *and our own contemporaries* by fusing him not with our own (now bygone) reading interest but
with those of others around us whose difference from us is that they cannot
or do not read (well) (other Americans, named Bush—or not). As Waters
says, with a poker face: Delano "is my compatriot." Either way, these interpretations allow the novella's two readings (the disposable and the durable,
the initial flawed reading and the second corrected reading) to sit in dis-
integrated relation to one another: either the former is embraced and the
latter refused within one reader, or the latter is embraced and the former
is simply reassigned to the next reader, another reader, a less enlightened
reader nearby (a "compatriot"). Such readings not only preserve but resur-
rect Delano's own peculiar version of myopia in the guise of criticizing it,
reconstructing the story's false front by reproducing new other not-slave-
revolts (like airplane hijackings) that take the place of Delano's preferred
red herring: piracy. But the point of the story is not that we should imitate
any one its characters or that we should lament what we know that others
don't. The point is that we should be changed by our reading. The ethics
of this double reading is a problem I will return to at the end of the essay.

The Time of Reading and the Time of Writing

In a recent talk Jonathan Elmer used *Benito Cereno* to theorize what he
called "the literary event," and he pointed out that literary history has always

tended to be more attentive to the history of production than to the history of reception, in large part because, he suggested, the point of production tends to be knowable and finite while reception is theoretically infinite—a continuously ongoing and unfolding event that, were we to theorize it in its totality, would require a massive reconceptualization of the scale of "the literary event" called (in this case) *Benito Cereno*.[14] As Elmer notes, there are almost always many more sites of reception for any given text than sites of production. But the relationship between production and reception almost entirely disappears in presentist readings of *Benito Cereno*. In most of the examples cited so far, the moment of reception is actually given more primacy than the moment of production. Thus James's wonder at "the miracle" of Melville's ongoing relevance for his world and his insistence that *Benito Cereno* "seems as if it [had been] written not even after World War I but after World War II" (175, 110). The disjunction between the moment of production and the later moment of reception is swept away in such accounts, while the distance between the story's two potential readings is likewise collapsed. Yet the history of *Benito Cereno*'s earliest readings suggests that reception is always tied in some sense to production, and so I want to offer an experimental attempt to link the issues I've been describing to an account of the story's production and early reception in 1855 and '56.

It's hardly a coincidence that *Benito Cereno* has called forth so many presentist readings. The story itself is very much occupied narratively with the slow passage of time on board the ship where it is set. The famous first words of the story are "In the year 1799," a gesture that seems to embed the story in History with a capital H. But, in fact, much of the story turns out to be not about epic historical time but about the quotidian painfulness of a more everyday kind of time. As students almost always report about their own (usually disposable) first reading, the story creeps like a caterpillar the first time through—so that the time that passes in the plot as we read it (before we know what is really happening) seems almost to line up with the time of reading, marked as that time is by a sense of profound disorientation as to why we are reading what we are reading and what the different details being described mean. The slowness both of Captain Delano's perception and of the narrative unfolding of the action is marked repeatedly in Melville's prose by the use of the words *at present* or *presently* to describe the slow unfolding of the story's (non)action for its first two-thirds. Indeed, some variant of the word *present* or *presently* is used fifty-two times in as many pages. As I will discuss at more length in a moment, it is almost as if the story actually *were* being read in the present tense—even though, of course, it isn't. But the fact that it isn't is, of course, crucial to the overall effect Melville seems to want to generate.

The discomfort of reading this story is connected in part to the discomfort Melville was beginning to feel about writing books that readers could not appreciate or understand. Indeed, it seems safe to say that Melville's experience of his own present tense was not really a comfortable one. The rise and decline of his authorial fortunes are well known: from popular romancer of the South Seas in *Typee* to literary experimenter in *Moby-Dick* and *Pierre* to increasingly frustrated and penny-pinched hack magazinist in the later 1850s to depressed poet (and state bureaucrat) in the last thirty years of his life. At the center of this declension narrative is the poor reception of *Pierre*. At the time Melville began writing magazine stories like *Benito Cereno*, he was routinely being described in newspapers and magazines as "exhausted," "insane," and "finished" because of the failure of *Pierre*. In 1853, in fact, *Putnam's* printed a critical assessment of Melville that essentially amounts to an authorial obituary: describing Melville's career as one of steady decline (from the productive "ferment" of *Typee* to the staggering "poison" of *Pierre*), Fitz-James O'Brien warned that "Mr. Melville . . . totters at the edge of a precipice, over which all his hard-earned fame may tumble with such another weight as *Pierre* attached to it."[15] But Melville could not have produced another *Pierre* even if he had wanted to, because after 1853 he had trouble getting freestanding novels published and turned instead to the serialized forum that more successful writers (like Hawthorne—and Stowe) were, by the mid-1850s, leaving behind: the middle-class magazine.

   Benito Cereno is one of these post-1853 magazine fictions, and its reception proved to be as mixed as anything that came before it.[16] George W. Curtis, who eventually assumed the editorship of *Putnam's*, warned his friend Joshua Dix, the publisher, to "decline any novel from Melville that is not extremely good." Though Curtis appeared to be warning Dix away from publishing *Benito Cereno* as a freestanding novel, he was nevertheless instrumental in getting the novella serialized in *Putnam's* in late 1855. Having read the story himself, Curtis assured Dix that "Melville's story is very good," even though he pointed out two notable aesthetic problems that bothered him in his reading: first, the problem of the story's disconnected parts and, second, the problem of pacing. Though Curtis thought the story "very good," in other words, he also found it frustratingly fragmented and slow and would not take the risk of publishing it as a novel. "It is a great pity," he writes, that Melville "did not work it up as a connected tale instead of putting in the dreary documents at the end.—They should have made part of the substance of the story." He ultimately judged it to be "a little spun out" but insisted "it ought not to be lost" (*Log*, 2:501).

Besides Curtis, we have few other records of the earliest readers' responses to *Benito Cereno*. It's not mentioned in Melville's correspondence or in any surviving correspondence between the magazine and its readers. The only other place to look for early readings is to the published puffs and barbs received by the collected *Piazza Tales*, which we might think of (using my earlier vocabulary) as the (durable) collection of all of Melville's (disposable) *Putnam's'* tales.[17] The reviews for *The Piazza Tales* tell us that *Benito Cereno* was neither Melville's best nor his worst received piece of writing, but many remark, as Curtis did, on its oppressive difficulty. One appreciative reviewer called it "a thrilling, weird-like narrative; which, read at midnight, gives an uncomfortable feeling" (*Log*, 2:516). Another found the story "most painfully interesting," noting that "in reading it we became nervously anxious for the solution of the mystery it involves." As if stumping for two readings, this reviewer concludes: "the book will well repay a perusal." But the reviewer for *Godey's* was less willing to put up with the discomfort that every other reader describes: there, the whole book is simply described as "confused and wearisome" (*Log*, 2:523).

Though such responses form an inevitably partial record of the story's first reading(s), they sound a remarkably unified note: the story is as disconnected, "spun-out," "dreary," "weird," "uncomfortable," "painful," and "anxious[-making]" as it is "thrilling" or "interesting." The uniformity of these early responses aside, however, few (if any) more recent readers have treated *Benito Cereno* as anything other than holistic monument. Its genre is often in question—it is variously described as a story, a tale, and a novella— but its aesthetic oneness with itself is rarely questioned. When it is conceived of as having parts, they are formalist projections: we sometimes speak of a "frame" for the scene on board the *San Dominick* or of the "appendage" (or "insertion") of certain legal materials near the story proper's end.

But there is another way to think about the parts of *Benito Cereno*, and that is to consider its original serialization. We do not really know how Melville composed the story, but we do know how it was composed in type for *Putnam's* and then reset (virtually as is) for publication in *The Piazza Tales*.[18] It appeared piecemeal in three successive issues of *Putnam's* in October, November, and December of 1855, and the narrative caesurae that interrupt each section would appear to be as purposefully staged by Melville as many of the *San Dominick*'s spectacles are staged by Babo. For example: the break that ends the first installment feels very like a conclusion, as if Melville knew he were writing the end of the first installment when he composed it (which, indeed, he may have). Thus *Putnam's* readers who read the entirety of the October 1855 section of the story were treated to the following summation on its final page: "Such were the American's thoughts. They were tranquillizing [*sic*]. . . . Nevertheless, it was not without something of relief that the good seaman presently perceived his whaleboat in the distance. Its absence had been prolonged by unexpected detention at the sealer's side, as well as its returning trip lengthened by the continual recession of the goal."[19] Most readers who get to this point in the narrative are tranquilized, if not numb, by the interminably slow pacing of the plot. The story's drifting winds and tides naturalize Delano's wait, but they also serve to extend our own reading time, which, like Delano's unexpectedly long visit to the *San Dominick,* is "lengthened by the continual recession of the goal" (narrative development, even more so than resolution). Progress of any kind, in other words, is entirely arrested in part 1 as plot and text align (uncomfortably) in the real time of reading. The crippling collapse of our own aesthetic reading time with Delano's diegetic boat time is just one of many "tautologies" identified by Eric Sundquist in his magisterial new historicist rereading of the story, creating a shared tempo that forces every (first-time) reader into uneasy alignment with Delano and continually reminds second-, third-, and fourth-time readers of that initial mistake.[20]

Quite remarkably (for a serial fiction meant to attract further consumption), almost nothing happens in this first installment. *Benito Cereno* begins with Delano being awakened to observe the mysterious *San Dominick,* and the whole action of this section involves Delano getting up, getting dressed, journeying over to the mystery ship in a whaleboat, listening to Cereno's story, and then observing a small number of inexplicable actions while he waits for his crew to return with water and food. By far, the primary action of part 1 involves the painstaking unfolding of Delano's cognitive processes as he compares Cereno's "tale" to the "stories" he has heard elsewhere. Delano's "singularly undistrustful good nature" comes into direct conflict throughout this section with "the sort of stories" he has heard about "impostor[s]," "low-born adventurer[s]", "conspirators," "burglar[s]" "assassin[s]," and (most recurrently) "Malay pirates" (Oct.: 364, 365, 366). Hence the story flip-flops repeatedly, creating a tedious narrative zigzag: Cereno is a murderous "impostor" at one moment and merely a needy "invalid" the next (Oct.: 364, 357, 360). For readers of the first installment on first (or later) reading, there are few overt markers of a slave revolt. Suspense, such as it is, is entirely generated through Delano's fantasy that he might have stumbled into some interracial pirate plot (after the fashion of *The Many-Headed Hydra*).[21]

Indeed, if part 1 has a theme, it is the slow pall of temporality itself. Perhaps this is why the most notable "event" in part 1 involves the appearance of Atufal, who stands before us as a marker of both boat time and our own elapsed reading time. As Cereno explains: "'I could not scourge such a form. But I told him he must ask my pardon. As yet he has not. At my command, every two hours he stands before me'" (Oct.: 362). What Cereno draws attention to as "form," Delano dubs both a "time-piece" and a "punctual shadow" (Nov.: 472 and Dec.: 633). Atufal is thus a sort of narrative clock, and, as readers, we can, if we like, mark time either by the narrator's many careful and seamanlike references to the placement of the sun *or* by keeping track of Atufal's staged appearances, which occur twice over the course of Delano's visit—timing that (again) neatly coincides with our own reading time of that particular stretch of story. In this way, boat time becomes "now-time" (as Dana Luciano has called it)—for characters and readers alike.[22]

Against the temporal crawl of part 1, the second and third installments of *Benito Cereno* unfold—a little less slowly—the epic signs of a less phenomenological temporality, arriving finally (if uneasily) at the version of time that Homi Bhabha identifies with modern nationalisms—a time its adherents are willing to submit to because it promises to contain both the everyday and the hereafter of history.[23] The slave revolt that is so well camouflaged in pirate's dress in the first installment of the story comes much more clearly into focus in the second, which contains the story's most celebrated and politically charged scene—Delano's visit to the cuddy, where he clearly intuits the revolutionary potential of what Babo calls "shaving-time," a powerful moment in which Delano finally/for the first time sees "in the black . . . a headsman, and in the white, a man at the block," an insight which is then tranquilized (as the narrator might say) by the arrival of the long-awaited whaleboat in the closing pages of part 2 (Nov.: 467, 473). The second installment of the story thus ends with the following sentences, each given its own paragraph, perhaps because they compress time so much more radically than other parts of the story: "The ship was now within less than two miles of the sealer. The whale-boat was seen darting over the interval. // To be brief, the two vessels, thanks to the pilot's skill, ere long in neighbourly style lay anchored together" (Nov.: 473).

It is not hard to imagine how exasperating it would be to be left hanging at precisely this juncture—not because of the exquisite production of aesthetic suspense but because of the continual return of its lack. Perhaps it is not so surprising, then, that just as the endings of the first two installments seem intentionally to spoil the story's potential for desirable suspense, so the opening pages of the third installment defy the conventional rules of narrative plotting by giving away the solution to the plot in the first pages, rather than building and then releasing narrative tension over the course of many pages. For the stalwart reader who was still following along with the serialized version, the third installment opens almost immediately with the revolt's unraveling and the mystery's denouement. Having spent several months reading a story in which nothing happens—for the first two installments have virtually no action, little discernible suspense, and hence almost no potential for serialized pleasure—the reader is bombarded almost immediately with a dense succession of information and events— a radical shift in tempo from either of the earlier installments. Thus, as Babo's plot is revealed, time compresses and collapses for both Delano and the reader (as the narrator famously remarks, "past, present, and future seemed one"; Dec.: 635). Indeed, the bulk of part 3, which focuses almost entirely on the legal disposition of the people and things "rescued" from the *San Dominick,* might be said to negotiate the present-tenseness of part 1 and the messianic (or revolutionary) temporality of part 2. It is here that Melville's first reader, George W. Curtis, found aesthetic fault (finding the "dreary documents at the end" distastefully disconnected from everything that came before) and it is here that many recent readers have sought to allay that formalist criticism by making sense of the law as the key to the story's various historical, philosophical, and theoretical (if not narrative) puzzles. It is here too that the narrative point of view shifts from a focalization on Delano to a more omniscient position. And it is here that Delano insists that "the past is passed," while Cereno continues to morosely grieve (Dec.: 643).

I will resist the temptation to make every part fit, in the interest of making the opposite point, which is that the story ends in pieces: bones scattered across different burial sites, point of view shattered, Cereno's mind unstrung, the *San Dominick's* wealth redistributed, and a large number of the surviving slaves deported to different foreign markets. More notably, perhaps, Babo's body is violently divided from itself (as slave rebels' bodies often were), with his head, that powerful "hive" of collective "subtlety," left on a stick in the town plaza, an ambiguous sign of his ongoing psychic power over Benito Cereno and his physical subjection to the power of the law, the state, and the paramilitary might of liberal seafarers like the American Captain Delano. In the end, the master plotter is dismembered, just as the story itself was published in three aesthetically unsatisfactory parts, subjected to the piecemeal logic of antebellum print culture and all its various generic expectations, which Melville by turns fulfills and frustrates. Scholars have frequently noted Melville's alignment with Babo, the plotter (and the reader's alignment with Delano, the naive reader). Here, the body of brilliant Babo is made commensurate with the material shape of an ungainly aesthetic object, its beautiful "form" (like Atufal's) constrained by the temporal conditions of what can and can't be said, by whom, and how.

Thus, as Maurice Lee has perhaps most powerfully noted, the story is as much about the theoretical conditions of certain forms of historical speech as it is about a particular slave revolt or social injustice.[24] But if this is true, it makes the time of writing a matter of no less importance than the time of reading. As trivial as the conditions of a text's publication and reception may seem hundreds of years after the fact (and as unseemly as it is to compare a fictional man's corpse to a real man's corpus), antebellum print culture—its commitment to disposable seriality and its fetishization of the freestanding and hence more durable book— forms the conditions of Melville's ability to speak, to give an account of himself and of his contemporary world. The status of cultural production and consumption is very much on Melville's mind here. It is no mistake that Delano repeatedly soothes himself, throughout his many anxious cognitive meanderings, by rehearsing a number of middle-class norms, pop culture commonplaces that float freely through the story, scattering themselves through Delano's thoughts like a "tranquillizing" [*sic*] narcotic. When brought below deck (to the same place where Don Aranda has recently been flayed alive), Delano prefers to imagine that he is visiting the country house of some "eccentric bachelor-squire" straight out of Jane Austen (or a rural Ik Marvel), a man of leisure "who hangs his shooting-jacket and tobacco-pouch on deer antlers, and keeps his fishing-rod, tongs, and walking-stick in the same corner" (Nov.: 466).[25] In this perilous setting, he likens Babo to a domesticated family pet (a "Newfoundland dog"), dubbing him a "natural valet[] and hair-dresser[]" while at the same time rationalizing the tension he observes (when Babo actually cuts Cereno in an effort to subdue him) as "a sort of love-quarrel" (Nov.: 463, 467, 469). Likewise, at the highest pitch of his suspicion in part 1 (just before the first installment breaks off—for a month—in the October issue of *Putnam's*), Melville writes:

> Scarce an uneasiness entered the honest sailor's mind but, by a subsequent spontaneous act of good sense, it was ejected. At last he began to laugh at these forebodings; and laugh at the strange ship for, in its aspect someway siding with them, as it were; and laugh, too, at the odd-looking blacks, particularly those old scissors-grinders, the Ashantees; and those bed-ridden old knitting-women, the oakum-pickers; and, in a human way, he almost began to laugh at the dark Spaniard himself, the central hobgoblin of all.
>
> (Oct.: 366)

Bachelors, dogs, servants, lovers—as well as minstrel-like "scissor-grinders" (earlier called "organ-grinders"), Dickensian "knitting-women," and even Irvingesque "hobgoblins"—are the stuff of middle-class culture, reductive stereotypes and caricatures that Delano must labor to paste onto and over the scene he sees unfolding before him throughout those painful hours we spend with him aboard the *San Dominick*. Indeed, it hardly seems unlikely to imagine that Delano himself might have enjoyed a *Putnam's*—or a *Harper's*—subscription. He is *that kind* of cultural consumer, that kind of invested and willful mis/reader.

The pained and irritated responses of *Benito Cereno*'s early reviewers tell us that the narrative dialectic of disposable to durable reading with which I began was being played out very meaningfully in Melville's material life as an author who was coping not just with the transcendent issues we associate with aesthetic masterpieces but with the material details of everyday life. It is clear from Melville's correspondence that he wanted to publish his magazine fiction as a freestanding (and more durable) object and that he anxiously awaited news about *The Piazza Tales*' early reception—whether in the form of praise or royalties. He queried his publishers in writing as early as August 1856 (only a few months after the book was in print), asking them to calculate its sales for him. The clerk who responded to his correspondence noted that sales were "dull," but urged the author not to read too much into the present accounts, which were then forwarded to him (showing that the book was still in the red), and he pointed instead to the pure potentiality of the book's future sales, which he assured Melville would be brisker in the fall season (*Log*, 2: 520).[26]

Melville's clerk turned out to be wrong—or merely polite. Consumers in 1856 were not ready to make *Benito Cereno*—nor, indeed, any of the *Putnam's* tales—appear immediately and obviously durable through a spontaneous act of conspicuous and enthusiastic mass consumption (like the remarkable one granted to *Uncle Tom's Cabin* a few years earlier). Indeed, if Melville saw in book (as opposed to magazine) publication a potentially more durable artifact than the ephemeral mode of serial publication in magazines, his historical readers and reviewers steadfastly refused this distinction by continually marking the collection's origins in the pages of various serial publications (like the ones their reviews appeared in). As one reviewer wrote in the *New York Times*: "Herman Melville's *Piazza Tales*, taken as a whole, will not augment his high reputation. . . . 'Benito Cereno' is melodramatic [and] *not* effective. . . . The author of *Typee* should do something higher and better than Magazine articles."[27] In 1856 the more durable form of a book could not overshadow its origin in the more disposable form of mere "Magazine articles"—even though the formalist bias of almost every review insists on taking the collection (and each story, whether serialized or not) "as a whole."

As such details suggest, Melville was enmeshed, like every writer, in the everyday minutiae of composition, publication, and reception, but, as his best readers have always recognized, he was also thinking on a grander scale than the problem of how one survives his (or her) own present tense in stories like *Benito Cereno*. Here he forces his reader to experience the discomfort of being in the present tense, but he also defers the value of his writing to a later moment of reception, playing with the very idea of a deferred interpretation (and thus reevaluation) in the diachronic structure of the two reading experiences he joins under one title. I have called these two readings the "disposable" and the "durable" readings, purposefully evoking the language of the ephemeral versus the language of the permanent in an attempt to capture not just how the technique works for readers but why Melville executed the story in this way. On one level, the story is Melville's attempt to negotiate the quotidian everyday pain of his own experience of the antebellum present through a temporal deferral of the potential reception of his text. In doing so, he actually appears to have alleviated his own present tense pain as the author of several failed texts by creating what amounts to a painful reading experience for his readers (thereby redistributing some of the discomfort associated with writing texts for readers who do not appreciate them). But, as Elmer argues, the moment of production only forms a part of the literary event, which means that the meaning of the story is still unfolding with every new reading.

Today Again: When Double Reading Is a Dated Reading

I began this essay in 2007 and I complete it today in 2009. In the months and years that have intervened between drafts, epic historical changes have changed the way the world looks and the way we write and think in universities as well in newspapers, blogs, magazines, and books. This continues to be true, even though America has, in recent decades, repeatedly been told (or told others) that it (or they or we) have come to the end of history, a claim that (ironically) has attached itself to a series of unfolding events: the end of the cold war, the painful events of September 11, the decline of the interminable (double) Bush regime, the election of Barack Obama—all distinct events that have been accompanied along the way with the so-called decline of the nation-state, the rise of globalization, and the onset of global recession. The keywords of my lifetime, once I write them down, promise to make this essay another piece of ephemera in a world of disposable ideas, events, people, and things. Those keywords (this morning) are: Twitter, Madoff, Britney, healthcare. These four, and others like them, make up (or made up) the present tense of the essay you are reading, at the increasingly distant site of its production.

Like us, Melville experienced history in his own present tense, and his absorption in his own unfolding world is marked throughout *The Piazza Tales* in any number of highly contemporary allusions. "Bartleby," most especially, makes explicit reference to the material everydayness of Wall Street, to "the late John Jacob Astor," and to recent newspaper fodder (such as the Colt-Adams murder).[28] *Benito Cereno* seems to intentionally place itself on a more vast historical (and geographical) stage, alluding to deep historical time through a series of references to church and state and insisting on a more distant date (1799) than the historical Delano and Cereno inhabited (though notably, the fictional Delano refuses to acknowledge himself as a character in history and instead posits himself as part of some dime novel plot). But the grandness of its temporal scale aside, *Benito Cereno* has been no less situated, for the last thirty years or so, in local discussions of United States slave culture. To good historicists, the keywords of the 1850s have seemed for some time rather obvious: *Uncle Tom's Cabin*, Bleeding Kansas, Harpers Ferry. My earlier list (Twitter, Madoff, Britney, healthcare) would seem to suggest that, at the start of the twenty-first century, history is not all that historical in the present tense. But the world of *Benito Cereno* is only historical in a way ours is not (yet), simply because of our distance from it. We are still (always) naive readers of the present tense, which must submit itself to a second (or third) reading before we can, as Delano says, "be certain" of what matters most to the future (Oct.: 365).

The story raises a series of questions about how one should deal with the uncertainties of the present. Readers can choose between two character positions, identifying with the cornered Benito Cereno (as Carl Schmitt did) or the naive Delano (as more contemporary readers sometimes do). But they can also choose between two interpretive positions—the naive or the knowing. As Dana Luciano has noted, the story is not invested in modeling "a new kind of character but a new kind of *reader*."[29] Yet Melville prescribes no clear directives here (short of rereading), which are left instead to be settled over time, again and again, in every new reading. Indeed, as the examples of Schmitt, James, Waters, Barber, Doolen, and Delbanco demonstrate, the answer to these questions must always be historical ones, depending on the fatal intersection of who and where (and when) we are. That aspect of the time of reading, once again, shadows the time of writing. The story is about what we can say *and* what we can know (or are ready to know) at any given point in time.

In the end, Melville models in *Benito Cereno* a version of a historicism that tarries—for the few hours when we are reading it—in the present. In doing so, the story collapses aesthetic reading time with historical time, making itself unsettlingly available to any reader's everyday, no matter the decade or the century in which the story is consumed. Melville thus seems to point knowingly to the philosophical problems of time, of progress (or enlightenment), and of everyday life, but then again leaves them as he found them, unsettled. And why not? To do otherwise would be to enunciate a kind of temporal or developmental fanaticism, one not unknown in the West, either in 1855 or in 2001 or today—whenever that might be.[30] That fanaticism is what we call modernity, and it's safe to say that in whatever world my printed essay about Melville's printed text circulates, some form of it is nearby, because print is, as a rule, a tool of such fanaticism, as are the conventions, in some sense, of literary criticism, which speaks always in the present tense of fictional plots, whether insurrectionist or not. In the end, *Benito Cereno* is "implicated in a social temporality that exceeds its own capacities for narration"—and, while Melville seems to know it, we often do our authors and ourselves the favor of trying not to notice that fact.[31] It is a necessarily partial account of the enduring conditions under which we might give an account of ourselves in our own present tense—and, as such, it is a kind of social theory of nonfanatical progress, one that takes into account the many different cultural forms and artifacts through which any one person's historical experience is first articulated and then, forever after, archived.

Notes

I thank the friends who helped me with this essay—Lara Cohen, Elaine Freedgood, Siobhan Somerville, and Joe Valente—as well as the participants, organizers, and audience of the American Literature's Aesthetic Dimensions conference and the members of my spring 2009 "Scenes of Reading" seminar at the University of Illinois.

1. Herman Melville, *Pierre, or The Ambiguities*, ed. Harrison Hayford, Hershel Parker, and G. Thomas Tanselle (Evanston: Northwestern University, Press, 1971), 209.

2. On Schmitt, see Jan-Werner Muller, *A Dangerous Mind: Carl Schmitt in Post-War European Thought* (New Haven: Yale University Press, 2003) 3, 40; Gopal Balakrishnan, *The Enemy: An Intellectual Portrait of Carl Schmitt* (London: Verso, 2002), 182–83; and Barbara Boyd, "Dick Cheney's Éminence Grise," *Executive Intelligence Review* 33, no. 1 (2006): 35–36.

3. Tracy B. Strong, "The Sovereign and the Exception: Carl Schmitt, Politics, Theology, and Leadership," in Carl Schmitt, *Political Theology: Four Chapters on the Concept of Sovereignty*, trans. George Schwab (Chicago: University of Chicago Press, 2005), viii.

4. All Carl Schmitt passages cited here appear in German in Thomas O. Beebeee, "Carl Schmitt's Myth of *Benito Cereno*," *Seminar* 42, no. 2 (2006): 114–34. German portions of this essay were translated for me by Adam Chambers.

5. C. L. R. James, *Mariners, Renegades and Castaways: The Story of Herman Melville and the World We Live In* (Hanover, NH: University Press of New England, 2001), 5.

6. For three more examples, see Maurice S. Lee, "Melville's Subversive Political Philosophy: 'Benito Cereno' and the Fate of Speech," *American Literature* 72, no. 3 (2000): 513.

7. Lindsay Waters, "Life Against Death," *boundary 2* 29, no. 1 (2002): 281, 283.

8. Benjamin Barber, *Fear's Empire: War, Terrorism, and Democracy* (New York: Norton, 2004), 72.

9. Andy Doolen, *Fugitive Empire: Locating Early American Imperialism* (Minneapolis: University of Minnesota Press, 2005), 189.

10. Andrew Delbanco, *Melville: His World and Work* (New York: Vintage, 2005), 231, 242.

11. Waters, "Life Against Death," 281.

12. Delbanco, *Melville*, 239.

13. For a more dialectically dense version of this same maneuver, see Paul Downes, "Melville's Benito Cereno and the Politics of Humanitarian Intervention," *South Atlantic Quarterly* 103, nos. 2/3 (2004): 465–88. For another example of a purely allegorical substitution of one reader's own historical moment for Melville's (or Delano's), see Robert Lowell's 1965 theatricalization of the tale in *The Old Glory: Endecott and the Red Cross; My Kinsman, Major Molineux; and Benito Cereno* (New York: Farrar, Straus and Giroux, 2000), which stages Babo as a 1960s civil rights figure.

14. For conference proceedings, see Jonathan Elmer, "A Response to Jonathan Arac," *American Literary History* 20, nos. 1/2 (2008): 12–21.

15. Jay Leyda, ed., *The Melville Log: A Documentary Life of Herman Melville*, 2 vols. (New York: Harcourt, Brace, 1951), 1:466–67. Further page references to *The Melville Log* will be cited parenthetically in the text.

16. There is only one extended account of the contemporary reception of Melville's magazine fiction: James L. Machor, "The American Reception of Melville's Short Fiction in the 1850s," in Philip Goldstein and James L. Machor, eds., *New Directions in American Reception Study* (New York: Oxford University Press, 2008), 87–98.

17. Serial publications in the nineteenth century were literally more disposable than they had been even fifty years earlier. Before 1820 it was not uncommon for families with subscriptions to newspapers and magazines to keep the entire run of such objects as family heirlooms—often binding them in leather folios for posterity. By the 1850s, serial publications were much less likely to be preserved. Even as early as 1839, Theodore Weld was able to compose most of his *American Slavery As It Is* by picking through the trash at Manhattan's mercantile libraries, bringing home discarded newspapers and recycling them into clippings that would later form the bulk of *Slavery As It Is*. Even invested readers threw out their magazines: Melville himself, when putting together a clean copy of his *Putnam's* stories for publication in *The Piazza Tales*, forwarded a request to *Putnam's* for clean copies of the issues his work had appeared in, because he had not saved them: "upon looking over my set of magazines," he wrote to his publisher, "I find two Nos., that I want, gone:—Dec. No. 1853, and Ap. No. 1854. Will you be kind enough to send those two Nos. to me by mail, so that I can do my share of work without delay" [*sic*]. Herman Melville to Dix

and Edwards, Publishers (January 7, 1856) in *The Letters of Herman Melville*, ed. Merrell R. Davis and William H. Gilman (New Haven: Yale University Press, 1960), 177.

18. We know the serialized version formed the exact basis for the later version included in *The Piazza Tales*, because Melville used the magazine's printed pages as his proof sheets when preparing the collection for publication. Herman Melville to Dix and Edwards, Publishers (January 19 and February 16, 1856), in Davis and Gilman, *The Letters of Herman Melville*, 177, 179.

19. *Putnam's Monthly Magazine of American Literature, Science and Art* 6, no. 34 (October 1855): 367. Further citations to the story will be inserted parenthetically in the text, with the month of publication and page number.

20. Eric J. Sundquist, *To Wake the Nations: Race in the Making of American Literature* (Cambridge: Harvard University Press, 1994), 135–225.

21. Peter Linebaugh and Marcus Rediker, *The Many-Headed Hydra: Sailors, Slaves, Commoners, and the Hidden History of the Revolutionary Atlantic* (London: Verso, 2000).

22. Dana Luciano, *Arranging Grief: Sacred Time and the Body in Nineteenth-Century America* (New York: New York University Press, 2007), 209.

23. Homi K. Bhabha, "DissemiNation Time, Narrative, and the Margins of the Modern *Nation*" in Homi K. Bhabha, ed., *Nation and Narration* (London: Routledge, 1990), 291–322.

24. Lee, "Melville's Subversive Political Philosophy," 495–520.

25. On Melville's attention to middle-class discourse, see Samuel Otter, *Melville's Anatomies* (Berkeley: University of California Press, 1999).

26. The August 30 statement showed that the tales cost $1048.62 to print and distribute, while sales had accrued $628.20 to the account, leaving the book over $420 from turning a profit. The ensuing season showed no better results for either Melville or his firm. In April of 1857, Melville's publisher failed and sold the stereotyped plates of *The Piazza Tales* (and *The Confidence Man*) to another firm, which likewise failed in August of the same year. The plates were offered to Melville for purchase, but on September 15, 1857, Melville wrote to George Curtis saying that he "could not at present conveniently make arrangements with regard to [the plates]. . . . Do with [them] whatever is thought best." Accordingly, on September 19, they were offered at auction. Though some plates sold for as little as $15, no one bid on Melville's, and their disposal is unknown. See Herman Melville to George William Curtis (September 15, 1857) in Davis and Gilman, *The Letters of Herman Melville*, 188–89.

27. *New York Times*, June 27, 1856.

28. On these and other allusions to the contemporary world in Melville's short fiction, see Dennis Berthold, "Class Acts: The Astor Place Riots and

Melville's 'The Two Temples,'" *American Literature* 71, no. 3 (1999): 429–61; Barbara Foley, "From Wall Street to Astor Place: Historicizing Melville's 'Bartleby,'" *American Literature* 72, no. 1 (2000): 87–116; and T. H. Giddings, "Melville, the Colt-Adams Murder, and 'Bartleby,'" *Studies in American Fiction* 2 (1974): 123–32.

29. Luciano, *Arranging Grief*, 210.

30. I owe the concept of temporal fanaticism to Elaine Freedgood.

31. Judith Butler, *Giving an Account of Oneself* (New York: Fordham University Press, 2005), 8.

What Maggie Knew

Game Theory, The Golden Bowl, and the Critical Possibilities of Aesthetic Knowledge

JONATHAN FREEDMAN

> The eloquent models provided by economists are not limited to economics. Henry James's *The Wings of the Dove* is one of the greatest modern works of art based on interdependent wills, reciprocal uncertainty, incomplete information, principal-agent relations, moral hazard, hidden actions and information, with one disastrous outcome holding in its net five persons whose wills have become interdependent in this game.
>
> —Philip Fisher, *The Vehement Passions*

It's a sign of the times: critics have been busy filling in the once-formidable crevasse between the ideal of the aesthetic—with an attendant sense of capacious consciousness, moral insight, expansiveness of perspective, affective appeal—and that of the economic—thrower of a Weberian net of instrumentalism, embodiment of sterile, dry rationalism. Nowhere has this project been more strenuously pursued than in the study of the Victorian novel, where the economic wing of the critical edifice has been built with remarkable energy by critics like Regenia Gagnier, Catherine Gallagher, and Mary Poovey.[1] Their work differs considerably from the previously dominant conceptualization of the interplay between the economic and the literary, that on offer in the Marxist tradition, Frankfurt school variety. This field has turned against Marcuse's or Bloch's or Adorno's invocation of the aesthetic in general, and literary art in particular, as providing a critique of and a utopian alternative to bourgeois, capitalist culture.[2] Instead, these critics stress the imbrication of the literary itself with the discourse of political economy, rather than its critical or utopian function.

Although it's rarely invoked by these critics, the case of Henry James is extraordinarily apposite to their project, confirming but complicating their insights. For just as he stood on both sides of the Atlantic (as biologically impossible as that may be), James stood firmly on both sides of the putative aesthetic/economic divide and deconstructed it *avant la* critical *lettre*. This is the writer who crafted for himself the position of High Culture novelist in the field of contestation that was late Victorian and early Edwardian letters; who articulated, in works like "The Art of Fiction" or the prefaces to the New York Edition, an elaborate formalist vade mecum not just for novelists but for those academics who followed in their path; and who spoke the aesthetic with extraordinary eloquence.[3] But James was also a figure who openly did his best to realize "interest" on an investment in a literary life in the economic sense of the word. To read James's letters or notebooks is to encounter the artist as avid professional, one who understood perfectly well that his art was a commodity and who attempted to sell it for the highest price on the open market: complaining about his failure to receive American royalties on his best sellers, *Daisy Miller* and *The Portrait of a Lady*; struggling to regain this audience by writing naturalist fiction or for the theater; wheeling and dealing with journal editors and publishers; turning with a mixture of despair and defiance to what I've called elsewhere a high art professionalism.[4]

James's fascination with the economic dimensions of his vocation extended into the texture of his work as well. No writer I know has a greater sense of the power and possibilities of money to effectuate change in the world, in both a positive and a negative direction: wealth or the lack of it, the possession of money or the want of it, not only trace the limits but also limn the possibilities of freedom in James's novels. No writer I know has at his disposal a more extensive arsenal of economic metaphors, particularly as he meditates on the nature and value of his own art itself. James's life and work alike raise the very possibility Poovey in particular rules out of bounds: that writers of the high art variety did not need to "cloak their participation in the literary marketplace" but rather celebrated it; that a version of the literary that "emphasized originality and textual autonomy" can nevertheless offer a critical knowledge of the world not despite but by means of its tendencies to valorize itself as a closed system.[5]

In what follows, I want to use James's *The Golden Bowl* both to explore these matters and to regard them with a different optic. Rather than looking at James through the lens of economic history, as do critics like Gagnier, Gallagher, and Poovey, I want to view James through that of economic theory, at least as economics has been theorized for the past five decades: abstractly, mathematically, even algebraically. Specifically, following but moving beyond Fisher's suggestive but brief comments cited in the epigraph to this chapter, I want to weigh James's representation of human behavior in the light of economic game theory—roughly speaking, the attempt to describe in symbolic or mathematical terms the strategies or "moves" that individuals pursue as they compete against or cooperate with each other to achieve a certain goal or end. James, I want to suggest, understands much of what game theory came to explore—and, more important, understood the things that game theory *can't* address. My aim is not just to explicate James, but to trace the outlines and integuments of the aesthetic itself, at least of its literary incarnation. Rita Felski has recently argued—in highly, if unwittingly, Jamesian terms—that giving us a greater knowledge of the world is one of the things that literature can do: "The worldly insights we gain from literary texts are not . . . stale, second-hand scraps of history or anthropology. Rather, through their rendering of the subtleties of social interaction, their mimicry of linguistic idioms and cultural grammars, their unblinking attention to the materiality of things . . . they do not just represent, but make newly present, significant shapes of social meaning."[6] In what follows, I want to see how far Felski's argument might be extended when literature as such is brought into contact with other disciplinary ways of knowing. The comparison, I hope to show, is not entirely to literature's discredit.

To invoke game theory in the context of James is to embrace anachronism, since the text to which Fisher refers appeared in 1944, and the kind of game theory I will be describing was developed in the subsequent decades. So before proceeding, I need to sketch briefly the *longue durée* of systematic thought about games and competitive strategy and suggest how James enters into dialogue with that tradition. Games are, of course, as old as human beings; in the West they developed into an intimate part first of courtly then of middle-class life as part of what Norbert Elias called "the civilizing process." Thereby, they accomplished the domestication of the warlike. What Elias sees as progressive movement from war to tournament to chess and cards—all of which mimic war (checkmate means "the king is dead")—betokens the gradual development of culture toward mediated forms of combat.[7] The same movement can be seen in the explicit theorizing about strategy. The early modern armchair general could, should he be interested in such matters, consult Caesar's *Commentaries*, Flavius Veg-etius's *De re Militare*, or even Machiavelli's *The Art of War*. Or that courtier, taken with the modish game of chess, could have studied the *Roman de la Rose*, in which the chess allegory mimics the battles of Charles d'Anjou; he might also have consulted *De ludo scachorum*, a thirteenth-century treatise that applied the rules of chess to the orders of medieval society. A few centuries later, a mathematically inclined cardplayer could have consulted a 1713 letter by mathematician James Waldengrave outlining a solution to a card game puzzle that historians take as the origins of game theory. A nineteenth-century intellectual could witness the application of these principles to other arenas of thought—Cournot's *Researches Into the Mathematical Principles of the Theory of Wealth* (1838) or Francis Ysidro Edge-worth's *Mathematical Psychics: An Essay on the Application of Mathematics to the Moral Sciences* (1881). The theorization of strategy moves from war to warlike games to the precincts of the library or the drawing room—and then back out again into a place where the public and the private, the domestic and the political, merge: the newly understood sphere of political economy.[8]

The same movement is evident in the elaboration of game theory. Originating in the research of brilliant (and fiendish poker-playing) mathematician John von Neumann, bearing fruit in 1944 with von Neumann's publication (with Oscar Morgenstern) of *Theory of Games and Economic Behavior*, game theory moved quickly into the sphere of national security, especially via the efforts of the RAND Corporation, which, consulting with the defense department, used it to "game" the nuclear arms race of the 1950s. In the last twenty years or so, the theory that "won" the cold war has been utilized most fruitfully in the social sciences—political science, sociology, and especially economics, where its applications have been fruitful both in modeling large-scale systems and strategies of individual business-people. Indeed, it is in the last-named discipline that game theory has seen its most intense elaboration. With good reason, since in capitalism, every unit, as small as a Mom and Pop grocery store, as large as a multinational corporation, needs to anticipate the moves made by the competition and game out the best response.[9]

The same pattern is played by games qua games in the novel. For games of all sorts are foregrounded throughout *The Golden Bowl* in ways that bring the strategic and the social, the intimate and the economic, together. This transfer is fairly clear when, for example, the relatively transparent maneu-verings of Fanny and Colonel Bob are depicted as moves in a game or when Guterman-Seuss, the Jewish antique dealer, lays out the object he has to sell, the damascene tiles, before Adam and Charlotte and is compared to a cardplayer laying down his hand. The most remarkable of these is a metaphor packed in near the end of the novel, where Maggie experiences a sudden pang of doubt as to whether Amerigo really will return to the room as they are saying farewell to Charlotte: "Closer than she had ever been to the measure of her course and the full face of her act, she had an instant of the terror that, when there has been suspense, always precedes on the part of the creature to be paid, the certification of the amount. Amerigo knew it, the amount; he still held it, and the delay in his return, making her heart beat too fast to go on, was like a sudden blinding light on a wild speculation. She had thrown the dice, but his hand was over the cast."[10] The passage bristles with conflicting economic forms of risk, ranging from lack of payment into the language of "speculation"—hers is a venture like all of those that had made fortunes for robber barons like her father, then morphs with a flick of the Jamesian wrist into the most speculative game of all, that of dice. And it's this last metaphor—the one drawn from gaming—that unites all of these into one amalgam of behavioral, psychic, and economic intensities.

Not just the metaphoric but the actual representation of games enters into the text in the bridge-playing sequence at Fawns. Maggie is happy to be left out of the game, claiming to be singularly unequipped for cards and all they connote. Yet this is the sequence in which she scores one of her absolutely greatest triumphs: where Charlotte slips the bounds of propriety and confronts Maggie directly, and where Maggie successfully convinces Charlotte that she has no reason to reproach her. This scene suggests that James juxtaposes one set of ludic behaviors bounded by rules yet open to multiple strategizing—bridge—with another, equally rule-ridden game, that of custom. And, tellingly, when Maggie faces her first crisis—when she begins to suspect Amerigo of sleeping with Charlotte—she drops false modesty and uses precisely the language of cardplaying to gloss her response. "So had the case wonderfully been arranged for her; there was a card she could play, but there was only one, and to play it would be to end the game. . . . To say anything at all would be, in fine, to have to say *why* she was jealous; and she could in her private hours but stare long, with suffused eyes, at that impossibility" (349). Now there's nothing surprising in the recognition that games play a crucial role throughout this novel, placing it in the tradition of the card-game-ridden novels of Austen, Dickens, Trollope et al.[11] But the gap between Maggie as actual and metaphorical cardplayer points to the quality of *The Golden Bowl* that brings it closer to the world-view of economic-drive modernity than do even von Neumann and Morgenstern: its recognition of the *divergence* between games and competitive strategies. Maggie may or may not be all that good at the former, but she is a genius with the latter. What's remarkable in the second book of the novel, after all, is that this seemingly naive, artless girl outmaneuvers the infinitely more sophisticated players who face her at the card table, including a supersubtle Roman Prince, a world-historically successful millionaire, and a penniless beauty who has had to live by her wits. Maggie does so precisely because, while they play, she thinks ("you know it's my nature—I *think*"), and Charlotte and the Prince, clever though they may be, underestimate this capacity: they "thought of everything but that I might think" (569). Crucially, "thinking" here is not defined as an Isabel Archer–like accession to an amplitude of consciousness but rather a cold assessment that leads to the formation of a plan of action. However emotional she may be, Maggie also anticipates, assesses, strategizes: "She had a plan, and she rejoiced in her plan" (343). And in so doing she transvalues the idea of strategy itself, augmenting its move from the warlike to the economic by extending it into the realm of intimacy.

I want to gloss Maggie's actions in the novel—and the responses they elicit—by means of two quite basic abstractions offered in the game theory tradition, the game tree and the Prisoner's Dilemma game. The idea of the game tree is deceptively simple: it traces out the possible moves one player can make in a game, each move setting up in turn another series of choices (represented as nodes) to which one's opponent can respond . . . and so on to the end of the game, at which a win, a loss, or a draw can be easily represented with a symbol like, say, +1, -1, and O (for win, lose, and tie respectively). Since each set of initial decisions creates a series of ensuing moves, following out each branch of the game tree in each case can suggest to a given player what the likelihood of success might be in a given move. A game tree for, say, tic-tac-toe is relatively simple (see addendum); a game tree for chess, with its greater number of variables, is infinitely more complex, and so must be the attempt to harness game theory to the behavior of those infinitely complex entities, human beings. But there's yet one more complexity relevant to James's novel. Game theory also accounts for situations of asymmetric information—situations in which one player has more information than the other, as when a player cannot know what move his or her predecessor has already made. In such situations, the second player has only one recourse: to work *retroactively*—to attempt to calculate probabilistically on the basis of what a player is doing, what that player has already done. The more one can grasp about what a player does in the present, the more one can construct the strategy he/she has followed in the past, and the more accurately one can anticipate his/her moves in the future.

This describes Maggie's situation exactly and suggests the kinds of tactics she adopts. Her situation is that of the player in a game in which the other players have already initiated the action, to which she is compelled to respond in a kind of epistemological void. "Moving for first time as in the darkening shadow of a false position" (329), Maggie decides to do something "just then and there which would strike Amerigo as unusual," "small variations and mild manoeuvres" undertaken however "with an infinite sense of intention" (331). She sets out quite consciously to undertake actions that will provoke a response and she gets one: the momentary flicker of uncertainty that greets her presence at their house, where in any normal relation she would be, rather than at her father's and Charlotte's, where he expects to find her. And she displays a subtle calculatingness in this process. "She had only had herself to do something to see how *promptly* it answered," Maggie muses (343, emphasis mine): in other words, she makes a move not just to bring about another move but in order to assess, via the *rapidity* of Amerigo's response, what is motivating him—what, in other words, his original move (the affair with Charlotte) had been. After betraying himself with his initial hesitation, Amerigo's countermove is brilliant: he embraces her. By thus acting as if nothing has happened between them, as if the status quo of their relationship could be restored with a simple embrace, he deprives her of any further information she needs to plan her own response. As he continues to do: pages later, Maggie muses over his changed behavior: "He was acting . . . [on] the cue given him by observation; it had been enough for him to see the shade of change in *her* behaviour: his instinct for relations, the most exquisite conceivable, prompted him immediately to meet and match the difference, to play somehow into its hands" (353). The point to be made here is double: not only is the Prince able successfully to counter Maggie by "meeting" and "matching" the difference in her behavior, but Maggie *understands* this about him. There's an element of detachment in her love even as there's an element of love in her detachment.

Amerigo's countermove blocks hers, as if he plays an *o* in a tic-tac-toe game that prevents the *x* from filling a row—a stratagem which, however, doesn't cause the game to cease, but freezes it in place, allowing her only to fill in more x's to be countered by more o's and so on to infinity. In order for her to break the stalemate, in order for her to attain the kind of knowledge she needs—in order, that is, to *win*—Maggie needs to test Charlotte, as she proceeds to do: "Of that inevitability, of such other ranges of response as were open to Charlotte, Maggie took the measure in approaching her, on the morrow of her return from Matcham, with the same show of desire to hear all her story" (346). Her cleverness here consists in making Charlotte go over the narrative ground of the affair not so much to hear the truth about it, since Maggie knows that Charlotte would never communicate *that*, but to be able to "take the measure" of Charlotte's "ranges of response"—to figure out what kinds of moves she is making in the present in order to understand the moves she has made in the past and hence what Maggie can do in the future. And after Charlotte responds more or less as the Prince has done, happily recounting a lying version of their time in Gloucester, Maggie counters by conspicuously spending time with her stepmother, assaying "the experiment of being more with her" (349). The alacrity of Charlotte's response to Maggie's overtures, like the Prince's embrace, allows Maggie to measure them: such sudden shifts in behavior indicate to Maggie that their "demonstrations" are "determined": willed, strategic.

They thereby designate that there is something for Maggie to be suspicious *of*: "By the end of a week, the week that had begun especially with her morning hour in Eaton Square between her father and his wife, her consciousness of being beautifully treated had become again verily greater than her consciousness of anything else . . . [of the] impressions fixed in her as soon as she had so insidiously taken the field, a definite note must be made of her perception, during those moments, of Charlotte's prompt uncertainty" (349–50). And from this she is able to move further, to the recognition that Charlotte and the Prince are acting together—a perception that nails into place her sense of their commonality:

> The word for it, the word that flashed the light, was that they were *treating* her, that they were proceeding with her—and for that matter with her father—by a plan that was the exact counterpart of her own. It wasn't from her they took their cue, but—and this was what in particular made her sit up—from each other; and with a depth of unanimity, an exact coincidence of inspiration, that when once her attention had begun to fix it struck her as staring out at her in recovered identities of behaviour, expression and tone.
>
> (354)

Brilliant as the deduction is, something in Maggie hesitates here to take matters to their logical conclusion, a hesitancy that lasts many chapters. This can be read as a sign of the persistence of her flawed innocence—of that state of blissful ignorance that has helped to construct the problematic ground of both of the marriages that structure the book and from which she needs to grow in the rest of the book. But when viewed in game theory terms, we can understand Maggie's passivity more fully. Maggie's options exist, as it were, on the left side of the tic-tac-toe game outlined earlier. One option is to lose the game (-1; or even -2): should she confront the two, either they would continue to deny her suspicions and make her look ridiculous or, worse, confirm them, costing her her marriage and, perhaps more problematically, wounding her father. A second option is to do nothing; a course that seems irrational, to be sure, but preferable to the alternative. In this version of the game, Maggie's moves are matched symmetrically by the Prince and Charlotte's countermoves, leading inevitably to a draw, the reassertion of the status quo (which would be expressed mathematically as the outcome o). Maggie's behavior, then, is perfectly rational—a o outcome being preferable to a –1. But to say this is, at the same time, to confront the harsh quality of the choices that confront her. After all, the status quo that is the source of the problem is, in the first place, a life in which Maggie is fixed, isolated: "The ground was well-nigh covered by the time she had made out her husband and his colleague as directly interested in preventing her freedom of movement. . . . Of course they were arranged—all four arranged; but what had the basis of their life been precisely but that they were arranged together? Ah! Amerigo and Charlotte were arranged together, but she—to confine the matter only to herself—was arranged apart" (357). Her strategic insight, in other words, only reveals to Maggie the bars of her prison, not a way to escape it.

But there is another way to succeed. The basic presupposition of hers, as of all games, is that its players are rational—that they play within the constraints set by its rules (e.g., *x* and *o* alternate turns in tic-tac-toe; knights move differently from rooks). What happens, however, when one player starts breaking the rules—moves out of turn, advances a pawn three spaces instead of one? According to von Neumann and Morgenstern, the game as such is over: "the rules of the game . . . are absolute commands. If they are ever infringed, then the whole transaction by definition ceases to be the game governed by those rules."[12] This is what happens when Maggie discovers the depth and extent of the Prince and Charlotte's history with each other via her visit to the antiquario's shop and the antiquario's return visit to her. The constraints of the game up until now have been that she can make no direct accusation of Charlotte and the Prince —as she puts it, "she had but one card to play, and to play it would be to end the game" (349). But in this moment she shockingly does just that, first to Fanny, then to the Prince himself. In so doing she breaks this formal vessel of the game structure as thoroughly as Fanny has done the bowl.

But to recognize this is to imply as well that a new game can then be established, one in which there are new rules, rules that might potentially be more advantageous to the player stalemated by the old ones. And this is what Maggie does, constructing a game that was later to be labeled the Prisoner's Dilemma. In that grim structure we are asked to imagine that two people suspected of a crime together are imprisoned separately. Both are told that there's enough evidence to convict them, but that their testimony against the other would clinch the case. They are then given the same set of choices: rat out their collaborator and, if the collaborator remains silent, go free; remain silent and, if their collaborator is also silent, receive a lighter sentence; remain silent and, if their collaborator confesses, receive the heaviest sentence possible. The optimal outcome for *both* is to remain silent—an alternative we might think of as cooperation in the economic and human spheres alike. But the optimal outcome for *each* is to confess and so implicate the other, since this will result in, at worst, a light sentence and at best freedom—an alternative we might think of as competition, again in both the economic and human spheres. As each contemplates his or her choices, then, betrayal seems the only rational thing to do, however dismal a comment this might be on human nature: as the Prince tells Maggie, "Everything's terrible, cara—in the heart of man" (582).

Maggie creates a version of the Prisoner's Dilemma—with an insidious twist. Having herself known what it is like to feel imprisoned and isolated by conditions of asymmetric knowledge, she turns these conditions on those who made them for her and offers the Prince a Prisoner's Dilemma choice. When she indicates to the Prince that she has evidence of his perfidy—the shards of the Golden Bowl, the testimony of the antiquario—and then immures him in a state of epistemological doubt when she answers his question, "does anyone else know?" with the challenge "I've told you all I intended. Find out the rest—!" (472), James's metaphorical language is explicitly that of enchainment: she feels "with the sharpest thrill how he was straitened and tied, and with the miserable pity of it her present conscious purpose of keeping him so could none the less perfectly accord"

(465). But the implication is that, in so framing the matter this way, she is offering him a bargain. Maggie will returns to the status quo if he will forsake Charlotte and return as an engaged participant to his marriage:

> "Yes, look, look," she seemed to see him hear her say even while her sounded words were other—"look, look, both at the truth that still survives in that smashed evidence and at the even more remarkable appearance that I'm not such a fool as you supposed me. . . . Consider of course as you must the question of what you may have to surrender on your side, what price you may have to pay, whom you may have to pay with, to set this advantage free; but take in at any rate that there is something for you if you don't too blindly spoil your chance for it."
>
> (461–62)

It's true that what Maggie wants least is an outright confession—"if that was her proper payment," she thinks at the end of the novel, "she would go without money" (595). What she wants instead is an acknowledgment of her change, an acknowledgment that will facilitate the construction of a new marital relation of equals; this would come, however, at the price of his tacit acknowledgment of wrongdoing and his abandonment of Charlotte. The alternative is a much heavier, even unthinkable, punishment: an outright breach, which would presumably leave the Prince impecunious and disgraced. Now, as in all Prisoner's Dilemmas, there is the chance the Prince might be able to bluff his way through, especially given the tacit understanding on the part of everyone that Adam is to be spared the knowledge of the perfidy of his wife and his son-in-law—this seems to be the implication of the Prince's first question to Maggie when she confronts him. But such a chance depends on too many variables. Under the circumstances, he makes the right choice, abandoning Charlotte and accepting the lighter sentence, a future in which he knows his wife knows that he is capable of betraying her but chooses to be with him anyway.

But Maggie's efforts do not halt here. She also constructs a twist on the Prisoner's Dilemma scenario: she offers only one of the prisoners a choice. Maggie isolates Charlotte, imprisoning her as effectively as she does Amerigo; but she never offers Charlotte the bargain that she presents to her husband. Indeed, to the contrary, she systematically withholds the very possibility of choice from her betraying friend: although Charlotte, a brilliant reader of others, knows that something has changed in Maggie, and knows as she must that Amerigo is no longer her collaborator, she is kept from the knowledge of exactly what has happened between them through lies at once explicit and implicit. This condition, explicitly understood as an imprisonment—the "cage" of a "deluded condition" (493)—reproduces, ferociously, the conditions to which the Prince and Charlotte have submitted Maggie ("Maggie, as having known delusion—rather!—understood the nature of cages" [493]): like Maggie in the first half of the second book, Charlotte is put in the position of the second player in a game who has to guess at what the first player has done in order to make her own moves.

Unlike Maggie, who is throughout, without perhaps realizing it, the subtler strategist and the better mind, Charlotte opts for direct confrontation, "a grim attempt" (493) at breaking out of the prison cage, first in the card game scene, then in a direct sally as she hands her back a book. Indeed, forcing Maggie either to accuse her or deny that she has any such accusation to make is precisely the move that Maggie had decided early on *not* to make with the Prince; when Charlotte makes it, she doesn't see, or doesn't care anymore to see, that the chain of decision nodes works in such a way as to suggest that she keep quiet. Assuming the worst—that Maggie knows—she faces the following possibilities: if Maggie accuses her, she and Maggie both lose (-1, -1); if she doesn't, Maggie may win or she may not, the status quo will at any event be preserved (-1, 0). Either way, the smart move is to do nothing: although this too might lead to a loss, it might prove to be closer to a draw than a loss.

Alternatively, Maggie might *not* know, and the changed behavior that Charlotte observes might be due to any number of factors; in this case, Charlotte and she will either keep the status quo, or Charlotte will give away her own guilt by word or deed in order to confirm a knowledge that is only, at the present, a suspicion; we would represent this as a decision matrix of (0, -1). Here again, the wise course of action is to do nothing, to remain suspended in a state of epistemological vertigo, which is the cruel price the situation demands. But, as it was for Maggie, the rational course of action is also the unendurable one—and unlike Maggie, who possesses both epistemological and financial power, Charlotte is not in a position to change the rules of the game.

Which isn't to say that she doesn't try. Her direct confrontation at Fawns is also an attempt to get Maggie to offer her some clear choice, like the one that Maggie has offered the Prince with her challenge:

"I'm aware of no point whatever at which I may have failed you," said Charlotte; "nor of any at which I may have failed any one in whom I can suppose you sufficiently interested to care. If I've been guilty of some fault I've committed it all unconsciously, and am only anxious to hear from you honestly about it. But if I've been mistaken as to what I speak of—the difference, more and more marked, as I've thought, in all your manner to me—why obviously so much the better. No form of correction received from you could give me greater satisfaction."

(506)

The word *correction* brings together the thematics of truth, knowledge, and punishment that play against each other throughout the novel: what Charlotte challenges Maggie to do is to offer her a version of the deal Maggie has sketched for the Prince, "correction" in exchange for a light sentence. We can see why she would wish to do so. Charlotte has, even more perhaps than the Prince, something to offer in exchange: Maggie's continued access to her own father. By implicitly turning to blackmail, Charlotte is pushing on the edge of the game, just as Maggie has; she's like a prisoner quite literally here, but one who is trying to turn the tables on her captor in the interrogation room. Again, Maggie proves to be the superior player. Although she is indeed willing to pay this price, she won't make that willingness explicit, preferring instead to keep Charlotte captive, controlled, corrected in the prison of her ignorance and her love. She does so perhaps out of a bit of cruelty—what better revenge could there be than to use the victimizer's tactics against her?—but also out of a sound strategy. That she has something to bargain with suggests to Maggie that Charlotte needs to be kept out of even a Prisoner's Dilemma choice: it suggests to Maggie the depths of Charlotte's guilt, the dimensions of her betrayal, and hence hardens her heart against her former friend. It also suggests to her Charlotte's courage, her bravery, and hence further positions Maggie in a situation where she daren't show any vulnerability.

Her next move is fully, forcefully, and explicitly to lie—an act that bests Charlotte irrevocably, for, not only does it render any of her countermoves irrelevant (what does she have to move against?), it formally reties the bond between Maggie and the Prince on their shared complicity in the gulling of Charlotte:

Maggie had to think how he on his side had had to go through with his lie to her, how it was for his wife he had done so, and how his doing so had given her the clue and set her the example. . . . They were together thus, he and she, close, close together—whereas Charlotte, though rising there radiantly before her, was really off in some darkness of space that would steep her in solitude and harass her with care. The heart of the Princess swelled accordingly even in her abasement; she had kept in tune with the right. . . . The right, the right—yes, it took this extraordinary form of humbugging, as she had called it, to the end. It was only a question of not by a hair's breadth deflecting into the truth.

(507–8)

The point is clear: Maggie's strategic genius shows her how to operate within the socially constricting rules as well as within the affectional confines of her own weird family; but its chief use is to demonstrate to her the limitations of the games she has been forced to play. It's not until Maggie starts breaking the rules, becoming an irrational player, and then making up new ones that her efforts are crowned with success.

To be sure, the novel registers victory in the conjoined language of game playing and economics I have been stressing, first in the metaphor of dice throwing I have previously quoted and then in Amerigo's embrace of her one last time, when the "truth" of her triumph "so strangely lighted his eyes that as for pity and dread of them she buried her own in his breast" (595). At this final moment all the themes I have been trying to bring together here are reprised, one last time, and brought together in a unity that proposes they are all versions of the same thing. If Maggie has triumphed through her gamesmanship, then she has both won her husband and, as her father does in his own way, transformed him into an object, a pawn, or a card in her hand.

It's this moment, I think, that not only validates the aesthetics/economics link but also extends it into our own time. Maggie's successful deployment of ludic strategies anticipates the kinds of intrusion of economic strategizing into the precincts of private life that is the hallmark of the current moment. James's novel adumbrates the kind of work done by Nobel laureate Gary Becker, who famously suggested just how much of what passes for responses to the people we love and desire—our fathers, our lovers, our partners—is shaped by the same tactics that govern the actions of hedge fund managers, millionaire investors, entrepreneurs, and so on. But, in so doing, *The Golden Bowl* also provides a powerful critique of those tactics and their results, and on two counts. First, it's important to remind ourselves that Maggie only wins the game by fixing it—by altering its rules to fit her own agenda, and she can do this not only because of her superior savvy (her recognition that continuing to play by the rules will lead to defeat) but also because her wealth and position give her the power to make a new game. The only way to be sure to win, in other words, is to make sure that yours is the only game in town; and the only way to do *that* is have the power to set the rules themselves—a power granted Maggie in no small measure because of the dependence of the Prince on her fortune.

Second, there is a very real question about the nature of her victory. What, exactly, *has* she won? Contra some readers of the novel and the triumphalist rhetoric of the last pages, it seems clear in the final lines of the book that she has achieved, more or less, nothing. Her father and her best friend are lost to her, immured in an exile to which she sends them as sacrifice and punishment; she has won again the love of her husband, but he seems to be as much a hypnotized automaton as an active participant in their marriage. Having been acquired by Adam as a present to his daughter, all but seduced by his passionate former lover, the Prince now switches his allegiance to his wife, but doesn't seem to display any more will than he had previously. What Maggie learns, in other words, is how to win at the game of her life and her marriage; but this is a loss-loss outcome (-1,-1). To win is to lose; it is to best Charlotte but to become troublingly akin to her; to regain your husband, but at the price of rendering him an inert object of your own will rather than the passive object of someone else's.

Anticipating the brave new world of game theory that was to prove so important to contemporary economic thought, and anticipating even more acutely the extension of economic analysis into understandings that have followed it of the transactions of everyday life, the novel thus presciently critiques these developments, putting in their place a view of life in which precisely the means that assure victory ensure defeat, those that allow for the accomplishment of gain negate it. And in doing so *The Golden Bowl* vividly displays the kinds of knowledge that fiction has to offer in a world where the economic has risen to social hegemony, as it was beginning to do at James's moment, as it has done more thoroughly over the course of the long twentieth century to our own. But, to conclude with one last turn of the screw, by making this gesture of critique, James anticipates one of the directions in which economic thought is beginning to travel. Underneath the rise of economism in the past thirty years as I've adverted to it, there has been another tide rolling through the field, a critique of the model of rational choice and marginal utility upon which game theory relies and to which James's novel poses pointed questions. The former has undergone sustained critique by the school of behavioral economics that poses the Jamesian question, in the words of Richard Thaler and Sunil

Mullainathan, of "what happens in markets in which some of the agents display human limitations and complications?"[13] Far from being rational agents capable of making the best possible choice from available alternatives, human beings are driven by cognitive frames and emotional needs into wholly irrational, self-balking behaviors. Recent work in economics has included stringent criticisms of the reigning models of economics on the score of information control. Understanding that the most basic claims of economics rely on the impossible ideal type of perfect transparency of knowledge between partners to any transaction, large or small, economists like Joseph E. Stiglitz (awarded the Nobel Prize in 2001) have stressed the ways that asymmetries of information play out in matters as crucial as the setting of wages and as mundane as bargaining at used car lots; in a more popular vein, Steven D. Levitt and Stephen J. Dubner have written a national best seller devoted to probing such questions as how real estate brokers use their greater knowledge of the market to more attractively price their own houses than they do those of their clients.[14]

The point here isn't that James anticipated *Freakonomics* or should have shared in Stiglitz's Nobel; it is, rather, that the self-critical turn in recent economic work brings it into territory that has been explored by James: a world in which the line between the intimate and the economic has been irrevocably blurred; a world where a complex blend of the rational and the irrational guides the strategies that individuals pursue as they enter into complex blends of competitive and cooperative behaviors; a world in which competitive strategies are shaped by asymmetries in information; a world, indeed, where information is capital itself, to be hoarded when possible, deployed with devastating effect when necessary.

But there is one more turn to this particular screw. For economists have been reconsidering the making of their own discipline, seeing the literary as offering precisely the terms and capacities for explicating the nature of the field, for explaining the economic behavior of individuals, or—most important—for providing vital access to knowledge in and of itself. The first of these moves I associate with Deirdre McCloskey, who has been writing of economics as a rhetorical and narrative practice for many years (although, admittedly, with less effect within her profession than she would have liked).[15] The second I associate with Robert A. Shiller, mainstream Yale economist (and the man who called correctly not one but two bubbles, that of the stock market of the 1990s and the real estate market in the 2000s), who has given narrative—that is, collectively authored stories without any necessary reference in fact—pride of place in accounting for the shaping of the irrational action of markets.[16] For the third, I would cite Tyler Cowen, a Harvard-trained libertarian at George Mason University, who compares literary with economic modeling and sees the former as providing what the latter lacks.[17] Representing heterodox, mainstream, and neoclassical schools of economics, respectively, their endeavors taken together suggest that the future of economic theory may well lie in the attempt to rethink the basic tenets of the discipline in such a way as to recognize the power of that species of knowledge production (i.e., narrative or literary) that seems most antithetical to it. What Maggie knew, or what Henry knew, in other words, suggests to them what the literary knows, what the aesthetic can teach: that art makes interest in all senses of the word, reflecting and reflecting on how we buy and sell, capitalize and consume, and that, in so doing, it makes knowing our currency and information our futures.[18]

Addendum: The Prisoner's Dilemma in *The Golden Bowl*

Nan Zhang Da

As noted, Maggie waits until the golden bowl is broken to design a Prisoner's Dilemma (PD) for Charlotte (CH) and Amerigo (A). She opts to use this strategy to corner CH and A because, while the golden bowl is evidence of their relation, in itself it is insufficient as a piece of incriminating evidence. A PD is usually only employed if the interrogator does not have enough evidence to punish the prisoners for their suspected crimes and/ or desires additional information. The beauty of this, as of all game theory, is the principle of mechanism design. By designing a game and coercing/ asking players to participate, the mechanism design can always get players to reveal the truth, whether or not there is in fact a falsehood: hence its optimality for Maggie's unusual situation.

By definition, a PD has to be performed simultaneously: each prisoner given the same amount of time and information, each denied access to the other. James models this as closely as possible by having M approach A and CH with the shortest possible time gap, while making sure A and CH cannot collaborate and, more important, give each other emotional/psychic/ facial signals that might let the other know where one's true preferences lie.

The logic behind M's PD is as follows:

A prisoner in the PD must always find his optimal strategy in confessing (C) even though his team's optimal strategy is to not confess (D/C).

This has to hold even given the following caveats: 1. uncertainty on the part of any one or both of the prisoners in a PD over the preferred treatment of the other (uncertainty signified as μ); 2. the probability that the other prisoner has more or less information (information asymmetry).

Or, represented below in a PD payoff matrix:

Viewpoint Amerigo	Charlotte C	Charlotte D/C
Amerigo C	3, 3	0, 5
Amerigo D/C	5, 0	1, 1

For Amerigo and Charlotte, for each to confess while the other one remains silent is the optimal payout (0); to both remain silent is less optimal (1), to both confess is even less optimal (3), and to remain silent if the other confesses the most punitive (5).

Confession is all but beside the point in the PD M designs for A. The true "mechanism design" of the PD for A is the conveyance of a message from M, who needs to formulate and deliver the message when she is *in the state of not knowing* A's true preferences. That message is deceptively simple: I will stay married to you no matter what. Its genius is that the open-endedness of the promise also has buried within it a time constraint: Maggie implicitly adds: "or so it seems, for now."

In dealing with CH, M's tactic must consist of two parts:

1. M has to convince CH that A is not on CH's team anymore, so that CH will cease to consider a scenario in which she leaves Adam but runs off with A. If, though, A has "confessed," she cannot be sure that an interlude with CH will not see an impulsive change of heart.

2. M can never know for sure what A's true preferences are and thus can never know for sure if CH knows what A's true preferences are. Simply "telling" CH that A is no longer her partner has its obvious risks. M can only convince CH that A no longer prefers to play with CH by conveying the impression to CH that A similarly went through a PD (with a clearer payout structure) and made his decisions against CH.

M creates a modified PD for CH, where one of the prisoners (here, A) receives preferential treatment not in the terms of the payout structure but in having more (or more complete) information about that payout structure than the other M cannot create a true PD for CH because, unlike the interrogator in the classic PD, she has constraints that sharply limit the extent to which she can enforce her "punishments." In technical terms, she does not have the ability to make good on certain parts of the payout structures she has designed for A and CH—and CH knows this. The genius of PD, though, is that the minute one of the prisoners in PD confesses, the enforceability of the PD for the second prisoner becomes irrelevant. The outcome is the same.

Notes

1. Regenia Gagnier, *The Insatiability of Human Wants: Economics and Aesthetics in Market Society* (Chicago: University of Chicago Press, 2000); Catherine Gallagher, *The Body Economic: Life, Death, and Sensation in Political Economy and the Victorian Novel* (Princeton: Princeton University Press, 2005); Mary Poovey, *Genres of the Credit Economy: Mediating Value in Eighteenth- and Nineteenth-Century Britain* (Chicago: University of Chicago Press, 2008).

2. See inter alia Georg Lukács, from his pre-Marxist "romantic anticapitalist" phase, *The Theory of the Novel* (Cambridge: MIT Press, 1974); Walter Benjamin, "The Storyteller: Reflections on the Work of Nicolai Leskov," in *Illuminations*, trans. Harry Zohn (New York: Schocken, 1970), 83–110; Herbert Marcuse. *The Aesthetic Dimension: Toward a Critique of Marxist Aesthetics* (Boston: Beacon, 1979); Theodor Adorno, *Aesthetic Theory*, trans. Robert Hullot-Kenter (Minneapolis: University of Minnesota Press, 1998); and, perhaps more relevantly, Adorno's gem of a discussion of Dickens in "On Dickens's *Old Curiosity Shop*," in *Notes to Literature*, vol. 2, trans. Sherry Weber Nicholson (New York: Columbia University Press, 1992), 171–77. For Fredric Jameson, see *Marxism and*

Form: Twentieth Century Dialectical Theories of Literature (Princeton: Princeton University Press, 1974), and *The Political Unconscious: Narrative as a Socially Symbolic Act* (Cornell: Cornell University Press, 1985).

3. Henry James to H. G. Wells, July 10, 1915, quoted in Philip Horne, *Henry James: A Life in Letters* (London: Penguin 1999), 555.

4. Jonathan Freedman, *Professions of Taste: Henry James, British Aestheticism, and Commodity Culture* (Stanford: Stanford University Press, 1990). Michael Anesko has shown how James's early and middle years comport withto this pattern in *"Friction With the Market": Henry James and the Profession of Authorship* (New York: Oxford University Press, 1987). For the effect of this on his work, see Marcia Jacobson, *Henry James and the Mass Market* (Tuscaloosa: University of Alabama Press, 1983).

5. Poovey, *Genres of the Credit Economy*, 418.

6. Rita Felski, *Uses of Literature* (Oxford: Blackwell, 2008), 104.

7. These themes are developed most fully in Norbert Elias and Eric Dunning, *Quest for Excitement: Sport and Leisure in the Civilizing Process* (Oxford: Blackwell, 1986).

8. See Robert W. and Mary Dimand, "The Early History of the Theory of Games from Waldengrave," in E. Roy Weintraub, ed., *Toward a History of Game Theory* (Durham: Duke University Press, 1992), 15–29.

9. John von Neumann and Oskar Morgenstern, *Theory of Games and Economic Behavior* (Princeton: Princeton University Press, 2004 [1944]). As William Poundstone has observed, this may be the most unread famous—and famous unread—book of the twentieth century, and while the author of this essay has made a valiant try, he can't claim to have followed its mathematical proofs with the greatest of acuity. Indeed, he has followed the advice of the authors, who suggest that the mathematical proofs need not necessarily be followed for the argument to be persuasive (11). He has relied on secondary works to flesh these out, most notably William Poundstone, *Prisoner's Dilemma: John von Neumann, Game Theory, and the Puzzle of the Bomb* (New York: Anchor, 1993), which offers a lucid explication not only of von Neumann but of the Prisoner's Dilemma problem set, and Morton Davis, *Game Theory: A Nontechnical Introduction* (New York: Dover, 1997).

10. Henry James, *The Golden Bowl*, ed. Ruth Bernard Yeazell (London: Penguin, 2009), 594. Further citations in the text will refer to this edition.

11. For a good summary of these, see Michael Flavin. *Gambling in the Nineteenth-Century Novel: "A Leprosy is O'er the Land"* (Brighton: Sussex Academic Press, 2003).

12. Von Neumann and Morgenstern, *Theory of Games*, 145.

13. Sendhil Mullainathan and Richard Thaler, "Behavioral Economics,"

262 AESTHETICS AND THE READING OF FORM

MIT Department of Economics Working Paper Series, Working Paper 00–27, September 2000. http://www.economics.harvard.edu/faculty/mullainathan/papers_mullainathan (accessed April 15, 2011).

14. See, for example, Joseph E. Stiglitz, *Whither Socialism?* (Cambridge: MIT Press, 1994); Steven D. Levitt and Stephen J. Dubner, *Freakonomics: A Rogue Economist Explores the Hidden Side of Everything* (New York: William Morrow, 2006).

15. This has been a constant theme in McCloskey's writing of the last twenty-five years. See "The Literary Character of Economics," *Dædalus* 113 (1984): 97–114; *The Rhetoric of Economics* (Chicago: University of Chicago Press, 1985); *Knowledge and Persuasion in Economics* (Cambridge: Cambridge University Press, 1991).

16. Shiller elaborates on the role of narrative in George A. Akerlof and Robert J. Shiller and Akerlof, *Animal Spirits: How Human Psychology Drives the Economy, and Why It Matters for Global Capitalism* (Princeton: Princeton University Press, 2009).

17. Tyler Cowen, "Is the Novel a Model?" in Sandra J. Peart and David M. Levy, eds., *The Street Porter and the Philosopher: Conversations on Analytical Egalitarianism* (Ann Arbor: University of Michigan Press, 2008), 319–37.

18. A shorter and somewhat different version of this essay was delivered at "American Literature's Aesthetic Dimensions," a conference held at the Huntington Library in 2007; I profited from numerous comments and questions from the audience there. Thanks to Sara Blair, Kerry Larson, Cindy Weinstein, and Christopher Looby for reading this essay, in some cases numerous times, and for making helpful suggestions for its revision, some of which I've even followed!

[12]

Upon a Peak in Beinecke

The Beauty of the Book in the Poetry of Susan Howe

ELISA NEW

A scrap of Emily Dickinson's "cream laid" notepaper traced with graphite, the face of the manuscript buffed and eroded by time and the friction of the oblong envelope (acid free) in which it is stored.

A strip of denuded gray homespun or of the muslin once used for bed curtains, the fabric threshed by time to a mere crosshatch of warp and woof: porous, skeletal.

The ambered tissue of a nineteenth-century frontispiece overleaf.

A crushed, torn origami, one friable finger's length, shaped like a weathervane, ripped from a Webster's dictionary, 1840 edition, tiny crumbles sifting from the edges.

The black-and-white photograph of a young blonde girl with a shoulder-length pageboy hairdo, wearing a toga. The photo is not actually black and white, but rather a study in grays brightened by a black backing or a white detail. Here it is a warm—nearly brown—gray pebbled with darker graphite, and there pale steel clouded with ivory. In folds and yokes of the girl's clothing, and the clothing of the others shown with her, various matte mid-grays cue us to see red, blue, or green. Only at the composition's center, where a gleam from below lights up the girl's hair and bodice, is there a true pearly white.

What else? A Xerox-shaped rectangle, a photo offset or photocopy of a microfiche strip, the rectangle bordered black and centered on one thick ivory page of a book of published verse. Within the gray rectangle separate words (*praises, thunders, kills*) are repeated according to some pattern, with discrete words enclosed in thick lozenges of border.

A fraying square of white silk from the wedding dress of a Connecticut minister's wife. The image of a man, walking abstractedly, random pieces of paper pinned to his coat. He wrote on every inch of paper he could find and then came home to his wife, after days of hard riding, with his coat covered in scraps.

Can words composed in holy awe betrothe him to Christ, marry his sin to redeeming graceful love? He prays it might be so, for his tradition tells him the Word is a wedding garment. Along with his wife's wedding garment, some of his scraps may still repose in drawers in Yale's Sterling and Beinecke libraries.

Such delicate and perishable objects, their structures resolving to non-structure, or nonstructures to structure, are central in Susan Howe's poetics.[1]

Typically, these objects to which Howe gives a nearly ritual power are ones she has personally salvaged and then subjected to a unique process of composition. Trained originally in the visual arts, Howe makes poetry (rather than merely writing it) as painters make art. From the personal libraries and scrapbooks of her own parents and forebears, from local libraries in small Massachusetts, Connecticut, Berkshire, and Adirondack towns, and from the great institutional archives where books deemed worthy of keeping reside—Harvard's Houghton and Yale's Bei-necke—Howe retrieves the articulate textual remnants of her New England past. Later, at home at her table, sitting near a window that brings in light broken by tree shadows, she coaxes these objects into second growth. She exposes their surfaces to the changing light on her desktop and then the technological light of the photocopier. After she has copies in hand, she begins the delicate grafting and quilting operations that give her pages loft and texture, and even a sort of grade, and she also composes the meditative or lyrical stanzas closest, in traditional terms, to what we call poetry.

Legibility, transparency, and even navigability are aspects, but hardly the most salient, of her poetry's features. How could they be, in this poetry so many featured, this poetry ambitious of exceeding, while including and honoring lyric form?

By and large, English readers expect that poems shall express the personality of an individual self, a self for whom the lyric "I" is spokesperson and whose subjectivity is represented by the supposed transparency of print. Poetic success, in the traditional model, is achieved best when the set of highly dense and quite material conventions, the poetic apparatus, can be made to seem sheer. For the extent to which print can be a communicative medium depends upon the individual voice that confers beauty by washing the world with vision, leaving it glistening. Traditional books of poetry will, in fact, contain any amount of obscure printed matter, but all such matter will be suspended within the life-giving fluidity of the lyric voice that contains and masters them. "Readings" are generally expected to enhance this experience of absorption, translating poetry on the page into sounds whose referential rather than acoustic or musical qualities will pierce the intervening crowded space of the room full of chairs, persons, microphones, and hearing aids.[2] One hears a poem at a "reading," or reads a poem in one's own mind, but the poem, we presume, is not altered. Only the delivery system is different.

Moreover, in America, poetry is often justified, if at all, only for its capacity to elevate us morally, to offer edification or moral improvement. It is expected that, as the poet aims his work at producing insight, his reader travels via printed lines on a journey whose end will be his own deeper understanding. As the popularity of explicit hortatory themes withered in America, it nevertheless remained a given that poetry and philosophy were hortatory forms. For instance, readers accepting that an arrangement of lines need not mimic a "psalm," that lines need not scan or count off in numbered stanzas to earn the right to be called poems, still wanted their poems to end with a redemptive bang. Readers assumed that the lines of a poem would conduce toward growing clarity, its progress initiated from the left and going to the righthand margin of a single page. Development on the page, in other words, would mimic growth or revelations within the psyche or soul of the reader, with destiny of poet and soul joined. The traditional poem ministers to this destiny.

What makes the poetry of Susan Howe so different is that the poem is not a minister or medium of transparency. The poet does not stand outside. She is, often at much risk, vulnerability, and exposure to herself, inside the poem, her voice one tactile, historical object among other objects in the poem. Her quest for the beautiful poem is not for what frames or contains. If the lyric speaker is usually outside her book, her "voice" containing the poem's contents, here the lyric voice sounds from within, and lyric consciousness has no special privileges.

> If the book is to be opened
> I must open it to open it
> I must go get it if I am to
> go get it I must walk if I
> walk I must stand if I am
> to stand I must rise if I am
> to rise I had better put my
> my foot down here is where
> consciousness grows dim[3]

Howe shows in such lines that poems have a weight and volume, palpabilities and opacities running counter to trained expectations. Though her poems can be called experimental and seem, on first glance, radical, this Connecticut poet is a secret sharer dwelling in the neighborhood of Wallace Stevens, who wrote that "the greatest poverty is not to live in a physical world."[4] As in Stevens, so in Howe. Not only is it axiomatic, in Howe, that the greatest poverty is not to live in a physical world but also that the physical world is historical. Such convictions have implications. To journey into the literary past is not, and will never be, for Howe, a matter of mere exercise of mind. The intellectual life of the poet will need more than clarity of vision, will be held accountable to disciplines more palpable than the cerebral ones—to farming, quarrying, harvesting; to the work of pioneer wives packing and unpacking, storing and arranging; even to uncomplaining attendance in a Hartford office. Even when the tools she uses are electronic—and she does use them—the most dematerialized of processes will retain its tactile feel or else lose purchase on the beauty of the objects it seeks. Even a Google search does, for Howe, retain the palpable labor intensiveness of mining or agriculture or an arduous handicraft.

It is no surprise, then, that Howe lets us see the process of making poems as painstaking, even excruciating. The poet's greedy raid on the archive will always uncover more of the disintegrating paper mobiles, each lovely in its way, than can ever be represented adequately. There is a certain pathos attached to work of this kind, for there will always be a fatter pile of photocopies, a taller haystack of the lovely mobiles, than any publisher will ever include in a book, always the prospect of diminishing returns for labor expended. Sometimes one feels how charily Howe has set down words, feels a Frostian thrift implicit in Howe's craft of honoring diminished things. And sometimes one senses, conversely, a certain luxuriousness in the enterprise, so lavishly deliberate, even prodigal.

Which fossil-like sprays of print, some black and distinct, some blurred and eroded, will find a place within the area of Howe's page? How to "frame" these? Shall the simple window-sized rectangle of a single page best frame the scrap or image, or ought the scrap instead form, say, part of a diptych, conversant with its facing page? If part of a diptych, shall the shard or flake be shadow, or herald announcing, or its coeval, and, if so, shall it appear in line with or raised above or below? Should the font or typeface be as distinct, more distinct, or less distinct than that on its facing page?

What of the rhymes or patternings, the principles of coagulation and scattering, that unify or loosen the pages? Shall there be threads of theme carrying through an actual narrative story line, or shall images pool in coagulant interknit structures—verbless, objectless, and yet visually or sonically dense? To what extent shall individual words comment on, reflect each other through sonic imitations or visual punning, and to what extent shall the individual line, or even the grammatical sentence, frame a given stretch or movement of the poem? When, and with how much information, shall the poet offer teacherly exposition; when should she narrate in a twenty-first-century plain style what she experienced when she wrote the poem? How much weight should she give to such passages?

What about the physical book as it organizes and is itself altered by an interval of reading? Books are read, Howe lets us see, by sunlight or lamplight, on divans or in bed or at library tables, for work or diversion. What about the weight or importance of any one page within the mobile architecture of the book itself? Pages may be flat, but books are made of 180 degrees; every page traces the arc from 0 degrees to 180 every minute or so. As the page turns, the reader's fingertip active, the geometries of relation between eye and print alter. Light dawns or spreads its bloom out from the spine of the book to the edge and then light is sucked back into the thin crevice. We block it out, but each page we press to 180 flat narrows back to nothing before it reopens. Reading constantly hazards triangles as well as rectangles. Only when we fail to open a book fully enough on the photocopier are we reminded of the way print slides on the diagonal down into a closed book, the inner margin an angled slope into the dark spine.

The mobile sculpture of the book is, what's more, a technology encased by and dwelling in the more complex architecture of the library. Houghton

Library at Harvard, no less than Mt. Vision in the Berkshires, is a complex site, creviced and craggy and promontoried. Nature and culture are inter-leafed and mingled to a far greater degree than we admit. Howe shows how certain "natural" spots on the North American crust—tracts of Adirondack acres where Protestants met Indians in war, for instance, or the Cape Cod coast, or certain becalmed Pennsylvania foothills where religious pilgrims preserved extreme cultural quietus—are textually fecund, full of articulate sounds, and sedimented with printed matter the poet can detect and carry into the future. Conversely, she disallows merely mental or intellectual spaces. Libraries, and especially the great ones like Houghton and Beinecke, are features of an environment composed out of material indigenous and transplanted, made by persons native or migrant, of stone and wood, their door frames and elevator shafts constructed once and forever changing, though less perceptibly. In banks of oak shelving on slate floors, in their cooling systems and Dewey decimal systems and maps, these buildings have declivities and broad plateaus, accessible pathways and unnavigable outcroppings, which, like a mountain or body of water, facilitate or impede, filter or speed engagement with their contents.[5] Like Keats who, in reading Chapman's Homer, compared it to the enlarged vistas "stout Cortez" beheld as he stood "Upon a Peak in Darien,"[6] Howe stands upon her peak in Bei-necke Library and surveys the American canon.

Susan Howe has written far more books than can be explicated here, and so I shall confine myself to looking at the last four, two from the 1990s and two from the early twenty-first century. These books will serve to repre-sent Howe's mature work. *Singularities* (1990) and *Pierce-Arrow* (1999); the small, privately published *Kidnapped* (2002); and, finally, *Souls of the Laba-die Tract* (2007) allow us to watch Howe's mature techniques in motion and development. I shall concentrate on describing the poet's relationship to precursors and history in the volumes *Singularities* and *Pierce-Arrow*, and, more concisely, in *Kidnapped,* before going on to analysis of Howe's most recent work, *Souls of the Labadie Tract.* There the poet becomes the courier between two Connecticut forbears, Wallace Stevens and Jonathan Edwards, making her own verse conversant with theirs.

Along with her colleagues of the L=A=N=G=U=A=G=E school, and in the tradition of William Carlos Williams, Howe's work has not only questioned the associated ideas of lyric subjectivity and self-possessive, self-assertive individualism but has also traced both to certain aggressive syndromes of the Puritan mind. This given, Howe has also cherished Prot-estant thought and, especially in the traditions of Protestant literacy, has created an aesthetic field with semaphores up, attuned to beauty and prolific in producing it.

Illustrating this point is the cover of Howe's *Singularities*, a cover that does not just illustrate but initiates and inaugurates the reading process. Tinted an antique powder-puff pink, the book's cover typifies books as decorative elements that furnished refinement as they "civilized" and domesticated the wilderness. Meanwhile, the cover's woodcut illustration tells a more violent story. The woodcut depicts a phalanx of black-hatted marksmen taking aim across what seems either a rolling sea or a planted field—in either case, someone is dying or drowning in the billows. Ambiguity also surrounds what lies between the shooters and their targets: sheaves, women, swaddled babies, or merely compacted leaves. Are the shooters in the woodcut perhaps uniformed British soldiers aiming at colonials in woodland settlements or, perhaps, colonials taking aim at Indians in longhouses? Battlefield and planted field share the same outlines, suggesting agriculture's slow-growth aggression, while the stylized foreshortened compression of the battles between whites and Indians, particularly those taking place around Deerfield at the commencement of King Phillip's war, suggests a telescoping of many battles and of history itself as battlefield. The woodcut seems (in the manner of Williams's prologue to *In the American Grain*) to expose the fear of contact, to represent the cold blossom of pride that allowed Americans to treat the earth as—in Williams's words—"excrement of some sky."[7]

European trashing of the American wilderness, a despoiling as old as the first Europeans' arrival but renewed in every century, is a theme Howe develops, especially in the second long poem of the volume, "Thorow." There Henry David Thoreau's alienation from the despoiling of America by commerce prefigures her own alienation before the cheap motels and gimcrackery of modern day Lake George. Again one hears echoes of Williams, as Howe finds that the "pure products of America go crazy."[8] The very entering of the wilderness and settling it is a form of madness that wreaks vengeance on the land itself, turning it to ugliness for the sake of private possession and discreteness of soul. This does not mean, however, that the poet marooned by Lake George, living out a winter in cold winds next to glittering ice, denies sympathy with the volume's central perpetrator-victim, the seventeenth-century minister Hope Atherton who, lost in the woods during King Phillip's war, was finally set aflame and ran to his death. Howe lets Atherton's purity of belief, his naked fear, his Protestant aloneness abide within and ignite her own lyricism. Through Atherton's stiff but lovely archaisms, Atherton's genuine if myopic convictions, his

Figure 12.1. Cover image of Susan Howe, *Singularities* (Middletown: Wesleyan University Press, 1990), copyright © 1990 by Susan Howe. Reprinted by permission of Wesleyan University Press.

chilled and threatened accents, Howe finds a certain redemptive womanliness in Puritan clerical speech. Also, Atherton's womanish name, Hope, softens the barriers of time and alienation so that the poet, in effect, takes him in. Howe, the lonely poet holed up in the frozen woods, is no stranger herself to defensiveness, to wondering who is her enemy and who her friend.[9] It is a milder version of wilderness panic she experiences during her sabbatical in the Mohawk wilderness, but she too fears marauders and girds herself defensively. She too suffers the syndromes of individualism, spasms of singularity.[10]

This "singularity" is at least part of the problem. Hence the plural title of the volume, *Singularities*, a title that deexceptionalizes while it also takes names and apportions accountability. *Singularities* gives the lie to the Puritan settler's assertions of chosenness, it exposes the modern advertiser's exploitation of the niche and it endeavors to find a place of kinship between the two aggressive proponents of chosenness, the Reverend Hope Atherton and his later-day nemesis, the woodland sojourner, Henry David Thoreau. To both of these, and channeling the communicative Whitman as well (for Whitman, as Christopher Looby notes, is interleafed with Howe's verse, as all poets, and persons, are tucked into his *Leaves*), the poet declares:

> You are of me & I of you, I cannot tell
> Where you leave off and I begin
>
> (58)

This relationality is crucial to the volume and to historical understanding as Howe seeks it. Historical consciousness is a remedy for excesses of singularity and a means of entering and sympathizing across lines of estrangement or aggression. It teaches us that we are interleafed, softens the distinctions of persons according to and along coordinates of proper identity, historical epoch, language, and compass points: Hope Atherton, a seventeenth-century English speaker living in western Massachusetts, is usually held distinct from Henry David Thoreau, a nineteenth-century English speaker living in eastern Massachusetts, who is ordinarily held distinct from Susan Howe, a twentieth-century English speaker living in southern New England. But these distinctions are nullified by language, which connects us all.

Only the most meager, most nonhistorical, uses of language, Howe shows, will confine themselves to expressions of a placed and mortal subjectivity—a person of one time and place. Poetry's richer capacities, its more elastic talents, may be used to achieve the resonant scattering, to help us hear sound forms that persist across spaces unbound by occasion. Indeed, the only kind of verse one hardly ever finds in Susan Howe is the "occasional." Rather, the single, double, and multiple panes of paper surface offered by a printed book are like springboards and landing spaces. The pages of a book entertain the commerce of syllables and nomenclatures. A page is where idioms and linguistic changes still in process leave their prints.

Howe's refusal of lyric singularity in favor of the space of the book may eschew the privileges of the individual, but it is anything but impersonal. As she carries Hope Atherton's pitiable, poignant singularity, she carries, too, that of her lyric forbears whose conventions of authorial power and forward thrust are her historical inheritance: "Work penetrated by the edge of author, traverses multiplicities, light letters exploding apprehension suppose when individual hearing" (41). But, beyond this, Howe's emotional, even plangent tonal register reminds us that writing does not slake but extends need; writing consists in a disarmed exposure of the writer's mind, psyche, and heart to the unknown. The seignorial distance and cutting frontage of authorship is always, happily, subject to ambush by reading, which turns the self into a throughway, a way of admitting the dead to take up habitation within one. Reading opens the book of the self to other leaves, which then dwell somewhere therein, their force liable to discharge at any moment.

Thus the fascination with "Thorow," Howe's scout and guide, in *Singularities*. During her visiting professorship at an upstate university in winter, the poet finds not Thoreau but "Thorow." Thorow clears trails, we might say, within the imagination of Susan Howe, who becomes disidentified with her "self" just as "Thorow," spelled with an English rather than French set of ending vowels, is disidentified from his. Not identical with his name, Thor-row is now, as one correspondent puns, a god-like "Thor" who "rows" (down the Concord and Merrimack). Not only does Thoreau row, but he rows on *eau*. Indian place names end with the suffix *et* and his ends with *eau*—both are words for water. Whatever the biographical personality Thoreau had, "Thorow" has riverine fluency and ready translatability; his name, like "Hope" Atherton, becomes not a singular label but a place of passage, a sort of pump. With "Thorow" at her back, the poet barricaded in her cabin ventures out, moves into "the weather's fluctuation"; she gets the Indian names "'straightened,'" by which she means "more crooked." Now she may read American history differently, allowing the language of one epoch to wash over that of another, admitting the past to the present.

A sequence of examples will demonstrate how this all plays out within the volume. The setting is northern New York, mid–twentieth century, the Adirondacks, where a poet, sometimes lonely, lives in a primitive cabin through a cold winter. Indian wars were fought in this place, as they were along the wide belt of the Mohawk lands extending east to Concord. And so the poet, through the winter, keeps the Reverend Hope Atherton, who fled from Indians through the woods, and the naturalist Henry David Thoreau, in mind. The battles between whites and Indians, part of the archaic

American experience, are yet more archaic, these conflicts now including the whole American continent and the epic history of war and terror. Howe endeavors to represent—all at once—the regular cycles of snow on earth, centuries of English and Indian habitation, fluctuations of fear, anger, and reverence. The ancient clash of bloodied arms achieves lucidity when, in Hope Atherton's "voice," it records:

> Loving Friends and Kindred:—
> When I look back
> So short in charity and good works
> We are a small remnant
> of signal escapes wonderful in themselves
>
> (16)

Yet Atherton's lucidity is achieved at the cost of much ambient depth of echo and many other sounds—of Indians, of woods, of seasons flowing through. It is as though the poet restricted language to the narrowest chamber to leave it in the care of the subjective voice. Thus, Howe lets the sound scatter, retrains it not only through the singular consciousness of a man's particular event, Hope Atherton's, into a larger surround, bouncing and rebounding off his cherished books and his dreams of Atlantic passage, his still-and-never-to-be unlearned Continental and filial humility, the slow occlusion of European memories by New World flora and fauna, and these off each other, since sounds compose their own relations.

> Otherworld light into fable
> Best plays are secret plays
>
> ————
>
> Mylord have maize meadow
> Have Capes Mylord to dim
> Barley Sion beaver Totem
> W'ld bivouac by vineyard
> Eagle aureole elses thend
>
> (11)

Atherton's humility before old forms of authority, his instinctual awe before the dazzle of New World heights and expanses, his natural reaching for biblical vocabulary to express exaltation, all these are compressed in these lines, the echo between worlds giving rise to a music no more crowded than history is. Obscurities in Howe are rarely opaque, although they may be refractory. What is "thend"? Perhaps it is "the end" subjected to the rules that allow "would" to be represented as "w'ld." Or something else—the thrumming sound, perhaps, of that eagle's wing, the concentric inexactitude of the eagle aureole sharpened, sleeked by the *d* to a feathered edge. That *d* cinches rhymes that wavered in one line; read down the strophe's edge and you will find that, as *dim* is to *vineyard, totem* is to *thend*.

A few more pages and more radical crosscuttings and interleafings break the integrity and decorum of the page. The poem itself becomes a tool of crosscutting, a chisel releasing the plural singularities that populate false singularities. A vertical oblong of couplets, with white ribbons of double space between each and a theme of "marching," give page 12 a forward leaning, epic-feeling surge across the gutter and between the leaves, impossible to ignore. Instead of ribboned lines, words not yet given semantic purpose, words not yet phalanxed or devoted to a cause, are arrayed in their native spirits—"Nature without check with original energy," as Whitman had it.[11] "Epithets young in a box" (13), the poet calls these syllables, these hard sounds unused to use, electric and many edged. Brilliant tessellated puzzle pieces milling in a square without the protocols of right to left to define their order, these words regain the density of epithets. Pictographic diagonals have just as much charge or more than laterals. Hence

       architect
         euclidean curtail

(13)

Or

     a
severity whey crayon

(13)

Or

                  shad sac stone
               recess

(13)

These little chimnied or cellared sheds of sound do not refuse all denotative gestures. They conjure, for instance, the actual phenomena in a primitive world (human settlement staked out through geometry, the oblong whey squiggles of loose bowels, a lovely sunlit pond incubating aquatic life), but their visual and aural shapes, stacked or leaning pyramids of *c*'s and *s*'s, latinate clusters starting back in the palate, have an interknitness of their own.

In *Singularities* the poet who was a visual artist has much to teach us about how forms confer beauty on other forms simply through patterns of resemblance and variation. For once, as she shows, thor ow (or eau) bursts the bounds of the singular person, once poetry leaps the fences of the lateral and the boundaries of the page, then, with the up-and-down joists of the book loosened, new species of poetic gravity, accountability, and kinship may descend. Once it is no longer human consciousness, with the lyric speaker in loge (lofted above, driving thought left to right in obedience to intention, past to future from nascency to destiny), words and thought may be seen in their more natural state. They splay and spread like lichen growth or tree fall, half living, half dead, turned face up, face down, some above and some below ground. From inside language's thicket, voices—even the poet's own voice—may be heard.

Choral, transtemporal, chthonic, language is beautifully crooked, branching and unlinear, turned and turned by tropings, cognitions, and recognitions.

That persons can never be transparent; that poetic "speakers," like philosophical "thinkers," are only by the most extreme suspension of disbelief reckoned to master, guide, or control materials; that there are other offices for the poet than Cartesian reflection or—even in America!—rhetorical (national) or homiletic (religious) persuasion—such convictions of poetry's coextensive relation with matter and complex ethical action inform *Pierce-Arrow* and *Kidnapped*, both of which highlight the poet's role as actor, reactor, and accountable ethical subject rather than pure supervisory will. Indeed, as Stephanie Sandler has noted, the accountability of Americans, including intellectuals and the institutions organizing intellectuals, to the exertions and dispositions of American power is a topic vital to Howe.[12] We have seen this in her treatment of scenes of war in *Singularities*. The idealized transparency or transcendent quality of the intellectual life are, as Howe shows in *Pierce-Arrow*, belied by how intellectual careers actually play out, with the levers and gears, the individual career trajectories and high stakes power struggles of university life mimicking those less idealized.

A career within the "ivory tower" is, as Howe reminds, a trade like any other, where ideas may be pressed into service as tools and the growth or stasis of disciplines liberated or impeded by demands of ego. And, of course, competition between disciplines, like the age-old contest between poetry and philosophy, deprives both of claims to any transcendent poise and restores them to history.

Poetry itself, these books remind, is a production, a profession, an institution. Thus *Pierce-Arrow*, largely set in the academy (art's patron and paymaster), finds Howe reflecting, as she had in other volumes, on the boundaries, constraints, and strictures governing creative life in New England's capitals of intellect.[13] Howe is not shy about allowing the tension between and among members of the intelligentsia to enter her poetics. Not for nothing does she, riffing on Thorstein Veblen, title the second part of *Pierce-Arrow* "The Leisure of the Theory Classes," as not for nothing had she given over pages of her work *The Birth-Mark* to exhuming and working through her own memories of Cambridge, Massachusetts in the 1950s. There, as daughter of a law school professor and an Irish actress, she came of age amid the posturing, genius, and tipsy grab-ass of the cold war academy.[14] Not unambivalent, but also not dismissive of her own opportunities, Howe makes her poems reflect the experience of one born into not only her own life but into a way of life. Like Mather and Eliot children, Holmes and Lowell and James children—privileged for being what is called, in academic parlance, "legacies"—Howe, daughter of a Harvard law professor, is informed by the name she bears and forever marked by the grid of Cambridge streets. To have come of age as a daughter of American law and the Irish stage, to be the sister of a poet and also an actor, are not incidental attributes but conditioning facts that Howe makes use of in her poetry. The fraught, if often fruitful, tensions between creative temperaments and the bureaucracies that pay their livelihoods; the national, ideological, and religious imperatives or fashions that may elevate one strain of thought over another; the inverse or torqued relation of genius to success; the sharp byplay between intellectual centers and hinterlands; the ups and downs and variances within and between intellectual careers; and, finally—of a salience nearly impossible to exaggerate—the kinship customs and rituals of bequest, the protocols of transmission, inheritance, and memory that enable or interrupt the flow of ideas across time—to all these Howe opens her verse. A true New England native and student of its intellectual and poetic history, Howe appears in her verse as just that, representing the interimplicated history of intellectual life, poetry, and the professoriat.

Throughout her career, Howe has mapped with great precision the consequential descent of American poetry, like American philosophy, from American theology. Indeed, Howe has reckoned more precisely than any other contemporary poet the exquisite trade-offs and paradoxes of such an inheritance. "God's Altar needs not our polishing." Thus Cotton Mather had once inveighed against Anglo-Catholic aestheticizations, while Jonathan Edwards, of the same Calvinist tradition and a key figure for Howe, saw in "the beauty of the world" the Divine maker's Hand. Either way, the Calvinist-Cartesian regime required poetry's justification to be found outside the realm of art, its office outside the purely aesthetic. Ideally, poetry was countenanced as a device for producing inspiration, whether national or religious or both. Or, elevated language was to be a medium of praise and glorification, a means and mechanism of revelation, or a help toward godly conduct.

"From 1860 on in nineteenth / century American colleges / philosophy was an apology / for Protestant Christianity," writes Howe in *Pierce-Arrow*.[15] A little later she quotes Charles Sanders Peirce admitting, "One of my earliest recollections was hearing Emerson deliver his address on 'Nature' and I think on that same day Longfellow's 'Psalm of Life'" (116). In these quotations we see that not only are poetry's and philosophy's hereditary American duties fulfilled, their manifold accountabilities to standards ethical and improving summed up, but also their tutelary function is carried out, one institutionally insured. The great institutions of culture that provide Howe her key mise-en-scènes do not leave disciplines to their own devices. At Harvard and Yale the homiletic imperative is never far off.

Half of the company
would try to portray
some abstract quality
Fear Courage Ambition
Love Conceit Hypocrisy

(72)

In *Pierce-Arrow*, a poem with Charles Sanders Peirce at its center, Howe finds numerous ways to give density to the persons and forms of academic instruction, using the transgressive, brilliant antihero Peirce as avatar of this density. Peirce's most lasting contribution as philosopher may have been to prove the irrelevance, to question the existence, of such abstract qualities when estranged from practice. The mere idea of instruction—the transmission of mental matter via and through the institution of the professoriat (an idea parallel, in Howe's understanding, to poetry as a transparent medium for the conveyance of feeling or beauty)—was one Peirce doubted and dismissed, that vocal dismissal doubtless compromising and eventually dooming his claim to an office of "instruction" at a university. As Howe mordantly informs, Peirce regarded the notion of the university as "institution for instruction . . . grievously mistaken" (7). She lets Peirce's companion, Juliet, define his more intimate relation to ideas: "He loved logic" (1). Of course Peirce's own lifestyle, in particular his relationship with Juliet, a woman not his wife, made him notorious and lost him several academic posts, but Howe focuses more on the scandal of Peirce's pragmatism. To "love logic" in this sense is a classic, pre-Socratic activity in which things are as they appear. For Peirce, the activity of pursuing the logical across a page of paper is an enterprise of the "passion-self" as edged and decisive as any march of epic warriors.

Each assertion must maintain its icon

(3)

As she develops her complex meditation on Peirce, a poem doubling as her own elegy to the departed husband, David, Howe gathers in a larger community of departed singers and thinker-lovers, communicants of Peirce and David. Howe herself writes that such poems as "The Triumph of Life" and "A Leave-Taking" comforted her during years of loneliness in Buffalo, Swinburne's loverlike fluency and plangent ripplings recalling her husband's skill at the tiller. George Meredith, and Swinburne, Peirce's late-nineteenth-century contemporaries, function in the book as his adjutants and secret sharers, all three blessed with a pleading that does not efface itself. Meredith is revealed through various personal effects, pens, pencils, and a period silhouette fashioned by Sir John Butcher, Swinburne through his desk and the discarded, much-edited, unfinished manuscripts he left. All three men are examples of unmetaphysical, untranscendent forms of immortality, as her husband's art—sculpture—exemplifies the idea persistent in material form. The poetic work does not transcend, does not "pierce" (Howe plays on Peirce's name here) or find some metaphysical persistence outside its physical form. But, in some essential way, as Peirce's philosophy remains immanent, secreted or "pursed" within the vascular tissue of the manuscripts, within the expectant point of the pen, within the storehouse of the archive, so does Howe's poem. If conventional notions of poetic immortality make it depend upon transcendence of print, paper, and ink, these are turned on their head. In *Pierce-Arrow* the arrow that would pierce is revealed as a purse, love still moist within. For it is, in the end, the great ardor of Peirce (for language, for his aptly named Juliet) that is expressed and reciprocated. Poetry itself, Howe shows, is inevitably an act of love.

The holder of such a view as Howe's will necessarily submit to wearing her own heart on her sleeve. The book, dedicated to the poet's late husband, the sculptor David von Schlegell, has Howe wearing herself on the cover and the back flap. Specifically, on the front we see a photograph of the young Howe in 1947 in a Cambridge, Massachusetts performance of *The Trojan Woman,* while the back flap shows her, in sunglasses, in front of the remains of the Pierce-Arrow automobile factory in Buffalo, New York, the struggling rust belt city where Howe taught until her retirement in 2008.

Figure 12.1. Cover image of Susan Howe, *Pierce -Arrow* (New York: Directions, 1999) copyright © 1990 by Susan Howe. Reprinted by permission of New Directions.

This book of poetry, written between childhood and adulthood, Cambridge and Buffalo, is her vehicle too. The poet does not deny that as a writer of poems she plays a dramatic, a performative role, one among others in a lifetime of roles. This book, *Pierce-Arrow*, traces a poignant trajectory, that of the poet's own growth. The tender curve of the maturational arc—the arc of a girl's growth in and through forms of art, in and through stages of love—the nakedness and guardedness of the artist, the nakedness and guardedness of the woman—these themes lend a terrible tenderness to *Pierce-Arrow*. Liaisons with books and encounters with lovers share vectors. Both human and intellectual love aim dead at the heart.

As a younger poet, and one associating with the poets of the School of Poetry and Criticism at SUNY, Buffalo, Robert Creeley, and Charles Bernstein, and as a member of the loose confederation known as L=A=N=G=U=A=G=E, Howe has, throughout her career, engaged in a certain amount of quiet polemicizing against the expectation that poetry should be weightless. Given the separation of the critical and the creative that has evolved in universities, the way Howe sends criticism to the school of poetic craft has put her, along with others, in a position of opposition. She found a kinswoman in Emily Dickinson (*My Emily Dickinson*), plus an alter ego in the Indian captive, Mary Rowlandson, and she has found foils and also valued interlocutors in such scions of the academy as Perry Miller and Helen Vendler.

Miller, author of *The New England Mind: The Seventeenth Century*, treated Americans as Augustinean agonists, lonely churches of one (in Niebuhr's phrase), and he dematerialized the Puritan inheritance by turning New England history into a history of ideas.[16]

Helen Vendler, the twentieth century's most celebrated defender of the subjective lyric, has argued for forty years in favor of the individual agency and necessary boundedness of a poem. Poems are, Vendler eloquently argues, what "soul says," the particular textural and thematic signature of a poet's style confirming and affirming the unique texture of the individual.[17]

Not so, Howe's stylistic crossweave demonstrates. Universities, intellectual communities, the professoriat, are not merely the settings in which minds operate, providing rooms for them to train limpid vision on objets d'art. Universities with their libraries and offices, their copiers and faxes, their sprawling neighborhoods of rental housing and substantial real estate, and not least their demographic instability and their transatlantic traffic, are part of the texture, entering the pure realm of ideas. Was America ever really America, its soul ever its own, Howe asks, when Boston rips off London? Nor is Harvard Harvard, nor Yale Yale, when Yale makes itself not-Harvard, Harvard makes itself not-Cambridge, Henry makes himself not-William or precisely William. National identities, like personal ones, are all so much annexation and occupation, so much ransoming, you kidnapping me, me you, every poet made out of her sisters and her uncles, volume after volume of imitation and theft down the years.[18]

Kidnapped demonstrates. In her first book of the twenty-first century, published in a limited edition of three hundred, Howe rewrites the American story of migration with materials from her own mother's family archive. In Howe's hands, the Manning family's journey to that most quintessentially American place, Massachusetts, is no Milleresque errand into the wilderness, no pilgrimage of individuals yearning for solitary redemption on the North American strand. The Manning immigration is best seen as a set of performances, of plays by a family of traveling actors. What is a family but a set of players? We feed each other lines. What are poets but estranged kin, kidnappers of the word?

Such scatterings and reunions of kin are themes that continue into Howe's most recent book, *Souls of the Labadie Tract*. The volume is her simplest to navigate and, in many ways, her most beautiful; it may provide a good starting place for readers who are wary of postmodern experimentalism, but lovers, as Howe is, of Wallace Stevens and Jonathan Edwards. As *Kidnapped* traced back along the branches of Howe's own family tree to Irish poets and playwrights, the title poem of this book traces Wallace Stevens to the Pennsylvania lands of his sectarian forbears, thus allowing Howe to press into new tracts of Anglo-Protestant America. The central poem in the book, "118 Westerly Terrace," ties Stevens to Jonathan Edwards, and both to Howe herself. Imagine the book as a group portrait of three Connecticut poets sharing one ecstatic linguistic raiment and you have its central conceit.

I mean the image literally, for in this book Stevens and Edwards and Howe herself are literally dressed in verse and, too, in the formalized apostrophes of poetry. The language of address, the elevated discourse— whether of poetry or theology or America's characteristic fusion of the two—adorns the history of Connecticut as a bridal gown adorns a bride.

Both Edwards and Stevens had the kind of intimate physical relationship with the poetic word Howe cherishes, which she credits in part to having learned from them. Edwards rode into the Connecticut hills with scraps of paper pinned to his coat, so that he came back from rides in the hills white-garbed, papered with godly sayings. Edwards's notebooks and miscellanies, collected at Yale, are still in the process of being finished, since pages of his thoughts from the 1740s are still being puzzled out and transferred into the modern form of a scholarly edition. Where does his real "writing" therefore abide? Stevens, whose ramblings in the envoi to "118 Westerly Terrace" Howe evocatively called his daily "Errand,"[19] also had a peripatetic and distributed habit of composition. Thoughts that occurred to him on his walks back and forth to the Hartford Insurance Company where he worked were recorded on "two by four inch scraps" (73), which he would then give to the secretaries in his office to transcribe onto 8 1/2 x 11 sheets. The transcribed scraps then became grist for Stevens's nighttime and weekend bouts of composition, when he "transformed the confusion of these typed up 'miscellanies' into poems" (73).

Although Stevens's poems have a monumental solidity that belies a liveness and quickness Howe rediscovers in their history, she uses the poem to follow this emergence of the poem "qua" from its many scattered incidents of cohering existence. Where and when does the poem acquire its "is," its thereness or address? At 118 Westerly Terrace? What then of the walks, where the ideas first emerged, or the office where they became print through the ministrations of stenographers? Or, at Howe's desk where, reading them, she also writes them? What is the poem's spatial and temporal address—the manuscript, the printed book? What of the house where the poem was written or the countryside around and about that touched the poet's mind? Are these some of its genuine addresses? Do these addresses still speak, some speaking to us in tones soliciting response? Might not, for instance, the feeling that we "love" a poem or a poet, or can see the scene it depicts, or, even more obscurely, feel "moved" by its language, confirm the existence of still active address from these other sites?

Such questions established, the book's sections seem to guide the reader toward the wedding of poet and landscape, matter and mind, present and past, theology and poetry that Howe has always endeavored to represent. The pages of *Souls of the Labadie Tract* amount to a lovely fusion or wedding of adhesive media, percept, thought, printed word yearning and straining toward each other. And the book's final poem, "Fragment of the Wedding Dress of Sarah Pierpont Edwards," appears in various guises. We see it literally, in the title of the book's final poem, and in a ghostly gray photocopy, a postage-stamp-sized square showing a thready edge of Sarah Pierpont's actual dress.

And then appears a set of lacelike, pressed, delicate catalog entries on the Edwards family. In the compost of book pressed on book, ripened by time, this detritus quickens into new delicate life. As Williams might have said, they grip down and awaken. These are not merely found objects or bibliographic refuse but a new wild growth, like wild ferns or thistles, sprouting from the page.

Though elliptical, full of gaps, the texture of a Howe poem is not less for being akimbo or tilted on the up-down axis, but more alluring,. An appreciative reader of Howe now knows and comes to crave the tension of letting the eye catch in one of her tactile, bristling installations. There is, in the end, great aesthetic satisfaction in looking through the openwork, the pierced slubby lace of historical knowledge embodied in historical texts. One looks through the fabric as through a veil, the beauty not beneath but abiding in the crush and weave of the historical fabric itself. Nor is this activity simply retinal or visual or aloof. Humane, and good humored toward the lyric speaker, Howe does not exempt herself from the somnam-bulistic focus, the clenched drive of the rational self, the "workaholic state of revery / Destitute of Benevolence" (85). Burning her candle down, trac-ing the up and down aspirational phallic linear motions, as if ardor of quest could guarantee success proportional to noise of effort. The poet has a sub-ject self but also suffers; she is relieved to meet her nightgowned forebears.

> For a long time I worked
> this tallest racketty poem
> by light of a single candle
> just for fun while it lasted
> Now I talk at you to end
> of days in tiny affirmative
> nods sitting in night attire
>
> (94)

It is a happy thing when the predecessors appear, Edwards or Stevens. To live in a world singly, unidimensionally, is to remain single and lonely when one might lie "happy down the grain." Everyone in his or her pres-ent time—Edwards, Stevens, Howe herself—had to live in a "house-island" (92), inside the shells of the one body, one gender, one historical moment, one house and family. And yet, Howe discovers, literate civilization creates openings for us—thresholds, doors—within the conversant architecture of the stanza. "Stanza" means room, of course. The poetic stanza, unen-closed, is naturally hospitable to poetic converse across time, as in Wallace Stevens's "rooms." Walking through them, the poet lets her voice loosen and receive. She utters but is also blessed by apostrophes—"Back to the doorway flow / of life's energy" (82); "Afternoon at its most glossy / The foyer seems to smile" (92). Every poem, Howe's own included, is in receipt of inheritances that pass from ancestors, and every poem will become, in time, what Whitman called "nourishment." Stevens also wrote, in "Post-cards from the Volcano," of children who would never know we were once "quick as foxes on the hill."[20] Poetry brings living and dead to dwell on one plane: "In the house the house is al / l house and each of its authors / pass-ing from room to room" (77). But it also begins to show the present the way into archive and earth, into sedimented rather than singular existence.

> Two ages overlap you and
> your predecessors—where
> they go to where far back
> becomes silent and all lie
> happy down the brain and
> barrier self-surrender for
> then all doors are closed
>
> (95)

To see, and to gain help from other poets, to see "what is secret, wild, double and various in the near-at-hand" (74), is what Howe honors Wallace Stevens for giving her in the central poem of the volume, "118 Westerly Ter-race." Time, which laps us together, allows more still to be accomplished of the apparently finished than we think.

What makes us still consider Susan Howe an "experimental" or "avant-garde" poet is our preference for the beauty of authors over the beauty of books. Physical aspects of the poetic volume are still meant, in contem-porary habits of reading, to evanesce. We expect that if the poem extends beyond the page, surely other recognizable closing devices will signal its beginnings and ends, edges and centers. We assume that the paper, leather, glue on which thoughts are stored are not part of the poem—that a poem is not a work on paper so much as a work despite paper. Notwithstanding that poems are made of black, clustered, twiggy, looped budwork of print of such impact they swim on our eyelids when we close our eyes; notwith-standing the sound individual pages make as they slip against each other, or the decisive thump they make clapping themselves closed after a session of silent reading; notwithstanding how the hands and the fingers experi-ence, second by second, tactile contrasts between the stiffened leather or cloth or glazed paper cover, which catch and brace the fingers, and the matte or silken page, smoothed to propel them—notwithstanding all this, poems are expected to transcend this embodiment, to present as little distraction as possible to the work of reflection. But the physical density and sensate clamor raised by the objects we use to read poetry can never be set to the side in the poetry of Susan Howe. The beauty of the book is in the book, in its itness and in the itness of the author who, in looking through is also seen in the pane, the lens, on which she leaves her own print.

> Face to the window I had
> to know what ought to be
> accomplished by predecessors
> in the same field of labor
> because beauty is what *is*
> What is said and what this
> *it*—it in itself insistent *is*
>
> (97)

Within the true world of what "is," Howe denies living in a world in which nothing has ever died out. What "is" is never achievable by the singular self, sitting by its rackety candle. This particular book is made of particular materials and relationships, by books that precede every poet's own book, the dictionaries full of words that precede her words, the libraries in which these books are held. Also of the cloverleafs on the highways spooling toward the libraries, the winter or spring or summer stand of trees growing around the libraries, and the leaves pressed and composted under the trees. And those buried under the trees with the dead.

Notes

[1]. For other treatments of the material aspects of Susan Howe's work, see Marjorie Perloff, *Radical Artifice: Writing Poetry in the Age of Media* (Chicago: University of Chicago Press, 1994), and *Twenty-First-Century Modernism: The "New" Poetics* (Malden, MA: Blackwell, 2002); Susan M. Schultz, "Exaggerated History," *Postmodern Culture* 4, no. 2 (January 1994); Stephen Collis, *Through Words of Others: Susan Howe and Anarcho-Scholasticism* (Victoria, BC: Department of English, University of Victoria, 2006); and Peter Quartermain, *Disjunctive Poetics: From Gertrude Stein and Louis Zukofsky to Susan Howe* (Cambridge: Cambridge University Press, 2009). See also Howe's own Web site at the Electronic Poetry Center (http://www.epc.buffalo.edu/authors/howe) and

the site at Penn Sound (http://writing.upenn.edu/pennsound/x/Howe.php). Walter Benn Michaels has argued that the emphasis on the materiality of texts is misguided. See his provocative *The Shape of the Signifier* (Princeton: Princeton University Press, 2004).

2. "Transparency" gets a powerful and sustained critique in Charles Bernstein, *A Poetics* (Cambridge: Harvard University Press, 1992). See also Marjorie Perloff's sustained analysis of the value, and limitations, of transparency in *Radical Artifice*.

3. Susan Howe, *Pierce-Arrow* (New York: New Directions, 1999), 57. Further page references will be given parenthetically in the text.

4. Wallace Stevens, *The Collected Poems of Wallace Stevens* (New York: Vintage, 1990), 325.

5. Libraries are crucial spaces for Howe, and the experience of navigating a library as important as any similar experience of navigating through "natural" space. A good place to begin investigations into the material aspects of the American library is Thomas Augst and Wayne Wiegand, eds., *Libraries as Agencies of Culture* (Madison: University of Wisconsin Press, 2003).

6. John Keats, "On first looking into Chapman's Homer," *Complete Poems and Selected Letters of John Keats*, intro. Edward Hirsch (New York: Modern Library, 2001), 43.

7. William Carlos Williams, *The Collected Poems of William Carlos Williams: vol. 1, 1909–1939*, ed. A. Walton Litz and Christopher MacGowan (New York: New Directions, 1986), 218.

8. Ibid., 217.

9. Howe's "autobiographical impulse," to use Hawthorne's phrase, complicates her eschewal of lyric subjectivity in interesting ways. Plainspoken scene setting and contextualization of a given poem within Howe's life and career are as common and persistent as more difficult features of her work. She is a cooperative and quite enlightening interviewee: see Susan Keller, "An Interview with Susan Howe," *Contemporary Literature* 36, no. 1 (Spring 1995): 1–34, and Schultz, "Exaggerated History." Along with Hejinian, Howe is often of interest to critics of women's autobiography: see Rachel Blau DuPlessis, *The Pink Guitar: Writing as Feminist Practice*, 2d ed. (Tuscaloosa: University of Alabama Press, 2006), 123–39. Kathy-Ann Tan goes so far as to devote a book-length study to the "Poetics of Autobiography": *The Nonconformist's Poem: Radical "Poetics of Autobiography" in the Works of Lyn Hejinian, Susan Howe, and Leslie Scalapino* (Trier: Wissenschaftlicher Verlag Trier, 2008).

10. See Peter Nicholls, "Unsettling the Wilderness: Susan Howe and American History," *Contemporary Literature* 37, no. 4 (1996): 586–601; Tan, *The Nonconformist's Poem*; Collis, *Through Words of Others*; Ming-Qian Ma, "Poetry as

History Revised: Susan Howe's "Scattering as Behavior Toward Risk,'" *American Literary History* 6, no. 4 (Winter 1994): 716–37; and, again, Perloff, for treatments of Howe's materialist approach to history.

11. Walt Whitman, *Complete Poetry and Selected Prose*, ed. Justin Kaplan (New York: Library of America, 1982), 188.

12. I am grateful to Stephanie Sandler for illuminating conversations on Howe's work, including several with Howe herself, and for many suggestions that much improved this essay. I am immensely grateful to Susan Howe for an unforgettable afternoon in New Guilford—including the opportunity to see her workspaces, her personal library and beautiful environs—and for her visit to Harvard and reading in the spring of 2009.

13. See Nicholls, "Unsettling the Wilderness"; and Schultz, "Exaggerated History."

14. Howe's great attachment to, and ambivalence about, Harvard and the Cambridge of the fifties is most on display in *The Birth-Mark: Unsettling the Wilderness in American Literary History* (Middletown: Wesleyan University Press, 1993).

15. Susan Howe, *Pierce-Arrow* (New York: New Directions, 1999), 71. Further page references will be given parenthetically within the text.

16. Perry Miller, *The New England Mind: The Seventeenth Century* (Cambridge: Belknap, 1983).

17. Helen Vendler, *Soul Says: On Recent Poetry* (Cambridge: Belknap, 1996).

18. On the other hand, Howe is as generous at acknowledging her own intellectual debts as she is incisive about the ransomings and thefts of academic/poetic practice. Acknowledgments of a kind other writers might put in citations—including mention of the printers, copyists, research assistants, editors, secretaries, and other amanuenses who turn a poet's fugitive thoughts into cogent, complete readable print—frequently become primary in Howe's work. It is an irony, then, that my own thanks to Charlotte Maurer, Madeleine Bennett, and Christopher Looby—through whose intelligent good offices this essay appears—should be filed in notes.

19. Susan Howe, *Souls of the Labadie Tract* (New York: New Directions, 2007), 71. Further page references will be given parenthetically within the text.

20. Stevens, *Collected Poems of Wallace Stevens*, 158.

PART 4

Aesthetics and the Question of Theory

[13]

Warped Conjunctions

Jacques Rancière and African American Twoness

NANCY BENTLEY

Have literary and cultural studies become disenchanted with disenchantment? There is evidence that, at least in some quarters, ideology critique may be losing the dominance it has enjoyed for the last two or more decades. Bruno Latour's 2004 essay, "Why Has Critique Run Out of Steam?" now tops the list of the most frequently cited essays ever published in *Critical Inquiry*. Eve Kosofsky Sedgwick, too, suggested that the dominant critical disposition fueling the "hermeneutics of suspicion" may have exhausted itself. And Peter Sloterdijk's 1988 treatise *A Critique of Cynical Reason* is enjoying new bibliographic life in a number of recent critical conversations. The reception of these and other works suggests a new wariness—or at least a certain weariness—with the project of exposing the ideological forces at work in art and culture. Will the pendulum then swing back toward the more "theological" criticism that preceded the turn to ideology, criticism in which expressive culture is prized for possessing not just a unique set of properties but a transcendent aesthetic ontology, inimical to the worldly preoccupations of the political? Will a thousand (Harold) Blooms flower?[1]

Such is the fear—or, alternatively, the hope—for critics who anticipate that giving greater critical attention to matters of form and aesthetic effect will detach the discipline of American literary studies from any overt political concerns. But a return to aesthetic form does not necessarily mean a return to the same *configuration* of forms that made up the field before the historicist emphasis on ideology. If it did, the consequences would be politically dire indeed, inasmuch as whole disciplinary areas—such as African American literature, a concern of this essay—would all but disappear from the field. But rather than reestablish an earlier configuration of the literary field, renewed attention to the aesthetic might demonstrate instead that the political force of art lies precisely in its power *of* configuration, its use of sensory forms to reorder what is perceptible—and hence contestable—about a given social order. In this view, the faculties and forms we call aesthetic are actually the conditions of possibility for the political.

This notion—that aesthetics are the ground for politics—is at the heart of Jacques Rancière's theory of democracy. Sensory forms are necessary for making political claims, Rancière argues, because any assertion of a wrong is also a picture of what is not—an absence in the world (a missing equality, a stolen freedom) intelligible only through the virtuality of a discernible form. Equality is a democratic truth while inequality is a historical fact, so only counterfactual images and *as if* locutions can speak across the gap that separates these otherwise incommensurable orders. Neither an unmasking of ideology nor a utopian counterworld, the aesthetic dimension of the political is a conjunctive space of appearance ("the polemical space of a demonstration that holds equality and its absence together") where the presumption of equality in the *demos* is linked with a perceived inequality in the polity, through an expressive troping that allows for the naming of a wrong. Aesthetic forms are thus necessary to articulate the "warped conjunction" of what is and is not.[2] Only figures, tropes, and the "quasi-bodies" visible in writing and images—inscriptions that do and do not refer to the facts of the world—are adequate to the task of formulating proper political speech.[3]

To anyone familiar with the current precepts of cultural and literary studies, these (still fairly gnomic) ideas about the relation between the aesthetic and the political are likely to appear counterintuitive, if not flatly wrong. Modern politics in particular has seemed far removed for the domain of aesthetics, attuned as the aesthetic is to contemplation rather than struggle and to form rather than history. For the "new revisionism" that has dominated literary scholarship in recent decades, aesthetics is usually treated as a "screen for unacknowledged ideological interests."[4] Acts of critical disenchantment thus typically aspire to strip away aesthetic illusion, setting politics and aesthetics in sharp opposition to one another. Can art and aesthetic experience—the enchantment produced by the senses—really conduct the agonistic contests of politics?

The prospect seems even more unlikely for any analysis of African American expressive culture, inasmuch as the black subject has been made to carry the stigma of bad particularity within the universalist schemas of Western aesthetic thought. As a result, the black diasporic artist, it seems, cannot *but* perform political work—the work of resistance, subversion, ironic signifying—whenever she takes up a pen or paintbrush, a fact that redeems her art from the false front of the aesthetic. The political dimension of most African American art is clear enough; from Phillis Wheatley and William Wells Brown to Edmonia Lewis and Jacob Lawrence, black artists have refuted white supremacist tenets and undermined demeaning conventions. But when we cast this art as performing chiefly a politics of resistance, we risk erasing the sometimes extravagant investment black artists have shown in art's positive powers of enchantment—including some of the most suspect of Kantian powers: beautiful semblance (*schöner Schein*), claims to universal taste, and the consent made possible by an aesthetic community. Rancière's way of conjoining the political and the aesthetic, I contend, can be illuminated and tested through examples from African American art, a body of cultural expression and thought that is itself an illuminating test of the way politics and art are configured in the broader field of American literature. Without dodging the damning complicity of aesthetic thought with histories of oppression, I probe Rancière's ideas about the aesthetics of politics and the politics of aesthetics by exploring certain key ideas through the work of contemporary painter Kehinde Wiley. I then address a number of selected literary works from the turn-of-the-century moment in which an emphasis on shared perception in art is simultaneously a political assertion and the "twoness" of African American double consciousness is also a reworking of universalist ideas about beauty and sense perception. Common to both Wiley's contemporary portraiture and some of the literary experiments in the era of Du Bois is an aesthetic of warped conjunction that merges the truth of democratic equality and the facts of historical inequality into a single compelling, enchanting form.

The paintings of New York artist Kehinde Wiley, many of monumental size and scale, reproduce an enduring tension between conventions of humanist art and the figure of the black subject. In Wiley's paintings, young black men wearing hoodies, low-slung jeans, and throw-back jerseys materialize in the traditional spaces of European art history. They appear in the concave spaces of rococo ceiling murals, floating in air or resting on clouds. They emerge in the poses of painterly saints and martyrs, evoking the beauty of male suffering in the unending instant just before transcendent redemption. Wiley's subjects claim the thrones and horses of royals who demonstrate sovereignty by merely presenting their bodies before the vision of their subjects. They occupy the allegorical landscapes in which beautiful bodies allow the idea of grace to speak through numinous flesh and appear amidst the props of wealth and power that distinguish the portraits of burghers and dukes. And Wiley's figures don't just occupy traditional scenes and styles of representation; they are also accorded the literal materials of this tradition: the hinged panels of a triptych, the massive gilded frame of the royal portrait, the intricate stitching of Old World tapestry.[5]

Lustrous and startling, these works display what Wiley calls a "contested relation" to a history of Old World portraiture and iconology, even as the paintings disable familiar habits of ideological analysis.[6] It is quite possible to suspect a version of critical parody at work here, a playful yet aggressive puncturing of the grandeur and the claims to global dominance inherent in these European conventions. But dwell for even a short time on the care Wiley gives those conventions and their invocation begins to feel distinctly more loving than hostile. Visual incongruities, it is true, are what set the pictures vibrating with life. But those incongruities seem less like an attempt at deflation and more like a gesture of appropriation, a practice of creative anachronism designed to lay claim to a history of preexisting forms and the concepts they convey—the concepts of sanctified suffering, the human dignity affirmed in luxury, the inviolability of a sovereign body (a status that once belonged only to the body of the sovereign).

And yet, just as parody is an inaccurate description of Wiley's practice (he is a self-described "contemporary descendant of a long line of portraitists, including Reynolds, Gainsborough, Titian, [and] Ingres, among others"), the notion of appropriation does not seem entirely apt, either, at least not if appropriation is understood as a correction of what has been false or exclusionary or a fulfillment of unrealized ideals.[7] According to Wiley, "my intention is to craft a world picture that isn't involved in political correctives or visions of utopia." The aim is rather to practice "a craft that has evolved into a vocabulary of signs that tells one the subject is important."[8] The operative principle here, it would seem, is not the exposure of art's blindness or bad faith but the principle of art itself, its apparent powers of signification, enchantment, and transport.

Wiley's paintings are not best read as a correction of concepts, then, but as a practice of aesthetic play—in his words, "a perpetual play with the language of desire and power." As I later show, in his eager embrace of Old World conventions of "the heroic, powerful, majestic, and the sublime" for painting contemporary black men, Wiley's portraits resemble the willful, almost gleeful satisfaction evident in a number of narratives from the turn of the century that similarly insert black subjects into unlikely settings or spaces—counterfactual stories, mixed geographies, and speculative or fantastic histories.[9] What is needed first, though, is a sharper understanding of how Wiley's self-vaunted affiliation with European art history—not just with its forms and themes but also its tangible materials and textures— can be understood as political. The energies animating Wiley's paintings are not energies of critical deflation but aesthetic intensity; how, then, can we consider these seductive surfaces, derived from hierarchical European vocabularies of "desire and power," part of a politics that is not reactionary or quietist?

In trying to answer this question, we can turn to Rancière's reinterpretation of aesthetic mimesis. Rather than thinking of art as a species of representation (imitation of an identity, an object, an ideal), it can be reconceived as a field of sense experience, a map or "distribution" of perceptible images and signs. What matters is not just the image or locution that appears but the economy of visibility that *allows* it appear, the more or less tacit "parcelling out" (*PA* 19) of different roles and abilities, delimited spaces and times, and intelligible possibilities as distinct from unthinkable events or impossible histories, that together make up the structural conditions of a given image or text. Every painting, novel, or film will thus model a "regime of sensible intensity" (*PA* 39) that connects facts, images, and concepts with intelligible forms of subjectivity and distinct relations of belonging. But, crucially, such structuring of sense experience is not merely the province of art. Every community or social order also rests on a distribution of the sensible: the slave understands the speech of the master but she cannot freely speak; the worker belongs to the polity but cannot leave the site of labor to appear in the places of governance because "work will not wait" (*PA* 12). Within a given social order, capacities of speech, appearance, and occupation are distributed according to a seeming law of necessity. But whereas rulers have resources (law and police powers) to ensure clear partitions between the spaces and allotments of sensory appearance and speech, works of art, with their birthright to commandeer the senses, can effect a material rearrangement of images and signs. (Hence Plato's expulsion of the poet for the untethered source of his speech.) Art thus allows for variations in the perception of trajectories of history and the capacities of persons. In a formulation especially resonant for interpreting Wiley, works of art are really "ways of declaring what a body can do."[10]

What, then, is "declared" about the bodies in Wiley's paintings? In art, of course, declarations are not propositional but formal; they rely on sensuous forms to fuse the semantic and the expressive. Through his unabashed invocation of the formal textures and traditions of canonized art, Wiley is clearly making a declaration of beauty. Standing before these paintings, we have left behind the law of necessity—the rule that has governed black diasporic life for much of the history of modernity—and we've entered the domain of the beautiful where, according to the humanist aesthetics Wiley directly cites, we activate possibilities of freedom whenever we experience the uncoerced judgments that are based in aesthetic feeling. Wiley draws on a species of painterly beauty, moreover, that had adopted the highest powers of speech and action for the medium of the painted portrait. According to Rancière, the optical depth discovered and then perfected in Renaissance perspectival painting represents a key moment in the political possibilities of Western art. Mastering three-dimensional space allowed the mimetic surface of a painting to lay claim to powers of meaningful speech and action—the disclosure of a significant "'scene' of life" (PA 16)—that had previously been evinced only in the living speech and acts of aristocratic rulers. Even when a canvas depicted a king or a duke, painting as an artistic practice still retained for its own perceptual surface a depth of significance that could be endowed on any figure permitted to appear there.

The glamour of three-dimensional depth in traditional portraiture is a touchstone in Wiley's bid for achieving beauty (the "luminosity I'm obsessed with, that light popping off bodies, that brings a certain hopefulness to something").[11] But it is precisely by recalling this high-water mark era of perspectivalism that Wiley triggers a crisis in the very aesthetic values that animate his portraits. For the original viewers of rococo murals or glossy Flemish portraits, of course, a black body could not have appeared in these spaces without violating exactly those canons of beauty that qualified the pictures as art in the first place. Or, more precisely, the figure of the black man or woman could appear and often did, but, according to those canons, the black subject can be beautiful only in selected postures and roles—the servile attendant, the stranger, the distant exotic or mythical chieftain. Suddenly, the quality of beauty seems to force on us a critical dilemma. If Wiley's paintings are beautiful, then, as Kant instructs, all human subjects ought to be able to see the entrancing "luminosity" he has attempted to capture on his canvases. And yet such universal agreement is demonstrably untrue. But if the perception of beauty is therefore nothing more than the perceptual habits belonging to a particular place and age, then the crucial principle of aesthetic consent—the kind of judgment we affirm freely, uncoerced by the demands of necessity but also distinct from merely arbitrary or singular likings—is exposed as hollow. The distinct freedom belonging to the aesthetic begins to seem more like "a taste for necessity," in Pierre Bourdieu's resonant phrase, and aesthetics becomes no more than a law of historical necessity passed off in the guise of consent.[12]

Whereas aesthetic experience had previously seemed like a zone of freedom from necessity, it suddenly seems implicated in the work of naturalizing the sensory order of a given community. The implication seems clear. Do not trust your senses; they can only trap you in the untruths of ideology. What does the beauty of a Franz Hals painting offer his Flemish patron but proof, through the observer's own eyes, that child slaves from the West Indies are as naturally pleasing as pet dogs are—and just as naturally unfree? And what does Wiley's canvas show, for that matter, but that beauty (or "beauty") is now only possible through the antiaesthetic knowingness of postmodern pastiche? When we reach this point, the critic who wishes to withstand the demand to confirm truth through an assent to beauty will be drawn down the rabbit hole of eternal political vigilance, consigning scholarship to unending acts of critical disenchantment.

Historical research in epistemology and perception, moreover, only gives further evidence of the need to bring a hermeneutics of suspicion to aesthetic experience. As Donald Lowe has shown, a profoundly different perceptual field emerged in European societies during the period Wiley references. The typographical revolution of the fifteenth century and the print culture it spawned, the discovery of the rational space of infinite extension and universal measurement, a shift in the hierarchy of the senses that gave primacy to vision, techniques of analytical reason that could detect connections and functions across different points in objective time and space—these and other related developments created an epistemic field in which sense experience must find its place in accord with the field's spatiotemporal norms or lose any secure claim to offering real knowledge. Most important, the factors that shaped this dominant field of perception also shaped the epistemic foundations for art. Empty three-dimensional space and a universal model of history supplied a new foundation for "bourgeois perception" at the same time that they gave rise to new styles and genres of art.[13]

More recent scholarship in postcolonial history raises the same warning from a geopolitical angle. The styles Wiley references—Italian rococo, Dutch portraiture, English and French romanticism—originate at precisely the historical moment when, from out of a world of multiple civilizations, the European conceptualization of knowledge was both expanded and narrowed. Expanded because Western epistemology left behind knowledge organized by traditions of rhetoric and the personal transmission of wisdom in favor of operations of reason that detach knowledge from the knower and seek impersonal truths that pertain for all places and times. As Walter Mignolo summarizes it, "At the moment when capitalism began to be displaced from the Mediterranean to the North Atlantic, the organization of knowledge was established in its universal scope." But the same expansion of knowledge through universalism also narrowed the geographical locale in which knowledge could be recognized as such. That is, while the rationality based on what Michel-Rolph Trouillot calls the "North Atlantic universals" opened up potent and even emancipatory formations of knowledge, it also closed out others that belonged to different geopolitical places. Thus when the scope of epistemology was reduced to the geopolitical spaces of Western Europe, Mignolo writes, it "erased the possibility of even thinking about a conceptualization and distribution of knowledge emanating from other local histories" of such places as China, India, and Islamic Africa. Given the structuring constraints for perception itself, the very possibilities through which sensory experience could generate aesthetic judgment or knowledge seems to have been restricted in advance, with damning implications for efforts to use aesthetic judgment to find and affirm truth.[14]

Yet it is also in precisely this context that the specificity of Wiley's historical references begins to take on new significance. Wiley does not merely allude to the Atlantic history that grounded these structural categories of space and time. He also *uses* those perceptual spaces for his own images and the beauty he hopes they convey; three-dimensional space and linear historical time allow Wiley to position himself as a "descendant" of Old World masters. But a close examination of his paintings shows that he does not finally affirm or fulfill North Atlantic universalism so much as exceed it, through a logic (or illogic) we might call extra-universalism. The result is a new epistemic perspective disclosed through the commonality possible in sense experience, an aesthetic disclosure that closely matches Rancière's definition of the political as "the art of the local and singular construction of cases of universality" (*D* 139).

The first clue to this political difference is the peculiar way Wiley's subjects inhabit space. Like all subjects of portraiture after the introduction of perspective, the three-dimensional nature of Wiley's black men emphasizes their emplotment in a world of bodies, objects, and landscapes akin to the world inhabited by the viewer. The perspectival resources of painting allow Wiley to underscore the way his subjects are possessors of bodies, living embodiments of the human. This way of occupying space, then, is one of the ways Wiley actively draws on the history of Western art as "a vocabulary of signs that tells one the subject is important," and he means to express this truth about the portrait subjects he finds in places like Harlem and Columbus, Ohio. A project like Wiley's thus helps to realize the aspirations of the European humanism that allocated for itself (and itself alone) the mission to discover and speak the truth about all mankind. And yet, in defiance of geometric logic, the bodies in these paintings do *and* do not belong to this representational space. In almost every Wiley painting, flattened patterns of ornamentation cut through the evocation of objective space, aligned neither with the background of the painted scene nor with the two-dimensional plane of the painting's frame.

The effect of this ornamentation is subtle but highly significant. The odd placement of the repeating pattern allows Wiley to insinuate a different spatial field that exists somehow outside (or is it inside?) the dimensional coordinates represented by the rest of the painting. The plane in which they appear, in other words, is integral to the representational scene and yet still lies athwart its spatial coordinates, breaking free from the axes that would measure the total height and depth of the depicted field. It is as if these repeating ornamental figures are the abstracted traces of an otherwise invisible domain that is hidden in inner space or in an unseen externality. And although Wiley's subjects have the "luminosity" and shaded contours of the traditional three-dimensional figure, they somehow emerge *out of* the flat surface of the ornamental plane, locating a kind of displacement or spatial syncopation in the field of rational geometric space.[15]

Floating both inside and outside the spatial extension of these scenes, intensely lifelike but somehow unconstrained by the coordinates of rational space—what kind of human subjects are these? How are we to locate them within the spaces and icons of a European humanism that allows them to be seen, yet seen only when objective space is folded or torn so as to disclose another dimension? These subjects belong to a more extensive perceptual world that somehow outstrips the *merely* three-dimensional world implied by these European scenes and styles. By becoming visible in this weird, almost unnameable spatial plane, they make perceptible what is otherwise invisible—a zone or dimension that the epistemic field structured through North Atlantic universals had erased or suppressed, or simply never dreamed of. Put another way, Wiley's black generals, burghers, and saints are not fantastic or anachronistic; they are catachrestic. They give intelligible form to what is illogical or impossible for a given system or language. Wiley's subjects show us forms of knowledge, spirit, or beauty that arrive from outside the bounds of the universal, which by definition has no bounds, no outside. In Wiley's paintings, an Old World language of freedom and beauty comes to life as a global black vernacular, an expressive mutation that asserts a continuity between royal scepters and NBA jerseys, between iconic postures of kings and saints and the now global iconicity of hip-hop poses and fashions.

The continuity Wiley forges between these different distributions of the sensible is not smooth or uncontested. Some who gaze at his paintings, Wiley notes, see an artistic tradition "brutalized by someone who has a contested relation to it."[16] Such disagreement, moreover, is one sign of the political stakes at issue in perceptual experience. But, in creating what Rancière calls a "warped conjunction" of two different sensory regimes, Wiley has viewers perforce take part in the strange kind of polity that is an aesthetic community in which shared sense experience becomes a test of value and meaning apart from the world of necessity ("the world of commands and lots that gives everything a use" [D 57]). Thus while the universality of aesthetic experience is never achieved— and even Kant recognizes that agreement is "a mere ideal norm"—the *appeal* to a universal sense of beauty in any work of art becomes the basis of a demand for shared judgment about who and what can count, who can appear and speak, who can act and in what roles.[17] The political force of the aesthetic, then, lies precisely in the "empty" idea of the universal, even as a given expression of it can only be a singular construction that particularizes the universal.

Hence the importance for Wiley of a nonironic idea of beauty. (He declares himself against "the type of artistic malaise" in which "joy is suspect and where absolute beauty is regarded with disdain.")[18] The axiom of universal beauty, like the principle of equality in democratic politics, is the site at which new or excluded particulars are able to appear and claim a place in a common world. Although the bid for aesthetic agreement may fail, in art as in political expression the domain of sense perception is a communal stage on which to include the uncounted, the "part of those who have no part" (*D* 30). Thus Rancière's description of political expression can read like a gloss on the warping of humanist identities and roles disclosed on Wiley's canvas: "Political activity is whatever shifts a body from the place assigned to it or changes a place's destination. It makes visible what had no business being seen, and makes heard a discourse where once there was only place for noise" (*D* 30).

Wiley's singular construction of the signs of North Atlantic universalism uncovers impossible subjects and deformed histories not as foreign contaminations of European spaces but as "warped deductions and mixed identities" (*D* 139) discovered by bending Europe's own coordinates for defining beauty and knowledge. When a black subject in Wiley's painting appears atop Jacques-Louis David's uprearing horse from *Bonaparte Crossing the Alps at Grand-Saint-Bernard*, for instance, it realizes the impossible subject of a heroic black revolutionary, a figure that could not exist according to Enlightenment epistemologies—could not exist, even when that figure did exist. As Trouillot has demonstrated, the Haitian revolution was "unthinkable even as it happened," a struggle for republican freedom that could not register in the cognitive coordinates of European history except as the unfreedom of savage revolt.[19] Thus when Wiley's canvas makes a young man from Ohio into a gorgeous Napoleon, the painting also gives an uncanny visibility to a historical black Napoleon who had long been uncounted in the archives, the revolutionary general Toussaint L'Ouverture, who was not recognized as a freedom fighter even as Napoleonic troops were struggling to defeat his fight for freedom. And it is not merely the outlines of codified masculine prowess that are the intelligible forms for black subjectivity in these paintings. Young black men are also the models for Wiley's paintings of wealthy matrons and female saints and muses. His painting *Passing/Posing (Female Prophet Anne, Who Observes the Presentation of Jesus on the Temple)*, for instance, features a thin young man in an Astros shirt gazing heavenward with arms outstretched, placing black masculinity under a sign of feminine grace and giving this portrait subject a singular appearance that cannot be parsed through a binary logic of sex. Although these images locate a wayward destination for David's stormy image of Napoleon or for the likeness of Saint Anne, they demand of a community of viewers a judgment

Figure 13.1. Kehinde Wiley, *Napoleon Leading the Army Over the Alps*, 2005. Brooklyn Museum, collection of Suzi and Andrew B. Cohen, L2005.6, copyright ©Kehinde Wiley. Used by permission.

of agreement—literally, a new common sense—about the human form and the forms of the human.

If Wiley is a "contemporary descendant" of Velázquez and Gainsborough, he is also an heir to the aesthetic experimentation of earlier diasporic intellectuals who drew upon art to give deformed form to the equality—axiomatically true, historically absent—of the black subject. Du Bois is the best known, but he can be counted as one of a generation of writers and artists who looked to the sensory properties of art to pry open, through incongruous folds in time and space, the closed universalism of North Atlantic history. To compare Wiley's visual art with literary production by writers such as Du Bois, Sutton Griggs, James Corrothers, and Pauline Hopkins is not to argue for either a uniform black aesthetic or a static history of political subordination stretching between Du Bois's moment and our own. It is instead to focus on the ability of art itself to insist on relations between otherwise incommensurable fields of sense experience as a

Figure 13.2. Kehinde Wiley, *Passing/Posing (Female Prophet Anne, Who Observes the Presentation of Jesus on the Temple)*, 2003. Brooklyn Museum, Mary Smith Dorward Fund and Healy Purchase Fund B, 2003.90.2, copyright © Kehinde Wiley. Used by permission.

way of making those relations seen by a community of readers or viewers. If formal discontinuities of this kind are especially pronounced in postmodernism, that is because the art of our time often exploits art's inherent potential to display or distort—and not just to reproduce—the categories of time and space that condition modern "bourgeois perception."

Literature, too, possesses these resources. In fact, the reflections on and disruptions of sensory perception in Wiley's canvases may owe a special debt to literary art and the transformations it can deploy through what Rancière calls the field of "unsensed sensation" unique to the literary.[20] Du Bois, the sociologist turned novelist, is a telling case in point. In an essay on the black public sphere, Houston Baker makes his own asynchronous fold in cultural history by comparing the compositional principle in *Souls of Black Folk* to the technique of cinematic montage, and the analogy is apt. Superimposing Berlin social science and Black Belt communal life, merging the lyricism of the sorrow songs and Richard Wagner's stormy melodies, *Souls* presents a composite form of literary analysis that makes critical revelations by way of conjoined incongruities.[21] For a reader versed in film history, then, a visual technique like montage captures well the formal interface between different sensible orders that Rancière identifies as the political potential of art. But, even as it anticipates cinematic montage, *Souls of Black Folk* can be seen as exploiting already existing aesthetic resources, namely, the formal resources of the novel. In fact, in Rancière's account it is actually the nineteenth-century novel that first innovated the formal possibilities that are later realized visually in modernist painting and film. As a species of writing that broke free from the rule-bound decorum of higher genres, the novel seized the chance to bring forms of intelligibility to a body of empirical materials—commonplace objects and ordinary actions—that previously had no place in established hierarchies of artistic form. Exploiting this capacity, the "triumph of the novel's page" (*PA* 17) was its ability to act as a space of interface and exchange between incommensurate distributions of signs and literary images.

Thus the "literary heterology" (*D* 59) of the novel allowed writing to break up and reconfigure approved allotments of speech and appearance. When the fiction of Flaubert depicts instead of instructs, when Melville's "Bartleby" distills the power of indeterminacy to break up well-ordered distributions of subjectivity and metamorphose strange new speaking bodies, then the page of the novel becomes an open space for making legible new maps of the visible and the sayable.[22] If *Souls* looks ahead to cinematic montage, it also looks back to the innovations of the novel inasmuch as Du Bois innovated a form able to make expressive black sounds and laboring bodies perceptible on the same plane as historiographical facts and already canonized lines of verse. It shouldn't surprise us, then, that even before he published the essays that would become *Souls of Black Folk*, Du Bois attempted to write a work of fiction that could capture what he saw as the "twoness" of African American experience, the heterogeneity built into the awareness that the subjective experience of the black American is cut off from the object of the "negro" as it is seen by white folks. In trying to give this heterogeneity a novelistic form, moreover, Du Bois's experimental narrative approached the problem of double consciousness precisely by transforming universal categories of rational space. Like a number of other speculative stories produced by African American writers during the same period, Du Bois's narrative allows uncounted bodies and counterfactual histories to emerge through the heterologies of the novelistic page.

In this never completed story (eventually titled "A Vacation Unique" by an editor), a white Harvard student is persuaded by a black classmate to undergo a "painless operation" that will make him temporarily black. Immediately after the procedure, however, the student is stunned to discover that there has been a profound rupture in his relation to time and space, a break or transformation that has brought him into a distinct spatial region. Already awaiting him there, the black classmate explains the mystery: this dimension is the space of blackness. "By reason of the fourth dimension of color," the black student informs him, "you step into a new and, to most people, entirely unknown region of the universe—you break the bounds of humanity."[23]

Scholars believe that Du Bois probably began his sketches for this novel when he was an undergraduate at Harvard himself, a time when he would have been busy mastering the epistemic principles of the highest transatlantic knowledge. But it is clear he was also reading novels. In fashioning his narrative, he was borrowing directly from the "scientific romances" of British writer Edwin Abbott and the American C. H. Hinton, fiction that had been widely read beginning in the 1880s. Abbott's novel *Flatland* tells of geometric races—circles, squares, and triangles—that live in a two-dimensional universe, whereas Hinton wrote sketches such as "What Is the Fourth Dimension," in which he speculates on the lives of "beings" who inhabit a four-dimensional world beyond our powers of perception. Even more starkly than other kinds of stories, these speculative tales of alternative geometric worlds demonstrate the ability of fiction to reconfigure the particulars of sense experience. While the zone of the fourth dimension has no "direct point of contact with fact," Hinton writes, the formal resources of fiction produce "a gain in our power of representation. They express in intelligible terms things of which we can form no image."[24]

But while Hinton's story abandons the three-dimensional space that structures "bourgeois perception" (and also anticipates the multiperspectivalism of perception in our age of new media), his fictional experiment actually affirms the idea of space as an infinite and homogeneous extension. It therefore retains the idea that the physical dimensions of the human world are already settled forever. In Hinton's fourth dimension, as in Abbott's *Flatland*, there are subjects but no humans. That is, when the form-giving power of fiction allows Hinton and Abbott to look into otherwise invisible domains in space, they discover there beings who possess bodies and creaturely life, but who are by definition nonhuman—triangles, for instance, or the qualitatively deeper "beings" of Hinton's fourth dimension, complex creatures for whom we humans are as shallow as triangles seem to us. In Hinton and Abbott, therefore, disclosing unseen spatial worlds only further proves that the world consists of a totality reducible to known geometric rules, a universe in which no region or zone—not even infinity—can exceed these existing powers of measurement. More important, any speaking beings discovered outside of the three-dimensional will be something other than human: any alterior zone in space has to contain an alterior form of creaturely being.

But, in contrast with Hinton and Abbott, in Du Bois fiction does not extend perception to new domains of nonhuman life, rather, it insists on a new way counting the human. For in Jim Crow America, where the black subject is "a thing apart," human life has been miscounted or mismeasured. As the narrator puts it to the newly inducted black student, "Your feelings no longer count, they are not a part of history" (223). Only when the lived experience of the black subject is disclosed in fiction do the real contours of the human appear, uncovering a distinct zone of human thought and feeling that is distributed throughout a three-dimensional world that still remains oblivious to it. Thus the fourth dimension of color is the surplus region needed in order to see the humanness of the black subject. Du Bois's model here is not a theoretical universality but a polemical one: it posits a human totality in order to make manifest the false delimitation in the way a given order has assigned purportedly natural properties and dwelling places to different bodies. Crucially, however, disclosing this dimension is not simply a matter of including what has been excluded, since the very discovery of an unseen and unimagined dimension of the human means that the existing metrics for identifying human life, its distribution of roles, capacities, and properties, is fundamentally wrong.

Picturing this wrong, giving it a form in fiction, is at once a political claim and an aesthetic expression, a formal demonstration of what the social order denied: that black subjects are "speaking beings sharing the same properties of those who deny them these" (D 24). Although Du Bois's unusual story never appeared in print, it shares the same feature of aesthetic warping with a number of other counterfactual stories by African American authors published not long after Du Bois worked on his narrative. In these narratives, fiction discloses invisible regions not of space but of history. Sutton Griggs's novel *Imperium in Imperio*, for instance, doubles the historical order of Jim Crow America by imagining a secret black republic dispersed throughout the United States, an organized polity of more than seven million black people with a constitution, an elected congress, a judiciary, and an army. Although this secret nation adheres to ideals of Jeffersonian liberty, faced with the failure of the U.S. state to protect black lives and rights, this republic is by the end of the novel poised on the brink of a war of insurgency against the United States.[25] Similarly, a story by the Chicago writer James D. Corrothers, "A Man They Didn't Know," tells of a military alliance of Japan, Mexico, and Hawaii, a joint Pacific force that recruits black deserters from the U.S. Army along with angry Japanese Americans for an invasion of southern California. A contingent of black fighters eventually becomes the decisive military unit in the invasion.[26]

As images of history and historical time, of course, these stories are wholly implausible. Newly disenfranchised, black men at the turn of the century enjoyed even less political agency and military standing than the freedmen who were their fathers. We might be tempted, then, to read these fictions as expressing a logic of wish fulfillment. But rather than signifying a flight from the real, the political valence of these stories lies precisely in their historical impossibility. By representing unthinkable events and tables-turned histories, the fictions allow black subjects to appear in the places they are supposed to be incapable of occupying. The narratives thus insist that the allotted positions of any subject or group are not determined by their different properties (as a law of necessity would have it) but only by history's contingencies. A more egalitarian order could have—indeed, necessarily *would* have—produced a different history. Alongside the history of what was or what is, there exist innumerable trajectories of what could have been, zones of counterfactual time and events that only fiction is capable of bringing before our senses. And, simply by presenting such fictions, Griggs and Corrothers insist on their own capacity as subjects of history, not merely as history's passive objects, thereby demonstrating political properties they are not supposed to possess and appearing in subject positions they are presumed incapable of occupying. Their stories can be refuted as mere fiction, but their own demonstration of political agency cannot—*that* agency can only be disputed, which dispute thereby confirms the black subject as a political interlocutor with those who would deny the very possibility.

Like the fourth dimension, these counterfactual histories are a site for enunciating a wrong, for speaking as part of a polity in which their authors have no part and thus introducing a "twist that short-circuits the natural logic of properties" (*D* 13). In another novel from this era, the same aesthetic turning or torsion allows fiction to reconfigure the human form itself, a transformation of the black body through which racial difference becomes a form of sheer surplus that demands a new logic of humanity. In her novel *Of One Blood; or, The Hidden Self*, Pauline Hopkins envisions a counterfactual that is simultaneously a hidden geographic space and an unthinkable history. Through the novel's complicated plot, Hopkins's African American protagonist, Reuel, finds his way to an ancient, hidden city surviving in modern Africa. Much of this section recycles the topoi of popular imperial romance, but formulaic exoticism eventually gives way to something stranger. Most strikingly, in this city, Telassar, there are forms of life that result from a kind of ancient cryogenics. The people of Telassar have been able to preserve the "natural appearance" of living organisms, for instance—not only organic life such as flowers but also human beings: "We preserve the bodies of our most beautiful women in this way," a priest explains to Reuel. And when Reuel is later introduced to Queen Candace (a descendent of the original Cleopatra), she is described in terms that evoke a similar idea of reanimation: "Yes; she was a Venus, a superb statue of bronze, moulded by a great sculptor; but an animated statue, in which one saw blood circulate, and from which life flowed." Candace's palace apartment is guarded by "beautiful girls" who seem likely candidates for the preservation program, if they aren't already its products: "Each girl might have posed for a statue of Venus."[27]

What are we to make of these strange fictional bodies, uncomfortably evocative of a collection of African Stepford wives? The women in Telassar seem largely consigned to the work of reproduction and preservation. But reproduction in Hopkins's novel is hardly the sort of passive transmission that makes women merely the bodily vessel of history. Instead, the strange bodies in Telassar seem to be a different order of life, even a unique ontology, for which there is no modern name. That is, they present people assumed to be long vanished who not only live and flourish in modern history but who possess knowledge of organic life superior to what is known by the inhabitants of "out-world" (130). Women are bodies that bespeak the forms of knowledge and human life unique to this "unknown" zone of world history.

The very strangeness of these figures, in other words, is the proof of their world historical significance. To begin to grasp this paradox, we can see these bodies as being akin to the "inconceivable bodies" that Judith Butler has discussed in her analysis of intersexed persons. For Butler, what makes these living bodies inconceivable is not anything inherently mysterious or unnatural about their status as human bodies but rather the position of those bodies outside a knowledge system that defines the exhaustive classes of the human through two sexes. Within that system, the intersexed body "becomes a point of reference for a narrative that is not about this body, but which seizes upon the body" in order to tell a story of what is conceivably human. ("They can't conceive of leaving someone alone," one intersexed person says of the medical establishment.)[28] Hopkins's fictional bodies, and the Telassar inhabitants generally, are hardly real in the same sense, but they *are* similarly "inconceivable"—that is, their status as unreal and fantastic has the same discursive origin in authoritative narratives within which they cannot be *other than* impossible or inconceivable objects.

Hopkins is emphatic on this point. As a living African civilization, fully coeval with European societies, Telassar is literally an inconceivable history. A white character declares that Africa is a "played-out hole in the ground" (159) holding "nothing but the monotony of past centuries dead and forgotten" (93). Hopkins knew very well that most contemporary scholarship assumed African peoples had long ago fallen out of the forward-moving currents of world history, and any effort to represent their ongoing life as coeval with Anglo-European history would be literally incredible; as her narrator puts it, "the modern world would stand aghast" (115). Quite simply, there is no conceivable realism for a story of Africans or African Americans who belong *as* Africans to modern world history. The novel's strange spaces and bodies are thus part of the inevitably fantastic language Hopkins invents for representing African humanness. Fantasy is here the realism of an impossible modern history.

Rather than insist that black people are just like white people, Hopkins presents the black subject as what Rancière calls a "surplus subject" (*D* 58), a figure inassimilable to the current configuration of the human who still must be counted as part of the whole. As with Wiley's black male prophetess, or Du Bois's white-turned-black student who dwells in the fourth dimension, in Hopkins's novel an aesthetic form is able to free sense perception from the "natural logic of properties" in order to see in a single image both what is and is not: the equality of the black subject. The century that divides Hopkins and Wiley, of course, introduced any number of significant changes in the political subjection and subjecthood of African diasporic peoples; Wiley's paintings are as concerned with male sexuality and intragroup relations as with the problem of the color line that is uppermost for Du Bois and Hopkins. If, as Rancière claims, works of art are "ways of declaring what a body can do," the declarations of these artists are also explorations of changing conditions that give ever new shapes to the souls and bodies of black folk. The *open* nature of art's declarations—openly claimed and open to change—is at the root of what makes a work of art political. Taken together, the catachrestic forms in these examples of African American expression allow us to see in a kind of heightened way the political dimension of all art, the domain that allows for the ongoing destruction and rearticulation of the human for the sake of opening a common perceptual world to what we do not yet know.

Notes

1. Eve Kosofsky Sedgwick, "Paranoid Reading and Reparative Reading; or, You're So Paranoid, You Probably Think This Introduction Is About You," in Eve Kosofsky Sedgwick, ed., *Novel Gazing: Queer Readings in Fiction* (Durham: Duke University Press, 1997), 1–37. Rita Felski discusses other influential works that criticize the hermeneutics of suspicion and addresses the question of "theological reading" in *Uses of Literature* (Oxford: Blackwell, 2008). Also relevant is Jacques Rancière's critique of Pierre Bourdieu, "Thinking Between Disciplines: An Aesthetics of Knowledge," *Parrhesia* 1 (2006): 1–12. Rancière criticizes Bourdieu's sociological analysis of culture and art as "the idle logic of demystification" (11).

2. Jacques Rancière, *Disagreement: Politics and Philosophy*, trans. Julie Rose (Minneapolis: University of Minnesota Press, 1999), 14. Subsequent page references, following the abbreviation *D*, will be cited parenthetically in the text.

3. Jacques Rancière, *The Politics of Aesthetics: The Distribution of the Sensible*, trans. Gabriel Rockhill (New York: Continuum, 2004), 39. Subsequent page references, following the abbreviation *PA*, will be cited parenthetically in the text.

4. Winfried Fluck, "Aesthetics and Cultural Studies," in Emory Elliott, Louis Freitas Caton, and Jeffrey Rhyne, eds., *Aesthetics in a Multicultural Age* (New York: Oxford University Press, 2002), 80–81.

5. Examples of Wiley's portraits are available at his Web site, http://www.kehindewiley.com (accessed April 22, 2011). Also see the publications Kehinde Wiley, *Columbus* (Columbus, OH: Columbus Museum of Art, 2006); and Kehinde Wiley and Brian Keith Jackson, *Black Light* (Brooklyn: powerHouse, 2009).

6. Kehinde Wiley, interviewed by Roy Hurst in "Painter Kehinde Wiley," National Public Radio, June 1, 2005.

7. "Biography," http://www.kehindewiley.com/main.html (accessed April 22, 2011).

8. Wiley quoted in "Exhibitions," *American Arts Quarterly* 21, no. 4 (2004): 51.

9. "Biography," http://www.kehindewiley.com/main.html (accessed April 22, 2011).

10. Rancière, "Thinking Between Disciplines," 11.

11. Wiley quoted in Lauren Collins, "Studio Visit: Lost and Found," *New Yorker*, September 1, 2008.

12. Pierre Bourdieu, *Distinction: A Social Critique of the Judgment of Taste*, trans. Richard Nice (Cambridge: Harvard University Press, 1984), 374ff.

13. Donald M. Lowe, *History of Bourgeois Perception* (Chicago: University of Chicago Press, 1982).

14. Walter D. Mignolo, "The Geopolitics of Knowledge and the Colonial Difference," *South Atlantic Quarterly* 101, no. 1 (2002): 57–96, quote from 59; Michel-Rolph Trouillot, "The North Atlantic Universals," in Immanuel Wallerstein, ed., *The Modern World-System in the Longue Durée* (Boulder: Paradigm, 2005), 229–37.

15. On the transformations modernist art made to the Kantian idea of space as "the realm of the external," see Susan Stewart, *The Open Studio: Essays on Art and Aesthetics* (Chicago: University of Chicago Press, 2005), 25. Stewart notes that when modernism made space a source of abstract figures, it was actually returning to what had long been the case for the way space functioned in Byzantine and Islamic art. While some of Wiley's patterns recall styles of ornamentation from French rococo or Victorian decorative arts, they sometimes invoke styles from Islamic cultures. Richard Iton discusses the "surreal" elements that have long been part of black expressive culture in his study *In Search of the Black Fantastic: Politics and Popular Culture in the Post-Civil Rights Era* (New York: Oxford University Press, 2008).

16. Wiley quoted in Hurst, "Painter Kehinde Wiley."

17. Immanuel Kant, *Critique of Judgment*, trans. J. H. Bernard (New York: Simon and Shuster, 1970), 76.

18. Wiley quoted in press release for DOWN, an exhibition at the Deitch Project Gallery, New York, 2008. See "The Art Blog: Roberta Fallon and Libby Rosof," http://theartblog.org/2008/11/beautiful-and-not-in-new-york (accessed April 22, 2011).

19. Michel-Rolph Trouillot, *Silencing the Past: Power and the Production of History* (Boston: Beacon, 1995), 73.

20. Jacques Rancière, "Deleuze, Bartleby, and the Literary Formula," in *The Flesh of Words: The Politics of Writing* (Palo Alto: Stanford University Press, 2004), 151.

21. Houston A. Baker Jr., "Critical Memory and the Black Public Sphere," in

Black Public Sphere Collective, ed., *The Black Public Sphere* (Chicago: University of Chicago Press, 1995), 23–25. I discuss Du Bois's strategic use of incongruities in *Frantic Panoramas: American Literature and Mass Culture, 1870–1920* (Philadelphia: University of Pennsylvania Press, 2009), 280–302.

22. For Rancière's discussion of Melville, see "Deleuze, Bartleby, and the Literary Formula," 146–64. For his extended analysis of Flaubert, see "Why Emma Bovary Had to Be Killed," *Critical Inquiry* 34 (2008): 233–48.

23. W. E. B. Du Bois, "A Vacation Unique," in the appendix to Shamoon Zamir, *Dark Voices: W. E. B. Du Bois and American Thought, 1888–1903* (Chicago: University of Chicago Press, 1995), 217–25, 221. Subsequent page numbers will be cited parenthetically in the text. I have discussed this text at more length in "The Fourth Dimension: Kinlessness and African American Narrative," *Critical Inquiry* 35 (2009): 270–92.

24. C. H. Hinton, *Scientific Romances* (London: Swan Sonnenschein, Lowrey, 1886), 30–31.

25. Sutton E. Griggs, *Imperium in Imperio* (New York: Modern Library, 2003).

26. James D. Corrothers, "A Man They Didn't Know," *Crisis* 7 (December 1913): 85–87, (January 1914): 135–38.

27. Pauline Hopkins, *Of One Blood; or, The Hidden Self* (New York: Washington Square Press, 2004), 131, 137, 136. Subsequent page numbers will be cited parenthetically in the text.

28. Judith Butler, *Undoing Gender* (New York: Routledge, 2004), 64.

[14]

Aesthetics and the New Ethics

Theorizing the Novel in the Twenty-First Century

DOROTHY J. HALE

In the introduction to a 2002 special issue of *diacritics* on ethics and inter-disciplinarity, Mark Sanders asks us to consider, "What points of contact, if any, are there between the current investment in ethics in literary theory, and the elaboration of ethics in contemporary philosophy?" Yet the question behind this question—the one that motivates his selection of essays for the issue—is why literary critics and theorists have drawn their ideas about ethics from Emmanuel Levinas, Jacques Derrida, Michel Foucault, Giorgio Agamben, and Alain Badiou with little or no felt need to consult past or present moral philosophers. As Sanders goes on to note, while "in North America and the Anglophone world generally, the tendency in ethics has been to bring moral reflection to bear on questions in political theory" there "has been relatively little attention among literary theorists to developments in disciplinary philosophy."[1]

Sanders's observation of this disconnect is particularly intriguing when we consider that the return to moral reflection in contemporary literary theory is in fact a double return: the pursuit of ethics has been accompanied by a new celebration of literature, and it is in the imbrication of these endeavors—the new pursuit of ethics leading to a new defense of literature—

that literary theory and moral philosophy find common ground in the twenty-first century.[2] No moral philosopher has been more enthusiastic or more vocal about the positive social value of literature than Martha Nussbaum. But the mere mention of the author of *Love's Knowledge* and *Poetic Justice* may seem to take the mystery out of Sanders's question. Isn't Martha Nussbaum—self-described humanist, avowed liberal, public excoriator of Judith Butler's "defeatist" feminism[3]—the prima facie evidence of moral philosophy's failure to get what is "new" about the new ethics? While literary theorists pride themselves in pursuing ethics and estimating literary value in light of and in response to complex and difficult poststructuralist truths, Nussbaum in particular and moral philosophy in general seem to remain, as Andrew Gibson has said, "pre-Barthesian."[4] While Gibson identifies the "pre-Barthesian" as a throwback to mid-twentieth-century naive humanism (epitomized for him by Lionel Trilling, with whom he groups Nussbaum), others have found Nussbaum so retro as to be antiquity itself: "Nussbaum is defiantly Aristotelian and therefore pre-Enlightenment; her slogan might be 'Antiquity—An Incomplete Project.'"[5]

Those hostile to Nussbaum find it fitting that the pre-Barthesian who unembarrassedly confesses her love of literature, who argues not just for the positive social value of literature but for the superiority of literature to other types of social discourse, and who even goes so far as to claim that "literary people" (authors and readers of literature) are "best equipped" to perform ethical inquiry, would be in love with Henry James.[6] It is one thing for Trilling in 1948 to hold up the Jamesian novel as an ethical ideal, to see literature generally and novels in particular as a moral corrective to what he calls the "cold potatoes" of social reform through government policies.[7] After all, Trilling's defense of the social value of literature is rooted in a prestructuralist sense of the liberal individual, usefully defined from the post-Foucauldian perspective of D. A. Miller as "the subject whose private life, mental or domestic, is felt to provide constant inarguable evidence of his constitutive 'freedom.'"[8] This is the kind of freedom that Trilling invokes when he argues that the imperialism of U.S. public policy can be checked only by the cultivation of the "free play of the moral imagination" and that "for our time the most effective agent of the moral imagination" has been a product of the literary imagination: "the novel of the last two hundred years."[9] For Trilling, the moral enterprise that is fiction—defined by its inutility, its anti-instrumentality, its inequivalence to state law—culminates in the work of an aesthete, Henry James.

But by 1990 shouldn't Martha Nussbaum have learned from literary critics the political lessons of Jamesian aestheticism? In *The Political Unconscious* Fredric Jameson declares James's creation of an aesthetics of the novel to have such profound social consequences as to be "a genuinely historical act," a crucial cultural formation in the development of late capitalism. For Jameson, James's refinement and glorification of point of view—both as a narrative technique and as a philosophy of perspectival individualism—serve as a "strategic loc[us] for the fully constituted or centered bourgeois subject or monadic ego," enabling capitalism to "produce and institutionalize the new subjectivity of the bourgeois individual."[10] In the twenty-five years since Jameson made this claim, literary critics have fleshed out the list of Henry James's political offenses. Many of these critics follow Jameson in their belief that James's formal practices—and the aesthetic value that James attributed to novelistic form—are the key to his bad politics. James's dedication to developing the novel into a high art form is understood as part of a more general effort on the part of nineteenth-century white male writers to make up in cultural capital what they were losing in sales figures. The ideological production of the aesthetic as a "discrete entity," Michael Gilmore and others have proposed, was the "creation of white male fiction writers reacting against the commercial triumphs of the feminine novel."[11]

In the post-Marxist and post-Foucauldian understanding of the development of the novel, James is indeed a culmination of the last two hundred years, and that culmination does produce, as Trilling believed, the liberal imagination. But for these critics the belief in the liberal imagination is precisely the problem that needs political reform. It has been the work of literary studies to show that the "free play" of the moral imagination is anything but free: it is an agent of regulation, discipline, instrumentality, and ideological delusion. Through its affective power and strategic representation of society, the novel creates a reader who (to quote D. A. Miller again) "seems to recognize himself most fully only when he forgets or disavows his functional implication in a system of carceral restraints or disciplinary injunctions" (x). In a similar line of argumentation, Nancy Armstrong finds the novel's social power to lie in its genre strategies of "disavowal," which transmogrify the "material body" as a social and political reality into a "metaphysical object" of "language and emotion"—an aesthetic act of partitioning that leads individual subjects to think of themselves as universal subjects.[12]

Is Nussbaum's defense of literature in general and Henry James in particular anything more than the disavowal of her own social positionality?

The literary values she admires, notes John Horton, "openness, subtlety of discrimination, a delicately nuanced understanding and a precisely graded emotional responsiveness [are] . . . perhaps not surprisingly, the virtues of a liberal literary intellectual."[13] And indeed Nussbaum's conception of literature generally and the novel in particular is predicated on the ethical value they confer upon private emotion: literature, she says, gives "ethical relevance" to "particularity and to the epistemological value of feeling" (*LK* 175). The novel distinguishes itself as a genre by its "profound" commitment "to the emotions" (*LK* 40). This means, for Nussbaum, that the novel both communicates its meaning through emotion and communicates the ethical value of certain types of emotion. One such ethical emotion is the feeling of possibility: novels, she tells us, engage "readers in relevant activities of searching and feeling, especially feeling concerning their own possibilities as well as those of the characters" (*LK* 46). Our feeling of possibility is, for Nussbaum, an outgrowth of a more foundational ethical feeling: love. To feel that we love is at once involuntary proof of our deepest values—what we authentically care about, what we can't not care about—and a means of developing better social practices since our love for others allows us to make their cares, their values our own, extending our experience by widening our "range of concerns" (*LK* 47). Nussbaum proposes that the art of the novel is first and foremost a performance of—and education in—the care we should have (and, for those of us who "love" literature, that we do have) for alterity, particularity, complexity, emotion, variety, and indeterminacy.

For the cultural critic, "love's knowledge," the care that on Nussbaum's view is inspired by and enacted through novel reading, stands as strong testimony to the particular way the novel performs its ideological work, the way that novelistic aesthetics accomplishes the project of universalizing the individual subject. The novel as a producer and agent of care certainly fits into D. A. Miller's account of the way the novel administers the "regime of the norm" (viii). For the Foucauldian, readerly love becomes the basis for (in Miller's words) "the subject's own contribution to the intensive and continuous 'pastoral' care that liberal society proposes to take of each and every one of its charges" (viii). Nussbaum's notion that the problem of human flourishing is first and foremost a private and "practical" affair, a problem pursued through and solved in relation to our emotional experience of "life" and, most intensely, through our emotional experience of life as represented in novels (*LK* 21), is for the political critic confirmation of the liberal subject's valorization of psychological interiority through its mystification.

A key moment in *Love's Knowledge* provides a powerful example of how novels might be said to lead Nussbaum herself into liberal disavowal. She quotes at length a passage from *David Copperfield* which describes the "comfort" David derives from the characters he meets through novel reading. The passage that Nussbaum cites ends with David's memory of "sitting on my bed, reading as if for life" (*LK* 230). For a chapter title, and elsewhere in *Love's Knowledge*, Nussbaum restyles Dickens's phrase "reading as if for life" as "reading for life." Her substitution seems to perform the erasure of the materiality of social reality by the "free play" of the liberal imagination. To forget the "as if" is to equate reading with life, is to disavow the ideological nature of reading, the particular social conditions that encourage Nussbaum herself to believe that there could be no significant difference between life and its fictional representation, between reading as a private and individual experience and reading as cultural work. To forget this difference is to project both life and the reader as mystified essences, metaphysical objects.

It thus may seem the logical conclusion of Nussbaum's liberalism that the political program she develops in *Love's Knowledge* locates the path to social reform in the consciousness of a fictional character, and a Jamesian consciousness at that. The first thing that contemporary literary critics should teach the world in order to improve it, Nussbaum declares, is how "to confront reigning models of political and economic rationality with the consciousness of Strether" (*LK* 192). The man of the imagination is for Nussbaum the epitome of right ethical value, brought into being by James's own ethical act: the creation of a novel that models through its narrative structure the "finely aware and richly responsible" acts of perception (the phrase is James's) that are for Nussbaum the key to human flourishing (*LK* 148). What do politicians and law keepers have to learn from James's representation of Strether's consciousness? That "the well-lived life is a work of literary art" (*LK* 148). That this sentiment echoes the villainous aesthete Gilbert Osmond, who advises Isabel Archer in *The Portrait of Lady* that "one ought to make one's life a work of art,"[14] seems to suggest the limits and dangers of living "for" life by living life "as if" it were no different from art. To want to confront power with Strether seems a confession of one's addiction to imaginary solutions to real political problems. In a postmodern world of pop culture, globalism, and multiculturalism, we might instead take it as a sign of our own cultural distance from the "genuinely historical act" of high capitalist subject formation that most readers today, academic and non-academic, feel the spectacular irrelevance of the Edwardian aesthete, either

Strether or his maker. We might take it as the end of disavowal that we can say with Cynthia Ozick, "The truth of our little age is this: nowadays no one gives a damn about what Henry James knew."[15]

But I want to argue that, even if no one thinks they give a damn about what Henry James knew, the modern novel that James helped to invent and the tradition of novel theory that he inaugurated provide a foundational aesthetics for the novel that underlies both Nussbaum's ethical philosophy and the new ethical theory that has emerged, especially in the past decade, in the attempt to articulate a positive social value of literature for our postmodern age. To mention J. Hillis Miller, Gayatri Spivak, Judith Butler, Derek Attridge, Geoffrey Galt Harpham, and Michael André Bernstein is to invoke some of the most influential contributors to the new ethical defense of literary value. And while these theorists do indeed, as Sanders observes, derive their ethics from diverse political theorists (Foucault, Agamben, Adorno, Benjamin, Levinas, and Derrida), what Sanders and others have yet to note is that the heterogeneity of these political influences has coalesced in a surprisingly unified account of literary value.[16] For these new ethicists, and a wave of others, the ethical value of literature lies in the felt encounter with alterity that it brings to its reader. It is the untheorized understanding of the form of the novel as inherently politicized that establishes a bridge between the poststructuralist ethicists and the "pre-Barthesian" Nussbaum. The development in the twentieth century of a novelistic aesthetics of alterity cannot be adequately explained (away) by the ideological notion of disavowal since the avowal of disavowal is part of what defines it as an aesthetics. I want to show how the achievement of alterity is, for both ethical camps, not only taken for granted as the novel's distinctive generic purpose, but understood to be accomplished through novelistic form. I then want to suggest how the aesthetics of alterity derives from James's own acute awareness that the politicized struggle between art and its ideological instrumentality is constitutive of novelistic aesthetics itself.

We can begin to chart the connection between Martha Nussbaum and the new ethicists by comparing her revision of Dickens's "reading as if for life" with the ethical value Judith Butler finds in the phrase "for life, as it were." The phrase that interests Butler is, importantly, Henry James's—and it ends the last sentence of *Washington Square*, the novel that Butler has used to make her own case for James's ethical insights. Here's the full last line of James's novel: "Catherine, meanwhile, in the parlour, picking up her morsel of fancy-work, had seated herself with it again—for life, as it were."[17]

Since I've discussed elsewhere Butler's new ethics in general and her investment in this line in particular, I want to draw forward here just the point of comparison with Nussbaum.[18] Butler understands the conditional phrase ("for life, as it were") as James's insight into the necessary condition of meaning making not just in literature but in life. Because Butler sees all meaning making as an act of figuration, of the "as if" imposition of order and coherence onto experience, not just reading but any act of knowing is, on Butler's view, created through the act of restyling "reading as if for life" as "reading for life." For Butler, human understanding comes into being through the oscillation between reading for life and reading as if for life. Reading for life, we ignore or forget the conditionality of our understanding. Reading as if for life, we are self-consciously aware that our certainty is all hypothetical: we understand that we create the meaning we think we find; we know that when we feel most certain we are taking for fact exactly what we pretend to be.

How are these moments of self-conscious apprehension achieved? As Butler describes it, we come to self-consciousness about our pretended certainty through the confrontation with alterity, an experience of the other that surprises us in its intractability, its refusal to conform to what we imagine we know—to fit into our own personal "regime of the norm" the expectations that we call knowledge. For Butler, *Washington Square* provides us with this confrontation with alterity by refusing to explain the motives that drive its heroine, Catherine Sloper, to reject her suitor and pick up her fancy work. In refusing to explain herself to the other characters, Catherine, according to Butler, defines her autonomy not through language but by "marking the limits of all speaking that seeks to bind her, that offers itself to her as a way of binding herself" (208). The reader's easy access to Catherine throughout *Washington Square* thus abruptly ends with her transmogrification from knowable point of view to unfathomable other. What Butler doesn't say, but what is an important feature of her account of alterity, is that it is precisely Catherine's move beyond social binding that binds the reader to her. Catherine's refusal to explain herself—and James's refusal to explain to us *for* her—is experienced by the reader as the emotional upset that reveals to the reader his or her own participation in the everyday binding we perform on the people we pretend to know. When James stymies our comprehension—in this case by substituting the ambiguating phrase "as it were" for the clarifying authorial judgment we expect and desire—Butler tells us "the reader is . . . left, in a sense, exasperated, cursing, staring" (208). On Butler's view, this emotional response is the precondition for ethical knowledge and choice: we are put in a position to "understand the limits of judgment and to cease judging, paradoxically, in the name of ethics, to cease judging in a way that assumes we already know in advance what there is to be known" (208).

To cease judging is, in other words, to cease trying to understand Catherine and instead, to use Nussbaum's word, to "care" for her as other. To the degree that the reader's judgment can be converted into recognition of/for Catherine is the degree to which we read not just "for life" but, in an even more spiritual way, "for *a* life" (214, my emphasis). Being bound (to the enigma that is Catherine, to the ambiguity that ends James's novel), the reader "has" (as James himself might say) her ethical experience: "we *undergo* what is previously unknown . . . we learn something about the limits of our ways of knowing; and in this way we experience as well the anxiety and the promise of what is different, what is possible, what is waiting for us if we do not foreclose it in advance" (209, my emphasis). Our experience of how literature binds us (binds us to characters, binds us to its emotional effects) is thus the happy psychological condition that frees us from our usual epistemological limits. The felt condition of our own binding makes possible, in other words, our knowledge of life "as it were." Incomprehension of the other yields knowledge of the self: we are made to recognize our operative interpretative categories as our own "regime of the norm." And this felt recognition of the limits of our ways of knowing opens up, for Butler, the possibility that we might change for the better, that we might actively try to judge less and undergo more.

But of course the psychological model that underpins Butler's theory means this ethical lesson cannot be learned once and for all. Our capacity for undergoing is dependent upon our continuing to judge: alterity can only be registered positively by our experience of its power to disrupt us, to leave us, in a sense, exasperated, cursing, staring. Our avowal of our epistemological limits is something that must be freshly performed, undergone again and again. Indeed, the hope of Butler's model lies in her belief that the ethical autonomy and significance of *a* life, of any one life, always exceed what D. A. Miller calls the social "system of carceral restraints or disciplinary injunctions" (x) by which we know it. For Butler, alterity is defined by the endless potential to resist comprehension, to trouble certainty. And it is precisely the endless possibility for psychological upset that creates the positive conditions for personal and social change. The end of the liberal subject's feeling of "constitutive 'freedom'" defined by private life (Miller) begins with the individual's emotional experience of the private life as confounded, invaded. Vulnerability allows change. Anxiety, promise.

How does Butler's "as it were" help us to understand Nussbaum's erasure of Dickens's "as if"? For Nussbaum the conversion of "reading as if for life" to "reading for life" is, as it is for Butler, grounded in two types of alterity: the reader's honoring of the characterological lives depicted in the novel and the work of literature as itself a "life." For Nussbaum, as for Butler, it is the encounter with alterity—with what Nussbaum calls the human—that produces "pains and sudden joys"—emotions that are themselves ethical in this context (*LK* 53) . The narrative strategies of the novel—"complex," "allusive," and "attentive to particulars" (*LK* 3)—position the reader to care "about what happens" (*LK* 3–4), to be "lucidly bewildered, surprised by the intelligence of love" (*LK* 53) into an openness to the new and different. Nussbaum says she learns from Strether the "willingness to surrender invulnerability, to take up a posture of agency that is porous and susceptible of influence" (*LK* 180). "The life of perception feels perplexed, difficult, unsafe. . . . But this life also seems to Strether—and to us—to be richer, fuller of enjoyment, fuller too of whatever is worth calling knowledge of the world" (*LK* 181). Literary "texts" thus display to Nussbaum what Butler's essay title terms "values of difficulty." For Nussbaum, novels engage the reader in "the complexity, the indeterminacy, the sheer *difficulty* of moral choice . . . the refusal of life involved in fixing everything in advance according to some system of inviolable rules" (*LK* 141–2). For Nussbaum, as for Butler, we negotiate between the "conceptions" (*LK* 29), the "rules and principles" (*LK* 44), the categories for judgment that we bring to the text, and our willingness to be "in some sense passive and malleable, open to new and sometimes mysterious influences" (*LK* 238). This vulnerability, she believes, "is a part of the transaction [with literary texts] and part of its value" (*LK* 238). To be truly vulnerable, to have authentically risked, is to honor the power of the life of the other through the feeling of "surrender," "succumbing."[19]

Nussbaum's account of the novel thus distinguishes itself from Trilling's—and does so, moreover, in a way that complements the political critique of Trilling. For Nussbaum, the reader's experience of the free play of her moral imagination ends in her experience of social restraint, of binding and of being bound to the life of the other.[20] In *Poetic Justice* Nussbaum comes even closer to Butler in her meditation on the way literary representation produces otherness through figuration. Nussbaum's term for figuration is "fancy"—and her definition of fancy neatly glosses why, in the James passage that so interests Butler, Catherine Sloper's act of refusal is accompanied by the picking up of her fancywork. Nussbaum tells us: "fancy is the novel's name for the ability to see one thing as another, to see one thing in another. We might therefore also call it the metaphorical imagination." For Nussbaum, as for Butler, figuration enables us not only to apprehend alterity (to see one thing as another, to see one thing in another)—but to inhabit the conditions of possibility that ensure a future different from our "now": that "other things [can be] seen in immediate things."[21]

One reason the connection between Nussbaum and the new ethicists might be hard to see is that the name given by poststructuralists to their valorization of readerly experience is anything but love. But to find this much common ground between Butler and Nussbaum puts us in a position to understand how the names poststructuralist theorists give to literary experience—names like estrangement, defamiliarization, and difficulty—are, like Nussbaum's "love," an attempt to answer Foucauldian and Marxist subjective functionalism by offering an alternative theory of private interiority. Rather than being the "constant inarguable evidence of . . . constitutive 'freedom,'" our interiority is, for Nussbaum and poststructuralist ethicists alike, the constant inarguable evidence of our constitutive sociality, a sociality felt as self-restraint. The disavowal of social positionality entailed by reading "for life" is countered by the avowal of social positionality necessitated by reading for life "as it were." The psychological necessity of oscillating between disavowal and avowal is, for both Butler and Nussbaum and in new ethical theory generally, what makes possibility possible.

After noting the disconnect between literary theory and moral philosophy, Mark Sanders declares, "Literature is an other-maker. It is to this activity that literary theory must attend."[22] But it seems that novel writers and readers have been attending to this definition of literature for at least a century. Sanders can take for granted that literature is an other maker precisely because in our own cultural moment the novel and its aesthetics of alterity define the literary for most readers. The new ethics helps us recognize novelistic aesthetics as an inherently politicized aesthetics by showing how novel form positions the reader to experience herself as "free" through her experience of being socially bound. The reader experiences the free play of her imagination as produced through a power struggle with a social other. The struggle to bind turns back upon the reader, enabling her to experience herself as unfree, as in a constitutive relation with the other who, in turn, binds her. And because the reader experiences her own binding as both a private and emotional condition, as a relationship with the lives represented by a novel and the literary text as itself a life, for the new ethicists literature is theorized as conferring a felt encounter with alterity that is not simply compensatory for social positionality but outside of systematic discipline. In the new ethical defense of literary value as the values of novelized form, reading produces not false ideology but a true experience of how possibility is produced in and through the operation of social constraint.

In new ethical theory, literature provides not just (or for some not even) the fictional imagination of social reform projected through the realist idiom of a story world. Novel reading does not yield a portable list of rules or tips to guide conduct. For the new ethicist literature does not technically teach us anything at all—unless we understand learning as the overthrow of epistemology by experience, the troubling of certainty by an apprehension that comes through surprised feeling. Ethical knowledge is the experience of irresistible encounter with what one does not try to know, what one cannot but help know. It is knowledge that is beyond reason, of the emotions, and so intuitive as to seem a bodily knowing. To formulate this knowledge as epistemology, as we must do, is to register the moment that we move from being bound to binding and back again. But the felt conversion of knowing into knowledge is what enables the process to continue—and to be felt as a progress. The reader feels she comes to know more each time her current knowledge is confounded. Knowing is made possible by every felt failure to know and made new through every repetition.

That the reader's ethical experience of alterity begins with the encounter with literary character is an aspect of poststructuralist ethics that provides the powerful link to James. James's creation of deep psychological characters leads readers, and himself as rereader of his own work, to regard these characters as possessing an autonomy of their own, an autonomy that encourages the cultural perception that fictional creations have a right to human rights. The centrality of characterological alterity to the modern novel has shaped its aesthetic problematic in two fundamental ways. First, the modern novel's commitment to the creation of autonomous characters positions any act of narration as a potential encroachment on the existential freedom of those characters. Second, the commitment to characterological autonomy positions literariness as itself inimical to novelistic mimesis. The new ethics helps us to see that the belief that characterological freedom should be honored and respected is made possible not just by the agency the story world accords characters but through the aesthetic functionalism the novel as an art form assigns them. Judith Butler can talk about Catherine as if she were an actual person not because James's use of point of view bestows upon her a full subjectivity indistinguishable from our own, but because, as point of view and in other ways, Catherine as character is also an instrument of the novel's form.

This is the ethicopolitical basis of novelistic aesthetics. The representation of character in the novel is never free from the threat of instrumentality, either from the subjective source of narration or by the threat of objectification posed by literary design. Fictional characters are produced as "human" precisely by the perceived limitation from both sources that novelistic form places on their autonomy. Fictional characters can be felt to be no different from real human beings to the degree that their functional positionality seems like a restriction of their subjective potentiality, a limit to the full freedom they have a right to enjoy beyond their representation by and within the novel. This double nature—character as a full psychology and character as an element of aesthetic form—has led in the twenty-first century to an understanding of novelistic narrative as inherently hegemonic. The all-too-visible incarceration of subjectivity by aesthetic form is decried as an abuse of representational power. The author who must more or less use his character for his own expressive ends is felt to be exploitative. The reader who identifies with a character worries about emotional colonization. And the reader and author who feel only the aesthetic thrill of a character's fate carry the guilt of the voyeur. The doubleness of novelistic subjectivity (as person, as artistic instrument) is perhaps best emblematized by the novel's third-person narrator, whose subjectivity is constantly imputed as the more than or the excess beyond the functional role as storyteller to which he is bound.

The politics of ethical possibility that the new ethicists find in literature generally are at the heart of Henry James's anxious consideration in his prefaces and elsewhere of the lives bound up in his fictions. The new ethical defense of literary value thus importantly casts light on the development of novelistic aesthetics into the twenty-first century. The aesthetics of alterity allows us to understand, on the one hand, the untheorized privileging of novel form that undergirds the cultural critic's interest in the novel and, on the other, the unacknowledged ethicopolitical values that inform the formalistic practice of teaching fiction as a craft. To show and not tell, to write what you know—such creative writing workshop dicta are connected to a conception of the novel as a social discourse different from other social discourses, made different by the aesthetic effects and ethical dilemmas particular to it. New ethical theory thus helps us see that what I have elsewhere called the social formalism[23] at the heart of the Jamesian tradition of novel theory —the belief that the novel instantiates social identity through its form—is not a logical confusion about the ontological status of literary form, but an aesthetic effect of the novel as the genre has been developed through the twentieth century and into our own cultural moment.

Notes

1. Mark Sanders, "Ethics and Interdisciplinarity in Philosophy and Literary Theory," *diacritics* 32 (2002): 3, 4. I am grateful to Charlie Altieri, Robert Caserio, Nancy Ruttenburg, Cindy Weinstein, and my graduate students at University of California, Berkeley for the exchange of ideas that enabled this project. I also want to thank the Berkeley Consortium for the Study of the Novel, the Huntington Library, the Stanford Center for the Study of the Novel, the University of Memphis, the University of Tennessee, and Princeton University for the opportunity to share work in progress. The version of "Aesthetics and the New Ethics" published here is based on the paper presented at the 2007 Huntington Conference, "American Literature's Aesthetic Dimensions." A subsequent version, edited by the author, appeared in *PMLA* 124 (2009): 896–905.

2. For recent work in moral philosophy on literary value, see Kwame Anthony Appiah, *The Ethics of Identity* (Princeton: Princeton University Press, 2005); Cora Diamond, "Henry James, Moral Philosophers, Moralism," *Henry James Review* 18 (1997): 243–57; Robert Eaglestone, *Ethical Criticism: Reading after Levinas* (Edinburgh: Edinburgh University Press, 1997); Jerrold Levinson, ed., *Aesthetics and Ethics: Essays at the Intersection* (New York: Cambridge University Press, 1998); Colin McGinn, *Ethics, Evil, and Fiction* (New York: Clarendon, 1997); Frank Palmer, *Literature and Moral Understanding: A Philosophical Essay on Ethics, Aesthetics, Education, and Culture* (New York: Clarendon, 1992); and Robert B. Pippin, *Henry James and Modern Moral Life* (New York: Cambridge University Press, 2000). For new ethical literary theory, see Charles Altieri, *The Particulars of Rapture: An Aesthetics of the Affects* (Ithaca, NY: Cornell University Press, 2003); Derek Attridge, *Peculiar Language: Literature as Difference from the Renaissance to James Joyce* (Ithaca, NY: Cornell University Press, 1988); Michael André Bernstein, *Foregone Conclusions: Against Apocalyptic History* (Berkeley: University of California Press, 1994); Lawrence Buell, "In Pursuit of Ethics," *PMLA* 114 (1999): 7–19; Todd F. Davis and Kenneth Womack, *Mapping the Ethical Turn: A Reader in Ethics, Culture, and Literary Theory* (Charlottesville: University of Virginia Press, 2001); Andrew Gibson, *Postmodernity, Ethics, and the Novel: From Leavis to Levinas* (New York: Routledge, 1999); Dorota Glowacka and Stephen Boos, ed., *Between Ethics and Aesthetics: Crossing the Boundaries* (Albany: State University of New York

Press, 2002); Geoffrey Galt Harpham, "The Hunger of Martha Nussbaum," *Representations* 77 (2002): 52–81; Stefan Helgesson, *Writing in Crisis: Ethics and History in Gordimer, Ndebele, and Coetzee* (Scottsville, South Africa: University of KwaZulu-Natal Press, 2004); Lynne Huffer, "'There is no Gomorrah': Narrative Ethics in Feminist and Queer Theory," *differences* 12 (2001): 1–32; J. Hillis Miller, *The Ethics of Reading: Kant, de Man, Eliot, Trollope, James, and Benjamin* (New York: Columbia University Press, 1987); J. Hillis Miller, *Literature as Conduct: Speech Acts in Henry James* (New York: Fordham University Press, 2005); Adam Zachary Newton, *Narrative Ethics* (Cambridge: Harvard University Press, 1995); Dominic Rainsford and Tim Woods, ed., *Critical Ethics: Text, Theory and Responsibility* (London: Macmillan, 1999); and Gayatri Chakravorty Spivak, "Ethics and Politics in Tagore, Coetzee, and Certain Scenes of Teaching," *diacritics* 32 (2002): 17–31.

3. Martha Nussbaum, "The Professor of Parody," *New Republic* (February 22, 1999): 37.

4. Gibson, *Postmodernity*, 11.

5. Harpham, "The Hunger of Martha Nussbaum," 57.

6. Martha Nussbaum, *Love's Knowledge: Essays on Philosophy and Literature* (New York: Oxford University Press, 1990), 192. Further references will be given parenthetically within the text following the abbreviation *LK*.

7. Lionel Trilling, "Manners, Morals, and the Novel," *Kenyon Review* 10 (1948): 22.

8. D. A. Miller, *The Novel and the Police* (Berkeley: University of California Press, 1988), x. Further page references will be given parenthetically within the text.

9. Trilling, "Manners," 27.

10. Fredric Jameson, *The Political Unconscious: Narrative as a Socially Symbolic Act* (Ithaca, NY: Cornell University Press, 1981), 221, 154.

11. Michael T. Gilmore, "The Book Marketplace I," in Emory Elliott, ed., *The Columbia History of the American Novel* (New York: Columbia University Press, 1991), 70–71. See Simon Critchley, *Ethics—Politics—Subjectivity: Essays on Derrida, Levinas, and Contemporary French Thought* (New York: Verso, 1999); and Howard Marchitello, ed., *What Happens to History: The Renewal of Ethics in Contemporary Thought* (New York: Routledge, 2001) for studies of the political theory underlying the new ethics. See Sara Blair, *Henry James and the Writing of Race and Nation* (New York: Cambridge University Press, 1996); Jonathan Freedman, *Professions of Taste: Henry James, British Aestheticism, and Commodity Culture* (Stanford: Stanford University Press, 1990); Karen Jacobs, *The Eye's Mind: Literary Modernism and Visual Culture* (Ithaca, NY: Cornell University Press, 2001); and Carolyn Porter, *Seeing and Being: The Plight of the Partici-*

pant Observer in Emerson, James, Adams, and Faulkner (Middletown: Wesleyan University Press, 1981) for particularly powerful political critiques of Jamesian aestheticism.

12. Nancy Armstrong, *Desire and Domestic Fiction: A Political History of the Novel* (New York: Oxford University Press, 1987), 6, and *How Novels Think: The Limits of Individualism from 1719–1900* (New York: Columbia University Press, 2005), 10, 18.

13. John Horton, "Life, Literature and Ethical Theory: Martha Nussbaum on the Role of the Literary Imagination in Ethical Thought," in John Horton and Andrea T. Baumeister, eds., *Literature and the Political Imagination* (New York: Routledge, 1996), 88.

14. Henry James, *The Portrait of a Lady* (New York: Norton, 1995), 261.

15. Cynthia Ozick, *What Henry James Knew: And Other Essays on Writers* (London: Jonathan Cape, 1993), 2.

16. See Critchley, *Ethics—Politics—Subjectivity;* and Marchitello, *What Happens to History* for studies of the political theory underlying the new ethics.

17. Judith Butler (quoting James), "Values of Difficulty," in Jonathan Culler and Kevin Lamb, eds., *Just Being Difficult? Academic Writing in the Public Arena* (Stanford: Stanford University Press, 2003), 208. Further page references will be given parenthetically within the text.

18. See Dorothy J. Hale, "Fiction as Restriction: Self-Binding in New Ethical Theories of the Novel," *Narrative* 15 (2007): 187–206.

19. Nussbaum, *Love's Knowledge*, 237, quoting Wayne Booth, *The Company We Keep: An Ethics of Fiction* (Berkeley: University of California Press, 1988).

20. See Bruce Robbins on binding in Nussbaum and Butler in "Pretend What You Like: Literature Under Construction," in Elizabeth Beaumont Bissell, ed., *The Question of Literature: The Place of the Literary in Contemporary Theory* (Manchester: Manchester University Press, 2002), 190–206; especially 199–203.

21. Martha Nussbaum, *Poetic Justice: The Literary Imagination and Public Life* (Boston: Beacon, 1995), 36. Further page references will be given parenthetically within the text following the abbreviation *PJ*.

22. Sanders, "Ethics and Interdisciplinarity," 4.

23. Dorothy J. Hale, *Social Formalism: The Novel in Theory from Henry James to the Present* (Stanford: Stanford University Press, 1998).

[15]

Postwar Pastoral

The Art of Happiness in Philip Roth

MARY ESTEVE

Esquire's January 1962 issue contained an excerpt from Philip Roth's novel *Letting Go* titled "Very Happy Poems." Taken from the middle of the novel, these are the words that the high-strung Libby Herz is reduced to uttering when encouraged by the representative of an adoption agency to describe the "kind" of poems she writes. None the wiser from his initial line of inquiry—"Do you write nature poems, do you write, oh I don't know, rhymes, do you write little jingles?"—the agent tries again, following Libby's breathy declarations of enthusiasm for Keats, Donne, and Yeats: "And how about your own poems? I mean—would you say they're, oh I don't know, happy poems or unhappy poems? You know, people write all kinds of poems, happy poems, unhappy poems—what do you consider yours to be?" "Happy poems," said Libby. "Very happy poems."[1] The situation is uncomfortable, not least because the flustered Libby desperately wants to demonstrate her motherly fitness to the adoption agent, an "easygoing" young man who nevertheless "intimidate[s]" her (*LG* 332). In turn, she perplexes the agent by disavowing being a writer of poems, despite having already told him she was writing a poem just before he arrived, which isn't the truth but not exactly a lie either.[2] Roth's intimate focus on Libby's perspective (for the first time in the novel) intensifies the sense of her agonizing difficulty countenancing the specific contingencies of her life—her husband Paul's sexual remoteness, her kidney ailment, their quasi-bohemian poverty and childlessness—and presenting a coherent version of herself to the external world. While such contingencies are presented as credible sources of frustration, Roth implies that Libby's emotional and psychic predicament is aggravated by an unrealistic expectation of ease and happiness, of ease *as* happiness. She would in fact like to wake up any given morning and, without prior effort or practice, compose some very happy poems.

Vividly portraying the near crack-up of this intelligent but misguided and overly sensitive character, the *Esquire* excerpt showcased Roth's talent for writing what might be called excruciating realism. But it also signaled that among the many concerns of the forthcoming novel (released later that year) was the relation between aesthetic value or quality and that paradigmatic postwar American feeling, happiness. What's particularly notable about the exchange between Libby and the adoption agent is not that it revolves around literary production, a self-reflexive theme that pervades Roth's fiction; nor that it engages the vocabulary of happiness in postwar America, which also recurs often enough in his work. Rather, it is the way this exchange imagines the two distinct pursuits of art and happiness as forming a compound precipitate, the happy poem. Forming, yet also deforming: for even as the two characters summon the happy poem into being, Roth suggests that it remains mere wish fulfillment. With Libby's happy poems claimed but disclaimed, not yet written but yearned for, genuinely esteemed by her but articulated as such only by echoing an affable social worker's prying terms, Roth places this imagined artifact under the pressure of multiple and conflicting valences.

This essay takes the *Esquire* excerpt's staged problematic as the point of departure for an examination of Roth's aesthetic and affective commitments at mid-century. At times Roth can be seen to join the era's intelligentsia and literati in dismissing happy art as a middle-class monstrosity, a kitschy blob threatening to suffocate postwar America. What might qualify as Exhibit A in the category of happy art monstrosity, as the historian of happiness Darrin McMahon suggests, is the "smiley face." It is in 1963 that an advertising executive invented this "modern icon," earning him a $45 commission, only to see it virally proliferate, selling annually in the form of 50 million buttons alone by 1971, and coming to rival "in certain quarters . . . the Cross and the Star of David."[3] But Exhibit B could well be drawn from one of Roth's early works, *Portnoy's Complaint*, where Portnoy extols his Jewish family's Thanksgiving tradition over and against that of his WASP girlfriend Pumpkin's, whose family in Davenport, Iowa, all look and act too much like folks in "a painting by Norman Rockwell."[4] At other times, however, happy art becomes for Roth an occasion to explore more deeply the existential and even ethical significance of both aesthetic and affective experience. In these instances, he puts into narrative play a range of conceptual, structural, and dispositional conditions that coalesce around the happy art object and test its precarious viability, thus revealing the potential for art and happiness to function as mutually animating values and qualities. Moreover, Roth draws attention to happiness's labile function within circuits of experience involving aesthetic engagement and arguably more mundane aspects of living a middle-class life, such as working at a white-collar job. He thereby registers a commitment to certain middle-class norms—a commitment, however, that is less concerned to reinforce and perpetuate postwar norms as they are than to imagine them as they might be.[5]

If happy art is subject to a rather withering trial by fire in *Letting Go*, its baptism in Roth's better-known earlier work, *Goodbye, Columbus* (1959), proves more promising. In this text historically actual artifacts such as Gauguin prints and Mantovani records vie for value priority, even if the contest is heavily weighted by authorial favoritism. Despite Roth's relish, as Jonathan Freedman convincingly shows in *Klezmer America*, for "popular and mass culture of the last century, particularly . . . [that of] the 1940s and 1950s," he clearly deems all too easy the mode of listening Mantovani music elicits.[6] And despite Roth's equally pronounced appreciation, as Ross Posnock richly elaborates in *Philip Roth's Rude Truth*, for high modernism and literary experimentalism,[7] Gauguin's paintings gain significance less for their modernist challenge or formal innovation than for the intense pleasure they bring to the uninitiated beholder and the genial dialogue they prompt. The happy art object's potential value, Roth implies, involves but is not reducible to its creator's expressive achievement; this value depends in no small measure on the beholder's capacities and ambitions as well as on the art object's relational function within a social system.

I

What might be called Roth's normative (as opposed to modernist or populist) challenge to happy art's smiley-faced normality takes shape within a broader discourse of happiness at mid-century.[8] The Declaration of Independence may have etched the right to pursue happiness into Americans' consciousness from 1776 onward, but not until the nation's claim to World War II triumph and the ensuing economic boom did happiness come to be equated with an American sense of entitlement, emerging as a kind of affective correlative of the nation-state. It thus became a social critic's veritable obligation to disparage happiness, stigmatizing it as the foremost index of middle-class conformity, complacency, and shallow materialism. In his 1953 book on the subject, *The Pursuit of Happiness*, the eminent historian Howard Mumford Jones summed up the conditions of happiness that rendered it a pox on the nation:

> The United States remains a happy land, the land of good cheer, God's country. It produces the Optimists' Club, the glad books, the Boosters' society, manuals on how to attain peace of mind, songs to the effect that though I want to be happy, I can't be happy unless you are happy too. . . . Advertisements reveal our folkways. They prove that the effect of purchasing American cigarets [sic], oil furnaces, laxatives, shirts, automobiles, house paint, television sets, coffee, nylon stockings, vacuum cleaners, chewing gum, coated paper, electric trains, and dog food is the instant creation of felicity.[9]

Not only advertisements, of course, but advice columns, children's books, stories in slick magazines, excessive leisure, indeed, the ubiquitous insistence on "having a good time," all contribute to "guaranteeing the American citizen the ghastly privilege of pursuing a phantom and embracing a delusion" (*PH* 138, 17). With this ominous witticism Jones manages to turn Kant's well-known statement about happiness's elusiveness on its head. Kant viewed happiness as a natural inclination, but one rendered elusively indeterminate by our cognitive limitations as to what would make us happy and by the gap between our empirical "wishes and wills" and "the idea of happiness." This idea "require[s] an absolute whole, a maximum of well-being" both in the present and the future, which is unknowable: "In short [the human being] is not capable of any principle by which to determine with complete certainty what would make him truly happy, because for this omniscience would be required." Kant thus considered happiness "not an ideal of reason but of imagination."[10] Jones, however, converts postwar happiness's elusiveness into gothic obsessiveness and imagination into a generator of patently false phantasms.

Jones's oddly good-natured book chronicles happiness's demise. It tells how a series of judicial decisions (involving such concerns as the right of inheritance and employment contract) conspired to render happiness a function of libertarian proprietary ideology; it also tracks pernicious shifts in cultural value, exemplified most dismayingly by Emerson's and William James's respective alignment of happiness with self-fulfillment and personal adjustment. By the postwar era, these propensities have devolved into navel-gazing self-expression and personal therapy. This "inheritance," Jones complains, has "translated the problem of the right to happiness out of ethics, out of law, and out of religion into a problem of both national and individual psychology, normal or otherwise" (*PH* 129–30).[11] Yet Jones is confident that the founders had more in mind than Locke's sense of privacy, that their declaration protecting the pursuit of happiness was predicated on Blackstone's natural-law assumption "that the law of nature being itself the product of divine benevolence, must be the only model for human law, so that in proportion as human law mirrors universal reason, citizens obedient to its ancient sanctions must secure felicity" (*PH* 105). By Jones's quasi-Aristotelian lights, then, genuine happiness must be keyed to public reason and virtuous action, inscribed within an empirically determinate teleology.

Other critics, even those with less pointed political concerns, developed a sharper social psychology than Jones's, as exemplified by the Princeton sociologist Melvin Tumin in a 1957 essay (he would befriend Roth some five years later). "A society is in real trouble with itself," he intones, "when its people get unthinking and unfeeling enough to consider 'happiness' as the prime goal in life. . . . The fact is simple: happiness is no guide to anything." Here happiness barely qualifies *as* a feeling; only "unfeeling" people pursue it, threatening open society by eroding "critical, reflective judgment based on sound experience."[12] According to the more radical left, middle-class happiness was essentially a symptom of false consciousness—thus an historical and ontological problem more than a psychological one—fictively exemplified by the pathetic figure Willy Loman who names his son Happy. The sociologist C. Wright Mills may harbor more empathy than Tumin for such "trapped" cogs of the military-industrial complex who generally "cannot overcome their troubles," but his verdict is similar: they are the ones whose "authority is confined strictly within a prescribed orbit of occupational actions," thus whose "power" is at best "a borrowed thing."[13] This quasi-Marxist sense of the white-collar worker's inability to be genuinely happy also dovetailed with the era's Freudian theorists for whom happiness is always already undone by the psyche's overdetermined, plea-sure-thwarting ways. Indeed, as Catherine Jurca has expansively shown in *White Diaspora*, the unhappier you found yourself at mid-century, the more distinctive and glamorous you might appear. Shored up by narcissistic self-pity, white suburbanites in gray flannel suits could join this special crew of *misérables* when their "houses and furnishings reflexively become evidence of and opportunities for alienation," thereby allowing them to count them-selves among the "malcontents" rather than the "mindless conformists."[14] In such accounts of alienation, Jurca suggests, there may be more bad faith than false consciousness at work.

For all the skepticism of mid-century happiness that Roth appears at times to share with the era's critics, he is less inclined to fix its position on the cultural landscape with witticism, ironic historiography, psycho-political complaint, or blanket stigmatization. "Everything will turn," Jones contended in his book's penultimate paragraph, "on the question whether happiness is construed in modern America as primarily an individual or primarily a social state" (*PH* 164). Roth doesn't disagree with this claim; but he doesn't share Jones's vision of rectifying the balance by reattaching happiness to its roots in Aristotelian virtue. He harbors some of Jones's suspicion of the postwar era's hyperpersonalization of happiness, but he doesn't abandon an essentially subjective orientation toward its meaning and value.

The alternative route to reinvigorating the idea of happiness that Roth's fiction fleshes out does resonate, however, with the work of other social analysts of the postwar era. These include Lionel Trilling, David Riesman, and William Whyte, who are often identified with cold war consensus ideology but whose ideas and arguments distinctly contest this ideology's blithe assumptions about American society's achievement of harmonious stability, its "indifferen[ce] to questions about the ultimate worth of capi-talism and the underlying values of American life."[15] Roth can be seen, in effect, to answer Trilling's chastening call, in his 1951 essay on William Dean Howells, to examine more critically the seductions of modernist aesthetics of extremity and to take more interest in Howells's depiction of "civil personalities" and their "moderate sentiments." Trilling's effort to rehabilitate the Howellsian aesthetic of "the 'more smiling aspects' of life" signals, as one sympathetic critic puts it, a "serious" but inadequate "attempt to recover the lost imagination of happiness."[16]

If Trilling's aesthetic revaluation remains overshadowed by his own mod-ernist commitments and polemics, Riesman proves a more illuminating

beacon. Better known for his critique of "other-directed" group identification (and conformity more generally) advanced in *The Lonely Crowd* (1950),
Riesman took "vitality and happiness, even in a time of troubles" to be a
sign of a person's autonomous potentiality.[17] He developed this point as
early as 1947 in "The Ethics of We Happy Few," evidently prompted by the
appearance the year before of the novel *We Happy Few* by Helen Howe
(and by Diana Trilling's review of it in the *Nation*), which satirized Harvard
humanities professors' smug and snobbish left-leaning elitism. In brief,
Dorothea, the faculty-wife protagonist who is the smuggest of them all, eventually comes to exalt the "truth" of self-sacrificing wartime service, namely,
that it requires "simply the power to forget yourself—completely." After a
series of personally humiliating and humbling experiences, Dorothea of
the Few is able genuinely to care about, succor, and even join the Many on
their knees in prayer because "the albatross of her self had gone."[18] In this
manner the novel imagines the discovery of true happiness as assuming
the force of a nationalist theology and personal obligation, articulating a
social logic that Riesman critiques and against which he advances an alternative set of political and existential propositions. He strenuously objects
to Howe's implicit endorsement of Dorothea's self-belittling, self-accusing,
and self-sacrificing means of self-correction, which he deems masochistic
and ultimately unethical. They reflect her surrender to the "phoniness of
'sharing' common experiences," her abdication of an intellectual's "critical
uniqueness" and "individuality of interpretation." With (quoting Howe) the
"burden of being one's own arbiter of taste and feeling" removed, Riesman
contends, the "ethical convictions that they [Dorothea and others] lack are
the belief in their own values."[19] By "belief" Riesman means a commitment
to the frame of mind and conceptual conditions that enable the validation
of one's values—in other words, not just having values but self-consciously
valuing one's values.

   This valuation logic thus entails an ethical component that subordinates the anthropological or naturalist fact of valuing (which amounts to
mere behavior) to the humanist fact of valuing (which is predicated on
self-awareness and endorsement). Echoing his mentor Erich Fromm, Riesman sees the acceptance of being one's own arbiter of taste and feeling
as a nonnegotiable element of a "rational individualist ethics." It is what
enables both the many and the few not just to feel but to assess their happiness. The belief in the value and human capacity of "self-love" is Riesman's ethical, existential, and political-economic starting point. Not to be
confused with selfishness or narcissism, Frommian self-love is more akin

to the concept of autonomy that Riesman elsewhere develops: "the self-loving person is confident of his own self-evaluation" and is thus "capable of loving [others] as he loves himself."[20] As a dimension of self-love, the pursuit of happiness doesn't threaten the critical faculty, as Tumin and others suppose, but rather enables its cultivation, thus playing a crucial role in the formation of an open society.

II

When Libby pronounces those three words, "very happy poems," she in effect allows the adoption agent to put words in her mouth; she thus commits Dorothea's crime of surrendering the arbitration of her own taste and feeling. To be sure, Libby is grasping here for anything on offer that might favorably impress the adoption agent; that is, her authorial claim to very happy poems looks something like the single remaining arrow in her quiver of positive self-projections. But this instrumentalization of her taste and feeling doesn't entirely exonerate her, for she has also committed the misdemeanor of biographical fallacy: she presumes (and wants the adoption agent to presume) that a happy poem reflects its author's happy disposition. Indeed, it is as though the falsity with which she releases the arrow—the falsity arising both from the fact that she hasn't written any poems and from this fallacy's illogic—causes it masochistically to reverse course, rendering Libby herself, along with her esteem for happy poems, its wounded target. Further deepening the wound is that inwardly, too, she seems to think that writing happy poems will make her happy. While theoretically possible—some writers of happy poems doubtlessly derive happiness from their creative production—her affective economy to date evinces its utter unlikelihood. She who is manifestly frustrated and miserable and who has a scheduled appointment with a psychoanalyst that afternoon thus entraps herself in a double bind: she can't write happy poems unless she's happy, but she can't be happy unless she writes happy poems.

At the same time, as Roth reveals the crippling aesthetic-authorial psychology underlying Libby's phantasm of the happy poem, he references a work of visual art that reveals Libby's concomitant inability to engage in any meaningful way with actually existing happy art. A painting by the picturesque impressionist Utrillo may not be as immediately recognizable a happy art object as the Norman Rockwell illustrations Alexander Portnoy loves to loathe, but in *Letting Go* a print by this painter, which Libby has tacked to her and Paul's various apartment walls since college, assumes this status, eliciting its beholders' undemanding, mildly positive engagement. However, it too proves problematic, but less on account of this engagement's mildness than its merely personal orientation. This comes into focus when Libby finds the adoption agent "standing before the Utrillo print," casually regarding it (*LG* 333). "Corny" is how Libby apologetically now assesses it, deploying a term that manages to elide the distinction between her judgment of the painting and her judgment of her personal history of owning the print. As they proceed to discuss its provenance and artistic value, with him suggesting that her fondness for the print is based on "sentimental reasons," she doesn't entirely succumb to the agent's attempt to put words in her mouth; but neither can she quite resist him: "'Well . . . I just like it. Yes, sentiment—but aesthetics, of course, too.' She did not know what more to say. They both were smiling" (*LG* 334). This halting response doesn't so much refute his notion of sentimentality as redirect it away from causal explanation and toward a sentimental aesthetic theory: just liking. As Roth implies by Libby's ensuing speechlessness and both characters' smiles, there's nothing exactly wrong with pleasing art objects, but an aesthetic engagement that involves no critical sense has severely limited social and even existential value. Such stunted engagement as just smiling risks reversion to the "phony" mode of sharing common experience that Riesman critiques. Reduced to just being liked by Libby, the Utrillo print begins to look at best like a prosthetic substitute for writing happy poems or a compensation for not writing them.

In broader aesthetic-theoretical terms, Roth's portrayal of Libby's predicament renders palpable the hazard of excluding the element of disinterest (in the Kantian sense of purposelessness) from aesthetic production and indeed from the affective experience of art: all too interested in determining her happy poems' cause and effect and all too personal in her response to happy paintings, Libby's aesthetic investments are destined to yield low returns. To put it another way, and to borrow Charles Altieri's provocative terms for theorizing "an aesthetics of the affects," Libby treats happiness too much like an "adjective," an empirical abstraction, rather than an "adverb," a quality of reflexive action. She converts it into a "fixed objective state," one that is describable in "standard adjectival terms" and that conforms too readily to an established belief system.[21] Though "just dying to be happy," Libby proves incapable of experiencing happiness reflexively because, for her, happiness isn't simply an inclination or an elusive pursuit; it *is* a belief system, as indicated by one of the nearly random thoughts that enters her mind right before she opens the door to the adoption agent: "She did not really believe in unhappiness and privation and never would" (*LG* 615, 332). But failing to key her affective and aesthetic belief in happiness to productive imagining, she reverts to the reductive paradigm of aesthetic fantasy and affective abstraction. More than an antidote to her husband's own melancholic "belie[f] in doom" and "mourning" (*LG* 615), Libby's obsession with happiness is a dispositional affliction that at once totalizes and diminishes her existence. As she replies to Paul's observation that she "think[s] too much about being happy," "that's all there is" (*LG* 616).

III

However negatively inflected, the aesthetic orientation exemplified in *Letting Go* helps to clarify the stakes of Roth's configuration, in *Goodbye, Columbus*, of art and happiness as mutually constructive, as values worth valuing. In this novella, moreover, Roth engages directly with the terms and arguments of the mid-century sociological imagination by situating the happiness problematic in the context of suburban domesticity and white-collar work—that is, where both happiness and art are putatively most compromised by compulsory normality.[22] The novella is contrapuntally structured around the main plot of Newark-dwelling Neil Klugman's summertime romance with suburbanite Brenda Patimkin and the subplot of his workaday tactics in the Newark Public Library to help a black boy maintain access to the art books he more than "just" likes. These narrative vectors pivot on Neil's sense of his employment as public librarian—in effect, as a white-collar bureaucrat. In Brenda's world, Neil is, as Althusser might say, occupationally hailed—and not without chagrin. His lowly job becomes a source of defensiveness, defining him as bereft of ambition and a career plan.[23] On the other hand, the work he takes upon himself to protect the black boy from his fellow librarians' narrow-minded rigidity and racism not only enables the boy's enjoyment of Gauguin reproductions of Tahitian paradise but turns out also to contribute to Neil's recovery of his own imaginative capacities.[24] Directly following the scene in which Neil finds the boy with the "expensive" art book and discusses the "pictures" with him (*GC* 37), Roth places Neil back "at the Information Desk thinking about Brenda and . . . Short Hills, which [he] could see now, in [his] mind's eye, at dusk, rose-colored, like a Gauguin stream" (*GC* 38). He stages, in effect, two different versions of pursuing happiness, imaged and twinned through the trope of paradise, with each version's stakes and contours rendered more visible by the contrast.

This trope of paradise further serves to intertwine the questions of happiness and art with that other postwar middle-class conundrum, leisure. Critics of all stripes fretted that Americans, rather than educating or cultivating themselves in their leisure time, "sought distractions . . . [and] the excitement, the spontaneity, and the 'immediate satisfactions' they missed on the job." Others "insisted that only when work and leisure were reintegrated could culture become an important part of, rather than a flight from, daily life."[25] In Roth's novella the fact that Brenda is home on summer vacation, and that the romance with Neil fully blossoms when he spends his two-week vacation with her at her parents' suburban home, reflects the abundance of their leisure time; it signals as well the degrading effect the syndrome of work-leisure segregation will have on both their work and leisure. Conforming to sociological type, Brenda and Neil do become each other's source of excitement and immediate satisfaction. Indeed, Roth appears to share Riesman's more specific criticism of contemporary youth for its "lack of imagination," for turning "sexual intimacy" into a "chief leisure resort" bereft of "joyful[ness]."[26] Neil and Brenda's sexual intimacy succumbs to this state as it gets bound up with the Patimkin family's entangled hierarchy of affection. The couple may well exploit the suburban home's ample opportunity for privacy, having sex for the first time in the spatially segregated TV room. But Neil can't disentangle the charm of this occasion from the mounting resentment he feels, having been peremptorily assigned to babysit Brenda's coddled little sister Julie, who feeds on the illusion of being the family's crack basketball and ping-pong player and is always allowed to win. "How can I describe loving Brenda?" Neil later mulls, "It was so sweet, as though I'd finally scored that twenty-first point" (GC 46).

Moreover, Neil's need to prove that he possesses a winning critical intelligence registers a kind of metasociological conformity. Throughout the affair with Brenda, he marvels at and indulges in the Patimkin family's overabundance of everything; but he is also apt to sneer at their country club attitudes, identifying their mindset with the herd mentality. Indeed, Neil creates opportunities to adopt the stance of a sociologist who witnesses—more precisely, pictures—affluent suburbanites at their most herdlike. Hence his afternoon drive to a nearby deer park where he sees in close proximity the "tawny-skinned mothers" of young deer and the "white-skinned mothers" of young children feeding them popcorn (*GC* 95). For Norman Rockwell this scene would be pastoral perfection. But, for Neil, these are mothers who "compared suntans, supermarkets, and vacations," whose "hair would always stay the color they desired," whose "clothes [were] the right texture and shade," whose "homes . . . would have simple Swedish modern when that was fashionable"—in sum, whose "money and comfort" had rendered their individual differences "microscopic," thus whose "fates had collapsed them into one" (*GC* 96). With this conspicuously severe but also boilerplate analysis, Neil betrays a willingness to parrot the critical condescension of such mid-century analysts as Jones, Mills, and Tumin, an attitude that prepares them to read all evidence of abundance as symptomatic expressions of mindless complacency and/ or illusory happiness. This condescension later informs the "psychoanalytical crap," as Brenda calls it (*GC* 132), Neil wields to explain her actions, provoking their recrimination-filled dispute over her mother's outraged discovery of the diaphragm that he persuaded her to obtain. After the break-up he finds himself staring at his reflection in the darkened window of Lamont Library, asking himself circular questions: "What was it inside me that had turned pursuit and clutching into love, and then turned it inside out again? What was it that had turned winning into losing, and losing—who knows—into winning?" (*GC* 135). Such questions reflect the couple's failure to reach beyond predictable, indeed almost compulsory, norms of flirtation and passion, to access what Riesman would deem a more joyful and imaginative level of intimacy.

Roth, however, doesn't let his protagonist languish in a logic of self-loathing, where winning and losing determine the measure of self-worth. The longer Neil stares at his reflection, the more he sees something else: "I looked hard at the image of me, at that darkening of the glass, and then my gaze pushed through it, over the cool floor, to a broken wall of books, imperfectly shelved" (*GC* 136). Literally, of course, the darkness of the glass makes it difficult for Neil to see what's behind it, an optical reality that figuratively corresponds to his fixation on the surface psychology of injured vanity. But the glass's heightened state of qualitative transformation, its darkening, also prompts Neil to "push through," which figuratively maps onto his more searching inner examination. Only a seasoned librarian would notice shelving imperfections; but only a self-loving white-collar aesthete would be drawn to the impersonal furniture of his work-time consciousness—to books in a library—in search of an objective correlative of his affective plight. As Neil transfers this observational sensitivity to his inner world, taking inventory of what might be called the library of his soul, he discovers it in disarray but not beyond repair. For as though in aesthetic overdrive, Neil turns this crisis-induced introspection into an occasion for the subtle but dramatic revaluation of his own sense of postwar bounty, of plenitude: "I did not look very much longer, but took a train that got me to Newark just as the sun was rising on the first day of the Jewish New Year. I was back in plenty of time for work" (GC 136). Here, at narrative's end, in addition to converting selective details of reality into shopworn tropes of renewal (the rising sun, the New Year), Neil more inventively uncouples the phenomenon of abundance from suburban affluence and draws it into his own sphere of life. Leisure time may be no less a commodity than Swedish furniture, but having "plenty" of it is a function of a prospering mixed economy, of having a public service job that turns the empty anxious time of the unemployed into positive time off.

For Neil, then, the relation between leisure and work undergoes crucial recalibration. Whereas the romance with Brenda at first serves as an escape from the job that Neil has "beg[u]n to fear" is "pump[ing]" him with "numbness" (GC 33), his almost eager thought of returning to work suggests that he now views it not so much as a segregated alternative to a botched love life, but as a place for self-validation based on renewed appreciation for the library and his own function in it. Such is the retrospectively implied effect of his earlier solicitude toward the black boy, who continues over the weeks to linger in his mind. During his vacation in Short Hills, for instance, Neil has a somewhat troubling dream of being on a boat with the boy in the harbor of a Pacific island; later, when he's back at work and Brenda back at school, he observes that he "never did see the colored kid again," wondering if he "discovered" another painter's work or went "back to playing Willie Mays in the streets" (GC 120). These imagined scenes form a temporal continuum extending to (and reinforcing the significance of) Neil's later sense of work-time plenitude, with his reflexive "gaze" into the "darkening" window of another library supplying the realist-symbolic relay between the boy's "playing" and Neil's work.

In other words, Neil's job doesn't so much hail him into occupational identity as open up a world in which he functions as a productively imaginative municipal agent. Neil goes to a lot of trouble to protect the black boy from the other librarians, anxious and racist as they are. Indeed, he engages in what the Howells-reading Trilling might call a civil person's intuitive acts of righteous disobedience to prevent the boy's favorite book of Gauguin reproductions from being checked out by another, far less needy patron—acts that are retroactively made good by the boy's explanation that he can't take the book home because "somebody [would] dee-*stroy* it" there (*GC* 60). While it is possible to criticize Neil for this subterfuge and arguably even more for fueling an impoverished kid's desire for unattainable tropical fantasies—as Neil himself momentarily and half-heartedly does when he thinks back on his dream (*GC* 120)—these fallibilities (if they are such) stand in tension with the immensely valuable role Neil plays in the development of the boy's self-sourced faculty of imagination.

Neil's initial encounter with the boy takes place on the library steps outside, where he spies him playfully tormenting one of the "pale cement lions" (*GC* 31): "He would growl, low and long, drop back, wait, then growl again," earning Neil's epithet, "the lion tamer" (*GC* 32, 33). In his taunting and taming play, the black boy registers a capacity for what Riesman calls "good play," which involves the "excited concentration" of "tasks" that are neither "too demanding" nor "not demanding enough"—a kind of "new-found mastery."[27] Later directing the boy to what Neil himself playfully hears him call the "heart section" (he could have opted for the more prosaic phonetic spelling, "hart"), Neil then finds him there with an open book on his lap and in deep enchantment: "[his] lips were parted, the eyes wide, and even the ears seemed to have a heightened receptivity. He looked ecstatic" (*GC* 34, 36). Creating opportunities for this activity's repetition and expansion seems the least a creatively conscientious bureaucrat can do; indeed, it is the sort of engagement that enables (in an existential if not remunerative sense) "the boundaries between work and play [to] become shadowy."[28] Neil himself suggests as much in another evocative pun. Hoping not to appear suspicious of the boy and interrupt his contemplative ecstasy, he pretends to search for a book: "I fished around the lowest shelves a moment, playing at work" (*GC* 36).

To be sure, the boy's ecstatic state falls more easily into the category of vehement passion than alongside such moderate feelings as happiness. In his recent book, *The Vehement Passions*, Philip Fisher distinguishes vehement states (such as anger, shame, fear, and wonder) from emotional ones (particularly happiness, discussed in the concluding chapter) on the basis of their multiple demands on subjectivity: undivided involvement, suspension of temporal consciousness, abolition of privacy by inducing bodily (i.e., publicly evident) expression, to name the most extreme. These demands work to "reinstall an absolute priority of the self, with its claim to be different from and prior to others both in the claims of its will and in its account of the world."[29] Roth might appear, in his portrayal of the black boy's ecstatic state, to endorse Fisher's valorization of vehemence over such "middle-class categories" as emotions and feelings, which instead give priority to "the everyday world"—a world that threatens, in its legislation of reciprocity and good will, the self's singularity, that is, its experience of "nonreciprocal intimacy."[30] But as the scene with the black boy unfolds, Roth reveals not only that the library, this paradigmatic middle-class institution, serves as a kind of curatorial site of vehement wonder, but also that reciprocity and good will themselves enable an enlarged or intensified experience of singularity within the affective realm of happiness. Reciprocity and singularity need not be mutually exclusive, as Neil's orientation toward the black boy makes visible.

To begin with, Neil's interest in the black boy goes well beyond institutional solicitude; it could indeed be called aesthetic. Attending to the curious particulars of the boy's painterly appeal, Neil converts him into a work of happy art: "By the light of the window behind him I could see the hundreds of spaces between the hundreds of tiny black corkscrews that were his hair. He was very black and shiny, and the flesh of his lips did not so much appear to be a different color as it looked to be unfinished and awaiting another coat" (GC 36). Here Neil exhibits, in distinct contrast to Libby, a capacity for careful but disinterested aesthetic appreciation, enhancing his own self-loving singularity. Roth's emphasis on Neil's reflexive perspective—"I could see," "appear to be," "looked to be"—suggests that the boy's incarnation of the happy art object doesn't *cause* Neil's appreciative pleasure so much as occasion or inspire Neil's attentive regard, which Neil then relishes for its own, productively imaginative, self-prioritizing sake. In other words, this mode of appreciation may be intimately keyed to Neil's good will to promote the boy's happiness, but it cannot be reduced to it.

In similarly pronounced contrast to Libby's doomed aesthetic logic—in which, to recall, her speechlessness signifies an overpersonalization of aesthetic sentiment—the ensuing dialogue between Neil and the black boy indicates their reciprocal engagement as well as their preservation of singularity, of intractable particularity and self-directed intimacy. As ecstasy modulates into more moderate good feelings and communicative agency, much of what transpires assumes a pedagogical cast. Neil supplies the geographical facts of Gauguin's work and attempts to correct the boy's terminology and sharpen his grasp of the distinction between taking a picture and painting one, while the boy absorbs the facts and remains largely indifferent to the corrections. An irony lost on both, though perhaps not on Roth, is that the ecstasy-inducing images are in fact pictures taken—that is, reproductions—as well as shrunken to 8 1/2 x 11 book proportions, another indication that for Roth the art object itself matters not nearly so much as the conceptual and subjective conditions underlying the beholder's orientation.

Here the pedagogy contributes to both interlocutors' affective enhancement as well as to their critical sensibility. Learning that Tahiti is in fact a "place you can go" to, the boy's inclination to vehemence resurfaces as "euphoria," prompting an unguarded expression of delight: "that's the fuckin life" (GC 37). Less communicative than exclamatory and self-concentrating, this comment tellingly elicits no response from Neil: the more forceful the vehemence, Roth suggests, the closer Gauguin's work will indeed have to suit the claims of the boy's will and his account of the world (which might be called "just enthusing"). While the boy doesn't exactly relinquish this claim—implied by his continued idiosyncratic reference to Gauguin as a "picture taker" rather than a painter (GC 37)— one could say he tempers it with faint expressions of reflective judgment. However underdeveloped, this capacity emerges when he descriptively expounds on one Gauguin image of "three native women standing knee-high in a rose-colored stream": "These people, man, they sure does look cool. They ain't no yelling or shouting here, you could just see it" (GC 37). As in Neil's description, cited earlier, of the boy himself, the perspectivalist vocabulary—"look," "see"—suggests the introduction of an interpretive or judgmental orientation, but one relaxed by communicative happiness.

Trading nonreciprocal intimacy for intimate reciprocity, the black boy thus enters the sphere in which critical or interpretive disagreement becomes possible—where, for instance, an interlocutor might opine that the women look benumbed or sedated rather than cool. Neil turns out not to disagree, but, as though completing a circuit of pedagogical reciprocity, he arrives at a slightly more sophisticated version of the black boy's account: "It *was* a silent picture, he was right" (GC 37). Here Neil shifts attention away from the appealing absence of noisy actions by particular "people" in the painting toward its overall mood or atmosphere; but he also preserves the boy's initial intuition. Similarly, when the boy asks, rather than exclaims, "Ain't that the fuckin *life*?" Neil finds himself able at least laconically to respond: "I agreed it was and left" (GC 37). No wonder he appears happy, weeks later, to be "back in plenty of time for work" (GC 136).

At the same time, the fact that Neil will soon never see the boy again suggests the functional limitations of Neil's municipal agency: his work as librarian may be valuable, even crucial, but it remains, like Kantian happiness, elusively indeterminate. For better and worse, training will never be everything. Rather, the important thing in this novella is to illustrate, whether in the form of a public institution's statuary decoration that in part signifies "pale" culture's self-lionizing ways or in the form of expensive reproductions of a "white man['s]" modernist paintings of "young brown-skinned maid[s]" (GC 37), how much the aesthetic object's capacity to elicit its beholder's affective and imaginative engagement depends on the beholder himself or herself, along with the social value of (and institutional support for) that engagement. The contrast could hardly be greater between the black boy's aesthetic play or Neil's aesthetic work and Brenda's brother Ron's mode of aesthetic engagement: he is only too complacently happy to hear again and again the easy-listening records of Mantovani or the "soft patriotic music" of "his Columbus record" before "rumbling down into that exhilarating, restorative, vitamin-packed sleep" of an athlete (GC 74). Like Libby's and the adoption agent's speechless smiles before the Utrillo print, Ron's sleepiness exemplifies engrained habits of overpersonalized normality that appear beyond the reach of Roth's normative challenge.

These scenes notably take place in the relatively segregated privacy of domestic dwellings. For in Roth's hands the public library becomes one of the "new 'symbols of happiness'" that, as historian Richard Pells explains, John Kenneth Galbraith hoped to see Americans invest in.[31] Public service institutions like libraries, parks, and mass transit systems could help to counterbalance what Galbraith saw as the American economy's overemphasis on the private-sector production of goods at the expense of social health. In addition, Roth suggests that the institutional logic of the public library combines public disinterest and subjective particularity, with aesthetic engagement, properly understood and undertaken, serving as his paradigmatic figure of this valued potential. In a 1969 New York Times editorial on the virtues of the Newark Public Library, then under threat of closure, Roth gestures toward this ideal as lived reminiscence: "For a ten-year-old to find he actually can steer himself through tens of thousands of volumes to the very one he wants is not without its satisfactions. Nor did it count for nothing to carry a library card in one's pocket; to pay a fine; to sit in a strange place, beyond the reach of parent and school, and read whatever one chose, in anonymity and peace."[32] In Goodbye, Columbus Roth enlarges this personal anecdote by reassigning its appeal to virtually anybody—young Jewish men and black boys alike—with a respect for "municipal citizenship" and for "aspiration and curiosity and quiet pleasure, for language, learning, scholarship, intelligence, reason, wit, beauty, and knowledge."[33] By distinguishing and evaluating modes of aesthetic receptivity and, like the black boy with his pale cement lion, by taunting and taming the specter of normal happiness, Roth manages to push through its dark glass, as it were, and retrieve its underlying normative value.

Notes

I am grateful to the Social Sciences and Humanities Council of Canada for funding this project and to Adam Carlson for his superlative research assistance. I wish also to thank Cathy Jurca and Stephen Schryer for their astute comments and suggestions on earlier drafts.

1. Philip Roth, *Letting Go* (New York: Ballantine, 1985 [1962]), 340, 341. Hereafter cited as *LG*, with page references appearing in the text.

2. Seized by a sudden inspiration to write a poem, Libby manages only to write down and weirdly cobble together famous lines from poems learned in college.

3. Darrin McMahon, *Happiness: A History* (New York: Grove, 2006), 463.

4. Philip Roth, *Portnoy's Complaint*, in *Novels 1967–72*, ed. Ross Miller (New York: Library of America, 2005), 435. A devotee of FDR's "Four Freedoms," which Rockwell illustrated to much popular acclaim, Portnoy seems to have in mind one illustration in particular, namely, the freedom from want (466). Rockwell had depicted this freedom as a privatized and thoroughly American affair: a cheery Thanksgiving feast, with family posed agreeably around the supper table while Grandma sets down the platter of roast turkey and Grandpa prepares to carve. Of course, Portnoy himself is another kind of middle-class monstrosity; and, as though not wanting him to have the last word on the Rockwell aesthetic, Roth revisits this scenario decades later in *American Pastoral* (New York: Vintage, 1997). In voluptuous and ambivalently loving detail, Roth portrays the Swede, who reveres Thanksgiving, as yearning to inhabit a Rockwell picture forever.

5. Cf. Stanley Cavell: "the achievement of human happiness requires not the perennial and fuller satisfaction of our needs as they stand but the examination and transformation of those needs." Cavell, *Pursuits of Happiness: The Hollywood Comedy of Remarriage* (Cambridge: Harvard University Press, 1981), 4–5. Length restrictions preclude elaboration of the influence of Cavell's insights on this essay. The same can be said for Robert Kaufman's account of a constructivist-idealist aesthetics in "What Is Construction, What's the Aesthetic, What Was Adorno Doing?" in Pamela R. Matthews and David McWhirter, eds.,

Aesthetic Subjects (Minneapolis: University of Minnesota Press, 2003), 366–96; for Christine Korsgaard's account of normativity as first-person reflective endorsement in *The Sources of Normativity* (Cambridge: Cambridge University Press, 1996); and for Andrew Hoberek's account of Roth's relation to mid-century institutionalism in *The Twilight of the Middle Class: Post-World War II American Fiction and White-Collar Work* (Princeton: Princeton University Press, 2005). For a very different view of Roth's early view of happiness, see Bernard Rodgers's book, *Philip Roth* (Boston: Twayne, 1978). He sees a parallel between Roth's orientation and Chekhov's suggestion that "behind the door of every contented, happy man there ought to be someone standing with a little hammer and continually reminding him with a knock that there are unhappy people, that however happy he may be, life will sooner or later show him its claws, and trouble will come to him" (171–72).

6. Jonathan Freedman, *Klezmer America: Jewishness, Ethnicity, Modernity* (New York: Columbia University Press, 2008), 164–65.

7. Ross Posnock, *Philip Roth's Rude Truth: The Art of Immaturity* (Princeton: Princeton University Press, 2006).

8. That Roth sought in *Letting Go* to explore the status of art in the context of this mid-century discourse of happiness was certainly not lost on one of his friends from his Chicago years, on which much of this novel was based. Thomas Rogers, in his own fifties-era Chicago novel, *The Pursuit of Happiness* (New York: New American Library, 1968), has one character, Jane Kauffman, settle into Roth's novel while the central character, her boyfriend William Popper, selects Croce's *Aesthetics* for bedtime reading (11).

9. Howard Mumford Jones, *The Pursuit of Happiness* (Cambridge: Harvard University Press, 1953), 131–32. Hereafter cited as *PH*, with page references in the text.

10. Immanuel Kant, *Groundwork of the Metaphysics of Morals*, in *Practical Philosophy*, ed. and trans. Mary J. Gregor (Cambridge: Cambridge University Press, 1996), 70, 71.

11. Similarly viewing America as having traded in its founding documents for a mess of happy pottage, Hannah Arendt, who quotes Jones's passage on phantoms and delusions in *On Revolution* (1963), longs for the eighteenth century, when "Americans knew that public freedom consisted in having a share in public business, and that the activities connected with this business by no means constituted a burden . . . [but rather] a feeling of happiness." Arendt, *On Revolution* (London: Penguin, 1990), 119.

12. Melvin Tumin, "Popular Culture and the Open Society," in Bernard Rosenberg and David Manning White, eds., *Mass Culture: The Popular Arts in America* (New York: Free Press, 1957), 554, 551.

13. C. Wright Mills, *The Sociological Imagination* (New York: Oxford University Press, 1959), 3, and *White Collar: The American Middle Classes* (London: Oxford University Press, 1951), 80.

14. Catherine Jurca, *White Diaspora: The Suburb and the Twentieth-Century American Novel* (Princeton: Princeton University Press, 2001), 19, 147.

15. Richard Pells, *The Liberal Mind in a Conservative Age: American Intellectuals in the 1940s and 1950s* (New York: Harper and Row, 1985). 146.

16. Lionel Trilling, "William Dean Howells and the Roots of Modern Taste," in *The Opposing Self* (New York: Viking, 1955), 103; Mark Krupnick, *Lionel Trilling and the Fate of Cultural Criticism* (Evanston, IL: Northwestern University Press, 1986), 110, 98.

17. David Riesman, "The Saving Remnant: An Examination of Character Structure," in *Individualism Reconsidered, and Other Essays* (Glencoe, IL: Free Press, 1954), 120.

18. Helen Howe, *We Happy Few* (New York: Simon and Schuster, 1946), 250, 342. No relation to Irving Howe, Helen Howe was the sister of the eminent Harvard law professor (to whom Howard Mumford Jones dedicated his book) and thus also the aunt of Susan Howe and Fanny Howe.

19. David Riesman, "The Ethics of We Happy Few," in *Selected Essays from Individualism Reconsidered* (New York: Doubleday, 1954), 42, 41, 43.

20. Ibid., 45, 30.

21. Charles Altieri, *The Particulars of Rapture: An Aesthetics of the Affects* (Ithaca: Cornell University Press, 2003), 10. Building on Kant's ideas of art's expressive particularity and aesthetic judgment's purposiveness without a purpose, Altieri aims analogously to redeem reflexive, imaginatively productive, affective experience for its own existential sake (14–16). This is precisely what Libby, redounding as it were aesthetic purposiveness *with* affective purpose, cannot accomplish.

22. The argument I advance here contrasts with Joseph C. Landis's. He claims that "what grieves Roth most is the awareness that normalcy has, like a Procrustes' bed, truncated the range of life, excluding on the one hand the embrace of aspiration, the exhilaration of wonder, and on the other the acceptance of suffering." Landis, "The Sadness of Philip Roth: An Interim Report," in Sanford Pinsker, ed., *Critical Essays on Philip Roth* (Boston: Hall, 1982), 165.

23. Philip Roth, *Goodbye, Columbus and Five Short Stories* (New York: Vintage, 1993), 51. Hereafter cited as *GC*, with page references appearing in the text.

24. The fact that Neil seems not to know the name of the "boy" says less about a possible racist habit of mind that deindividuates male blacks (after all, Neil doesn't call the boy "boy" to his face) than it does about the limitations,

for better and worse, of institutional solicitude. On the one hand, there is only so much Neil as librarian can do to improve the lot of a child from the housing projects; on the other hand, institutional surveillance is checked and the black boy's privacy is protected by his anonymity.

25. Pells, *The Liberal Mind*, 222, 228.

26. David Riesman, "Some Observations on Changes in Leisure Attitudes," in *Selected Essays from Individualism Reconsidered*, 129–30.

27. Ibid., 145.

28. Ibid., 147.

29. Philip Fisher, *The Vehement Passions* (Princeton: Princeton University Press, 2002), 46.

30. Ibid., 45, 218.

31. Pells, *The Liberal Mind*, 170.

32. Philip Roth, *Reading Myself and Others* (New York: Farrar, Straus and Giroux, 1975), 176. In a footnote Roth reports that the "vehement" protest against closure led the Newark City Council to rescind the decision (175).

33. Ibid., 176, 175.

[16]

Perfect Is Dead

Karen Carpenter, Theodor Adorno, and the Radio; or, If Hooks Could Kill

ERIC LOTT

For Tom Smucker

The only philosophy which can be responsibly practised in face of despair is the attempt to contemplate all things as they would present themselves from the standpoint of redemption. Knowledge has no light but that shed on the world by redemption: all else is reconstruction, mere technique. Perspectives must be fashioned that displace and estrange the world, reveal it to be, with its rifts and crevices, as indigent and distorted as it will appear one day in the messianic light. To gain such perspectives without velleity or violence, entirely from felt contact with its objects—this alone is the task of thought.

—Theodor Adorno, *Minima Moralia*

The Carpenters seem made to order for what Theodor Adorno in a famous essay called "the fetish-character in music and the regression of listening."[1] Nothing in the smooth, reified, even fetishistic sheen of songs such as "Close to You"—a brand of Los Angeles vernacular sentimental poetic production for the airwaves—suggests the potential for authentic aesthetic experience or expression. The apparently unbroken surface of this industrially manufactured sound, however, is in fact riven by longing, constriction, and discomfort, and I will argue that it constitutes a kind of negative dialectic of the L.A. that had so revolted Adorno during his exile there in the 1940s and early '50s. In this sense the Carpenters provide an excellent

test case for Adorno's ideas about structural listening and the fate of aesthetic responsiveness in the age of radio (one of Adorno's first activities
upon his arrival in the United States was of course his work with Paul
Lazarsfeld's Princeton Radio Research Project). In *Dialectic of Enlighten-*
ment (an L.A. story if ever there was one), Adorno and Max Horkeimer use
the parable of Homer's Sirens to theorize sonic experience in capitalist
society, the only options being dogged sublimation (the rowers' stopped-up
ears) or beauty without consequence (Odysseus strapped, motionless, to
the mast);[2] it is tempting to suggest that by the time the Carpenter family moved to Downey, California, in 1963, the agon of Odysseus and the
Sirens had been reduced to the upbeat oblivion of surfers and the Beach
Boys. Yet when the Carpenters hit it big in 1970, deuce-coupe Fordism
was already undergoing significant strain, and the contradictions of capital,
urban space, cultural abundance, the nuclear family, and female power
were registered—hideously, magisterially—in music that was calculat-
ingly designed for the car radio and the quadraphonic sound system. The
Caucasian blues of "Superstar," "Rainy Days and Mondays," "Goodbye to
Love," "Hurting Each Other," and others project the suburban whiteness of
Downey—known for its aerospace industry, its surfing, its pioneering fast-
food chains, and its racist police force—into a soundscape of pain and self-
negation whose real-life counterpart came in Karen Carpenter's notorious
death from anorexia at the age of thirty-two. Read right, in other words, the
Carpenters' music speaks symptomatically of the "damaged life" Adorno
espied in L.A.'s endless summer.[3]

It is amusing, I'll allow, to catalog some of the ways in which the Carpenters story suggests a willfully antiliberatory ethos—political, personal,
and musical. The brother-sister duo looked almost freakishly alike, their
visages on album covers and in photo shoots frozen into the same rictus
of compulsory cheerfulness. This aura of sibling sameness is often represented pictorially and musically as a marriage of true talents, an endoga-
mous involution that further resists the incursion of difference. The motivating product behind—or consequence of—this imaginary is a series of
hit songs overdetermined by repetition, calculation, sameness: the same
sweet bummer vibe in song after song of lost or unrequited love set to
arrangements that blur one into the next, featuring Phil Spector–like cho-
ruses of background vocals made up solely of Karen and Richard Carpenter's multiply overdubbed voices. One of their first big hits, "We've Only
Just Begun" (1970), was originally a bank commercial jingle—at a single
stroke fulfilling exponentially Adorno's nightmare of culture-industry

commodification. By all accounts, Richard Carpenter and his lyricist, John Bettis, not infrequently wrote to a precise formula. Richard and Karen both insisted that their stage show perfectly reproduce—without variation from show to show in a punishing touring schedule—their already overcalculated recordings. Their record company, Herb Alpert and Jerry Moss's A&M Records, was careful to market the group only in terms that conformed to the public's perception of them as bland and square.[4] In 1973 the Carpenters accepted Richard Nixon's invitation to perform at the White House during a state visit by West German chancellor Willy Brandt and basked in the president's description of them as "young America at its best," thus officially becoming the musical face of Nixon's "silent majority."[5] The group dominated early seventies easy-listening FM radio formats, which had been built on the kind of administrative audience research Adorno decried in his work with Lazarsfeld.[6] If to Adorno standardization was the watchword and the death knell of cultural forms produced by industrial means, the Carpenters embraced those means perhaps more fully than any best-selling pop band of their moment.

The fetish-character of the Carpenters sound is evident all across the hits they carefully packaged in 1973 as *Singles 1969–1973*, which sold many millions of copies upon its release. In the very first notes of the album's brief opening snippet of "Close to You" comes a piano-and-vibraphone isomorphism whose crystalline ring sounds like a perfectionist's manifesto. (Since the song in its entirety closes the album, the placement of this little excerpt out front, an interesting packaging move in its own right, makes the record go in a self-enclosed circle, ending where it begins.) The cordoned-off "classical" piano-and-strings segment that opens the group's dolorous cover of the Beatles' "Ticket to Ride" could have given Adorno the fatal heart attack he suffered the year they recorded it; nor is the band above studio tricks such as the overamplified closed hi-hat strikes that begin each verse of "Superstar," only to recede deep into the mix. The absurdly incongruous fuzz-guitar solo on "Goodbye to Love" is so deliciously overwrought that you can hear the guitarist's pick torturing the strings. And the Herb Alpert/Tijuana Brass horns that come out of nowhere in the middle of "Close to You" sound like nothing so much as a gold-plated gearshift thrown in to drive the tune into a new key. Even these obvious examples of Richard Carpenter's gifts as an (over)arranger understate his ability to turn calculated simulation into a brand: the "Herb Alpert" horns I just mentioned were played by Chuck Findley, since Alpert himself wasn't available the day of the session.[7]

Meanwhile, Karen Carpenter's voice is unmatched in its ability to summon a languid melancholy that is somehow at the same time evacuated of personality. This is what Robert Christgau was referring to, I think, when he spoke long ago of "Karen Carpenter's ductile, dispassionate contralto."[8] Aside from the self-mortgaging "We've Only Just Begun," the unconvincingly upbeat "Top of the World," and the infantile "Sing," all the songs on *Singles* are downers—full of rainy days, Mondays, fugitive rock star lovers, so-longs to love, embraces of loneliness, nostalgia for better days, romantic skepticism, pain, and longing. Yet you never get the sense that the persona being crafted is really going through anything; as Roland Barthes says in "The Grain of the Voice," "everything in the (semantic and lyrical) structure is respected and yet nothing seduces, nothing sways us to jouissance." The art is, as Barthes could justifiably have said of Karen Carpenter, "inordinately expressive (the diction is dramatic, the pauses, the checkings and releasings of breath, occur like shudders of passion) and hence never exceeds culture: here it is the soul which accompanies the song, not the body"—an effect of breath, not the grain of the voice. "The lung, a stupid organ," writes Barthes, so unlike the throat.[9]

Fetishized, segmented, voided: a perfect case, one would think, of Adorno's contention that to broadcast (and by extension record) music in the commercial culture industries is to make it impossible. Adorno's work on aesthetics and the radio came at the intersection of three closely related concerns: a post-Hegelian philosophy of music, both serious and popular; a philosophical and methodological critique of the culture industry and its own commercial research practices as well as prevailing U.S. trends in social research; and a critical encounter with U.S. cultural life, first in New York City and then in Los Angeles, in which German fascism seemed recapitulated in laissez-faire leisure society. The conjuncture of at least these matters put Adorno on high-minded lookout for art forms that in their structural integrity could produce part-and-whole dialectics that resisted the wholly administered tendency of modern Western societies and the increasingly one-dimensional political economies that characterized them. The administrative research of Lazarsfeld's project, as David Jenemann splendidly documents in *Adorno in America*, struck Adorno as "sneering empiricist sabotage" that, instead of examining radio programming in the context of a total social situation of production, distribution, and consumption in whole social fields structured in precisely identifiable if contradictory ways, took audience likes and dislikes at their word, among other things mistaking values for facts—a conspiracy of bean counters complicit with the logic of social domination.[10] The radio as he found it upon his arrival to the United States in 1938 not only used aesthetic forms to sell products but thereby turned those forms themselves into commodities, canceling their aesthetic value and binding them and their listeners ever more firmly to the everyday harmony of unfreedom. It was the task of criticism to expose this:

> Chesterfield is merely the nation's cigarette, but the radio is the voice of the nation. In bringing cultural products wholly into the sphere of commodities, radio does not try to dispose of its culture goods themselves as commodities straight to the consumer. In America it collects no fees from the public, and so has acquired the illusory form of disinterested, unbiased authority which suits Fascism admirably. The radio becomes the universal mouthpiece of the Fuhrer. . . . The gigantic fact that the speech penetrates everywhere replaces its content, just as the benefaction of the Toscanini broadcast takes the place of the symphony.
>
> (*Dialectic*, 159)

This is doomy, no doubt; but here and elsewhere Adorno's insistence on the dialectical rehearsal of the entire situation of entertainment reception is, I would argue, crucial to any lasting sense of aesthetic possibility. I have argued elsewhere that, contrary to thinking of aesthetics as a ruse or repository of ugly political animus—antidemocratic investments in "standards" or normative notions of taste, for example—we should pursue its democratic reclamation. The problem with aesthetics is not (pace Terry Eagleton) that it's a bourgeois illusion but that it's too often a bourgeois reality; we ought to be arguing for more of it for more people, not less of it for the few.[11] To the extent that the culture industries debase aesthetic possibility, Adorno is there, with no little sympathy I might add, to suggest why. "The customers of musical entertainment are themselves objects or, indeed, products of the same mechanisms which determine the production of popular music. Their spare time serves only to reproduce their working capacity. It is a means instead of an end. . . . Popular music is for the masses a perpetual busman's holiday."[12]

For working people beaten down by the same political economy that sponsors (in every sense) their leisure time, the labor of aesthetic responsiveness takes a backseat to escape and distraction—which in turn delivers them each Monday to the same labor routine. Inducing relaxation because its products are patterned and predigested, according to Adorno,

"The culture industry perpetually cheats its consumers of what it perpetually promises. The promissory note which, with its plots and staging, it draws on pleasure is endlessly prolonged; the promise, which is actually all the spectacle consists of, is illusory: all it actually confirms is that the real point will never be reached, that the diner must be satisfied with the menu" (*Dialectic*, 139). However much Adorno's approach could slide into somewhat moralistic condemnations of everything from jazz to astrology, it would be silly to discount the pressures he outlines on the creation of a genuinely popular aesthetic—just as Adorno's framing of such pressures here will return to animate—and haunt—the work the Carpenters produced in the 1970s.

If that work depends on the techniques or at least commercial requirements of repetition, standardization, and the other culture-industry attributes Adorno relentlessly critiqued,[13] might it be worth looking further into their shape and resonance and effects in the contexts that produced and embraced them? I am inspired here by Adorno's remarks about "immanent criticism" in his essay "Cultural Criticism and Society," written in Los Angeles in 1949. There Adorno argues that the contradictions or inadequacies of form or meaning in artistic products may dialectically suggest the social forces that deformed them—by indicating how "untrue" they are to the social field they claim to represent. The forms themselves are not untrue, writes Adorno, but rather their pretension to correspond to reality: "Immanent criticism of intellectual and artistic phenomena seeks to grasp, through the analysis of their form and meaning, the contradiction between their objective idea and that pretension. It names what the consistency or inconsistency of the work itself expresses of the structure of the existent."[14] What is worst about the Carpenters' music, in other words, may also be what is best about it; in so fully giving form to one wing of the culture industry of its time, the group might be said to have "produced the concept" (à la Althusser) of turn-of-the-seventies Southern California unfreedom.[15] On this view, it is less important to note the ways the Carpenters amount to a sort of sonic servitude than to look into how they cognitively map through aesthetic inadequacy the culture and subjectivity of one aspect of their historical moment. "A successful work, according to immanent criticism," Adorno writes, "is not one which resolves objective contradictions in a spurious harmony, but one which expresses the idea of harmony negatively by embodying the contradictions, pure and uncompromised, in its innermost structure."[16] I'd like to try to show that the Carpenters, while seeming to opt for a "spurious harmony," are all about its negation.

The sort of dialectical treatment Fredric Jameson describes—which would aim "not so much at solving the particular dilemmas in question, as at converting those problems into their own solutions on a higher level, and making the fact and the existence of the problem itself the starting point for new research"—is, I would contend, something to which the Carpenters have not as yet been subjected.[17] This is not strictly true: there is the brilliant and corrosive 1987 Todd Haynes short film *Superstar*, which features Karen and Richard played by Barbie and Ken dolls (as Karen gets sicker the doll's face is gradually whittled and sanded away) and which Richard managed to suppress in 1990 (though it's now easily available on the Internet); there is Sonic Youth's 1990 song "Tunic (Song for Karen)" (more on which later), an equally brilliant meditation on the singer's fame and physical frame; and there is the 1994 tribute compilation, *If I Were a Carpenter*, of Carpenters songs covered by bands like Sonic Youth (an incredible reading of "Superstar") and Babes in Toyland, which on the whole attempts to retrieve the group's dark side. For that matter, Ray Coleman's biography of the Carpenters is full of (usually oblique) testimony by fans and friends alike concerning the pain and emptiness of its principals' inner lives and music. The present attempt draws on these readings to analyze further the ways in which something was very wrong in Downey.

I say in Downey rather than in the Carpenter family because the deformations that beset the family—and they were many—were endemic to the post–World War II suburban settlement. Downey, incorporated in 1956, lies in southeast L.A. at one of the busiest intersections in 1950s America: the crossroads of U.S. Highways 19 (the through route from Laguna Beach to Pasadena) and 42 (the road from L.A. to San Diego). Once the Interstate Highway System (officially authorized, probably not coincidentally, the year of Downey's incorporation) had been completed, Downey was bordered by federal highways 710, 105, 605, and 5—perfectly plotted, that is to say, on the postwar map of state-sponsored highway construction under Eisenhower that helped push-pull suburban/inner-city racial and class formations into being. (Downey is cheek-by-jowl with relatively isolated Watts.) Eric Avila's *Popular Culture in the Age of White Flight* offers an excellent account of the way in which this dialectic of chocolate city and vanilla suburb came about. Studying such institutional formations as Hollywood, Disneyland (opened in 1955), Dodger Stadium (built in time for the 1962 season), and the freeway system, Avila shows how mid-century L.A. was self-consciously made into a white or white-dominated city.[18] As in other U.S. conurbations, housing in Los Angeles was concertedly racially redlined by a host of agencies and activities, not least among them the New Deal's Home Owners' Loan Corporation and Federal Housing Authority. Disney's choice of Orange County's Anaheim for the location of Disneyland certified the sanitized suburban ethos he meant to foster there. Dodger Stadium was set down atop a working-class Chicano neighborhood in an attempt by city fathers to "renew" the historic downtown area. Key to this entire system was the freeway, whose supplanting of an extensive, demographically diverse, public streetcar system cemented the new urban regime of privatized, racially segmented living. (As California historian and activist Carey McWilliams put it in 1965, the "freeways have been carefully designed to skim over and skirt around such eyesores as Watts and East Los Angeles; even the downtown section, a portion of which has become a shopping area for minorities, has been partially bypassed.")[19] The figurehead for these developments, Avila observes, was Ronald Reagan, who aided the House Un-American Activities Committee in its quest for "subversive" influences in Hollywood, emceed the televised opening ceremonies at Disneyland, and appeared on live television to promote the building of Dodger Stadium (7). Reagan was of course governor of California from 1967 to 1975, precisely the years of the Carpenters' ascendance.

The Carpenter family parachuted into this context from New Haven, Connecticut, in 1963, partly to get to better weather and partly to bolster Richard's budding musical career (Richard was seventeen, Karen was thirteen). What they encountered in Downey was a city like the whole of L.A. on the cusp of post-Fordism, poised between the suburban commute, the service shop floor, and the entertainment business on one side and factory work (Karen and Richard's father, Harold, worked in industrial printing) on the other. The very first Taco Bell had just opened there (in 1962; the fourth-ever McDonald's had gone up there in 1953), and suburban homes and aviation factories had recently replaced the area's farms. Two years after the Carpenters' arrival, the 1965 uprising in next-door Watts made spectacular protest against the racial entailments of the area's suburban splendors. The Carpenter family's response to the cumulative force of these structures, as we will see, was to circle the wagons into a highly strung centripetally focused family unit that more or less ravaged its members, however upbeat they appeared on the surface. On the face of it, the kids reveled in clean-cut postwar L.A. youth culture: Karen's lifelong affinity for burger joints (till the onset of her illness) and both siblings' love of cars (Richard to this day remains a collector), while certainly not unique to Downey, are hardly coincidental. Of course L.A., perhaps more than any other city than

Detroit, is the urban monument to the automobile. The Beach Boys memorialized that fact in "Little Deuce Coupe," "Fun, Fun, Fun," and at least a dozen other great songs that undeniably capture a moment and an ethos of suburban white abundance and mobility. The Carpenters picked right up on this soundscape, similarly sublimating the blackness of car music such as Ike Turner's "Rocket 88" even as they offered a broadly whitened defense against it in the musical context of the late 1960s. If they turned it to the account of a very different sound, it's worth noting that, like the Beach Boys' Brian Wilson (and what the hell, the rest of them, too), each of the Carpenters caught the wave of catastrophe brought on by the ebullient sense, and sound, of plenty.

How this seeming paradox might have come about—that in a land and moment of abundance the result was constriction, loss, self-denial, and horror—has too often and too easily been ascribed to the bottoming out of the sixties into helter-skelter madness and murder, the now canonical (almost postcanonical) script to be found in, say, Joan Didion's dispassionate odes to dispassion and disaffection, *Play It as It Lays, Slouching Towards Bethlehem,* and *The White Album.* Not in the Carpenters' backyard did it happen this way, those moderate Republican friends of music bizzer (and sometime boyfriend of Karen's) Mike Curb, leader of the popular whitebread middle-of-the-road singing group the Mike Curb Congregation, chair of the California Republican party during Reagan's tenure as governor, and later himself the state's lieutenant governor. So what was it? Clues exist everywhere in the Carpenters' music: the sense of (suburban? automotive?) isolation conveyed in "Close to You," an apparently dreamy evocation of intimacy that is in fact its opposite—"just like me / they long to be / close to you." The sense there, too, of personal interchangeability, or the everyday monotony of routine and repetition that defines "Rainy Days and Mondays" (which "always get me down"), the latter a weekly certainty sure to give the singer, as she sings, "what they used to call the blues" (don't they still?); or, again, the fragile (and rather frightening) hope articulated in the forced antidepressant "Top of the World" that, like the sudden joy of today, "tomorrow will be just the same." We're treading on pins and needles here, and it's not a little ominous. Whence the will to melancholy in a willfully upbeat world? Did the Carpenters intuit something about the culture that produced them?

In my view, the Carpenters songs that thematize and, as it were, self-reflexively theorize their sound are those that speak most interestingly to the underside of El Dorado. "Superstar," for example, these days surely the Carpenters' signature song, limns the story of a groupie longing for the eponymous guitarist to come back to her: "Long ago, and, oh, so far away / I fell in love with you before the second show. / Your guitar, it sounds so sweet and clear, / But you're not really here, it's just the radio."[20] All somewhat ludicrous—she fell in love that fast? she forgot she's listening to the radio?—until you consider that this is nothing less than a set of reflections on the culture industry itself: its promissory note that never delivers, its illusory compensation, its perpetual confirmation of frustration. "It's just the radio": one hell of an indictment of the commercial universe it was Richard and Karen Carpenter's every ambition to enter. Presence of guitar is here absence of star, ironic commentary indeed on what I've noted about the withholding quality of Karen's voice, to say nothing of her gruesome disappearing act. The song appears to work like this: girl falls in love with guitar superstar, and they have a brief moment in the flesh; she later hears him on the box, which makes her feel even more abandoned and wanting than she already did; she longs for his return so that she can hear him "play [his] sad guitar" in person once more. One big culture-industry circle, the outcome of which is frustration and even a desire for further sadness, which Adorno argues was guaranteed to happen in the first place.[21] And as for one's demeanor in the face of that frustration and sadness? "The pathos of composure justifies the world which makes it necessary" (*Dialectic*, 151).

But there's more. A dialectic of the live and the commercially reproduced here structures the responses of the singer, who is also a listener like us (in serial regress, we listen to her as she listens to the guitarist; her experience is a stand-in for ours). The live is itself, of course, commercially mediated; otherwise the guitarist wouldn't be a superstar. But when his sounds take to the airwaves, an evacuation—of presence, of flesh—occurs. This is in the nature of radio, as Allen Weiss has written, this is how it works: "Recording and radio—through a sort of sympathetic magic—entail a theft of the voice and a disappearance of the body, a radical accentuation of the mind/body split, with its concomitant anguish." The crush that the radio fosters is by definition unrequited: that is what the song says. Some understanding of this on the singer's part may be why she desires the superstar to come back and play his guitar for her—he's less a person now than a sound. If, as Weiss argues, "recording produces an exteriorization and transformation of the voice, a sort of dispossession of the self," we can observe here not only the guitarist's but also the singer's dissolution into sound, the flat magic of lyrical repetition in her multiply articulated desire, as in some fort-da game of the soul, that the superstar come back again, the very word *again* repeatedly punctuating the insistence of desire until articulation fails: "Baby, baby, baby, baby, oh, baby." The attempt to cling to an absence by such means only ensures the fate of all such radio-produced evacuations: "Radio-phonic airspace is a necropolis riddled with dead voices, the voices of the dead, and dead air—all cut off from their originary bodies, all now transmitted to the outer international and cosmic airwaves only in order to reenter our inner ears."[22]

Meanwhile, a similar decomposition-by-culture-industry occurs in the song "Yesterday Once More." As the early '70s reclamation of 1950s Americana—think *American Graffiti* and *Happy Days*—kicked in, the Carpenters produced a song (this one by Richard Carpenter and John Bettis) that addressed this nostalgia with striking self-consciousness: "When I was young / I'd listen to the radio / Waitin' for my favorite songs / . . . / How I wondered where they'd gone / But they're back again / Just like a long lost friend / All the songs I loved so well. / . . . / Just like before / It's yesterday once more."[23] Once again the substitution of sound for "friend" via the radio. And, here again, this time in the nostalgic embrace of oldies (or their re-creation in current music), the industrial production of sound establishes a closed circuitry of repetition—of the past, of former feelings, of period musical refrains themselves (so commercially familiar that the singer can short-hand them with a "sha-la-la-la")—summed up in the title's "once more." Not least, the singer's allegedly happier times are marked by the tears of musically induced heartbreak. Culture-industry seriality: all is unchanging, and invariably downcast, in the radio's orbit. I am arguing that the Carpenters' music depends on a soundscape of structured disappointment and disillusion, but also that this soundscape offers them an occasion to reflect on and willfully perpetuate that disillusion. As succeeding lines of "Yesterday Once More" have it: "Lookin' back on how it was / in years gone by / and the good times that I had / makes today seem rather sad / So much has changed."

The self-annihilation that the Carpenters, particularly Karen, enacted by way of radiophony is eerily evoked in such songs. In retrospect it is as though they lived the sublating maxim expressed in one of their titles, that "All You Get from Love Is a Love Song." Yet it must be said that the Carpenters' intended response to an administered world they espied even in their own music was homeopathic—a striving for perfection and extreme exertions of studio (and stage) control; I think you can hear it (and its essentially negative outcome) in the music. Sound quality was prized so far above performance aura that the Carpenters' stage show (until they made drastic changes to it in 1976) was widely considered a dud.[24.] (Check them out on YouTube: Richard sits inertly at the keyboard; Karen sighs into the mike like a willow in a mild breeze.) The word *perfection* peppers the accounts of their studio methods and output. A revealing 1971 article captures their compulsive meticulousness:

> What the Downey pair will do tonight is put the finishing touches to [the song "Hurting Each Other"], adding things none but the best-trained ears will even hear. But Richard hears, and Karen hears, and they are perfectionists. . . . To the average listener the song was already complete, and even those of us watching and listening were unable to perceive why the Carpenters would suddenly stop, say "no, that's not right," and start over again. . . . With a technician standing by, the Carpenters entered the sound booth and the 16-track tape containing their latest release was started. It will sound like 12 to 15 voices on the radio Friday, and all of them are Richard's and Karen's.[25]

The nonchalance of the Carpenters' music is belied by a straitjacketed production ethic that undermines the desired effect; it sounds manufactured, airless, the swelling vocals less like rock 'n' roll background singers than the Mormon Tabernacle Choir, which, come to think of it, may not have been far from the desired effect.

The article from which I just quoted was aptly called "Can't We Stop?" and it rightly suggests the out-of-control, compulsive quality of perfection's lure for the Carpenters. Again, this has its dialectical counterpart in the Carpenter family unit and the destructions it wrought or for which it provided the scene. For whatever combination of reasons, that family was an impacted, armored horror show in the guise of suburban rectitude (but aren't we all?). Allow me just to telegraph the dimensions of the Carpenter family lockdown. Agnes Carpenter ruled the household with more vigor than warmth. The family ethos dictated that Karen and Richard live at home with their parents—not only when they first became stars at nineteen and twenty-three, respectively, but also for many years after. When they did move out, Karen and Richard bought a house and lived together. Even then, one tiptoed around Agnes's dictates. Richard complained bitterly for years that Karen had adopted Agnes's mother-function, policing in particular his romantic life (she broke up more than one of his relationships).[26] The aura of incest that hung over the group was conveyed pictorially on album covers, on stage in the hand-holding they indulged at certain moments during their shows, and musically in the marriage-minded "We've Only Just

Begun," which of course they sing with, if not exactly to, each other. (As Richard put it in 1988, "I called her K.C., and she called me R.C. It seems as if we did everything together. We loved cars and went bowling and listened to Spike Jones, Nat King Cole and Elvis, among many others. More than brother and sister, we were best friends.")[27] After Karen's death, and only after it, Richard got married—to his cousin Mary. Both siblings appear to have had obsessive-compulsive disorder, and both became drug addicts, though in Karen's case the consequences were deadly. One might say they responded in kind to an administered world, and it killed them.[28]

In 1979 Richard successfully kicked an addiction to Quaaludes in a Topeka, Kansas, rehab facility; Karen for many years took as many as one hundred Dulcolax laxative pills a day, together with syrup of Ipecac and thyroid medicine to speed up her metabolism. Later in her short life this five-foot-four-inch woman fluctuated between 106 and 77 pounds; her heart was so stressed by this regime that when in early 1983, after extensive psychiatric treatment, she managed to gain a considerable amount of weight, she suffered a fatal heart attack. The point of all this for me is not the usual Hollywood Babylon fable. When she wasn't in the bathroom, Karen obsessed over her needlepoint, and Richard mostly washed his cars. Rather, Karen met the culture industry on its own terms and lost. Operating at the intersection of show-biz spectacle and her mother's severe strictures on female power and autonomy, she strove to eliminate imperfection until there was no life left. Internalizing the business's murderous pressure on the female image, K.C. tore at herself to preserve an imagined innocence that amounted only to self-negation. Her fleeting romantic relationships were invariably unsatisfying, and her only marriage was abortive. Quite a good drummer as well as singer, she was implored by Richard to abandon the drums, crimping her musicianship and putting her out front, where her paralyzing self-consciousness was only redoubled. She made every attempt not to grow up, surrounding herself with her beloved stuffed animals and Disney paraphernalia. When, with Richard in rehab, she attempted a solo record with famed producer Phil Ramone (veteran of recordings with Bob Dylan, Bruce Springsteen, and scores of others), she did try on a more embodied, adult image, with songs like "Remember When Lovin' Took All Night" and "My Body Keeps Changing My Mind." The result was so ridiculously unconvincing that A&M refused to release it—yet one more moment of negation and waste that amounted, if only unconsciously, to an immanent critique of the industry norms the Carpenters had so embraced.

Enter Sonic Youth, whose "Tunic (Song for Karen)," released seven years after the singer's death, acutely renders the culture-industry death drive I have tried to capture in this essay. After a drilling, discordant opening, we find Karen in heaven, reflecting on celebrity, selfhood, music, body image, and—Agnes, her mother: "Dreaming, dreaming of a girl like me / Hey what are you waiting for—feeding, feeding me / I feel like I'm disappearing—getting smaller every day / But I look in the mirror—and I'm bigger in every way // She said: / You aren't never going anywhere / You aren't never going anywhere / I ain't never going anywhere / I ain't never going anywhere."[29] Fed on Hollywood dreams, Karen, as they say in the business, "blew up"—got as big as stars came in the 1970s. This, as "Tunic" rightly suggests, produced a series of self-alienations. It made it impossible for her to have a healthy relation to her size. The body that disappeared in radiophony and in commercial spectacle was also always outsized and therefore a problem in the flesh. At the same time, the song speculates, whether because of anorexia or fame, the singer felt dwarfed ("smaller every day"), a feeling contradicted by the mirror, which doesn't so much return the singer to her "self" as invert its image. And these dissociations are founded on the installation of Agnes in Karen's head as internal admonitor.

The only way out of this, the song asserts, is posthumous. "I'm in heaven now," Karen says, "I can see you Richard / Goodbye Hollywood, Goodbye Downey"; and she seems happy with "all [her] brand new friends," among them "Janis" (Joplin), "Dennis" (Wilson, the just-deceased Beach Boy, most likely—an inspired choice since he too was a drummer), and, inevitably, "Elvis." Karen's ambition ("dreaming, dreaming") has taken her to the ultimate firmament. "Hey Mom! Look, I'm up here—I finally made it / I'm playing the drums again too." Looking down from the house band of heaven: not a bad fantasy of omniscient restoration, complete with drum set. The result is a version of the Carpenters' "Top of the World," with K.C. literally "lookin' down on creation." Where in that song it was love that had lifted her, here it is death. Convincing first-person testimony of anorexia nervosa reveals precisely this: a withholding that delivers plenitude: "Anorexia nervosa isn't an attempt to make yourself suffer; it's an attempt, from a postlapsarian vantage point, to recapture Eden by revealing it; with pain you feel, with shivering cold, warmth becomes real and wonderful again. Food becomes delicious and gratifying. . . . It isn't that I wanted to be a child again. It's that I wanted to feel the way I felt when

I was a child in this asocial life, centered on my home."[30] This is indeed, as Adorno would have it, contemplating things from the standpoint of redemption. It draws on the tradition Joan Jacobs Brumberg describes as "anorexia mirabilis," which descends from the examples of fasting saints, though, as Gillian Brown observes, it is also taken with the Romantic imperative of self-expansion.[31] Brown's work directs us to the contradictory relations between consciousness, self-determination, and subjection to be found in the case of Karen Carpenter. The anorectic refusal of food amounts to a paradoxical attempt at self-assertion and self-maintenance; as Brown has it, "the anorectic projects a self that expands through its material reduction."[32] The assumption of power and control is produced by the anorectic as a disappearance; mastery takes the form of self-subjection, for as long as it lasts.[33] Thus is "alienation absolutely identical with self-possession,"[34] which, I have argued, is the Carpenters' distaff contribution to a critique of the culture industry. In this radical form of self-proprietorship—dispossession itself—is a kind of antihumanism that shines in every note the Carpenters put on record.

This is, finally, the "health unto death" of which Adorno acidly wrote in *Minima Moralia*. Karen Carpenter withdrew from feeding (and thus the mother) and musical coimplication (and her brother) into self-possession in extremis—slow starvation and a bad solo record. It may be that these were among the "libidinal achievements" Adorno speaks of as being demanded of an "individual behaving as healthy in body and mind," which can be performed "only at the cost of the profoundest mutilation."

> The regular guy, the popular girl have to repress not only their desires and insights but even the symptoms that in bourgeois times resulted from repression. Just as the old injustice is not changed by a lavish display of light, air and hygiene, but is in fact concealed by the gleaming transparency of rationalized big business, the inner health of our time has been secured by blocking flight into illness without in the slightest altering its etiology. The dark closets have been abolished as a troublesome waste of space and incorporated in the bathroom. What psychoanalysis suspected, before it became itself a part of hygiene, has been confirmed. The brightest rooms are the secret domain of feces.[35]

Not long before Karen died, the regular guy and the popular girl managed to release (in June 1981) their all-too-fittingly-titled comeback album *Made in America*. It was too little too late: there was nothing left to eat but the menu, and Karen found only in heaven the only perfection there is.

Notes

1. Theodor Adorno, "On the Fetish-Character in Music and the Regression of Listening" (1938), in Andrew Arato and Eike Gebhardt, eds., *The Essential Frankfurt School Reader* (New York: Urizen, 1978), 270–99.

2. Max Horkheimer and Theodor W. Adorno, *Dialectic of Enlightenment*, trans. John Cumming (New York: Seabury, 1972 [1947]), 32–37. Hereafter cited in the text as *Dialectic*.

3. Theodor Adorno, *Minima Moralia: Reflections from Damaged Life*, trans. E. F. N. Jephcott (1951; London: Verso, 1974).

4. Ray Coleman, *The Carpenters: The Untold Story; An Authorized Biography* (New York: Harper Collins, 1994), 163. See also Barney Hoskyns, *Waiting for the Sun: Strange Days, Weird Scenes, and the Sound of Los Angeles* (New York: St. Martin's, 1996), 230–31.

5. Coleman, *The Carpenters*, 143,

6. Joseph Lanza, "'Beautiful Music': The Rise of Easy-Listening FM," in Andy Bennett, Barry Shank, and Jason Toynbee, eds., *The Popular Music Studies Reader* (New York: Routledge, 2006), 161; see also Joseph Lanza, *Elevator Music: A Surreal History of Muzak, Easy-Listening, and Other Moodsong* (New York: Picador, 1994), 167–82.

7. "Chuck didn't play it that way at first, but I worked with him and he nailed it," said Richard. "A lot of people thought it was Herb—Bacharach thought so, too. But it's the way Findley is playing it." Quoted in Daniel Levitin, "Pop Charts: How Richard Carpenter's Lush Arrangements Turned Hit Songs Into Pop Classics" (1995), in Randy Schmidt, ed., *Yesterday Once More: Memories of the Carpenters and Their Music* (Cranberry Township, PA: Tiny Ripple, 2000), 219; originally published in *Electronic Musician*.

8. Robert Christgau, *Rock Albums of the '70s: A Critical Guide* (New York: Da Capo, 1981), 75.

9. Roland Barthes, "The Grain of the Voice" (1972), in *Image–Music–Text*, trans. Stephen Heath (New York: Hill and Wang, 1977), 183.

10. David Jenemann, *Adorno in America* (Minneapolis: University of Minnesota Press, 2007), 1; see also 45, 53–54. For an excellent account of Adorno in Los Angeles, see Nico Israel, "Damage Control: Adorno, Los Angeles, and the Dislocation of Culture," *Yale Journal of Criticism* 10, no. 1 (1997): 85–113.

11. Eric Lott, "The Aesthetic Ante: Pleasure, Pop Culture, and the Middle Passage," *Callaloo* 17, no.2 (1994): 546, 547.

12. Theodor W. Adorno, with the assistance of George Simpson, "On Popular Music" (1941), in Simon Frith and Andrew Goodwin, eds., *On Record: Rock, Pop, and the Written Word* (New York: Pantheon, 1990), 310.

13. E.g., Adorno, "On the Fetish-Character in Music," 306; *Dialectic*, 136.

14. Theodor W. Adorno, "Cultural Criticism and Society," in *Prisms*, trans. Samuel and Shierry Weber (Cambridge: MIT Press, 1981 [1967]), 32.

15. Louis Althusser, "On Levi-Strauss" (1966), in *The Humanist Controversy and Other Writings*, ed. Francois Matheron, trans. G. M. Goshgarian (London: Verso, 2003), 26–27.

16. Adorno, "Cultural Criticism and Society," 32.

17. Fredric Jameson, *Marxism and Form: Twentieth-Century Dialectical Theories of Literature* (Princeton: Princeton University Press, 1971), 307.

18. Eric Avila, *Popular Culture in the Age of White Flight: Fear and Fantasy in Suburban Los Angeles* (Berkeley: University of California Press, 2004); see also Cotten Seiler, *Republic of Drivers: A Cultural History of Automobility in America* (Chicago: University of Chicago Press, 2008), 1–16, 69–104.

19. Carey McWilliams, "Watts: The Forgotten Slum," *Nation*, August 30, 1965, quoted in Avila, *Popular Culture in the Age of White Flight*, 213.

20. Leon Russell and Bonnie Bramlett, "Superstar" (Embassy Music/Cherry River Music, 1971).

21. Adorno, "On the Fetish-Character in Music," 313–14.

22. Allen S. Weiss, *Phantasmic Radio* (Durham: Duke University Press, 1995), 32, 32, 79. See also, more generally, Susan J. Douglas, *Listening In: Radio and American Imagination* (Minneapolis: University of Minnesota Press, 2004).

23. Richard Carpenter and John Bettis, "Yesterday Once More" (Almo Music/Hammer and Nails Music, 1973).

24. For an account of the absurdity of those changes, see Ray Coleman's 1976 *Melody Maker* article, "Carpenters uber alles!" in Schmidt, *Yesterday Once More*, 137–43.

25. Dan Armstrong, "Can't We Stop? Putting the Finishing Touches on a Carpenters Record" (1971), in Schmidt, *Yesterday Once More*, 57.

26. See, for example, the revealing comments in Coleman, "Carpenters uber alles!" in Schmidt, *Yesterday Once More*, 140–41.

27. Richard Carpenter, "Karen Was Wasting Away . . . I Had a Drug Problem . . . and We Couldn't Help Each Other," *TV Guide* (1988), in Schmidt, *Yesterday Once More*, 193.

28. These more or less standard biographical details come from Coleman, *The Carpenters*, the Richard Carpenter–authorized biography.

29. Sonic Youth, "Tunic (Song for Karen)" (Savage Conquest Music, ASCAP, 1990).

30. "Norma," quoted in Hilde Bruch, *The Golden Cage: The Enigma of Anorexia Nervosa* (Cambridge: Harvard University Press, 1978), 71.

31. Joan Jacobs Brumberg, *Fasting Girls: The History of Anorexia Nervosa* (Cambridge: Harvard University Press, 1988), 44–45, 47–48; Gillian Brown, "Anorexia, Humanism, and Feminism," *Yale Journal of Criticism* 5, no. 1 (1991): 190. Brown's essay is brilliantly useful in the present context; for Brumberg's interesting remarks on Karen Carpenter, whose illness brought major public attention to anorexia, see *Fasting Girls*, 17–18.

32. Brown, "Anorexia, Humanism, and Feminism," 190.

33. See also, in this connection, Judith Butler, *The Psychic Life of Power: Theories in Subjection* (Stanford: Stanford University Press, 1997).

34. Brown, "Anorexia, Humanism, and Feminism," 196.

35. Adorno, *Minima Moralia*, 58, 58, 58–59.

[17]

Network Aesthetics

Juliana Spahr's The Transformation and Bruno Latour's Reassembling the Social

SIANNE NGAI

Whether regarded with optimism or ambivalence, the rise in the late 1960s of a "global network culture" characterized by an "unprecedented abundance of informational output and acceleration of informational dynamics" (and historically shaped by the late-twentieth-century restructuring of the capitalist mode of production),[1] is widely thought to have led to a "qualitative change in the human experience."[2] To be sure, networks as a form of social organization are by no means exclusive to postmodernity, though their thematic prominence in discourses ranging from Internet journalism to post-Fordist management literature—both part of what has come to be regarded as an entire "connexionist genre"[3]—often gives this impression. "The formation of more or less extensive networks is no more novel than commercial activity was when Adam Smith wrote *The Wealth of Nations*," as Luc Boltanski and Eve Chiapello note in *The New Spirit of Capitalism*. "But it is as if we had to wait until the last third of the twentieth century for . . . the art of making and using the most diverse and remote kinds of connection, to be autonomized—separated from the other forms of activity it had hitherto been bound up with—and identified and valued for itself" (108). More specifically, actors enmeshed in the social networks that played a central role in the early development of capitalism "did not describe their own actions on the basis of the network form, and above all, *did not appeal to the network . . . to deliver value judgments or construct justifications"* (151, emphasis added). It is thus not just that the "information technology revolution" has provided "material basis for [the network's] pervasive expansion throughout the entire social structure," as Manuel Castells has argued.[4] Since around 1965, what is genuinely new, Boltanski and Chiapello stress, is the rise of the network as a normative concept: the "formation of a mode of judgment which, taking it for granted that the world is a network (and not, for example, a structure, a system, a market or a community), offers fulcra for *appraising and ordering the relative value of beings in such a world"* (151). What is specific to our contemporary moment, in other words, is the rise of "connexionism" as an ideological worldview and thus as a basis for making evaluative judgments ranging from the ethical to the aesthetic.

What defines a network aesthetic? We know it must be, at the very least, an aesthetic that revolves around connection and information: what are its other formal qualities? In terms of offering a perspicuous representation of social relations in general, what are its advantages and limitations? In what follows I examine two twenty-first-century texts committed to a "philosophy of connection"—one literary, the other sociological—that explicitly take up the challenge posed by the network as form and in a way that directly links it to the challenge of creating a more lucid representation of individual and collective action. The first is Bruno Latour's *Reassembling the Social: An Introduction to Actor-Network-Theory* (2005), which Latour explicitly invites us to read as a literary as well as methodological treatise: "To put it in the most provocative way: good sociology has to be *well written;* if not, *the social doesn't appear through it."*[5] Making "the social appear" will thus entail writing "interesting" or "risky" texts (aesthetic judgments Latour uses repeatedly throughout his text and always interchangeably with the verdict "good"), and writing "interesting" texts will entail deploying actor-network-theory, a method that involves tracing ties between a radically expanded number of actors and agencies. My second text is American poet Juliana Spahr's *The Transformation* (2007), a generically ambiguous prose narrative featuring a radically heterogeneous collective protagonist: "they."[6] Narrated in a serial, repetitive, deliberately belabored style, *The Transformation's* story of the ontologically ambiguous "they," and their increasingly complicated relationships with a vast multiplicity of other agents across time and space, is also a formal experiment in what happens to narrative— plot and character—when a *protagonist* takes on the hybrid and spatially distributed form of a network. Read together, these two texts give us a sense of what an aesthetics or discourse of pleasure and evaluation based on networks might look and feel like, as well as a sense of the poetics of connectionism's limits.

"When we act, who else is acting? How many agents are also present? How come I never do what I want? Why are we all held by forces not of our own making?" As Latour writes, questions like these have fascinated people "since the time when crowds, masses, statistical means, invisible hands, and unconscious drives began to replace the passions and reasons, not to mention the angels and demons that had pushed and pulled our humble souls up to then" (43). But this should not lead to the conclusion that the true agent is a force called "the social," Latour argues. While it is true that "we are never alone in carrying out a course of action"—that action is always "othertaken"—explanations that appeal to "the social" as an underlying cause for these detours are "conspiracy theory, not social theory" (53). Thus, while the "sociology of society" tautologically appeals to a preexisting "social order" to explain the formation and behavior of collectives, the "sociology of associations" or actor-network-theory (ANT) maintains that one cannot study groups as autonomous and stable entities, but only the "ceaseless process" of group formation. Keeping its perspective strictly limited to what might be described as the social's most minimal unit, the inherently fragile and fleeting "tie," ANT further sets itself apart from both macro and micro sociological traditions by foregrounding nonhuman and even conceptual or imaginary objects as actors and by privileging the role of "mediators" over "intermediaries."[7] While intermediaries "transport" information and meaning "without deformation or transformation," mediators of action "translate"—deform and transform—the elements they are supposed to carry (38–39).

Having defined ANT as the activity of tracing links between a radically expanded set of actors, Latour's next move is to describe this activity as coeval with its representation: "What do we do when we trace social connections? Are we not, in effect, writing down accounts?" (122). Latour thus conflates doing sociology with writing in a certain genre or way (an "interesting" way), and both in turn with the reproduction of the social itself. "If the social is something that circulates in a certain way, and not a world beyond to be accessed by the disinterested gaze of some ultra-lucid scientist, then it may be passed along [that is, made to continue circulating] by many devices adapted to the task, *including texts, reports, accounts*"

(127).⁸ Texts, reports, and accounts are thus mediators in an unremitting process of tracing connections, and/or *ensuring a continuity of circulation* that amounts to "the social" itself. The painstaking tracking of the ANT sociologist, her *"continuous and obsessive attention"* to the "translations" of action by mediators (127), or to ties "that transport transformation" across a vast plurality of political, economic, legal, biological, psychological, geographic, and linguistic actors (108), will thus retroactively give rise to the very object initially pursued: "the social" qua "something *that circulates in a certain way.*"

Describing "the social" also as perpetually in process of being made and remade, ANT further aligns this with a mode of production and reproduction whose temporality we might describe as serial. This meticulous way of assembling the social—one tie after another—reinforces ANT's "continuous and obsessive" devotion to descriptive detail: "A good text should trigger in a good reader this reaction: 'Please, more details, I want more details" (137). The "tracking" ANT prescribes thus resembles the elaborate "writing-down system[s]" in the classic texts of "obsessional modernity" Jennifer Fleissner analyzes in her account of the latter; narratives such as *Memoirs of My Nervous Illness* or *Dracula* in which intensely recursive acts of writing and rewriting reflect the structural incompleteness of modern knowing itself.⁹ The serial connection-tracing of ANT seems haunted by a similar "feeling of incompleteness";¹⁰ as Latour puts it, "The presence of the social has to be demonstrated each time anew" (53).¹¹ For to "persist in its existence," the social "needs new associations," which can only be revealed through the ANT sociologist's labor, and "such a labor requires the recruitment, mobilization, enrollment, and translation of many others—possibly of the whole universe" (218). Because of this unruly proliferation, even "infinite regress" of agencies, such a labor will also require a radical commitment to doubt. Indeed, according to Latour, ANT requires a conscious decision to "feed off uncertainties," and in particular the "constant uncertainty over [whether actors are] behaving as intermediaries or as mediators," which he describes as "the source of all the uncertainties we have decided to follow" (39). As one might immediately grasp from its chapter titles—"First Source of Uncertainty: No Group, Only Group Formation; Second Source of Uncertainty: Action is Overtaken; Third Source of Uncertainty: Objects Too Have Agency; Fourth Source of Uncertainty: Matter of Fact vs. Matters of Concern; Fifth Source of Uncertainty: Writing Down Risky Accounts"—one of the main rules of *Reassembling the Social* is that "uncertainty should remain uncertain throughout" (47).

There is thus something "continuous and obsessive" not only about the sociological method prescribed in *Reassembling the Social*—with its commitment to serial activity, the generation of ever more descriptive detail, the multiplication of uncertainties, and the rigorous application of rules— but about its rhetoric and form. Adverbial phrases such as "ceaselessly tracing," "ceaseless upkeeping," "continuously upkeeping," and "patiently following" circulate throughout the text, reinforcing Latour's point that assembling actors into networks is *work,* which not only has to be continuously done but redone. This conflation of doing with redoing is highly consonant with the logic and temporality of retroactive constitution, in which to follow the links between actors that constitute the social, is effectively to make the social "appear."[12]

Underscoring Latour's proliferation of actors and agencies (human, nonhuman, imaginary, material), and placement of them on the same ontological footing in a way that enables them to be "cumulated, aggregated, or shuffled like a pack of cards,"[13] *Reassembling the Social* also abounds in lists of nouns: "Microbes, scallops, rocks, and ships" (10); "films, skyscrapers, facts, political meetings, initiation rituals, haute couture, cooking" (89); "fishermen, oceanographers, satellites, scallops" (106); "fetishes, beliefs, religions, cultures, art, law, markets" (101); "Monte Carlo calculations . . . mugs . . . quaternions . . . black swans" (114); "editorials, textbooks, party officials, strike committees, war rooms" (182); "written names, statistical charts, notebooks, documentation, blood samples, genetic fingerprints, and visual aids" (197). The poetics of the list or catalog often seep into the language of Latour's commentators, as Graham Harman self-consciously admits.[14] Harman argues that Latour's "rosters of being" should be viewed as a pointed intellectual intervention, however, rather than as a rhetorical quirk: "We cannot imagine Kant or Hegel invoking such a roll call of concrete entities, which shift the weight of philosophy toward specific actors themselves and away from all the structures that might wish to subsume them. . . . Instead of dismissing grass, gates, gravestones, radios, classmates, and courts of law as mere ontic details, he allows them to be topics of philosophy again" (102). Thus, while Harman admits that "some readers may tire (or pretend to tire) of these frequent lists, dismissing them as an 'incantation' or 'poetics' of objects," he also insists that "most readers will not soon grow tired, since the rhetorical power of these rosters of being stems from their direct opposition to the flaws of current mainstream philosophy" (102).

The rosters of nouns singled out by Harman, however (who also contributes many of his own) are not the only lists in *Reassembling the Social.*

Latour's prose is also replete with catalogs of actions (verbs): "If the social circulates and is visible only when it shines through the concatenations of mediators, then this is what has to be *replicated, cultivated, elicited, and expressed* by our textual accounts" (136, emphasis added). Even the word *action* triggers a rhetorical unfurling into a list of particular actions: "Action is *borrowed, distributed, suggested, influenced, dominated, betrayed, translated*" (46, emphasis added). This pluralization of *action* becomes particularly prominent when Latour makes lists of the *extra activities* that one becomes committed to doing when one commits to ANT: "To be sure, [the sociology of associations] requires more work: an *extension* of the list of actors and agencies; a *deepening* of the conflicts about practical metaphysics; a *pursuit* through areas scarcely visited until now; a *new practice* of finding controversies more rewarding and, in the end, more stable than absolute departure points; and, finally, an invitation to *develop* a puzzling new custom to *share* generously metalanguage, social theory, and reflexivity with the actors themselves who are no longer considered mere informants" (87, emphasis added). Latour's "poetic" catalogs of practices in *Reassembling the Social* mirror the expansion and proliferation of action that ANT itself requires: its "extension," "deepening," "pursuit," and "development." Lists in Latour not only multiply and gather up actors; *they enact an increase of activity* in the form of a series of new projects, like the extra "tinkering, reshuffling, crossbreeding, sorting" Latour calls for in *We Have Never Been Modern*.[15] There is thus a sense in which Harman's gallant insistence that "most" readers will not "grow tired" of Latour's "frequent lists" misses their stylistic point. For the multiplicity and seriality of the catalog (as Harman himself notes) mirrors the ANT principle that commits Latour to "follow[ing] the social fluid through its ever-changing and provisional shapes" in the first place—a project Latour explicitly describes as an "arduous task" (202). Readers will grow tired because, in Latour's own words, ANT "requires more work." *Reassembling the Social*, Latour lectures, is therefore not a book for those who are "lazy" or those who refuse to do their "accounting" and pay the "transaction costs for moving, connecting, and assembling the social" (17, 220). So for what type of person will this book be particularly suited? Those especially skilled at "accounting" and keeping track of their "transaction costs"; those willing to undergo "difficult trial[s]" while working continuously on projects (25, 30). In other words, the type of person Max Weber profiles in *The Protestant Ethic and the Spirit of Capitalism*: an important forerunner, as Fleissner notes, of the modern obsessive.[16]

The narrative task of making action perspicuous by "ceaselessly trac-ing" ties between a radically heterogeneous multiplicity of individual actors makes obsession similarly central to both the story and discourse of *The Transformation*.[17] Spahr's information-dense, 214-page prose narrative, which she describes in her afterword as a "barely truthful story of the years 1997–2001," begins as the story of three people of unspecified gender who move from New York to Hawaii to take a job teaching English literature at the state university, then back to New York in time to witness 9/11 and the first deployment of U.S. troops to Afghanistan. Through a series of events that make the three aware of themselves as actors whose actions are "borrowed, distributed, suggested, influenced, dominated, betrayed, [and] translated" by a vast range of other, similarly interconnected actors and agencies, the three expand into the even larger, more ambiguous collective "they."[18]

There are thus distinct stages of "transformation" in *The Transforma-tion*, beginning with the combination of two relationships (one between X and Y, the other between Y and Z) into a domestic arrangement involving three: "They decided to fix their relationship into a triangle" (15). When the three move to "the island in the middle of the Pacific," however, their already complicated kinship arrangement becomes complicated even fur-ther by other "patterns of relating" inflected by race, nation, and the his-tory and legacy of American imperialism (21). The experience of colonial complicity, in particular, causes the threesome to morph into the "gram-matically accusative" "they." The they's increasing awareness of them-selves as enmeshed in a web of connections ironically intensifies their desire to keep tabs on their actions—a task that becomes increasingly dif-ficult precisely because of the radical multiplication of actors and agencies to which they now understand themselves to be linked. As if to inculcate a "feeling of incompleteness" in the reader that will mirror the protagonist's way of writing with "endless qualifiers and doubts" (a description that also applies to the discourse of the anonymous narrator telling their story), we are often left uncertain who or how many agents "they" includes at a particular moment.

As "they" thus seems to proliferate into an increasingly heterogeneous network of human and nonhuman beings, the question of collective action and responsibility—of exactly who is acting when "they" act—increasingly becomes an object of obsessive worry for they. Ironically, the more "they" become aware of their ties to other actors, the more their collective agency spreads—much like the "expansionist language" which they see constantly overtaking or "translating" the actions they intend: "They realized that when they wrote their poems, their essays, their software programs, even their grocery lists in the expansionist language, they immediately became not only part of the expansionism by the accident of birth but they became the willful agents of expansion. When they wrote they wrote as war machine. When they wrote, they wrote as ideological state apparatus. When they wrote they wrote as military industrial complex. This list went on and on" (98). Tracing ties to others makes actions on the part of the "they" that were previously imperceptible to them perceptible for the first time. Yet this only seems to increase the power and size of "they" at the very moment they want to restrict both. In other words, the they's increased perceptibility of their actions extends their *agency*, but without increasing their *autonomy or self-control*. How will they try to compensate for this undesired expansion of action, or manage the guilt and anxiety it creates? By "compulsively collecting rules about what to write and what not to write about" (57); by "making elaborate charts" that "categorized the options for writers like them who came from afar" (92, see also 108). And by "compulsively" gathering these rules and options into lists like the one below:[19]

> The rules went like this. . . . Whenever they discussed the island, they had
> the responsibility to address the legacy of colonialism on the island. . . .
> They felt that any work they did about the island should somehow make
> clear that it was against colonialism. But at the same time this work
> should also make clear that they were not the only person who had ever
> thought up anticolonialism. They had to point out both that they sup-
> ported the movement and that this movement was larger than them so
> as to indicate that while they supported the movement they were not its
> spokesperson and were not a major or crucial part of this movement. . . .
> They also felt they should not claim to understand the culture that was
> there before the whaling ships arrived. And if they were for some reason
> going to write something set in the past, they should not set any of their
> work in the time before the whaling ships arrived.
>
> (109)

The narrator thus concludes:

> So they wrote no poems about how beautiful the bougainvillea was with-
> out also mentioning how the plant was probably brought to the island
> in 1827 by the first Catholic missionary to the island. And during this

time whenever they had to submit a biographical note to go with some publication they always wrote they were a continent haole so as to make clear that they did not have genealogical ties to the island from before the whaling ships arrived but most of the editors of the publications on the continent edited out this information.

(109)

If nothing else, "writ[ing] with endless qualifiers and doubts" results in the production of more writing: "They felt . . . that they could never have enough rules" (114). The they's "doubting mania" is thus compulsively countered by a graphomania which expands in tandem with their growing awareness of themselves as part of a larger collective—and particularly after the three make a formal agreement to "let the story they told about themselves . . . be interrupted by others."

This brings us to an irony which *The Transformation* self-consciously thematizes. As we have seen, "they" have an especially difficult time negotiating their role as carriers of "the expansionist language," which seems always to have effects outside and beyond their intentions. Yet as noted, the practices they turn to in order to control this expanding language—the "collecting and cataloguing of rules" (58)—result in more language. Discursive expansion is thus a key part of the plot of *The Transformation*, as we see "they" restlessly producing more and more lists, maps, charts, software programs, and other forms for synthesizing and displaying information in order to make the extent of their collective agency more perspicuous to themselves. It is also a feature of the language of Spahr's narrator, who systematically stretches short phrases out into much longer descriptions disclosing the presence of more actors and agencies than hitherto suspected. "Native Hawaiian" thus becomes "those with genealogical ties to the island from before the whaling ships arrived." "New York" becomes "the island in the Atlantic." "Working-class" extends out into "being of a working-class family of a small rural town in the middle of the continent, a town without libraries and bookstores." "Expansion" is not only a property of specific languages, *The Transformation* finally implies, but *of networks in general*: informational, social, and biological.[20]

It thus seems fitting that *The Transformation* culminates in a four-page list in which all the agencies gradually recognized over the course of the narrative as affecting or affected by the protagonist's actions are re-gathered and made to circulate in an imaginary network. This is a "monstrous" circulatory system consisting of several hearts, through which "they" imagine "pump[ing] through" all the mediating agencies encountered in the story: "They pumped the cracking Larsen B ice shelf through their right ventricles. . . . Pumped through the superior vena cavas the losses in the world caused by the military that currently occupied the continent. Pumped back around with the inferior vena cavas all they ate. And then pumped through their right atriums the expansionist language. Pumped with their tricuspid valves a vow not to think of themselves as separate from those killed by the military that currently occupied the continent. Then back around to another heart, through the pulmonary veins they pumped long sentences and lists of connections, both paranoid and optimistic" (213–14) and so on. The account of *why* it feels necessary for they to imagine this circulatory system in the first place is provided in the longest sentence in the book:

> They could not write about the *70 percent reduction of the ocean's zooplankton biomass* without having *one-way tickets for haoles off the island* in their heart and they could not write about one-way tickets for haoles off the island without having *the impositions of imperialisms and an understanding of how their legacies continued to shape them* in their heart and they could not write the impositions of imperialisms and their legacies without having the *expansionist language* in their heart and they could not write about the expansionist language without having *the arrival of the huehue haole* in their heart and they could not write about the arrival of the huehue haole without *the air from the fallen buildings that made them retch* in their heart and they could not write about the air from the fallen buildings without having *the ghosts and the DNA in the dust* in their heart and they could not write about the ghosts and the DNA in the dust without having the *operations that were already happening and operations to come with names like Operation Devil Thrust, Operation Aloha, Operation Centaur Rodeo, Operation Warrior, Operation Suicide Kings, Operation Tiger Fury, Operation Iron Saber, Operation Duke Fortitude, Operation Lancer Fury, and Operation Lancer Lightning* in their heart and they could not write about the operations that were already happening and operations to come with names like *Operation Rock Bottom, Operation Falcon Freedom, Operation Soprano Sunset, Operation Wonderland, Operation Powder River, Operation Triple Play, Operation Therapist, Operation Lanthonid, Operation Copperas Cove* without having the 70 percent reduction of the ocean's zooplankton biomass in their heart.

(210)

Only after assembling this list do "they" realize that "they had to stop making maps that were limited by their horizontal or vertical axes. Or charts that started with two options and then spread from there. They needed a new sort of conceptualization that allowed for more going astray than any map they had ever seen" (210). The list that brings "they" to this realization—and to the narrative's concluding four-page image of circulation—is not just an assemblage of things but of ties: things they find themselves compelled to write about precisely in connection with one another. It is also a gathering-up of agencies, since every phrase listed names an entity that has been affected by or somehow affected they, altering their bodies or mediating/overtaking their actions: from scientific facts ("70 percent reduction of the ocean's zooplankton biomass") to political slogans ("one-way tickets for haoles off the island").

Spahr and Latour thus undertake the challenge of representing/constructing the social—understood in both cases as a challenge of making *links between individual actors* more perspicuous—from opposing directions. While Spahr's narrative moves from a multiplicity toward a relatively enduring unity, Latour's first move is to dissolve "society" into a swarm of nonhuman and human actors connected only for a passing instant in time. Indeed, since ANT calls not only for a radical commitment to localism and presentism but for the immediate disintegration of any concept or structure, as Harman points out Latour's "philosophy of connection" can thus end up seeming oddly anticonnexionist: with his many individual actors left "island-like" in their "utter concreteness" (104, 105). As Harman elaborates, "Actors [in Latour] are defined by their relations, but precisely for this reason they are cut off in their own relational microcosms, which endure only for only an instant before the actor is replaced by a similar actor" (116).[21] Most surprisingly, *Reassembling the Social* claims to be indifferent to social *form*. Actor-network-theory tells us nothing about the *appearance* of the assemblages it describes, Latour stresses: just as one should not confuse "drawing *with* a pencil" with "drawing the *outline of* a pencil," we should not confuse "the network that is drawn by the description and the network that is used to make the description." When it comes to "making the social appear" by way of ANT, only the latter definition of "network" oddly matters: "ANT is a method, and mostly a negative one at that; it says nothing about the *shape* of what is being described with it" (142). Hence while real networks like subways and telephone systems "do not necessarily have to be described in an 'Actor-Networky' way," one can use "Actor-Network" to describe "something that doesn't look at all like a network"—such as a "state of mind" or "fictional character." In *The Transformation*, by contrast—a narrative whose main character looks and acts exactly "like a network"—the shape of "they" is of explicit interest to "they" (as we will soon see in more detail).

But for all these important differences in the way Spahr and Latour go about assembling collectives, their opposing trajectories end up converging in a similar affective and discursive space: one defined by the circulation and recirculation of information, by the series and its temporality of ongoingness ("the list went on and on"), by a style of writing marked by "endless qualifiers and doubts," and by a "continuous and obsessive attention" to descriptive detail. Marked as well by a distinctive set of affects and values—meticulousness, scrupulosity, self-vigilance, a strong work ethic, a radical commitment to doubt, an intense desire for order, and an arguably "inflated sense of responsibility"[22]—in Spahr and Latour's approaches to connexionism the writing of "interesting accounts" intensifies into a poetics of what Spahr calls "obsessive thinking about and revising rules" (113). What is the significance of this link? Of the fact that both Spahr and Latour's efforts to reduce the opacity of the social (by multiplying actors and making the links between them more perspicuous) result in what we might (problematically) call an obsessive-compulsive aesthetic? Why would tracing networks involve a shift from a relatively anodyne aesthetic of information, seriality, and circulation (what I have elsewhere called the aesthetic of the "merely interesting") to an intense and fervent version of the same?[23]

One answer is that the discourse of "continuous and obsessive attention" in *Reassembling the Social* and *The Transformation* points to a fundamental ambiguity about the *representability* of networks that we see each text grappling with in a different way. As Galloway and Thacker note, any "macroidentification of the network as a cohesive whole" is a "paradoxical move, since a key property of any network is its heterogeneity" (59). Since it is internal to networks to be continually "extended and altered"—and since it is also in the nature of networks to be "*internally* variable"—there is always a tension between the individuation of the network as a whole, and the individuation of "all the nodes and edges that constitute the system" (59). "Awareness of the increasing interconnectedness of our communications systems" has thus made it "increasingly difficult to think of [social] formations as distinct entities," as Tiziana Terranova notes.[24] How can a perpetually expanding collection of actors be properly formalized? How can the boundaries of a network be nonarbitrarily drawn?[25] As Boltanski and Chiapello put it: "Networks can be known only on a person-by-person basis. No one is in a position to totalize them" (130).

The only way in which networks can be given a certain finality in spite of their lack of empirical closure, as Spahr's text highlights, is thus through symbolization or metaphor. Indeed, it is exactly because "they" perceive the lack of closure in their web of associations that they feel anxiously compelled to search for reticular metaphors. *The Transformation* thus ends up self-consciously choked with not just metaphors for networks—plant species with reticular root systems, airplane and boat travel routes, fifty hand-holding skydivers, file-sharing computers, an octopus, the Internet, the human circulatory system—but for "the network" *as a particularly promiscuous and flexible metaphor.* Because growth is intrinsic to networks in the same way that movement is intrinsic to metaphor, most of *The Transformation*'s metaphors for networks in fact double as metaphors for metaphor, which, as the narrator informs us, has a tendency to "take over poems" in the same way the passiflora takes over indigenous plant species, "smother[ing] shrubs, small trees, and the ground layer" (31). Conversely, one of the most interesting metaphors for networks in *The Transformation* is "metaphor" itself, which Spahr explicitly aligns with transportation/transformation: "Their dreams were pressing but this period of moving from one place to another place *and having this motion take over their thoughts the way metaphor takes over poems* was only a brief period" (131). Here "metaphor" supplies a figure not just for a kind of "motion," but for the more specific motion of "taking over" something (thoughts, poems, actions, etc.): the "overtaking" Spahr refers to elsewhere as "expansion." Metaphors for networks thus expand and overtake the narrative discourse of *The Transformation* in a way that directly contributes to its obsessional quality. Indeed, one of the things the three obsess about most is *their very dependency on metaphor* for a sense of themselves as a network. Though "they did not want metaphors to matter," "they constantly rewrote metaphors to make them work for them" (17). Metaphor also appears to involve a kind of "overthinking" as well as constant rewriting, as when they reflect on the fact that the tallest building in the small rural town where they grew up was only six stories tall: "They thought a lot about this six-story-tall building even as they felt they were at a risk of overthinking it. But they couldn't stop from seeing it as a metaphor" (127).

As a strategy for negotiating the ambiguity surrounding the totalizability of networks, the compulsive proliferation of reticular metaphors in *The Transformation* seems to stand in sharp contrast to Latour's professed disinterest in the network as appearance or form. Indeed, if metaphorical "overthinking" abounds in Spahr's effort to combat social opacity by tracing networks, Latour's attempt to do the same involves a deliberate "underthinking," advocating an antlike focus on local connections over any "leaping" to structures. Yet one could view Latour's very dismissal of reticular form as irrelevant (as when he insists actor-network-theory tells us nothing about the look or shape of the assemblages it describes) as a response to precisely the same ambiguity that leads to the not entirely wanted proliferation of metaphors in *The Transformation*. In other words, it is perhaps exactly because of the formal problem posed by networks that Latour *brackets* the question of the network as form or appearance. How else explain the oddness of that bracketing, especially since elsewhere Latour suggests that the social is precisely that which can be made to "appear" through interesting or well-written accounts?[26]

Indeed, one of the strangest, even admittedly "tricky" moves Latour makes in *Reassembling the Social* is to use "network" as a "benchmark of literary quality," rather than as a reference to a structure or physical entity with a particular shape (131). Despite the acknowledged "disingenuous[ness]," not to mention grammatical awkwardness of using the noun *network* as a term of aesthetic evaluation, Latour is adamant that the concept should be reserved for the purposes of distinguishing a "powerful and convincing" account of the social from a "weak and powerless one" (in the same way one might use an adjective such as "interesting" or "good") and not to describe an entity with a particular shape (130–31). As he states plainly in a chapter section just as plainly titled "Defining at last what a network is": "The network does not designate a thing out there that would have roughly the shape of interconnected points, much like a telephone, a freeway, or a sewage 'network.' It is nothing more than *an indicator of the quality of a text* about the topics at hand" (129). In this manner, the network is that which distinguishes a "good text"—a "narrative or a description . . . where all the actors *do something* and don't just sit there" (128)—from one in which "only a handful of actors will be designated as the causes of all the others, which will have no other function than to serve as backdrop or relay for the flows of casual efficacy." A "bad textual account," in other words, is one in which actors "go through the gestures to keep busy as characters, but . . . *will be without a part in the plot*, meaning they will not act [without making a difference]." By contrast, a good or interesting text—one that combats the opacity of the social by disintegrating and then reassembling it—is "a string of actions where each participant is treated as a full-blown mediator" (128).

Network for Latour is thus an *aesthetic property of texts*, not what texts narrate or describe. As an "indicator of literary quality," it is more specifically an indicator of a kind of character system in which every individual actor makes a difference ("Remember that if an actor makes no difference, it's not an actor" [130]). Plural, heterogeneous, and nonhierarchical, this character system would stand in vivid contrast to the asymmetrical one of the classic realist novel, where a single actor or at most "handful" do the acting, while all the rest "will have no other function than to serve as backdrop or relay."[27] By the same token, "network" for Latour calls for a very specific kind of *plot*: a radically dynamic one where every single action by every actor will have a significant impact on the action of every single other. "Network" qua "benchmark of literary quality" when it comes to "assembling the social" (or making the social "appear" through well-written accounts) is thus bound up with explicitly narratological issues. As Latour notes, "ANT has borrowed from narrative theories" not because "sociology is fiction,"[28] but because the "diversity of the worlds of fiction invented on paper allow enquirers to gain as much *pliability and range* as those they have to study in the real world" (55). Flexibility is the key value here: "It is only through some continuous familiarity with literature that ANT sociologists might become *less wooden, less rigid, less stiff* in their definition of what sort of agencies populate the world" (55).[29]

And yet, in a telling contradiction, obsessiveness with its characteristic demand for rigor and specificity (the very opposite of "pliability") is clearly a positive literary value for Latour as well. This is evinced in Latour's repeated use of the adverb "obsessively" as a way of qualifying his practices, proudly referring to ANT's "obsessively blind . . . trail-following" (179) and way of "actively, reflexively, obsessively" making comparisons (149); and to Latour's own specific way of "obsessively [asking] questions" (187), his "obsessively literal" interrogation of "social explanations" (103) and commitment to keeping what he calls the "landscape" of ANT "obsessively flat" (174). Of a piece with *Reassembling the Social*'s idiosyncratic use of *network* as a term of aesthetic praise for texts in which "all the actors *do something* and don't just sit there," this discourse of obsession points to a general intensification of labor that the "new network morality" of post-Fordist capitalism at once helps mask and sustain: "To be doing something, to move, to change—this is what enjoys prestige, as against stability, which is often regarded as synonymous with inaction" (155). As Boltanski and Chiapello argue, "a premium on activity, without any clear distinction between personal and even leisure activity and professional activity," is one of the signature traits that distinguishes the current "spirit of capitalism" from the Weberian spirit, which advocates the separation of domestic and industrial life (155). As reflected also by the compulsion of "they" to make lists that "go on and on," which in turn mirrors how "they kept going, going with job application after job application" (65), the radical intensification of activity in the era of networks, due in part to the erasure of the distinction between "activity" and "work," points to the rise of "networking" itself as activity par excellence in a reticular world. As Boltanski and Chiapello write, "Activity aims to generate *projects,* or to achieve integration into projects initiated by others. But the project does not exist outside the encounter (not being integrated once and for all into an institution or environment, it presents itself as an action to be performed, not as something that is already there). *Hence the activity par excellence is integrating oneself into networks and exploring them*" (110). The politically ambiguous breakdown of the distinction between "work" and "activity" specific to the "new network morality" of late capitalism also points to the rise of *affective* labor, the putting-to-work of personal and subjective qualities. For "in a connexionist world, the distinction between private life and professional life tends to diminish under the impact of a . . . confusion . . . *between the qualities of the person and the properties of their labor power,*" Boltanski and Chiapello note, making it difficult to separate "affective bonds" from "useful relationships" in a historically unprecedented way (155).

Consciously or unconsciously, the way in which Spahr and Latour mobilize a poetics of connection that is noticeably obsessive—one marked by the "feeling of never enough rules"—thus discloses the link between the "new network morality" and the expansion of work as well as the labor that goes into building collectives in general and networks in particular.[30] As stands to reason, *The Transformation* takes up a more explicitly literary version of this problem: that of sustaining a reticular *protagonist* in a genre that exerts as much individualizing pressure as the memoir or novel (which is clearly why Spahr's allegiance to each stays equivocal).

The difficulty of *maintaining* "the social" qua network in this narrative is reflected most vividly by a certain slippage between the idea and reality of "they." As noted, the first half of Spahr's narrative is devoted to showing how the original "three" expands to *become* "they" after being affected/infected by the history, politics, and culture of the island—all of which "entered into their body and changed it." The whole point of this first section, with its multiplication of heterogeneous agencies, seems to be that of establishing that the membership of "they," while always changing and indeterminate, extends far beyond the "three" from which it starts out. After the move from the "island in the Pacific to [the] island in the Atlantic," however, the referent of "they" reverts back to *the initial three,* as if the development of "three" into "they" never really took hold (or, more disturbingly from *The Transformation's* own point of view, as if the experience of living in the "accusative" on the "island in the Pacific" was quickly forgotten on departure).

Theoretically, "they" still includes the flora, airplanes, desks, history, and all the human and nonhuman "actors" which the first half of the narrative works so hard to assemble, even after they return to New York. Yet as the second half of the narrative returns to a more detailed account of their domestic life together and its various formal organizations and arrangements, it is increasingly clear that "they" explicitly refers to "three":

> They settled into an apartment with upstairs and downstairs. One of them had a desk downstairs. Two of them shared a room with two desks upstairs. They all set up their computers and one of them built a network that connected all the computers.
>
> (130)

> One of them dreamed of being crushed by two big blue rubber balls. . . . One of them dreamed they were getting a tattoo of birds such as the hedge sparrow, the dipper, the peacock, the ostrich, and the bird of paradise, all of them in flight or walking, whatever the individual bird's preference, in a circle around their upper arm. One of them dreamed about Three Dog Night and the Three Stooges and opening and closing doors.
>
> (131)

Not only is "they" explicitly three people here, as opposed to a more ambiguous and heterogeneous "many"; three itself is shown to split easily into two and one (upstairs and downstairs desks) and into one, one, one (dreams). This slipperiness between they and three (or, for that matter, between three and two/one and one/one/one) points to yet another feature about networks that makes them especially challenging to traditional character systems. For networks are "multiplicities" not because they are constructed of numerous parts, Galloway and Thacker argue, "but because they are organized around the principle of perpetual inclusion" which is a "question of a formal arrangement, not a finite count." What this means is not just that "networks can and must grow (adding nodes and edges) but, more important, that *networks are reconfigurable in new ways and at all scales*" (60–61). In short, because of the "multiplicity that inheres within every network"(12), a network is never just one. In *The Transformation* this self-difference is dramatized not just by its oscillation between "they" as indeterminate/fluctuating many, and "they" as a fixed/exact three, but by the constant tension between singular and plural that runs throughout the narrative in the form of a lack of agreement between grammatical subjects and objects: "they were *a pervert*" (177) instead of "they were *perverts*." In addition to highlighting this *formal* ambiguity on the part of networks, the oscillation between the indeterminacy of "many" and the exactness of "three" mirrors one of the most anxiety-provoking contradictions in the world of networking, as described by Boltanski and Chiapello: the "tension between the requirement of *flexibility* and the need to be someone—that is to possess a self endowed with *specificity* (a 'personality') and a certain *permanency in time*" (461). As Boltanksi and Chiapello elaborate, adaptability is a "basic requirement for circulating in networks," since "to adjust to a connexionist world, people must prove sufficiently malleable to pass through different universes while changing properties." Yet, in order to "interest" others, the networker must at the same time "be someone": "If he is merely his faculty for adapting, if he isn't someone, why attach oneself to him?" (461).

Like the contradiction between "being specific" and "being flexible," the anxiety provoked by the tension between being exactly three and being many is thus yet another thing that the obsessive discourse in *The Transformation* arguably reflects and tries to negotiate. For *three is already as much of a reticular organization as they.* This is already evinced by the metonymy of the upstairs and downstairs computers, which while clearly referring to a "they" of exactly three (two upstairs, one downstairs) is also quite literally a network: "They all set up their computers and one of them built a network that connected all the computers." Instead of reading the slippage between "they" and "three" as the sign of a failed poetics of networks, then—a failure to take the "philosophy of connection" to its logical endpoint and then *sustain it*— we could read it as making a series of more polemical and interesting points about the limits of network theory.

One thing that the shift from "they" back to "three" highlights is how the "principle of perpetual inclusion" makes networks very badly suited for explaining why social ties may fail to form, break off, or disappear. Networks can help us schematize extremely dense and complicated social connections, but not the most basic rupture or gap. Because of the "diachronic blindness" of networks,[31] to become disconnected in the "reticular universe" is to have never existed; Latour's ANT is thus, as Harman points out, a "philosophy of isolated instants." Even aside from this inability to narrate dynamic processes, even *ongoing states* of disaffiliation, disconnection, or exclusion cannot be described by ANT: negative relations that are just as fundamental to the formation and nature of currently existing groups as the positively existing "tie." But, as if exactly to compensate for this relentless positivity (and representational exclusion of exclusion), Spahr's narrative exaggerates the *gap* between different reticular "regions." In a similar vein, the asymmetry between "they" and "three" in *The Transformation* works against a formal aspect of connectionism Latour deliberately embraces: flatness. Like Facebook, ANT recognizes no distinction between strong and weak ties, but in the interests of "networking" or "expansionism" treats all associations equally. A tie is a tie: all have the same affective intensity, the same transient and fragile quality.[32] In conjunction with widening the concept of "actor" to include a new variety of nonhuman agents, to treat all ties as equal encourages a worldview in which "everything is connected." But to say "everything is connected" is to make connexionism utterly banal, returning us to the blandness of "the social" as universal explanation, which Latour appeals to ANT to combat. How then to write a narrative with a reticular protagonist that doesn't lead to this conclusion? By emphasizing that network's internal variability; its capability of being "reconfigurable at all scales."

Mirrored by the "back and forth" of the protagonist's "obsessive thinking,"[33] the slippage between "they" and "three" more interestingly implies that while "they" is larger, more indeterminate, and more heterogeneous, *the network of three is just as difficult and laborious to maintain.* This is evinced by the intensity of the three's struggle simply to keep their relationship going, as underscored once again by rules:

> When they sometimes met others who also configured themselves in three, they longed to ask them things, like did they too have a schedule for who slept in what bed? What did they do about those awkward moments when colleagues invited them and their partner to dinner? Did they too have a rule that made them mumble something about having more than one partner and could all of them come? What did they do when they wrote their name plus two on the office sign up sheet for the holiday party and then got an email from the secretary that roommates were not invited, only spouses? Did they too have a chore wheel where the wheel was cut into three wedges? But usually they were too shy. And they avoided becoming friends with these others like them as if people would make even more fun of them if they saw them with others like them.
>
> (178–79)

Note how the difficulty of staying three is reinforced by the three's failure to establish relations with *other* threes, a socially meaningful *absence* of connection that could not be registered as meaningful or even visible by ANT.[34] Reflected thus in the story as well as in the belabored quality of the discourse, this struggle becomes especially pronounced after one of the three decides, after his/her experience in the Pacific, to move back to the "islands on the Atlantic." After a "physically and emotionally hard" period of "moving back and forth," the two follow the one; in part because "moving back and forth . . . wore them down," but also because "the islands on the Atlantic were known for their perversions and various sexualities and they wanted to live some place known for its perversions and various sexualities" (122). At the same time, even when ensconced there, the three struggle to find the right concept for their alliance or formation, leading to a "back and forth" on the word *pervert* in particular:

> They embraced the word pervert when really it was probably an overstatement and the fact that they felt that everything was a metaphor against them did not mean they were that abnormal, that unacceptable.
>
> (171)

> Although they frequently adopted a haughty tone and called themselves perverts when asked about their sexuality, they greatly feared appearing overtly lecherous or perverse and as a result they abandoned all flirting and innuendo even though they had enjoyed flirting and innuendo a great deal when they were just one of a couple.
>
> (20)

While "pervert" is thus described as an "overstatement," the three also view it as meaning the contrary of "anything radical." "Once a friend of theirs who had surgically changed their gender asked them why they did not speak more publicly and explicitly about their relationship. The implication behind their comment was that perhaps they were more in the closet even though their friend did not suggest what they should come out as. When their friend asked them this they immediately felt guilty and wondered at the same time if the reason they did not come out was that they saw themselves more as perverts than anything radical" (175). The three choose not to identify as queer on similar grounds: "they told themselves that they did this out of respect because they were not sexually involved with people of the same gender" (173).

Yet, as dramatized at the level of both discourse and story, the fact that the romantic/sexual alliance of three is just as difficult to maintain, conceptually as well as practically, as the larger indefinite "they" has politically queer implications. For one thing, in highlighting the repetitive, rule-based, obsessional labor involved to sustain both formations, it calls attention to the *intersection* between ANT and what feminists now broadly call kin work, which is both a reproductive and an affective labor. The explicitly gendered concept of affective labor, in turn, overlaps to some degree with the neo-Marxist concept of immaterial labor that figures prominently in network-oriented studies of post-Fordism and the global information economy: while both involve the production of affects, subjectivities, and social relationships, the latter models itself on labor in the culture industries as opposed to female reproductive labor in the household *and also across households*, as anthropologist Micaela di Leonardo noted in her 1987 paper originally defining "kin work" specifically as the "creation, maintenance, and ritual celebration of *cross-household* ties"—a concept of kinship that defines it explicitly as *both* labor *and* networking and thus cuts through what Di Leonardo describes as an impasse in feminism between "the 'labor' and 'network' perspectives on women's lives" or the divided focus on women's nonmarket activities as either exploitative work or as social altruism.[35] Though the "work of kinship" is thus explicitly gendered (and the conception of it feminist) in the way ANT is not, the practices they involve are strikingly similar. These politically ambiguous overlaps are brought out all the more strongly by *The Transformation*'s insistent gender neutrality, as if to confirm the hope, voiced earliest by Gayle Rubin, that alternative kinship arrangements—which is to say, alternative *social* arrangements—have the power to produce ideas of gender still yet to be conceptualized.[36]

The striking similarity between the *kinds* of work involved in kin work and ANT; the fact that the sex-affective alliance of three seems just as difficult to sustain as the larger network they, suggests that kinship is, in fact, a kind of networking. Though the shift from the large-scale, amorphous "they" to the smaller finite "they" seems quite pointed (as if to suggest that the former somehow blocked the story of the latter from being fully told), Spahr's text thus resists being read as simply pitting kinship against network or privileging the social arrangements and values particular to the domestic realm over those of the "reticular universe." In fact, as Boltanski and Chiapello suggest, as a "system of rules governing who can be linked or affiliated to whom through exchange and interactions," kinship implicitly remains connexionist culture's dominant *metaphor* for networking. As one of the management authors cited by them writes, "If links can be created in the name of friendship, work, fraternity, they remain of a *kinship type* in the first instance. To live a highly [professional] life, the best thing is a well-constructed family universe. For the family represents *a primary network* that is less outmoded than people think and which, on the contrary, is undergoing massive changes" (133).

"Kinship" and "network" are thus far from construed as conceptual opposites in *The Transformation*, but rather shown to be coimplicated in ideologically complex and politically ambiguous ways. It is only after having been turned into they, after all, that they can think about what it means to be three. Conversely, it is only by their reverting back to being three that the reader of *The Transformation* is able to grasp how much the connectionist "principle of perpetual inclusion" leaves out when it comes to understanding the conditions that make the formation of certain social entities possible. What this suggests is not just the limits of actor-network-theory for theorizing exclusion's role in the constitution of that "primary" form of social arrangement, kinship, but how new configurations of kinship might lead to a more critical and politically astute theory of networking.

Notes

This essay grew out of a talk for a panel called "Poetry and Complex Systems: Global Ecologies and Poetic Form" at the December 2008 MLA in San Francisco; my thanks to the organizers and audience members. I would also like to thank Alex Woloch and Eric Hayot for encouraging me to think harder about some of the issues raised in this text and Chris Looby and Cindy Weinstein for inviting me to contribute it to the volume.

1. Tiziana Terranova, *Network Culture: Politics for the Information Age* (London: Pluto, 2004), 1.

2. Manuel Castells, *The Rise of the Network Society*, 2d ed. (Malden, MA: Blackwell, 2000), 508.

3. Luc Boltanski and Eve Chiapello, *The New Spirit of Capitalism*, trans. Gregory Elliot (London: Verso, 2005), 138. Further page references will be provided parenthetically within the text.

4. Castells, *The Rise of the Network Society*, 500.

5. Bruno Latour, *Reassembling the Social: An Introduction to Actor-Network-Theory* (Oxford: Oxford University Press, 2005), 124. Further page references will be provided parenthetically within the text.

6. Juliana Spahr, *The Transformation* (Berkeley: Atelos: 2007), 188. Further page references will be given parenthetically within the text.

7. This macro/micro distinction has most defined the field of sociology in the twentieth century (with the abstract study of structures and systems by

Parsons and Luhmann, on one side, and the study of face-to-face interactions by Goffman and Garfinkel on the other).

8. For Latour, the aesthetic of the interesting is thus an aesthetic of circulation, underscoring a link I've suggested elsewhere. See Sianne Ngai, "Merely Interesting," *Critical Inquiry* 34 (Summer 2008): 777–817.

9. Jennifer L. Fleissner, "Obsessional Modernity: The 'Institutionalization of Doubt,'" *Critical Inquiry* 34 (Autumn 2007): 106–34, 118.

10. A translation of psychologist Pierre Janet's *sentiment d'incomplétude*. See ibid., 118. Also see Jennifer L. Fleissner, *Women, Compulsion, Modernity: The Moment of American Naturalism* (Chicago: University of Chicago Press, 2004), 10.

11. See Latour, *Reassembling the Social*, 37. Latour contrasts the idea of the social as a "building in need of restoration" with his own idea of it as a "movement in need of continuation" as in performance or dance.

12. The prominence of adverbs in general seems nontrivial, since *continuously* and *patiently* modify verbs like *upkeeping* in the same way Latour's "mediators" modify actions.

13. Bruno Latour, *Science in Action: How to Follow Scientists and Engineers Through Society* (Cambridge: Harvard University Press, 1987), 223. Quoted in Graham Harman, *Prince of Networks: Bruno Latour and Metaphysics* (Melbourne: re.press, 2009), 54.

14. Harman, *Prince of Networks*, 102.

15. Bruno Latour, *We Have Never Been Modern*, trans. Catherine Porter (Cambridge: Harvard University Press, 1993), 126.

16. Max Weber, *The Protestant Ethic and the Spirit of Capitalism*, trans. Talcott Parsons (London: Routledge, 1992). On Weber's text as a "precursor account of obsessional neurosis" see Fleissner, "Obsessional Modernity," 113.

17. This is the case even as otherwise the two texts could not be more different in tone: Latour's highly charismatic and irreverent, Spahr's flat and suffused with "guilt" (111).

18. It is tempting to read this problematic as an instance of the negative aesthetic experience Spahr calls "connective paranoia" or of Bruce Robbins's closely related "sweatshop sublime": a "moment of consciousness which will not be converted into action" that comes about as a result of one's recognition of one's place in the global division of labor (or upon glimpsing "for a moment, the unimaginable face of society as a whole" [88]). But though I've written about Spahr and these themes before, I do not think paranoia or sweatshop sublime are the best affective concepts for thinking about *The Transformation*. The problem "they" come to confront through their tracing of connections is the problem not of paralyzed or suspended agency, but of excessive,

uncontrollable action. And while paranoia indexes one of the defining existential dilemmas of postmodernity, which Fredric Jameson described as a
"growing contradiction between lived experience and structure, or between a
phenomenological description of the life of an individual and a more properly
structural model of the conditions of existence of that experience," the problem
of the networked universe in *The Transformation* involves an *excessive proximity*
and even conflation of the local and global, phenomenological description and
structural model that is arguably just as unsettling. See Bruce Robbins, "The
Sweatshop Sublime," *PMLA* 117, no. 1 (January 2002): 84–97; Fredric Jameson,
"Cognitive Mapping," in Cary Nelson and Lawrence Grossberg, eds., *Marxism
and the Interpretation of Culture* (Urbana: University of Illinois Press, 1988),
347–57, 249.

19. In the same vein, see also their rules for "writing in the complex" (57–
58); the "map of poetry" (80); and the "elaborate chart" categorizing "options
for writers like them who came from afar" (92–93). Spahr, *The Transformation*.

20. As Alexander Galloway and Eugene Thacker note, "networks exist
through 'process'"; they are inherently dynamic. See *The Exploit: A Theory of
Networks* (Minneapolis: University of Minnesota Press, 2007), 61–62. Further
page references will be given parenthetically within the text. Other accounts
emphasize the very opposite; see note 28.

21. Graham Harman argues that "Latour simply cannot be understood if
this Janus-headed principle is overlooked." See Harman, *Prince of Networks*,
116.

22. Ian Osbourne notes the "inflated sense of responsibility" of obsessives, "a
deep seated, automatic tendency to feel accountable for anything bad that might
happen." See Ian Osbourne, *Tormenting Thoughts and Secret Rituals: The Hidden
Epidemic of Obsessive-Compulsive Disorder* (New York: Random House, 1998),
59. Quoted in Paul Cefalu, "What's So Funny about Obsessive-Compulsive
Disorder?" *PMLA* 124, no. 1 (January 2009): 44–58, 49.

23. Ngai, "Merely Interesting."

24. Terranova, *Network Culture*, 2.

25. This problem of knowing when to stop, or how to decide nonarbitrarily
on the limits of an actor-network, is acknowledged in an offhand joking fashion by Latour, but never really seriously confronted. For a particularly telling
moment on this topic in *Reassembling the Social*, see the dialogue between Professor and Student on 148.

26. For, as Galloway and Thacker note, when it comes to networks, shape
or pattern is essential: "material instantiation is *coextensive with* pattern formation" (*The Exploit* 35). Latour argues that "network" is a benchmark of "interesting," "well-written" accounts of the social. It is only these network-like texts

that "make the social appear in a certain way." But since to write the social is in effect to produce it—since the social is precisely *that which is made to appear through a certain kind of writing*—why *isn't* the network a "real" thing "out there" *as well as* a property of writing (*Reassembling the Social* 93), since from the ANT perspective the real thing is at least in part *constituted by* the writing?

27. Alex Woloch, *The One vs. the Many: Minor Characters and the Space of the Protagonist in the Novel* (Princeton: Princeton University Press, 2003), 130.

28. See Latour, *Reassembling the Social*, 54, n 54: "It would be fairly accurate to describe ANT as being half Garfinkel and half Greimas."

29. We thus surprisingly find a discourse of literary value at the very heart of *Reassembling the Social*: a guide to how to write flexible, yet at the same time extremely concrete and specific, network-like accounts of social forma-tion which will by definition contribute to the reality of the entity described. Given this embrace of both aesthetic evaluation and literary theory as fully relevant to ANT, it seems worthwhile to note Latour's indifference to the dis-tinction between narrating and describing, as reflected in his definition of a network-like account of the social as a "narrative *or* a description . . . where all the actors do something and don't just sit there" (128). Latour's unconcern with the difference reflects an unconcern with the incompatibility between the kind of "character system" that ANT calls for—one in which the concrete and specific nature of each individual agent matters absolutely—and a plot so radically committed to "ceaseless," "continuous" transformation that it changes the identity of the actors from one moment to the next. While, according to Castells, the "network society" is characterized by the *"preeminence* of social morphology *over* social action" (508), privileging a static, formal arrangement of individual characters at the direct expense of narrative, Latour maintains that one can have both a radically open, enlarged, and heterogeneous character system, *and* a radically dynamic and active plot. Yet actors in ANT "have no choice but to occupy punctiform cinematic frames"; their "utter concreteness," with each defined entirely by the sum of their associations with others with "nothing held in reserve," requires that "they be incarcerated in an instant" (105). ANT could thus be described a poetics *of activity without development*. It is true that development is by no means a prerequisite for narrative: as Lukács and Fleissner show, naturalism is perhaps the handiest example of a kind of narrative filled with restless activity in which even major characters do not "grow." Yet at an even more basic level, one cannot represent "flows of causal efficacy" or actions *succeeding one another in time*, without individual agents who endure for more than just an instant. In spite of Latour's disregard for "mere displacements without transformation," then, transformation depends on a minimal degree of non-transformation (130). If everything acts upon or

effects everything at once, or if everything changes *all the time*, our experience of the world would be that of Hume's skeptic: with the entire world reinvented from instant to instant. There is thus a sense in which good ANT texts can really *only* be descriptions. And yet it is exactly narrative, not description, that Latour seems explicitly to call for when he praises a network-like account of the social as a text "where all the actors *do something* and don't just sit there."

30. Latour even advocates using the awkward term *worknet* because, unlike *network,* it highlights this relation rather than obfuscating it: "*Work*-nets could allow one *to see the labor* that goes on in laying down *net*-works; the first as an active mediator, the second as a stabilized set of intermediaries" (*Reassembling the Social* 132). Making this labor visible requires an *intensification of activity* that Latour seems to privilege for its own sake. "Work-net" is a better "benchmark of literary quality" than "network" *because the term itself* functions as an "active mediator" (131, 132). It is thus as if Latour wants to highlight the labor of "networking" less to critique the projective city's privileging of activity than to demonstrate his adherence to it. ANT—the production of network-like narratives/descriptions—appeals to Latour because it calls for *increased* vigilance and activity; because it calls on the sociologist/writer *to work harder.*

31. Galloway and Thacker, *The Exploit*, 33.

32. Flatness is a desirable quality for Latour, who refers to the need for "clamps" (174) to prevent "the social" from popping out from behind his traced connections and, in his own words, "keep the landscape obsessively flat" (174). See "How to Keep the Social Flat" in *Reassembling the Social*, 166–72.

33. While, on the one hand, they "worry people knew they were a pervert" and thus "resort to secrecy about their personal life when meeting new people," these anxieties are countered with "loud celebrations" such as "mak[ing] out in public while standing in line at the grocery" (177).

34. Again, due to ANT's "diachronic blindness" and inability to model negative relations—exclusions, disconnections—as significant factors in the formation of societies. Since, according to ANT, what the social consists of is only ties, there is no room in the theory to account for how the *absence* of a social tie might in itself be *socially meaningful* (or, indeed, relevant to the formation of groups). Latour, *Reassembling the Social.*

35. Micaela di Leonardo, "The Female World of Cards and Holidays: Women, Families, and the Work of Kinship," *Signs: Journal of Women in Culture and Society* 12, no. 2 (1987): 440–453, 442.

36. Gayle Rubin, "The Traffic in Women: Notes on the 'Political Economy' of Sex," in Linda Nicholson, ed., *The Second Wave: A Reader in Feminist Theory* (New York: Routledge, 1997), 27–62.

Afterword

Are Aesthetic Models the Best Way to Talk About the Artfulness of Literary Texts?

CHARLES ALTIERI

My strongest response to this book is surprise mixed with considerable admiration. These essays are strikingly inventive in exploring such a variety of possible uses for the aesthetic in relation to concerns shaped by social and political life. I am grateful to the authors for bringing such intelligence and energy to a topic that I had long abandoned as hopelessly vague and abstract. But I am still not convinced that discourses on the "aesthetic" can be very useful for literary work, especially for the novel, which has a long and troubled relation with its own artifactuality. (Cultivating intricate internal relationships seems both to produce and to obfuscate perspicuous relations with the actual world.) In fact these essays intensify my doubts because they seem to show that the only way, or the best way, a language foregrounding "aesthetic" can be effective in dealing with history and politics is to build predicates for social use into the definition of *aesthetic* from the start. The essays concentrate on how particular aesthetic properties might be appropriated for social use. But to achieve this goal they have to separate these properties from what I will call the more comprehensive aesthetic processes that give a distinctive cast to aesthetic experience as a synthesis of these various properties.[1] On one level this could be cause for criticism, because most of the essays talk about the aesthetic rather than demonstrate the power of texts to establish distinctive modes of experience. Yet I think this stems from an honest and intense realization that what matters in literary experience is not how the imagination aestheticizes but how the imaginative labor develops various modes of articulating significance for particulars by treating them as aspects of concrete ways of reflecting on and participating in experience. Were the essays to focus on a distinctively aesthetic cast to that experience, I think they would have to displace literary intensities into misleading analogies with the other arts and ignore what is distinctive for an art based on the medium of language.

These essays are often bold and precise in stating the importance of reconciling aspects of the aesthetic with the historical and political interests still dominating Americanist literary criticism. Bentley, for example, develops possibilities for countering our disenchantment with disenchantment, and Castiglia speaks for many of the essayists in his call for an "aesthetics beyond the actual" that might promise sources of enchantment and empowerment in what is felt to be a dark time for the society at large. But they do not allay my doubts that talk of the aesthetic will cure our sense of malaise, in part because they do so well in directly engaging materials for which the aesthetic is not in fact central. So one almost has to ask why it might matter that most of the essays fail to (or refuse to) honor a crucial distinction between aesthetic properties employed in texts and conditions of aesthetic experience in which a variety of properties function together to establish the kind of event that has traditionally been proclaimed as somehow denying referential functions because the state of attention becomes valuable in itself. In one sense this can be considered a typical problem when a discipline shaped by historicist concerns tries to expand to accommodate "the aesthetic." But I have become increasingly convinced that there is a significant positive side to the preference for aesthetic properties rather than aesthetic experience. Therefore I will try to show why "aesthetic experience" is not a very good way to talk about the power of literary work because that notion has been developed primarily for arts that do not have the advantages (and problems) of language as their fundamental medium. Then I will suggest as an alternative language for verbal art a simple focus on how we talk about imaginative labor to build worlds out of linguistic resources.

Since I cannot mount any argument at all if I attend carefully to individual essays within my space limit, I will have to trust that my gratitude to them is everywhere apparent. Yet I have to mention a more specific gratitude to two features of their arguments. Bentley's and Ellison's essays strike me as doing an especially good job of establishing a sense of the historical urgency informing our need to recuperate what can be accomplished by works of literature in a profession now disenchanted with disenchantment and eager to find new political implications for literary experience not pervaded by rhetorics of resistance and demand. Second, and even more important, there is a shared sense in most of the essays that this is a unique historical moment we would fail were we not to find ways to bring the aesthetic and the political into conjunction: with the election of Obama we can plausibly hope for improvements in social justice and in the U.S. renouncing some of its imperiousness toward the rest of the world. Therefore there can be a renewed sense of the stakes involved in thinking clearly about what roles our profession can play as the Obama years continue to unfold.

Given these stakes, it should not be surprising that most of the essays concentrate on developing possible immediate loosely political uses for specific aesthetic properties. The essays identify the aesthetic with dream states or play or revolution or counterfactuals or various kinds of knowledge as if a critical tradition weakened by aestheticization could recast the power of the "aesthetic." While this is a reasonable reaction to our disenchantment, it also generates a potential problem that we have to engage. Because of the urgency to find direct uses for these aesthetic properties, it turns out that what might make them distinctively aesthetic comes almost to disappear as any particular essay develops the practical functions. Let me try to illustrate the situation here by drawing an analogy with the philosopher J. L. Austin's concept of "trouser-words." Faced with the difficulty of fixing meaning for such a notoriously vague, equivocal expression as *real,* Austin argues that we should look for the implied concept or term that is actually wearing the trousers and asserting the authority (this is British humor after all).[2] Then we see that something is perceived as "real" because it is not fake or not illusory or not a forgery. The negative judgments wear the trousers.

In our essays we find that the aesthetic must be supplemented by positive rather than negative terms. But it remains the case that the supplements wear the trousers. As a test case, imagine how often you can proceed in these essays while simply ignoring or bracketing the language of "aesthetic" so that you can concentrate on the meat of the argument, especially when the author gets down to the particular case. At other times the aesthetic properties idealized prove difficult to reconcile with one another, so authors have a good reason to minimize the case for their distinctiveness.

For example, if we stress play and dream, what will we do with apparently justified claims that the aesthetic enhances our sense of the actual and cultivates a critical concreteness that exposes our quotidian imaginings as just fantasies? But if we stress knowledge, what difference in fact does the aesthetic component make in our gathering that knowledge, especially a knowledge that is suspicious of those other aesthetic properties?

The traditional solution to this problem has been to bite the philosophical bullet and insist that the aesthetic properties can have their full force only when they are features of overall aesthetic experiences. If we go this route, we probably have to stress various ways that this experience is different from practical experience. And this obviously complicates immensely any critical position that tries to reconnect this distinctiveness to political and historical projects. For example, if we go the traditional philosophical route we have to correlate two competing claims—that the arts "realize" a density within experience by developing modes of attunement to the world more sensitive than the instruments of empirical understanding, and that the arts have the power to separate themselves from or negate versions of the real produced by those understandings. And the efforts at correlation confront substantial problems. As Loughran shows, claims for aesthetic experience typically foster a contemplative, relatively timeless attitude toward histori- cal materials because the work presents a world for the imagination rather than representing a world for practical judgment. I would add that because of this stress on presentation, aesthetic experience is set against conceptual knowledge of all kinds: the work is singular, and its distinguishing quality is a synthetic or multivalenced expressiveness not reducible to the structures of oppositions on which concepts are based. Aesthetic experience need not be autonomous in the strong sense of claiming separation from life, but its connections to practical life require something like Hale's concern for alter- ity in relation to our standard practical discourses. Finally, aesthetic experi- ence makes the medium central to the expressive force of the presentation so that any language of "representation" will seem thin and insensitive.

The medium creates a subtlety of presentation where the aspects of color, line, tone, and movement at once establish their own expressive power and invite metaphorical uses of that power that are not reducible to concepts. So the theory of the arts must cultivate the language of non- discursive significance (now in the guise of alterity). And such a language will always be hard-pressed to avoid the temptation toward mysticism that emerges in the rhetoric of artists as different as Mondrian, Rothko, Martha Graham, or even classical masters like Beethoven.

I think we best honor the work in these essays if we allow ourselves to explore how literary experience might make use of aesthetic properties without necessarily submitting to the language of post-Kantian aesthetics, which is for most purposes simply to say "without submitting to aesthetics."[3] After all, while literary texts were central to Kant's and Hegel's formulation of aesthetics, the picture changed drastically during the course of the nineteenth century (where the popular writers simply refused to write as if they read German and French philosophical aesthetics). Aesthetic theory was primarily derived from and primarily applied to visual art and music, precisely because any "use" value would have to rely on models that challenged the priority of language. Music redirects sound by relying almost exclusively on its capacity to provide structure and suggestiveness to shapes and themes that exist almost purely in a realm where there can be very little talk of "meaning." And vision does engage the world of conventional meaningfulness, but it populates that world with details and with forces that clearly have no direct conceptual component. Literature has a different mode of mediation. So I propose that the cultural task provoked by this collection of essays is the experiment of seeing how differently we can talk about literary experience, because it is an art made of language and it is usually devoted to challenging not the resources of language so much as limited uses of those resources. The product will probably look a good deal like traditional aesthetics. But it might have at least two differences. It will foreground why language matters and so will grow much closer to rhetoric than traditional aesthetics allows because of its suspicion of language and the practical orientation language traditionally cultivates. Moreover, this experiment will have a more intricate relationship to the power of concepts. It can still emphasize concrete display rather than argument. But it might be able to show the sources of the display in argumentative concerns and take satisfaction in the ways that criticism tries to adapt what is displayed for participating in practical concerns.

Let me conclude by taking up the two differences that make the language of aesthetic experience problematic for literary experience. The traditional modernist in me is still disturbed by the willingness of several of the essayists to deny the basic differences between the rhetorical and the aesthetic on which idealist and romantic traditions of aesthetics were founded. But is traditional aesthetics sufficient grounds for denying how Cahill, Wilson, Castiglia, Bentley, and Ellison treat the aesthetic domain as a generator of properties to be assessed for their utility in public life? Their arguments seem to me fundamentally defensible if we see that at their core they are trying to get back behind Kant, to a time when the sharp split between the rhetorical and a commitment to something like the aesthetic did not exist. So long as the aim of literature was to move and to delight by marshaling the powers of language, literary art was fundamentally an extension of the power of rhetoric to persuade by appealing to concrete emotions. There could simply be different applications of rhetoric—to social agendas and to developing elaborate displays of behavior intended to exemplify the possible consequences of feelings and actions.

Of course we cannot quite go back behind Kant's disinterested "purposiveness without purpose." But we can explore different ways of cultivating that concreteness of the aesthetic object without basing our account on how the medium establishes alternatives to the domain of the concepts produced by the understanding. (After all, we have less faith in supplanting the understanding by higher powers of reason than Kant did; and we have stronger resources for concentrating on how language carries exemplary actions that need not produce true representations in order to be intelligible and significant.) So I will try to elaborate a different way of talking about the powers of concrete display that are central in literary experience's manner of implicating the practical world. This task I think can be handled simply by emphasizing what the imagination can produce when it concentrates on the powers made available by language. Then we need not treat the ontology of literary signs as parallels to the ontology of musical and visual signs. Literature redirects language by relying on its capacity to render worlds. And this capacity is best measured by the range of language games that can be elicited by texts and projected for audiences. Playing with the limitations of concepts is itself a language game fundamental to Wittgenstein's fascination with the difference between referential and expressive and modeling possibilities of linguistic practice.

On the simplest level, the labor of imagination evokes the various arts of ornament where the imagination becomes central for its ability to play with design and create variety in how we engage the world. As we get more practical, we can easily relate the literary to the rhetorical without identifying them entirely. Rhetoric becomes the imaginative labor of using particulars with persuasive force that supports and directs argument. In contrast, we take texts as primarily literary when imaginative labor is focused on the metaphorical elaboration of particulars so that they have force primarily through the concrete actions they display and elaborate. Then the fullest language for the labor of imagination is elicited by literature's many ways of using the hypothetical activity of practical speculation, typically constructed as the display of possible worlds. In literary experience it is crucial we admit two different foci of hypothesis, often fused by the richest texts. One is a performative level engaging the question who could I become or how could I act linguistically if certain conditions were presupposed and constructed to make a concrete world. The second focus locates hypothetical interest in how the values emerging in the concrete world displayed might affect the way in which we talk about possibilities in the world we have to live in. Here one could cite as an especially clear example of this kind of attention Beam's display of how intricacy of tone becomes a vehicle making mutual recognition possible in texts by Woolson and James.

On the microlevel I want to extend the language of the hypothetical to cover the full range of affective experiences created by the text, especially to its capacity to create empathy through the work these affects perform. After all, the primary question enabling empathic response is some version of "what would it be like for this person to have to face this situation and speak these words or have to deal with these persons and demands in the process?" Of course something like an aesthetic attitude has to be invoked if we are to dwell in empathy rather than insist on making up our minds about the best practical way to proceed. But, rather than base the contemplation on aesthetics, why not base it simply on the realization that we can be interested in empathy and a reflective attitude is necessary for its full elaboration? We refuse practical attitudes not because we are dealing with "art" but because we have an interest in testing what our imaginations can make of situations or of authors' engagements in those situations.

The corresponding macrolevel is a testing of imagination's capacities to totalize. Agents often hold off practical judgment to explore how various elements in situations might come together to provide the kinds of large pictures that provide contemplative frames in which we assess practical options. Again we have interests that can be activated simply by judgments that this particular textual situation affords reflective capacities that are worth our putting off any rush to practical judgment: the possibility of understanding historical contexts or contemplating possible long-term consequences because of what is implicit in the overt actions might make it worth our while to dwell on how this author develops the interconnections possible in the range of actions he or she brings together. If we attribute this reflective attitude to aesthetic forces, we cannot avoid the intellectual history that tells us how difficult it is to connect what refuses to represent the world to any language of values sustained by that world. So it might be better simply to derive the contemplative mode from a basic account of human interests in avoiding the consequences of shortsighted practical judgment. We could even bring the aesthetic inside our story of interests. For we can argue that because of the influence of the aesthetic in Western culture, writers have learned to provide cues inviting us to dwell in and dwell on their imaginative labors to provide large-scale contexts within which the actions take place. Literature learns from the aesthetic to make it own distinctive uses in accord with the powers of language to suspend practical reference—not for some other world of dream or beauty but for a richer sense of what we might do in the world we are given. Then even the aesthetic must stand before the tribunal of an enlightened pragmatic spirit that literary texts have the linguistic capacity to invoke.

There is no space for an elaborate application of this theoretical position. And I think there is no need for it because I am only trying to describe what we typically do as literary critics in a way that brings out how foreign the discourse of philosophical aesthetics is to that practice. There are similarities in our concerns for the performative and for the tension between display or presentation as opposed to representations that appeal to stable concepts. But there are much simpler and less problematic ways of accounting for these features of literary experience than we can develop once we make the fateful turn to invoking the discourses of aesthetics, especially if we want to talk about the novel. So, in lieu of a fuller argument, I will only point to what I see as exemplary qualities in two of these essays—one devoted to how the aesthetic becomes incorporated in imaginative action rather than being invoked to explain the status of that action and the other offering a way to develop a text's capacity to set action against the promise of conceptual models.

Castiglia's essay on *The Marble Faun* offers a powerful analysis of how an interpreter can use aesthetic categories to flesh out the imaginative action rather than provide the experiential frame for it. In fact, while his emphasis is on criticism rather than performance, he presents the text as the imagining of what the world would be like if certain conditions hold. Fundamental to these conditions is how the two main female characters in the narrative, Miriam and Hilda, are each shaped by competing "perspectives on aesthetics" (124). Each of these perspectives proves a block to developing their full capacity for intimacy. So in this case their aesthetic orientations provide a negative frame setting off how the action stages the major male characters' "possibilities for inventive intimacies" (122). These possibilities derive from "a new aesthetic theory that combines rather than separates, imagines rather than judges, and acknowledges that relationships" with what remains other to our moral orders "might transform, rather than confirm, our interior conceptions of truth and beauty" (128). He finds this theory in Schiller. But he does not spend time arguing that the shape of the reader's experience follows Schiller's model. Rather he shows that the actions of the male characters align with Schiller's aesthetic in order to achieve this intimacy and provide examples for the audience of dispositional traits that may well produce similar results. By shifting from readers to characters, Castiglia can stress how the narrative action exemplifies opening for social life "a space of negotiable and compensatory intimacy" (130) based on contiguity that avoids the oppositional orientation shaping the women's interactions with that society. The text is not an illustration of an argument, but does serve concretely to perform the rhetorical purpose of directing the imagination to attitudes worth reflecting on for the values they define as possible states of spirit.

Castiglia's essay nicely merges rhetorical and literary interests to project through the text the practical possibilities for idealized values. Freedman's essay on James's *The Golden Bowl* explores a contrary linguistic practice by setting James's constructed action against any concept that might sponsor rhetorical projections. So Freedman restores the fundamental power claimed for aesthetic experience to counter prevailing conceptual practices without any mystification about formal relations or claims to the status of distinctive experience that may require a language of autonomy. First Freedman establishes an admirably clear and subtle account of economic game theory. Then he turns to how the novel stages an action where Maggie wins because she is in an economic position to break the rules and act in a way that opens her to irrational risk. Freedman needs no claims for an additional aesthetic dimension because he can show how James's imaginative labor stages a complexity of embedded human relations for which almost any conceptual structure will prove inadequate. The conditions of persons triumph over the adequacy of ideas about these persons.

I will quote Freedman at length because I want readers to hear how much he can make of the power of concrete display without gussifying the picture with claims to distinctively "aesthetic knowledge":

Anticipating the brave new world of game theory that was to prove so important to contemporary economic thought, and anticipating even more acutely the extension of economic analysis into understandings that have followed it of the transactions of everyday life, the novel thus presciently critiques these developments, putting in their place a view of life in which precisely the means that assure victory ensure defeat, those that allow for the accomplishment of gain negate it. And in doing so *The Golden Bowl* vividly displays the kinds of knowledge that fiction has to offer in a world where the economic has risen to social hegemony.

(256)

Because of James's intense particularity, he develops the kinds of economic thinking that would ally him now with the school of "behavioral economics" that stresses how often irrationality and "self-balking" behaviors pervade our economic activity. But he does it in a way that also challenges those economist's staged expectations that rationality is an adequate ideal for practical economic decisions against which we judge that irrationality. Rationality and irrationality are themselves embedded inextricably in Maggie's trying to find a path of behavior she can live with.

I stress this particularity more than Freedman does because I think his provisionally taking on the economist cap blinds him to one dimension of the action in James's novel. This dimension matters because it has been a central theme for those who want to emphasize James's aestheticism—the possibility that the novel refuses to judge Maggie's action as a failure but instead just characterizes it as necessary for her as an extension of the character the novel has realized for her. I agree with this aspect of the aestheticist position. Even though Freedman persuasively argues that the outcome of Maggie's decision is not very desirable—exile of the two people with whom she was closest and regaining a husband's seemingly painfully desexualized and "hypnotized" love (256)—I think the important point is not the desirability of the outcome but its necessity. It seems to me that her decision was the only possible one for Maggie if she were to sustain a sense of herself. There is probably no point in judgment here because no alternative action by which to measure whether she succeeds or fails even becomes thinkable. But I do not think one has to base this argument on aestheticist concerns for singularity. We can attribute our sense of necessity for Maggie simply to how the hypothetical fictive world gets displayed. It is the specificity of our attention to Maggie that makes the action seem of a piece with her life and so resistant to any judgment that imposes conceptual contexts about desirable outcomes. And this particularity is where the Jamesian novel departs from even the work of the most radical behavioral economists: what readers of Maggie come to know is that justice is immanent to action. There is no Maggie outside this action—not simply because of the tautology that she lives a fictional life but also because she lives a life within a sense of necessity, and paradoxically of freedom to express that necessity, that qualifies and complicates what an economic judgment might be. Actions need not generate binary oppositions of success and failure: they are simply there, like our lives.

Notes

1. This tendency to isolate properties helps explain why the essays rely on a very small range of work done in aesthetic theory. The omission of Adorno as an aesthetic theorist (rather than the social theorist Lott invokes) is especially striking. And, while I do not want to be picky, the treatments of topics like Kant's disinterestedness or Schiller's sense of imagination seem something less than thorough. For example, Schiller stresses play, but makes play responsible for developing concrete universals where sense joins the domain of ideas. The only philosophers who seem to matter in these essays are Judith Butler and Jacques Rancière, probably because they do exactly what the essays do—promote social uses of the aesthetic without worrying about problematic linkages between how forms of organizing the senses work in particular art works and how they work in social life. And both combine phenomenology's concerns with intimate self-awareness with a Foucauldian attention to how culture produces categories for sorting experience.

EDITORS' NOTE: Circumstances prevented Altieri from reviewing some of the essays in this volume or taking into account the final revisions made by the authors.

2. J. L. Austin, *Sense and Sensibilia*, reconstructed from the manuscript notes by G. J. Warnock, 2d ed. (Oxford: Oxford University Press, 1962), 70. There is an interesting, almost literal, manifestation of this trouser phenomenon in Cavitch's citing of a late-nineteenth-century *Atlantic Monthly* statement that "aesthetics is still the vaguest and most fantastic branch of psychology," then Cavitch's adding, "It makes a good deal of practical and also political sense if, for 'most fantastic,' we hear 'riskiest,' and if, for 'psychology,' we hear 'the psychology of freedom'" (87). Notice here the strange affinity with Derrida's concept of the supplement, the qualifier that in the end determines the meaning, but always in a vulnerable fashion.

3. I think it is difficult to identify literary experience with aesthetic experience without running into the problem of just how other is the world of the aesthetic from the practical and therefore just how other is anything we might be tempted to recuperate as the knowledge deriving from the experience. Hale's essay seems a case in point because I worry that there is a

pervasive ambiguity in her two uses of the term *alterity*, which stems from how such experiences resist the authority of concepts. One sense is comprised by Nussbaum's claim that alterity is a productive difference calling attention to the mind's powers to work beyond the limitations of its conceptual structures and the other is Butler's poststructuralist sense where the alterity is absolute—one can see only the limits of one's own perspective and learn to let the other be. Here even a rhetoric of "care" would seem presumptuous because one would have no warrant to trust in one's own sense of the ethical power of that term.

Contributors

CHARLES F. ALTIERI is professor of English at the University of California, Berkeley. He is the author of *The Particulars of Rapture: An Aesthetics of the Affects* (Cornell University Press, 2003), *Painterly Abstraction in Modernist American Poetry* (Cambridge University Press, 1989), and many other books and articles.

DORRI BEAM recently published *Style, Gender, and Fantasy in Nineteenth-Century American Women's Writing* (Cambridge University Press, 2010). She is the author of a number of published and forthcoming essays, including "Transcendental Erotics, Same-Sex Desire, and *Ethel's Love-Life*," in a special issue of *ESQ* on women and transcendentalism, ed. Jana Argersinger and Phyllis Cole (2011); "Harriet Prescott Spofford and the Politics of Ornament," in Ivy Wilson and Dana Luciano, eds., *Unauthorized States: Antinomies of the Nation and Other Subversive Genealogies*; and "Fuller, Women Writers, and Feminist Idealism," in Brigitte Bailey and Conrad E. Wright, eds., *Margaret Fuller and Her Circles*.

NANCY BENTLEY is professor of English and chair of the English Department at the University of Pennsylvania. The author of *The Ethnography of Manners* (Cambridge University Press, 1995), she recently published *Frantic*

Panoramas: American Literature and Mass Culture, 1870–1920 (University of Pennsylvania Press, 2009) and is completing a book entitled "New World Kinship and the American Novel."

EDWARD CAHILL is assistant professor of English at Fordham University, and has completed a book entitled *Liberty of the Imagination: Aesthetic Theory, Literary Form, and Politics in the Early United States* (University of Pennsylvania Press, forthcoming). He has published essays in *American Literature, Early American Literature,* and elsewhere.

CHRISTOPHER CASTIGLIA is liberal arts research professor of English and senior scholar in the Center for American Literary Studies at Penn State University. He is the author of *Bound and Determined: Captivity, Culture-Crossing, and White Womanhood from Mary Rowlandson to Patty Hearst* (University of Chicago Press, 1996) and *Interior States: Institutional Consciousness and the Inner Life of Democracy in the Antebellum United States* (Duke University Press, 2008). He coedited Walt Whitman's novel *Franklin Evans, or The Inebriate: A Tale of the Times* (Duke University Press, 2007), as well as a special issue of *ESQ* on new approaches to nineteenth-century American literature and sexuality. His new book, coauthored with Christopher Reed (University of Minnesota Press, 2011) is called *If Memory Serves: Gay Men, AIDS, and the Promise of the Queer Past.*

MAX CAVITCH is associate professor of English at the University of Pennsylvania. He is the author of *American Elegy: The Poetry of Mourning from the Puritans to Whitman* (University of Minnesota Press, 2007) as well as essays on a variety of topics in *American Literary History, Contemporary Psychoanalysis, Early American Literature, Senses of Cinema, Screen, Victorian Poetry,* and numerous other journals and collections.

JULIE ELLISON is professor of American culture, English, and art and design at the University of Michigan, where she has taught since 1980. Her scholarly work focuses on two areas: transatlantic cultures of the eighteenth and nineteenth centuries, with particular emphasis on gender, genre, emotion, and politics, and, more recently, the impacts and implications of civic engagement in the production of cultural knowledge. The University of Chicago Press published her third book, *Cato's Tears and the Making of Anglo-American Emotion,* in 1999. Her articles have appeared in *American Literature, Studies in Romanticism, American Literary History, Critical Inquiry, ELH, MLQ,* and in a number of edited volumes. Ellison served as founding director of Imagining America: Artists and Scholars in Public Life, a consortium of ninety colleges and universities. Since 2003 she has worked on a number of collaborative projects with academics and artists in South Africa and Canada. She lectured in New Zealand as a Fulbright senior specialist in 2007.

MARY ESTEVE teaches in the English Department at Concordia University and is the author of *The Aesthetics and Politics of the Crowd in American Literature* (Cambridge University Press, 2003). She has published in *American Literary History, ELH,* and the *Yale Journal of Criticism* and is currently developing two research projects, one on narratives of redistribution in late nineteenth- and early twentieth-century American literature, the other on the literary and cultural discourse of happiness and normativity in the mid twentieth century.

JONATHAN FREEDMAN is professor of English at the University of Michigan. He is the author of *Professions of Taste: Henry James, British Aestheticism, and Commodity Culture* (Stanford University Press, 1990), *The Temple of Culture: Assimilation, Aggression, and The Making of Literary Anglo-America* (Oxford University Press, 2000), and *Klezmer America: Jewishness, Ethnicity, Modernity* (Columbia University Press, 2009).

DOROTHY J. HALE is professor of English and director of graduate studies at the University of California, Berkeley. Her books include *Social Formalism: The Novel in Theory from Henry James to the Present* (Stanford University Press, 1998) and *The Novel: An Anthology of Criticism and Theory, 1900–2000* (Blackwell, 2006). "Aesthetics and the New Ethics" is part of her current book project, *The Novel and the New Ethics*. Additional work related to this new project includes *"On Beauty* as Beautiful? The Problem of Novelistic Aesthetics by way of Zadie Smith" (*Contemporary Literature,* forthcoming) as well as recently published essays in *Narrative* and *The Cambridge Companion to the Twentieth-Century English Novel.*

CHRISTOPHER LOOBY is professor of English and the director of the Americanist Research Colloquium at the University of California, Los Angeles, as well as president of C19: The Society of Nineteenth-Century Americanists. He is the author of *Voicing America: Language, Literary Form, and the Origins of the United States* (University of Chicago Press, 1996) and he edited *The Complete Civil War Journal and Selected Letters of Thomas Wentworth Higginson* (University of Chicago Press, 2000). Recently he wrote an introduction for Robert Montgomery Bird's 1836 novel *Sheppard Lee, Written by Himself* (nyrb, 2009) and he coedited, with Christopher Castiglia, a special issue of *ESQ* on new approaches to nineteenth-century American literature and sexuality.

ERIC LOTT is professor of English at the University of Virginia. The author of *Love and Theft: Blackface Minstrelsy and the American Working Class* (Oxford University Press, 1993) as well as *The Disappearing Liberal Intellectual* (Basic Books, 2006), he is completing "Tangled Up in Blue: The Cultural Contradictions of American Racism."

TRISH LOUGHRAN is associate professor of English and history at the University of Illinois. She is the author of *The Republic in Print: Print Culture in the Age of U.S. Nation Building, 1770–1870* (Columbia University Press, 2007), which won the Oscar Kenshur Book Prize.

ELISA NEW is professor of English at Harvard University. Her books include *The Line's Eye: Poetic Experience, American Sight* (Harvard University Press, 1999), *The Regenerate Lyric: Theology and Innovation in American Poetry* (Cambridge University Press, 1993), and *Jacob's Cane: A Jewish Family's Journey from the Four Lands of Lithuania to the Ports of London and Baltimore; A Memoir in Five Generations* (Basic Books, 2009).

SIANNE NGAI is professor of English at Stanford University, and the author of *Ugly Feelings* (Harvard University Press, 2005). She has completed *Our Aesthetic Categories: The Zany, the Cute, and the Interesting* (Harvard University Press, forthcoming).

WENDY STEINER is the Richard L. Fisher Professor of English at the University of Pennsylvania, past chair of the Penn English Department, and founder of the Penn Humanities Forum. Among her books on modern literature and visual art are *The Real Real Thing: The Model in the Mirror of Art* (University of Chicago Press, 2010), *Venus in Exile: The Rejection of Beauty in Twentieth-Century Art* (University of Chicago Press, 2002), and *The Scandal of Pleasure: Art in an Age of Fundamentalism* (University of Chicago Press, 1997). Her cultural criticism has appeared widely in U.S. and UK papers. Most recently, Steiner has turned to multimedia opera, as librettist and producer of *The Loathly Lady* (2009; composer Paul Richards; artist John Kindness) and *Biennale* (in process; composer Paul Richards; artist Andrew Lucia).

CINDY WEINSTEIN is the author of *The Literature of Labor and the Labors of Literature: Allegory in Nineteenth-Century American Fiction* (Cambridge University Press, 1995) as well as *Family, Kinship, and Sympathy in Nineteenth-Century American Literature* (Cambridge University Press, 2006). She coedited *The Concise Companion to American Literature, 1900–1950* (Blackwell, 2008), edited *The Cambridge Companion to Harriet Beecher*

Stowe (Cambridge University Press, 2004), and has published numerous essays in *Leviathan, American Literature, Nineteenth-Century Literature,* and elsewhere.

IVY G. WILSON is associate professor of English at Northwestern University and the author of *Specters of Democracy: Blackness and the Aesthetics of Politics in the Antebellum U.S.* (Oxford University Press, 2011) as well as recent articles in *ESQ, Arizona Quarterly,* and *PMLA*. His other work in U.S. literary studies includes *The Works of James M. Whitfield:* America *and Other Writings by a Nineteenth-Century African American Poet,* coedited with Robert S. Levine (University of North Carolina Press, 2011), and *At the Dusk of Dawn: Selected Poetry and Prose of Albery Allson Whitman* (Northeastern University Press, 2009).

Index

Aesthetics *(continued)*
178, 291–92, 313; revolutionary, 20,
56–65, 70; of temporality, 22, 198,
211, 213; Western, 5, 293, 298–99,
400; *see also* Experience, aesthetic;
Network aesthetic; Properties,
aesthetic
Aesthetics of Cultural Studies, The (ed.
Berubé), 7
Aesthetics in a Multicultural Age (ed.
Elliott et al.), 7
Affect, 4–6, 9, 27, 64, 79, 105, 118–19,
124, 128, 242, 315–16, 322–23, 329–31,
335–38, 342–44, 347n21, 377–78,
385–87, 399
Affective labor, 385–87
African American art, 26, 60, 91, 293
African American literature, 3, 11, 17,
20, 26, 42, 56–70, 292–93
African Americans, 11, 17, 20, 41, 51,
55n24, 56–59, 96, 309–10; intellec-
tuals and artists, 66, 92, 101–2, 105,
107, 293–310
Agamben, Giorgio, 222, 313, 318
Agency, 20, 49–51, 92, 95, 105, 126, 187,
280, 307, 321, 323, 342, 373–75, 382,
389n18
Aldington, Richard, 167
Alison, Archibald, 46
All About My Mother (dir. Pedro
Almodóvar), 190
"All You Get from Love Is a Love Song"
(Carpenters), 359
Alpert, Herb, 351
Alterity, 22, 27, 128–30, aesthetics of,
316, 318–24, 396, 404
Althusser, Louis, 9, 28, 337, 354
Altieri, Charles, 28–29, 336, 347n21
Ambassadors, The (Henry James),
317–18, 321
America Project, The (Sundiata), 94,
96–100, 108n2
"America, the Beautiful," 104–5
America the Scrivener (Jay), 35n41

American Graffiti (dir. George Lucas),
359
American Literature, 7
*American Moral and Sentimental Maga-
zine*, 43
American Novel and Its Tradition, The
(Chase), 30n1
American Puritan Imagination, The (ed.
Bercovitch), 6
American Renaissance (Matthiessen),
30n1
American Revolution, 40–41, 58,
62–63, 65, 70
Anachronism, 24, 225, 244, 294, 300
Anatomy Lesson, The (Roth), 181
Anorexia nervosa, Karen Carpenter's,
350, 361–63
Anti-formalism, 10
Arab American National Museum
(Dearborn, Michigan), 94
Arac, Jonathan, 34n29
Archeology of Knowledge, The (Foucault),
13
Arendt, Hannah, 346n11
Armstrong, Nancy, 315
Art as Experience (Dewey), 31n14
"Art of Fiction, The" (Henry James),
243
Art Students League (New York), 87,
134
Association, of ideas, 42, 44–48, 50
Atlantic Monthly, 87, 403n2
Attridge, Derek, 318
Auerbach, Jonathan, 145–47
Austen, Jane, 233, 246
Austin, J. L., 395, 403n2
Autobiography of an Androgyne (Lind),
156–62, 164, 174n5
Avila, Eric, 355–56

Babe's Bed, The (Wescott), 171
Babes in Toyland, 355
Badiou, Alain, 313
Bailyn, Bernard, 52n3

"Philosophy of Composition, The"
(Poe), 80
"Philosophy of Furniture, The" (Poe),
69
Photovoice, 100, 112n29
Piazza Tales, The (Melville), 229,
234–36, 239n17, 240nn18, 26
Pierce-Arrow (Howe), 25, 268, 275–80
Pierre (Melville), 220–21, 228
Plato, 160, 171–72, 295–96
Play It as It Lays (Didion), 357
Pleasure, 4, 9, 18, 20–21, 39, 42–46,
49, 51, 119, 127, 157–60, 162, 171–72
Poe, Edgar Allan, 22–23, 69, 80, 104,
120, 197–214
*Poems on Various Subjects, Religious and
Moral* (Wheatley), 60–61
Poetic Justice (Nussbaum), 314, 321
Poirier, Richard, 2, 30n3, 32n14
Political Unconscious, The (Jameson),
30n5, 33n24, 315
Pollin, Burton R., 199, 214n3, 216n13
Poovey, Mary, 242–44
Pope, Alexander, 179
Popular culture, 2–3, 8, 17–18, 28, 164,
170, 180, 188, 308, 330, 352–57
*Popular Culture in the Age of White
Flight* (Avila), 355
Port-Folio, The, 45
Portnoy's Complaint (Roth), 330, 335,
345n4
Portrait of a Lady, The (Henry James),
138, 243, 247, 317
Portraiture, literary, 56, 58, 62–63, 65,
67; oratorical, 58, 65–67; visual,
294–96, 298–99
Posnock, Ross, 330
"Postcards from the Volcano" (Stevens),
284
Postcolonialism, 9, 298
Poststructuralism, 140, 221, 314, 318,
322–23, 404
Pound, Ezra, 167
Powell, Dawn, 171–72

"Powers of Genius, The" (Linn), 45
Practicing New Historicism (Gallagher
and Greenblatt), 33n28
Pragmatism, 25, 31n14, 278
Presentism, 23, 221–25, 227, 377
President's Council on Bioethics, 180,
185, 193n13
Price, Richard, 40
Prime-Stevenson, Edward, 171–72
Princeton Radio Research Project,
350–52
Print and publication history, 199, 201,
206–8, 219–20, 228–38
Prisoner's Dilemma, 247, 251–54,
258–60
Project, distinguished from piece by
Sundiata, 92–96
Project Row Houses (Houston, Texas),
93
Properties, aesthetic, 393–97, 403n1
*Protestant Ethic and the Spirit of Capital-
ism, The* (Weber), 372
Proust, Marcel, 13
"Psalm of Life" (Longfellow), 277
Psychopathia Sexualis (Krafft-Ebing),
158
Puritan Origins of the American Self, The
(Bercovitch), 6, 32n16
Putnam's Monthly Magazine, 24,
228–30, 234–35
Pygmalion myth, 184–85, 187, 193n17
Pynchon, Thomas, 188

Queer Beauty (Davis), 161, 175n14
Queers, 11, 153n5, 159, 163, 168, 172, 386;
queer reading, 148–49; queer style;
120; queering of literary and social
conventions, 148–52, 164; *see also*
Homoeroticism; Homosexuality;
Lesbian; Same-sex friendship

Race, 8, 51, 64, 98, 103, 105, 209–14
Radio, 100, 350–53, 358–60, 362
Radway, Janice, 11, 17–18

Silent Terror, The (Cotton), 95–96
Silverman, Kenneth, 48
Sinatra, Frank, 105
"Sing" (The Carpenters), 352
Singh, Nikhil, 107
Singles 1969–1973 (Carpenters), 351–52
Singularities (Howe), 268–75
Slavery, 20, 50–51, 65, 67, 70n3, 95–96,
    107, 212–13, 222, 224–26, 231–33,
    236, 295, 297
"Sleepers, The" (Whitman), 86–87, 103
Sloterdijk, Peter, 291
Slouching Towards Bethlehem (Didion),
    357
Smith, Adam, 367
Smith, James McCune, 58, 66–67
"Snow White," 179, 188
Sobel, Dava, 201–2
Somaesthetics (Shusterman), 5–6
Sonic Youth, 355, 362
Souls of Black Folk, The (Du Bois),
    303–304
Souls of the Labadie Tract (Howe), 268,
    281–85
Southern Literary Messenger, 199, 201,
    206–7
Southworth, E. D. E. N., 3
Spahr, Juliana, 3, 28, 367–68, 373–80,
    382–88
Spears, Britney, 236
Spectator, The, 42
Spheres of Liberty (Kammen), 52n3
Spivak, Gayatri, 318
Stanford University, 96
Steele, Thomas J., 71n9
Steiner, Wendy, 22
Sterling Library (Yale University), 264
Stevens, Wallace, 25, 266, 268, 281–84
Stewart, Susan, 311n15
Stiglitz, Joseph E., 257
Stoddard, Charles Warren, 21, 164, 167,
    171–72, 176n21
Story of American Freedom, The (Foner),
    52n3

StoryCorps, 100, 112n29
Stowe, Harriet Beecher, 2–3, 19, 57–58,
    63–65, 67, 69, 228
Strange Brother (Niles), 165–67, 171
"Street of the Hyacinth, The" (Wool-
    son), 141, 145
Strong, Tracy, 222
Structuralism, 10
Style, 1, 9, 119–20, 165–67, 169–70, 199,
    267, 280, 294, 298, 300, 311n15,
    368, 378
Sundiata, Sekou, 19–20, 91–108
Sundquist, Eric J., 230
"Superstar" (The Carpenters), 350–51,
    355, 357–59
Superstar (dir. Todd Haynes), 355
Surface reading (Marcus and Best),
    7–8
Suspicion, hermeneutics of, 5, 9, 291,
    297
Swift, Jonathan, 40
Swinburne, Algernon Charles, 278
Symposium (Plato), 172
Symptomatic reading, 7

Taste, 4, 9, 42–43, 45–46, 50, 166, 168,
    173, 293, 334–35, 353
Tate, Claudia, 17
Terranova, Tiziana, 378
Thacker, Eugene, 378, 383
Thaler, Richard, 256–57
Theory of Games and Economic Behavior
    (von Neumann and Morgenstern),
    245, 250, 261n9
Thomson, David, 103
Thoreau, Henry David, 269, 271–72
"Ticket to Ride" (Beatles, covered by
    Carpenters), 351
Titian, 294
"To the maiden" (Crane), 85
"To the Right Honourable Earl of Dart-
    mouth" (Wheatley), 48, 54n21
"To S.M. a young *African* Painter"
    (Wheatley), 59–62